Global Russian Cultures

Global Russian Cultures

Edited by

Kevin M. F. Platt

The University of Wisconsin Press

Publication of this book has been made possible, in part, through support from the University of Pennsylvania.

The University of Wisconsin Press
728 State Street, Suite 443
Madison, Wisconsin 53706
uwpress.wisc.edu

3 Henrietta Street, Covent Garden
London WC2E 8LU, United Kingdom
eurospanbookstore.com

Printed in the United States of America

This book may be available in a digital edition.

Library of Congress Cataloging-in-Publication Data

Names: Platt, Kevin M. F., 1967- editor.
Title: Global Russian cultures / edited by Kevin M. F. Platt.
Description: Madison, Wisconsin: The University of Wisconsin Press, [2018]
| Includes bibliographical references and index.
Identifiers: LCCN 2018011414 | ISBN 9780299319700 (cloth: alk. paper)
Subjects: LCSH: Russians—Foreign countries. | Russians—Ethnic identity.
| Russia—Civilization.
Classification: LCC DK35.5 .G56 2019 | DDC 909/.049171—dc23
LC record available at https://lccn.loc.gov/2018011414

ISBN 9780299319748 (pbk.: alk. paper)

To Russian cultures everywhere

Contents

Illustrations

Figures

Tables

Acknowledgments

My to-do list from some six years back includes the item "edited volume on peripheral Russian culture." While working on a book about Russian culture in Latvia, I had become interested in the broader problem of Russian culture outside of the Russian Federation, and in April 2013 I convened a symposium at the University of Pennsylvania to follow through on this intention, although by then without the term "peripheral." That event was titled "Global Russian Culture" (in the singular), and the "proper" definition of that term was the focus of energetic debate among its participants, many of whom would eventually contribute chapters to this volume. In the course of the next few years, at a series of panels at successive conventions of the Association for Slavic, East European, and Eurasian Studies, gaining new collaborators as we progressed, we arrived at one of the animating insights of our project: the realization that the symposium's title should have been in the plural and that even within Russia itself, not to mention on a global scale, we needed to speak of multiple Russian cultures. As is explained in greater detail in the introduction, it is our shared contention that culture is borderless and multiple until someone names it and claims a place for it within a geography, and that these acts of naming and emplacement are the work of history, power, ideology, and culture itself. This is the central topic of this book. Lastly, a second symposium in late 2015, also at the University of Pennsylvania, titled "Russian Cultures and Global Situation," allowed the authors to workshop draft chapters for this book, which finally found its proper name in our discussions then: *Global Russian Cultures.*

As editor, I wish first and foremost to thank my fellow authors, who took part in this multiyear discussion with energy, creativity, and patience. Special thanks must go to Philip Bullock, Natalya Kosmarskaya, Artyom Kosmarski, Ilya Kukulin, and Maria Rubins, who joined our authorial collective comparatively late and composed focused chapters "to order" with great efficiency. Their contributions gave the volume its finished shape—that of an intentional treatment of a complex field rather than a loose collection of conference papers around a common theme.

We owe a debt of gratitude to institutions that have supported us in our project's long gestation. First and foremost, this includes the University of Pennsylvania, funding from which made possible both symposia. Additionally, we thank the audiences and participants at those events, who all contributed to this work through their ideas and insights if not as part of our authorial collective. These partners in dialogue include Rossen Djagalov, James F. English, Olga Gershenson, Keith Gessen, Philip Gleissner, Peter Holquist, Michael Idov, Monica Kim, Kirill Medvedev, Benjamin Nathans, Eugene Ostashevsky, Serguei Oushakine, Peter Steiner, Dirk Uffelmann, Julia Verkholantsev, Ilya Vinitsky and Lisa Yountchi. We also extend thanks to the staff of the University of Pennsylvania's Department of Slavic Languages and Literatures (since renamed the Department of Russian and East European Studies), especially to Alina Yakubova, who organized the symposia.

Thanks must also go to Zoya Frolova, herself an emphatically global Russian (also American, Latvian, and Ukrainian), for permission to use her painting on this volume's cover, and to art director Jennifer Conn of the University of Wisconsin Press. Finally, we are grateful to the press's executive editor Gwen Walker for supporting this project so enthusiastically and shepherding it toward publication, to our project editor Sheila McMahon and copyeditor Judith Robey, and to the two outside reviewers whose advice helped sharpen our arguments and the volume's organization. One of these, Andy Byford, who revealed his name to us, graciously allowed insertion of a key phrase from his report in this volume's introduction.

A Note on the Transliteration of Russian and Other Matters of Style

The transliteration of terms, surnames, geographic locations, and cited Russian material in this volume follows the Library of Congress system. Yet exceptions abound. Very many of the cultural figures we treat live or lived in non-Russian societies and have been published in languages other than Russian, presenting their own names according to any number of transliteration systems—or without any system at all. In general, we adopt these transliterated forms in the pages that follow, applying the Library of Congress system for Russian names and material that we ourselves have transliterated anew. For identity terms such as "Russian-American" and "Russian-Israeli," our spelling includes a hyphen to reflect the concatenated, doubled-over nature of these identities for many individuals. For citations of poetry, ellipses in brackets indicate omitted material, while ellipses without brackets are carried over from the original text. In most prose citations we do not make such a distinction, presenting all ellipses simply, without brackets.

Global Russian Cultures

Introduction

Putting Russian Cultures in Place

Kevin M. F. Platt

In the past few decades, Russians have gone global. Millions of ethnic Russians and others who identify with Russian language and culture have fanned out across the world—to Europe, Israel, and North America. Millions of others, as a result of the USSR's collapse, were left stranded, as if by a receding tide, in the "near abroad"—to use the Russian name for the string of countries around the rim of the Russian Federation from the Baltics to Central Asia (Laitin 1998, 29–35; Brubaker 2000). These mass movements and changes of status have only added to populations of Russians and their descendants from previous waves of migration, which occurred in the wake of twentieth-century Russian history's serial cataclysms. Reaching a crescendo in the present, this process of global dispersion has produced novel and thorny questions concerning Russian culture and identity. And, in light of the recent Russian annexation of Crimea and Russia's efforts "to protect the rights of Russians" in eastern Ukraine, these questions are far from academic. Where is Russian culture properly located? What does it mean to be a hyphenated Russian or a "global Russian"? Who claims to speak for all Russians, everywhere, and to what end? Where are the "natural" boundaries of Russian territory and who has the right or might to impose them on the map? *Global Russian Cultures* addresses these and other questions concerning Russian cultural formations in multiple situations, across space and time—chiefly, however, from the perspective of the present moment. Our use of the plural "cultures" corresponds to our shared conviction that these formations must be seen as an interconnected web of distinct entities rather than a totality that can be captured in any definition or formula. In the following, I explain why.

The study of global or extraterritorial Russian cultures is analogous to a rapidly expanding set of similar subdisciplines—such as global Anglophone, Francophone, and Sinophone studies—and intersects with the intense scholarly discussions in the past decade of "world literature(s)" (Moretti 2000, 2013; Damrosch 2003; Casanova 2004). In our rapidly globalizing world, people, communities, and cultural life are more and more dispersed and mobile. We contribute, therefore, to a broader research agenda: the study of cultural life and communities distributed across territory and borders and on the move, physically and virtually. Yet beyond these cultural and scholarly trends, our attention is drawn to global Russians and Russian culture by more specific recent events and contexts. In Anglophone societies, the Russian-American writer has become a major feature of the cultural landscape, with best-selling publications by figures such as Gary Shteyngart, Lara Vapnyar, and David Bezmozgis. This phenomenon, which is matched in other contexts of Russian emigration such as Israel, Germany, and France, presents intriguing new problems of cultural translation, social and gender identity, and literary self-fashioning. Closer to the borders of the Russian Federation, Russian cultural production has also entered a new phase, in light of the enormous populations of Russian speakers now living in societies outside of the Russian Federation—in Israel, in the Baltic States, and elsewhere. Dwarfing previous Russian émigré communities in scale, these populations commonly retain their linguistic and cultural identity in what is a novel geographical situation. In an age when individuals (at least those with means) may move about the world freely (and this is even more the case with money and cultural products), the many locations of Russian cultural life present authors, artists, and institutions with new forms of circulation among dispersed audiences and markets. As never before, Russian writing, music, and art is being produced outside of Russia, crossing borders to reach audiences and creating new hybrid forms, institutions, and identities in the process. Finally, and most recently, ethnic and cultural identities have been weaponized, as the Russian state has come to recognize the power of cultural identification to influence political interest, loyalty, and even armed conflicts. As a result, global Russian and Russophone populations, especially in the Baltic, Central Asia, and—most spectacularly—Ukraine, have become the objects of intense propaganda and other projections of soft and hard power, which attempt to create and manage a "Russian world" in order to engineer geopolitical realities. For all of these reasons, it is clear that global Russian cultural life has emerged as an important and fascinating new field of research.

It is a highly complex area of study that varies across time, space, social environment, and the vagaries of individual cases. The chapters of this volume are calculated to explore the topic's many dimensions and variations. Individual contributions describe Russian culture in discrete locations across the globe, from America, where Russians and Russian speakers form a part of the melting pot society of rapid assimilation, to the divided identities of Russians in the Baltic and Central Asian Near Abroad, who live under the shadow of the neighboring Russian Federation, to Israel, where culturally Russian Jews have returned from the Jewish diaspora only to find themselves part of a Russian one. The genres under investigation vary from one chapter to the next—from film, to music, to literature, to cultural life per se—while methods of study range from literary criticism to discourse analysis, digital humanities, sociolinguistics, and cultural sociology. Finally, the cases we consider vary widely with regard to the status of Russian language and culture itself—from investigations of Russian-language cultural life outside of Russia to analyses of authors who retain Russian identity even though they write in English (e.g., Vapnyar or Bezmozgis). They also include explorations of "Russian" cultural production by authors and composers who may have no biographical or hereditary ties to Russia at all.

The cases we investigate are united by their common participation in the world of Russian culture as a whole. But "united" is a poor term to use here, as is "whole." Given the multifarious situations we study, how can we even posit a single entity called "Russian culture as a whole"? One obvious response to this question might refer to the language and cultural traditions of Russia itself as the root to which all the varieties of Russian diaspora may be traced in one way or another. Yet we take issue with this proposal. Last year, the poet and publisher Dmitry Kuzmin emigrated from Moscow to Riga, Latvia, in order to find a safe haven for his nonnormative approach to Russian literature and to family life, in both of which he embraces modes of sexuality and gender identity that are increasingly anathematized by the Russian state, the Russian Orthodox Church, and defenders of patriotic identity in Russia (see Platt, this volume). The case of Kuzmin starkly illustrates the problem of locating "the whole of Russian culture" in geography. Should we see Russian culture as properly centered in Russia, where it is at home in what appears to be its "natural" territory and society yet is also confined by political and social forces that police not only physical frontiers but also the ideological borders of cultural propriety? Kuzmin abandoned Russia precisely in order to produce Russian culture. Should we then, perhaps, treat the whole of Russian culture as somehow greater than the Russian Federation itself, or located more aptly beyond those borders, where it is freed from political forces that attempt to limit its development and expression?

Such a choice is instructive only via reflection on the degree to which it is reductive. Both within and without the Russian Federation, Russian culture is fragmented and multiple, and everywhere it is the object of diverse and contradictory institutional, political, and economic forces that seek to define and constrain it. Here, then, is the reality of culture and its emplacement in modern geography: it always exceeds any one location and presents a unity only in its perpetually renegotiated multiplicity. Émigré communities, especially under conditions of political emigration, frequently claim to represent a purer form of a national culture than what they left behind in the homeland—this was a foundational belief, for instance, in postrevolutionary Russian communities in emigration who "firmly believed that one of their primary tasks in exile was to preserve, carry on and create Russian culture" (Raeff 1990, 95). Yet even if my own sympathy is with Kuzmin's vision of Russian literature in exile, where it has escaped the patriotic institutions of contemporary Russian society, it would be a mistake to romanticize the condition of an "emancipated" Russian culture abroad as more authentic or complete than cultural life in the Russian Federation. Minority collective identities are no less subject to overt political regulation and tacit social pressure and definition than those of social majorities. In the same Latvia to which Kuzmin fled from Moscow, in an expression of the politics of post-Soviet nation-building, access to Russian-language education and the use of Russian in commerce are legally restricted (and Latvia's climate with regard to nonnormative gender and sexuality, too, is a matter of contestation). In Israel, a comparable yet distinct regime of Russian minority identity and social life is delimited by and shaped in response to majority cultural norms that reflect Zionist conceptions of Jewish collective identity and social tensions over the economics and politics of immigration (Moshkin, this volume; Rubins, this volume). And at a more localized level, immigrant communities everywhere bring normative conceptions of gender, identity, belief, and custom with them to their adoptive countries (Furman, this volume). In other words, "being Russian" or "performing Russian culture" is everywhere subject to local constraints, but those constraints, and therefore the content of "Russianness" as well, are distinct in each new context.

Yet global Russian cultural life is shaped not only by constraints but also by incentives. As is illustrated by the case of Gary Shteyngart and his 2003 hit debut novel, *The Russian Debutante's Handbook*, a Russian identity or mode of writing may be a savvy branding move, rewarded with book contracts and sales (Wakamiya, this volume). Books, songs, and cultural producers' public personae are almost always formed with an eye to audiences, markets, publishing houses, and reviewers. Yet these incentivizing contexts, too, are many and varied, encompassing American audiences eager for exotic and amusing tales of Russian-American immigration along with audiences in the Russian Federation seeking models of cosmopolitan transcendence of Russian parochialism. Examples of cultural products consumed by these audiences include the novels of successful Russian émigré writers such as the Israeli author Dina Rubina (Rubins, this volume) and poetry from the near abroad by Sergej Timofejev and other members of the Riga-based Orbita poetry and multimedia collective (Platt, this volume). Some cultural producers may address multiple audiences with a range of tailored versions of their own "Russianness." A case in point is Michael Idov, whose career reads as a string of ventures into new markets and personae: Russian-American author, American writer in Moscow and editor of Russian *GQ*, and Russian TV producer in Europe (Wanner, this volume). For others, market incentives may ultimately constrain possibilities. This returns us to Shteyngart, who has sought in recent years, with some difficulty, to shed his "Russian" persona. The cultural capital of a Russian or Russian-American identity can be both a boon and a burden for cultural producers.

Yet the increasingly concerted political instrumentalization and management of culture in relation to geography in recent years casts the question of the multiplicity or unity of global Russian cultures into the starkest relief. Since the Soviet collapse, the Russian state has been acutely sensitive to extraterritorial Russian populations, which it has sought to gather in, influence, and claim outright by a variety of policies that in the past decade and a half have fallen under the general conceptual umbrella of the "Russian world"—which is both a rhetorical commonplace and the name of a state-sponsored cultural outreach foundation (Gorham, this volume). Yet state efforts to define and manage this Russian world stumble upon its diversity and the impossibility of defining its "proper" place. In 2014, at the solemn ceremony with which the Russian state ratified the annexation of Crimea ("reunification," in Russian state and public discourse), Vladimir Putin referred to a deep history of national and religious events, which ostensibly demonstrated that "Crimea is a primordially Russian land and Sevastopol is a Russian city." But he also alluded to more recent history when he stated that with the collapse of the Soviet Union, the "Russian people became one of the largest, if not the largest, divided people in the world." These historical arguments culminated in his affirmation that "millions of Russian and Russophone people live in Ukraine, and Russia will always defend their interests by political, diplomatic and legal means" (2014a). To hone the precision of Putin's formulation, we might add "military" means to this list.

However, in spite of Russian aspirations to act on behalf of "Russians and Russophone people" in Ukraine, a great many of those very people were so passionately opposed to Russian meddling in Ukraine that they took up arms in the struggle with Russia-backed separatist forces in Donbas. By forcefully inscribing one vision of the territorial integrity and spiritual unity of the Russian people into geography, the Russian state alienated, perhaps permanently, a great many other potential members of their "Russian world." Furthermore, this rift between alienation and allegiance cuts across Russian communities in many other places as well, including Moscow itself, where those opposed to the annexation are calumnied as "fifth-columnists" and "national traitors." The more insistently one tries to contain a singular "Russian world" within any one border, definition, or concrete collective, the more one loses hold of many other Russian worlds.

In sum, for all of the various conceptions of Russian identity or cultural life across the globe, whether they are termed "diaspora," "national culture," "émigré culture," or "immigrant fiction," we take it as axiomatic in the following chapters that there is no "fundamental" or "natural" relationship between culture and geographical location. Such relationships are historically and contextually contingent. They need to be *made.* There is no single fundamental Russian cultural formation, in or outside of Russian territory. And the territories of culture have no natural or proper boundaries. Although the long era of nationalism granted general acceptance to the idea that culture is at home in the territory of a nation-state (French culture is made in France, just as Russian culture is made in Russia), this is an ideological illusion. As Putin's appeals to mythic history in his address on the Crimea demonstrate, the very category of "Russian territory" is itself produced by culture, and not the reverse. So too is the concept of wholeness, when applied to any singular national culture, a construct. Cultures are fragmented and placeless until someone calls them by name, defines their "essential" characteristics, and claims a territory for them. That these acts of naming and defining, in their most fundamental and authoritative forms, are accomplished by largely anonymous historical processes over the *longue durée* does not render them any less ideological in nature than more intentional and rapid interventions such as the aggressive Russian actions in contemporary East Ukraine or émigré claims to represent true Russian culture. The attribution of wholeness, unity, or a fixed location to Russian cultural production across the globe is analogous to the methodological problem of diaspora itself, which as Rogers Brubaker has argued, must refer in scholarship to "a category of practice, project, claim and stance, rather than . . . a bounded group. The 'groupness' of putative diasporas, like that of putative 'nations,' is precisely what is at stake in political, social and cultural struggles" (2005). While any one restricted vision of community or culture may have a fixed location, this is always only as a fragment of a larger, undefinable, and placeless whole. In other words, ultimately, cultures per se can only be global. The insight into cultural activity enabled by our globalized and interconnected era is that cultural life has always already occupied a superspatial, virtual dimension, defying our human, ideologically reinforced tendency to think in terms of space, place, and boundary.

Let us be frank about the political commitments of this volume. Our work stands in opposition to the bounded and unitary conceptions of culture and identity that are most often associated with national projects in and around Russia. In an era when some would build walls around ostensibly distinct cultures and societies and their own "primordial" territories, we insist that cultures are always plural, unbounded, and polycentric. As we will show, "Russian culture" projects may claim to be singular, correct in their constructions of geography, and authentic. Examples include the vision of "national culture within its boundaries" projected by Putin's speech on the annexation of Crimea, cited above; the cosmopolitan "global Russian culture" promoted by the glossy journal *Snob* for wealthy Russians shuttling between Moscow, New York, and Berlin; or the patriotic organizations supported by the Russian World Foundation that seek to claim the loyalty of Russians in the near abroad, to name a few. Yet all such claims are implicitly or explicitly acts of contestation—power grabs that may accompany land grabs or cash grabs. A poem written in Sevastopol may one year appear to be a product of "minority culture of Eastern Europe" or "Russian culture of the near abroad" and the next year be taken to exemplify "Russian national culture"—all as a result of the movements of soldiers and borders. Diverse conceptions of the geography of Russian culture are all, and all to the same degree, historically and politically contingent projects—in other words, there is no hierarchy of authenticity that makes "national culture within its boundaries" more authentic or just than diasporic or migrant culture. There can be, therefore, no nonideological distinction between Russian culture in the Russian Federation and Russian culture anywhere else. At base, there is no single thing that may be called "global Russian" culture. We therefore offer "global Russian cultures" as a master category that allows us to bring into focus the diversity and contingency of all conceptions of Russian culture across space and time. For us, the concept of global Russian cultures constitutes a "set of all sets" rather than a single entity. In short, ours is a study of how placeless Russian cultures are perceived in relation to geography and how geographies are inscribed with Russian cultural meanings. In this respect our subject goes beyond a study of "Russian culture abroad," which simply echoes the nationalist dictum that culture belongs to a nation and to its "rightful" place on the map.

The contributions to this volume are devoted to comparative and mutually cross-referenced studies of various forms of geographic placement of Russian culture, with attention to the *processes* and *purposes* behind the production, contestation, and dissemination of these situated cultural singularities as they come into being and eventually pass into history. Our starting point is the enormous present-day global dispersion of Russian communities, who generate their own cultural identities (e.g., as Baltic Russians or Russian-Israelis) or propose and contest shared ones (through phrases such as "global Russian," "truly Russian," and "Russian world"). The chapters take up a variety of distinct cases: contemporary diasporas, émigré culture of the twentieth century in various places and media, Russian culture "written in English and German," contemporary globe-trotting "global Russians," or the current Russian project of "Novorossiya" in Eastern Ukraine.

The volume's chapters are divided into two parts. Part One, "Mapping Russian Cultures," includes broad overviews of historical and contemporary conceptions of Russian culture in its relationship to geography, within and outside of "Russian" political unities. We offer a novel geocultural remapping of "the Russian world" across not only the "near abroad" (the former imperial territory) and the "distant abroad" (the territory of émigré dispersion) but also the current Russian state's own sovereign territory. Part Two, "Russian Cultures at Large," presents more focused case studies of particular authors, populations, and problems. This half of the book deconstructs the political projections and traditional cultural preconceptions of "the Russian world" to reveal how this "world" takes shape, exists in places, belongs to people, and is articulated in languages that would normally have been constructed as external to it, or even as its "Other." Part Two also considers how states and others contest and capitalize on this multiplicity of Russian cultures.

In order to describe and analyze global Russian cultures as they appear in the most diverse arenas of human experience, the chapters of *Global Russian Cultures* offer a broad range of disciplinary modes of inquiry. We track Russian cultures in literature, film, and music through analytic and historical methods particular to those forms of expression and communication; we also use tools such as ethnography, sociolinguistics, discourse analysis, and digital humanistic inquiry to understand public, everyday, and internet language use relating to our subject.

Part One begins with Maria Rubins's overview of the historical development of Russian cultures "abroad" over the course of the twentieth century. The century's revolutions, wars, and divided political geographies sent successive waves of emigration from Russia and the Soviet Union to locations across Europe and the globe—creating what Rubins describes as the "archipelago" of Russian cultural geographies. Her account, focused on case studies of Paris in the interwar period of the 1920s–30s, New York in the 1940s–50s, and Israel in the late twentieth century, explores the specific character of each location in time and space and the factors that shaped it. These case studies allow her to chart the changing conditions of global Russian cultures over the century while taking into account the varied circumstances of global geopolitics and cultural circulation. Thus in the 1920s the cultural and literary life of émigré communities was closely connected to life in the Soviet Union until Stalinist policies, followed by the Cold War, severed these close ties, dividing world geography into closed zones. The globalized post–Cold War world, featuring the rapid circulation of people and cultural goods, has propelled more Russians across the world's geography while at the same time tying the far flung islands of the archipelago more closely to each other and to the "continent" of Russia. Yet shifts in global and local ideologies and imaginings of cultural life have also shaped the place of Russian cultures in global geographies in various ways—from the situation of the first émigrés, who sought to preserve a "true" Russian culture that would one day be returned to "proper" Russian territory, to contemporary dispersed Russian communities who may revel in their freedom to create independent identities, books, poems, and music in new geographies—or to write books marketing their "exotic" existence abroad to audiences in Moscow and Ekaterinburg.

Other chapters in Part One report on the state of Russian cultures in widely varied present geographies. Vitaly Chernetsky examines the case of Ukraine, in which centuries of intermingling and rivalry between Ukrainian and Russian language, literature, and cultural production have culminated in the present-day contestation not only of borders but of state claims to populations. As Chernetsky shows, up until the Soviet collapse, in conditions of imperial domination by the "Russian" center of power, Ukrainian national identity was articulated as ethno-national. Being Ukrainian meant asserting one's non-Russian ethnic roots in a world where assimilation to Russian cultural life and institutions was the norm. In the post-Soviet era, Ukraine has been making the painful and complex transition to a civic conception of Ukrainian identity that is inclusive not only of assimilated members of other ethnicities but of Russians and others who retain their "Russianness" while still identifying with the project of Ukrainian independent statehood. As Chernetsky concludes, authors and other cultural figures in Ukraine are coming to the realization that a poem written in Russian in Kyiv may nevertheless be a Ukrainian poem.

Two additional chapters, one by Natalya Kosmarskaya and Artyom Kosmarski and the other by Kevin M. F. Platt, add descriptions of Russian and Russophone cultural life in two other regions along Russia's borders—Central Asia and the Baltics, respectively. Like Ukraine, both regions are viewed in Russia as parts of the near abroad, yet the status of Russian cultural life in the two could not be more different. As Kosmarskaya and Kosmarski show in a cultural-sociological analysis based on extensive field work, Russian influence in Central Asia during the era of imperial conquest and subsequent Soviet development resulted in the acculturation of urban social elites to Russian culture and language. Especially in Kazakhstan and northern Kyrgyzstan, where the modernization of formerly nomadic peoples rendered them especially responsive—or vulnerable—to the "gift" of imperial culture, and especially in cities, a Russophone cultural space inclusive of members of Central Asian, Russian, and other former Soviet ethnicities is to this day a vibrant scene of commerce, cultural life, literature, and cultural identification. In the Baltic, as Platt shows in his literary ethnography focused on Latvia, the situation could not be more distinct. Here, as a result of nineteenth-century national awakenings of the Baltic peoples in the context of the Russian Empire, interwar decades of independence, followed by years of Soviet occupation, Baltic national identities have been articulated as completely separate from, if not orthogonal to, Russian cultural identity: Russians and Russophones are largely tolerated in the Baltics, yet only as a "national minority" whose presence recalls the legacy of occupation. Over half of this sizable population is to this day composed of "noncitizen" residents whose peculiar legal status reflects their lack of political entitlement. Chernetsky's characterization of Ukraine applies equally to the Baltics: they comprise a territory in which the imperial claims of hegemony emanating from the centers of Russian political power come into conflict with distinctive local Russian cultural formations. For Baltic Russian populations, as Platt shows, the question of cultural belonging looms large: are they an anomalous population that will assimilate in time to local national identities? Are they a "displaced" population, a part of a greater "Russian world" that extends beyond Russian borders? Russian cultural life in the region pursues various strategies of inscribing the Russian community into these imaginary cultural wholes and fragments. The diverse disciplinary modes of these three chapters on near abroad territories demonstrate the distinctive significances that Russian cultures acquire when viewed in terms of everyday speech and practice, as in Kosmarskaya and Kosmarski's contribution, in which cultural hybridization occurs in an inchoate and historically contingent manner, as compared to when seen in terms of literary and other cultural production, as in Platt's and Chernetsky's chapters, in which writers and poets intentionally construct varieties of cultural, territorial, and political belonging.

Two other contributions study Russian cultural locations more distant from the Russian Federation. Alex Moshkin describes Russian-Israeli cultural life over the past three decades, focusing on the development in Israel of Russophone cinema, which has passed from the margins of Israeli cultural institutions to their center. As Moshkin demonstrates, Russophone Jews in Israel confront not one but two dimensions of geographical displacement: they are suspended between, on the one hand, the "typical" émigré experience of departure from their place of birth to enter the global Russophone diaspora and, on the other hand, an Israeli cultural geography that conceives of the gathering of Jews in Israel as an end to the Jewish diaspora. This "dual diasporic" condition plays out, in the films Moshkin examines, in negotiations of nostalgia, assimilation, and alienation, balancing the competing claims of two "homelands." Lisa Ryoko Wakamiya's chapter turns to the rise of "fourth wave" Russian immigrant fiction in Canada and the United States, which has brought names like Gary Shteyngart, Lara Vapnyar, and David Bezmozgis to the top of best-seller lists. In distinction to Russian cultural production in the near abroad and Israel, predominantly oriented toward writing in Russian and often aiming at markets that include the Russian Federation, these are authors who write "Russian-inflected" prose in English. Wakamiya examines the self-conscious responses of authors like Shteyngart to opportunities presented by American publishing markets and literary traditions, offering the popular genre of the immigrant tale as an entry point to successful authorship. Yet as she demonstrates, once one has fallen into a marketing niche, it can be hard to exit it in order to write simply as an "American author" and not in the expected mode of a Russian-American. The novels and films analyzed in Wakamiya's and Moshkin's chapters demonstrate how retelling the story of immigration can itself be productive of new formations of Russian culture. At the same time, such stories can constrain cultural creativity by supporting a mythic connection of culture to a point of origin in a distant homeland.

As argued above, conceptions of Russian diasporic culture as displaced from its "proper" location in Russia naturalize what is in fact a historically contingent linkage of culture with geography. The cultural life of Russia is, to borrow Rubins's formulation, simply the largest "island" in the archipelago of global Russian cultures. Furthermore, one can hardly understand Russian cultural life and its contestation in places like Latvia or Ukraine without comprehension of the history and actuality of Russian projections of cultural hegemony across territories near and far. Therefore, Part One of *Global Russian Cultures* would not be complete without Ilya Kukulin's chapter on representations and problematizations of the relationship between literary text and territory within Russia—in the Russian Empire, the USSR, and the post-Soviet Russian Federation. In resonance with Rubins's account of the global archipelago of Russian cultures, Kukulin offers an alternative construction of Russian culture within "Russian territory" itself as fragmented, multiple, and archipelagic. As Kukulin demonstrates, since the late premodern period Russian cultural life has alternately sought, on the one hand, to disseminate Russian culture broadly as an imperial formation, gathering people of many ethnicities together in loyalty to Russian statehood and social life, and, on the other hand, to define Russianness in national terms as an exclusive characteristic of ethnic Russians. This ambivalence is itself the subject of many Russian literary works that seek to champion expansionist claims to far-flung territories or to subvert those claims by describing a more circumscribed extension of Russian culture over space or by bringing to light other peoples who might lay claim to purportedly "Russian" lands—such as the Finno-Ugric ethnicities of the Russian Federation that are the object of Denis Osokin's story cycles and poetry. Taken together, the chapters of Part One map global Russian cultures across time and place, investigating the many and diverse islands of the archipelago described by Rubins, both within "Russian territory" and without, demonstrating in the process the historical and ideological contingency of any emplacement of Russian cultures in geography.

Yet the task of describing global Russian cultures, conceived as a plurality of claims and constructions of Russianness, is more complex than may be accounted for in any straightforward mapping or linear historical account. The chapters of Part Two are devoted to a range of more focused problems and cases that complicate and challenge the matrix of global Russian cultures described in Part One. Michael Gorham's chapter provides an account of the Russian Federation's "Russian World" project—a collection of strategies, programs, and policies pursued by the Kremlin over the last two decades to foster among the globally dispersed populations of Russians and Russophones a sense of community with and loyalty to the Russian Federation. Gorham's chapter demonstrates how Moscow's strategies with regard to Russians beyond its borders confront the conceptual impasse of the de facto fragmentation of Russian cultures and identities in neighboring territories such as Ukraine, the Baltic, and Central Asia, as described in Chernetsky's, Platt's, and Kosmarskaya and Kosmarski's contributions. As Gorham explains, the Russian World project has been fraught by a growing ambivalence between truly "soft" goals of fostering transnational cultural understanding or gaining access to Russian and Russian-speaking professionals and specialists, on the one hand, and "hard" projections of power, most fully evident in Russian territorial expansion and military action in Eastern Ukraine and in official statements claiming for the Kremlin the authority to "defend ethnic Russians in Ukraine" and elsewhere (Putin 2014c). Dirk Uffelmann's chapter complements Gorham's by analyzing "Russophone Russophobia" in the Ukrainian internet—Russian cultural life that explicitly renounces the politics and patriotic collective identity of the Russian Federation. As Uffelmann shows, the label of Russophobia is itself a powerful tool of Russian patriotic culture and propaganda that presupposes that Russian language and culture belong to the Russian state—that Russians everywhere who fail to identify with the politics of their "homeland" are tantamount to traitors, and that the expression of views opposed to the Russian state in Russian language and culture is a contradiction in terms—an "anti-Russian Russian culture." As we learn from Uffelmann's analysis, Russophone culture of the Ukrainian internet—in particular its rich store of jokes and poetry—demonstrates not only the logical absurdity and ideological basis of such claims but also the viability of alternate Russian cultures that are affiliated with other political and social collectivities, such as Ukraine. Furthermore, this material illustrates the availability and legitimacy of these "other Russian cultures" everywhere. Cultural life, once it becomes virtual, truly has no proper location. Who is to say, ultimately, that an internet joke originating in Kyiv or the anti-Kremlin writings of Odesa poet Boris Khersonsky are any less Russian than the jokes told in Moscow's Satire Theater or the poetry of Pushkin? Ukrainian culture is Russian, too, and both are equally global in reach.

Two other chapters are devoted to the implications of culture and human mobility. Adrian Wanner describes the career of Michael Idov, the "most global Russian of all"—a writer, editor, and film producer whose biography has taken him from the Soviet Riga of his birth to the United States, where he grew up and began a career as a novelist and journalist, after which he moved to Russia, where he became editor of the Russian edition of *GQ*. At that point he switched to writing in Russian and ultimately moved into film and television. Idov's path through language and geography, lending him the status of a cosmopolitan and worldly figure, has helped him to further his career in each new location. As Wanner shows, Idov's story demonstrates the way globalized human mobility allows cultural producers to engage in a sort of cultural arbitrage, plying the cultural capital accumulated in one location in a new location, to great effect. This is to say, physical passage from one island in the archipelago of Russian cultures to another is itself a strategy for cultural production and for the production of new identities. Lara Ryazanova-Clarke investigates the mobility not of producers of culture but of its consumers: Russian tourists in Scotland. Just as Kosmarskaya and Kosmarski's chapter complements the investigation of literary culture (with a capital *C*) in the near abroad with an examination of cultural life there as lived experience, so Ryazanova-Clarke's chapter complements Wanner's examination of Idov's highly intentional deployments of cosmopolitan identity with an alternative investigation of the experience of a broader population of mobile cultural consumers. Ryazanova-Clarke's sociolinguistic analysis of interviews gathered from Russian tourists demonstrates how they view their own place in the global community of cultures and how current populations of mobile Russians fashion their identities through access to non-Russian landscapes and cultures.

Three final chapters investigate "limiting cases" of global Russian cultures in relation to gender, genre, and identity, returning us emphatically to recognition of Russian cultural formations' multiplicity and uncentered, archipelagic dispersion that is, ironically, this volume's unifying topic. Yelena Furman's chapter studies literary works by Vapnyar and Anya Ulinich that critically examine Russian constructions of gender identity and question the extent to which, freed from Russian society in immigration, these constructions are subject to reconstruction. The chapters of *Global Russian Cultures* as a whole, and those of Moshkin, Wakamiya, and Wanner in particular, demonstrate that immigration and other forms of displacement make possible reinventions of Russian cultures in new forms. Furman shows that they also offer an opportunity to reinvent gender identities, although here, too, as in Moshkin's and Wakamiya's chapters, the mythical authority of the "authentic" cultural origin is a potent force that is not easily overcome. Philip Bullock's chapter turns to the question of Russian musical culture, and in particular song, in global circulation. The complexities of song, drawing variously on poetic texts, composers, and performers, render it an intriguing case of cultural production that may be distributed globally not only across geographies but also across the cultural identities of participants. This leads to intriguing indeterminate cases, such as those of the Russian émigré to Europe and later the United States Arthur Vincent Lourié, whose songs provided a vehicle for preservation of his ties to Russian cultural traditions in exile, and the English composer Benjamin Britten, whose settings of Russian texts have been canonized as part of the Russian song tradition, despite his having no genealogical linkage to Russia at all.

Completing our trajectory through, and unsettling, of global Russian cultures, Miriam Finkelstein's final chapter steps beyond even the limiting case of

Britten, an English composer of Russian songs, to investigate what may be the furthest frontier of our subject: "Russian literature" that is, paradoxically, written in non-Russian languages by non-Russian authors. If, as Rubins and Kukulin argue, Russian culture is scattered across time and space and fragmented within the ostensible whole of Russia proper, written in many versions of the Russian language, in English or in non-Russian languages of the Russian Federation, then how indeed may borders be inscribed around "Russian culture," and what is to be gained by such an inscription? Finkelstein examines novels and poetry written in German, French, English, Portuguese, and other languages. As she proposes in a counterintuitive, yet provocative and productive intervention, in an age of globalized cultural circulation, when constructivist conceptions of cultural identification have been popularized to an unprecedented degree and when authorship has been recognized as a function of fictional articulation by theorists taking their lead from Roland Barthes, Russian literature has been reimagined by some not just as a diasporic or global project but as a globally shared undertaking. In this view, any author, anywhere, may contribute to this project, inscribing him- or herself into Russian traditions of the author as moral exemplar whose writing articulates social conscience and political idealism in the face of suffering and oppression.

In sum, the chapters of *Global Russian Cultures*, applying a variety of disciplinary tools from the social sciences and humanities, map the multiplicity of cultural phenomena that may be called Russian through the dimensions of space and time. Furthermore, they trace their variation across media (film, music, literature, everyday culture) and language and identity (from Russian and Russophone, to "hyphenated" Russian-Israelis and Russian-Americans who may write in English or Hebrew, to "voluntary" authors who self-fashion themselves as Russians). Our project's central claim is that culture, while shaped by political and social institutions in definite locations, is ultimately autonomous from fixity in time and place. All cultures are global in their potential. Scholarly inquiry into their objective circumstances demands recognition that the location of culture in a definitive geography is a contingent result of human history, action, and ideology rather than a given of nature or destiny. In order to comprehend Russian culture anywhere, in or outside of Russia, one must first comprehend it everywhere. This is the task of this volume.

Part One

The Situation of Russian Cultures

A Century of Russian Culture(s) "Abroad"

The Unfolding of Literary Geography

Maria Rubins

The Archipelago of Russian Culture: Prologue

The global trends that informed much of the world's cultural production in the last hundred years—including massive migrations in the wake of major catastrophes and world wars, displacement of dissident intellectuals by oppressive political regimes, and intensified mobility after the breakup of colonial and totalitarian powers—have resulted in a proliferation of hyphenated, hybrid, translocal, and transnational identities. Russia has been no stranger to these trends, yet its unique experiences of revolution, war, the Cold War, and Soviet collapse have left their specific imprint on Russian cultural expression. Since the 1917 Revolution Russian culture has been moving progressively beyond metropolitan borders to recreate itself in diverse geographical, political, and linguistic contexts. And just as the content of cultural life in one location is distinct from that of the next, it has also taken on new forms in response to the changing meanings of emigration over time, reflecting both global and local historical and ideological developments. The present chapter offers an account of the shifting circumstances of this century of diasporization of Russian culture.

The process of emigration from Russia has conventionally been divided into several waves. The first wave started as a reaction to the Bolshevik terror and civil war that ensued shortly after the October Revolution of 1917, and it extended until the end of the 1930s. It was the most massive of the Soviet-era emigrations and included a significant percentage of artists and intellectuals. A key moment of the initial period was the Bolshevik expulsion from Russia in 1922 of 160 leading thinkers, including Nikolai Berdyaev, Sergei Bulgakov, Nikolai Lossky, Fedor Stepun, and Semyon Frank, on what became known as the "Philosophers' Ship." This wave of emigration included many other prominent individuals as well: members of the House of Romanov; the opera singer Fedor Shaliapin; the stars of Serge Diaghilev's *Ballets Russes*; and the recipient of the first Russian Nobel prize for literature, Ivan Bunin, are but a few of the renowned figures who contributed to the international visibility of "Russia abroad" during the interwar decades. The second wave was triggered by World War II. To a large extent, it consisted of displaced persons originating in territories occupied by the German army who followed it after its retreat or were compelled to move to Germany to work, as well as liberated concentration camp inmates and prisoners of war, who were reluctant to return to the USSR and risk prompt arrest. With some notable exceptions, this wave produced relatively few outstanding cultural achievements.

The third wave of Russian emigration started in the late 1960s following the end of the Thaw, a period of relative liberalization, and continued on and off, depending on fluctuating Kremlin emigration policies, until the end of the Soviet era. Not large in number, this emigration was primarily composed of dissidents, Zionist Jews, and high-profile defectors. It counted among its ranks many celebrity figures, including the thinkers Vladimir Bukovsky and Alexander Zinoviev; the poets Joseph Brodsky and Naum Korzhavin; the writers Alexander Solzhenitsyn, Andrei Siniavsky, Viktor Nekrasov, Vasily Aksyonov, Sergei Dovlatov, Sasha Sokolov, and Vladimir Voinovich; the sculptors Ernst Neizvestny and Mikhail Shemiakin; the ballet dancers Mikhail Baryshnikov, Natalia Makarova, and Rudolf Nuriev; the cellist Mstislav Rostropovich; and the opera singer Galina Vishnevskaya. Finally, the opening up of the USSR under Mikhail Gorbachev's perestroika policy and the Soviet breakup led to a vast exodus from Russia beginning in the late 1980s. This is often referred to as the fourth wave of emigration. It was, however, radically different from preceding waves, as most people left for economic rather than political reasons. In a new era of open borders and easy global movement of people and cultural goods, many of this contingent, especially prominent cultural figures, have preserved their Russian citizenship and do not consider themselves émigrés. This multidirectional cross-border migration, in other words, can be seen as a component of the globe-trotting cultural life that overtook the planet at the turn of the twenty-first century.

Until recently, scholars of émigré culture, regarding their subject of study as a finite phenomenon with well-defined chronological boundaries, postulated the ultimate merging of diasporic and metropolitan branches of Russian culture.[1] In recent years, however, emigration from Russia has surged yet again, bringing to the West scores of intellectuals, skilled professionals, and political activists fleeing Putin's regime. In the current political climate, this trend can be expected to intensify. It is therefore quite clear that Russian culture beyond metropolitan borders has outgrown the Soviet-era phenomenon to become a permanent and evolving formation.

Each locus of Russian life that has emerged over the last century generated its own models of extraterritorial identities, shaped by evolving relations with metropolitan space and local geography. For decades, critical constructions of Russian emigration were informed by the archetypal examples of diasporic experience, based on Jewish, Greek, and Armenian mythologies. Within this paradigm, the homeland is figured as an object of continuous longing, generating collective memories and commitment to an ultimate return (Safran 1991); displacement from the place of origin is interpreted as a trauma and the host country as a locus of exile. However, with increasing frequency over the last century, the teleology of origin and return has been displaced in Russian cultural discourse in favor of cross-cultural dialogue or circulations taking place within and across diasporic communities. Such patterns of collective identities correspond to alternative diasporic models more recently articulated by scholars along the following lines: reconfiguring "return" as "re-turn" (a rhetorical focus on the place of origin without the intention of actual repatriation, according to Tölölyan 2007, 649); postulating a spatially disseminated identity (Gilroy 1993); highlighting the important roles of a diasporic imaginary (Axel 2002) and the decentered, lateral sociocultural networks deployed across diverse territories (Clifford 1994, 308); questioning the "victim tradition"; and celebrating the "creative, enriching side of living in 'Babylon,' the radiance of difference" (Cohen 1997, 196).

The exilic "victim tradition" and the "radiance of difference" mark two opposite poles in constructions of émigré cultural life. In the following pages, each of three case studies, focusing on interwar Paris, New York of the Cold War era, and late twentieth- and twenty-first-century Israel, presents a distinct configuration of cultural, ideological, geopolitical, and institutional parameters. Rather than embedding these case studies within the more conventional chronology of successive waves of emigration (defined primarily by Russia's fluctuating historical and political situation), I prefer to view these cultural formations as a set of *chronotopes*, shaping discourses of identity and corresponding to each specific location.[2] This shift in perspective entails further reconsideration of hierarchical approaches to metropolitan vs. diasporic geographies. Soviet-era discourse construed diasporic cultural production as located on the periphery, thereby positing its inferiority vis-à-vis the metropolitan center and stressing its alienated or even non-Russian character. Despite dramatic reversals in ideological assessments during the post-Soviet period, this centripetal pattern endured.[3] The tropes of "return" and "homecoming" inevitably prevailed in any discussion of diasporic literary figures, while response to the national agenda remained the major theme in émigré scholarship.[4] Adherence to the self-imposed "mission" of preserving the classical national canon and dedication to "writing back home" were certainly not uncommon among émigrés themselves. However, such an exclusive focus on the metropolitan center often deemphasized the transformative potential of extraterritorial Russian cultures, including their ability to generate alternative historical narratives and geographical frames. As Homi Bhabha argued in *The Location of Culture*, peripheral locations are rich in innovation and can destabilize and refashion stagnating "centers" (1994). A polycentric, nonhierarchical model of global Russian cultures may be visualized as an archipelago, a chain of islands that appear independent and isolated but in fact are interconnected in space, as well as time, often owing their origin to a series of volcanic eruptions.

Recent academic focus on the archipelago has challenged colonizing grammars that reduce islands to peripheral locations whose meanings and identities are dependent on the remote mainland. In fact, islands, often lying at the crossroads of trade and migration routes, have tended to be dynamic, shaped in equal measure by local geographies and passing flows, and, at least in the Mediterranean context, capable of producing sophisticated civilizations long before the continent. The archipelago as a trope for extraterritorial Russian culture suggests exchange, multiplicity, and fluidity. On the one hand, each individual diasporic center may appear to be an "island" in the midst of the host society, with no visible links to the metropolitan "continent" or other sites of dispersion. On the other hand, like a chain of islands, these centers emerged gradually over the last century as a result of successive "explosions": revolution, wars, periodic closure or opening of the Soviet state borders, and so on. While these common origins contributed to their shared heritage, each center of

Russian culture has also been informed by a unique combination of local and global factors. Open to cross-cultural exchanges, hybrid island identities are in flux, subject to continuous redefinition. Just as the totality of an archipelago is constituted by the articulation of each of its islands, so global Russian culture can be represented as a dynamic totality of all of its interconnected yet autonomous and evolving "centers." Indeed, the interdisciplinary study of the archipelago has challenged the binary conception of mainland versus islands, recasting the entire cultural space as an archipelago (Westphal 2007). The metropolitan Russian "continent," reconfigured so many times over the last century, is revealed under scrutiny as far less monolithic than convention would have it; in effect, it can be seen as just the largest island within the global archipelago of Russian culture. The next three sections of this chapter will engage with three particular "islands," examining the original character of each within the broader context of local and global cultural geographies.[5]

Interwar Paris and the Creation of Extraterritorial Russian Cultures

In the years following 1917, the routes of postrevolutionary dispersal of Russian emigration traversed the entire planet. From the Far East refugees fled to Harbin and Shanghai; from Crimea boatloads of civilians and soldiers of the defeated General Wrangel's White Army set sail for Istanbul, and then onward to Europe; many fled from Petrograd via Finland and the Baltics. Soon, compact Russian-speaking communities sprang up all over Europe and Asia, with some refugees reaching North Africa, Brazil, the United States, and Australia. In Europe, in addition to Paris, sizable Russian communities were established in Berlin, Prague, Sofia, Belgrade, Riga, and elsewhere. These diasporas were distinguished by their urban context, not only offering more opportunities to immigrants but also inevitably facilitating preservation of a distinct identity. Essentially, Russian cultural life in each of these locations produced a variation of the same model. During the first postrevolutionary decade, Russian émigrés harbored hopes that Bolshevik rule would soon collapse, enabling their speedy return. Consequently, they focused mostly on building diasporic networks (publishing ventures, schools, libraries, churches) that would bind together Russian-speaking communities, preserve their heritage, and support a sense of unity and common purpose. The professed teleology of return slowed assimilation and often led to the deliberate isolation of Russians within their host countries. Another factor that contributed to this isolation was the absence of an adequate legal framework. The Nansen passport, introduced by the League of

Nations in 1922, granted refugees the right to reside in a state that had signed the relevant convention, but it did not solve long-term problems of cross-border movement and employment, and it significantly reduced the likelihood of naturalization in host countries. By the 1930s, the hope of quick return was largely abandoned, and the second émigré generation began to adopt more hybrid identities. At the same time, economic crisis; the rise of xenophobic and overtly profascist sentiments in many places of Russian dispersion, from Harbin to Paris; and ultimately the outbreak of World War II dealt a heavy blow to Russian diasporic social structures.

During the interwar decades, Russian life in Europe was remarkably dynamic. The volatility of the political situation often caused individuals and whole communities who had just begun to settle into one location to pack up and move on, usually westward. For example, the establishment of diplomatic relations between Bulgaria and the USSR in 1934 led to a considerable decrease in the number of Russians fleeing to Sofia, where some 30,000 refugees had settled in the first postrevolutionary years. The rich cultural life of Russian Berlin, with its population of nearly a quarter of a million, was dramatically curtailed in the mid-1920s when relations with the Soviet Union, which had sustained cultural activity, shifted radically and many leaders of the community departed for Paris. Many of those who stayed on, including Vladimir Nabokov and his Jewish wife, Vera Slonim, were compelled to flee Hitler's regime in the following decade.[6]

Even more impressive than human mobility was the circulation of texts and ideas between pockets of the European diaspora and across the Soviet border. For example, the Change of Landmarks (*smenovekhovstvo*) movement, advocating the return of émigrés to Russia and a peaceful transformation of Bolshevism, originated in Prague with the 1921 publication of the volume *Smena vekh*, which was soon reincarnated in an eponymous Parisian periodical, and in the Berlin-based daily *Nakanune*.[7] Likewise, Eurasianism, which advocated the idea of a "Russian world" stretching across Europe and Asia and comprising other ethnicities alongside Russians, was first popularized in Sofia and developed in the works of the linguist and historian Nikolai Trubetzkoy, who taught at Vienna University. Special Eurasian seminars were organized in Paris and Prague, and the *Versty* journal, which promoted the Eurasian agenda, was edited in 1926–28 in Paris by Dmitry Sviatopolk-Mirsky, who later continued his activities in London.[8] Periodicals published in these various "islands" were read across the entire diasporic "archipelago," offering a platform for ideological debates and showcasing artistic achievement. Any Russian-language journal was potentially open to all émigré authors, irrespective of place of residence. The Prague-based periodical *Volia Rossii*, for instance, particularly welcomed novice writers from the global diaspora. The perception of integrity of diasporic space was reinforced by the fact that cultural life in every Russian community was punctuated by the same key events, including the annual Day of Russian Culture on Alexander Pushkin's birthday (June 6); celebrations of Leo Tolstoy's centenary in 1928, and activities in the run-up to the centenary of Pushkin's death in 1937.

In the earlier 1920s, the dissemination of émigré intellectual production across European and Soviet metropolitan territory was quite easy. Due to good relations between the Weimar Republic and the USSR, Berlin became the main site of cultural exchange between Soviet Russia and Russia abroad. Many of its 188 Russian-language publishing houses had a Soviet branch office, as was the case with Petropolis, Gelikon, Epokha, and Grzhebin. The Soviet government routinely placed commissions with Berlin publishers, and some of them produced large print runs almost exclusively for the Soviet market. Russophone periodicals that came out in Berlin, too, targeted not only the émigré audience. Some, like *Novyi mir*, maintained an openly pro-Soviet stance, while *Nakanune* was practically financed from the Soviet budget and maintained a Moscow office. Formally Soviet writers and journalists (Sergei Esenin, Andrei Bely, Maksim Gorky, Ilya Erenburg, Viktor Shklovsky, and Aleksei Tolstoy, to name just a few) visited or lived in Berlin for extended periods of time, mixing with their émigré peers in the House of the Arts or the Writers' Club. This unique cooperation between metropolitan and diasporic literary cultures, replicated nowhere else until the end of the Soviet period, came to an abrupt end in 1925, when the USSR embarked on a policy of political and cultural isolation, and émigré cultural achievements became a taboo topic for many decades to come.

Having surpassed Berlin around 1925, for the next fifteen years Paris hosted the most vibrant Russian community in Europe. The Paris diaspora numbered 45,000 and equipped itself with a well-organized network of institutions: educational and theological establishments, publishing houses and libraries, and more than 60 Russophone periodicals, including *Sovremennye zapiski*, *Vozrozhdenie*, *Poslednie novosti*, and *Chisla*. Resembling Russia in miniature, the Parisian community was characterized by extreme diversity, and an attempt to map out every ideological and aesthetic position would be futile. The focus here will be on two contrasting literary trends and their respective lexicons of national and artistic identification.

The mainstream émigré cultural establishment was composed of an older generation of established figures who worshipped the Russian cultural legacy and practiced, to use Svetlana Boym's (2001) term, a form of "restorative" nostalgia. The utopian dream of return to a Golden Age informed their foundational "mission," which consisted in preserving the national cultural tradition in order to pass it on to future generations. Russia served as a vital center, while émigrés assessed their own exilic locations as remote outposts. Quite uninterested in the European avant-garde, senior émigré writers often limited themselves to reproducing familiar models drawn from the Silver Age. Their writing, ranging from nostalgic evocations of Russia to debates over the "national idea," reassessments of Orthodox spirituality, and explorations of the metaphysics of the revolution, demonstrated their loyalty to Russian themes. This conservative stance did not necessarily undermine artistic potential. Bunin's short story cycle *Dark Avenues* (*Temnye allei*, 1937–44), for instance, remains one of the greatest achievements of émigré writing and twentieth-century Russian literature as a whole. But these stories arguably represent an experimental development of the same aesthetic parameters that characterized Bunin's pre-emigration art. The impact of the new place and many years spent away from Russia was limited for Bunin to accentuating his tragic perception of the irreversibility of time and nostalgic longing for evanescent moments of happiness. Paris serves as a background only in one story ("In Paris"), and the conceptual and aesthetic languages of interwar Europe leave little trace on this masterpiece of the premier writer of Russia abroad.

Gradually, however, voices emerged in Russian Paris that transcended this national, retrospective cultural paradigm; increasingly, the émigrés' exilic sensibilities—with attendant feelings of loss, longing, and cultivated isolation reminiscent of "masochistic narcissism" (Said 2000, 183)—were attenuated by closer engagement with local cultural contexts. Naturally, this transition was effected more easily by the younger generation of Russian Parisian authors, who had left their country of birth as adolescents, were almost bilingual, and were intrigued by the French artistic environment. The hybrid nature of their writing reflected their fragmented, interstitial, bicultural identity. While older mentors steered them toward nostalgic re-creation of canonical Russian literary models, they sought to break away and turn to interwar European modernism.

In Modris Eksteins's view, the postwar ideological, philosophical, and aesthetic crisis produced a modernist "culture of nightmare and denial" (1990, 237). Younger Russian writers provided their own variation on this generational ethos by fusing it with their specific experience of exile and deracination.

The inevitable setting of their texts was Paris, conceived as a dehumanized urban metropolis but also as a source of creativity born out of trauma, rupture, and cultural alienation. The narrative rhythms of Gaïto Gazdanov, Boris Poplavsky, Vladimir Varshavsky, Vasily Yanovsky, Elsa Triolet, just like those of Ferdinand Céline, Henry Miller, Louis Aragon, or Philippe Soupault, are punctuated by random wanderings through defamiliarized, uncanny, nocturnal Paris. Obsessive peripatetic motion within the microcosm of the city became a trope for the itinerant identities of the uprooted "lost generation," including those Russian émigrés who preferred to refer to themselves as the "unnoticed generation." They found their *genius loci* in the Montparnasse district, with its cafés and bars, the epicenter of avant-garde art and international bohemian life. Speaking in the language of interwar European modernism, Russian Montparnassians addressed the main concerns and anxieties of their time. Although for the most part they composed in Russian, their texts departed from the "classical" literary idiom practiced by senior émigrés. Disavowing the canonical Russian view of the writer as prophet, moral guide, or social critic, they created semi-autobiographical first-person narrators who displayed intimate feelings and shameful confessions in a manner reminiscent of the human document. Their style was characterized by simplicity, physiological vocabulary, and code-switching, leading the guardians of linguistic and cultural purity in the Russian community to accuse them of "foreignness." The authors of Russian Montparnasse indeed violated many taboos that had persisted in the discourse of their elders and rearranged the canon, provocatively dismissing Pushkin in favor of Lermontov and Rozanov, whom they interpreted subjectively as precursors of twentieth-century existentialism (Rubins 2015, 165–230).

The diasporic condition of deracination, hybridity, and fusion was crystallized as well in the poetry of the Paris Note. The Paris Note emerged as a loosely bound group, mentored by the poet and critic Georgy Adamovich, and included Anatoly Shteiger, Lydia Chervinskaya, Perikl Stavrov, Irina Knorring, and Igor Chinnov. Viewing the Russian Silver Age conception of poetic craft as a theurgic activity with a great deal of skepticism, they transformed poetry into an intimate conversation about life, death, spiritual and physical malaise, and loneliness. In Adamovich's words, "The poet at first blush is talking to himself, often he talks only about himself; the era of oratory has passed" (Adamovich and Kantor 2005, 6). From the Paris Note perspective, contemporary poetry should be divorced from any philosophical, political, social, or even aesthetic agenda and rendered a "private affair." The diaristic modality of the resulting verse matched the human document style of Russian Montparnasse prose.

The Paris Note poems are distinguished by lexical poverty, confessional intonation, fragmentation, frequent pauses, and a near absence of figurative language and ornamentation:

> Words are sad and simple,
> The heart wants no highbrow words.[9]
>
> **Shteiger**, "Simple Landscape"
> ("Prostoi peizazh") (Kreid 2003, 118)

Such minimalism reflected the group's perception that all conventional forms of artistic expression had collapsed. As Igor Chinnov later recalled, "We believed that we should write as if there would be no more poetry after us" (Glad 1993, 33). The "exhaustion" of culture was encoded in metapoetic meditations on the inadequacy of the poetic word.

> I know the value of my poems.
> I'm sorry for them, that's all.
>
> **Adamovich**, "I know the value
> of my poems" ("Stikham svoim
> ia znaiu tsenu") (Kreid 2003, 51)

In the Paris Note verse, the negation of the cultural tradition and of any collective identity cemented by shared ideologies or national belonging reached a high point. In this sense, it can be defined as poetry of "counter-exile" (Hagglund 1985, 38–39) focused on the key moments of human experience per se and stripped of national, historical, or cultural specificity.

The watershed between exilic and postnational cultural identities did not strictly coincide with the generational divide. In fact, it cut across generations and even individual literary personae. In one of the most provocative texts produced by the first wave of emigration, "Disintegration of an Atom" ("Raspad atoma," 1938), Georgy Ivanov, who was closer to the older generation of émigrés, offered a hybrid discourse conflating the native tradition and the Western modernist crisis narrative, echoing T. S. Eliot's *The Wasteland* and Henry Miller's *The Tropic of Cancer*. In this work, Russian cultural collapse becomes just one case of the entropy engulfing all of European civilization. Ivanov's work challenges the Russian canon by violating major cultural taboos, evoking scatology, filth, and necrophilia, providing catalogues of rubbish alongside random allusions to high Russian culture. His narrator's misquotation of well-known poetic lines, from Pushkin to Kruchenykh, signals the extinction of cultural memory and the irrelevance of the literary tradition in exilic reality. Grappling with arbitrary cultural references crisscrossing his failing consciousness, the narrator is impotent to decipher the fragments or reconstitute a broken whole. The metaphor of atomic explosion is employed by Ivanov to underscore the imminent physical and spiritual disintegration of his narrator. Ivanov's controversial text, which he preferred to define as a *poema* (long poem), inaugurated a new dimension of Russian literature that would be explored more systematically in the later twentieth century, in particular by Viktor Erofeev.[10]

Another elder émigré, Vladislav Khodasevich, represents an even more striking and complex case of literary development. In emigration, he gained a reputation as a resilient conservative who insisted on preserving the national cultural tradition against all odds. In his influential extended polemics with Adamovich, Khodasevich was critical of poetic "innovations" and the diaristic trend, persistently calling upon younger writers to learn from the Russian classics—and above all from Pushkin. And yet, in his last major poetic cycle, "European Night" ("Evropeiskaia noch'," 1927), Khodasevich eschews the "'grand' lexicon of poetic speech" (Bethea 1983, 276) and renders the Zeitgeist through, in Nabokov's words, "optical-pharmaceutical-chemical-anatomical" images (cited in Bethea 1983, 276). This jarring discontinuity between his professed ideal of "classical" form and a profoundly modern expression of civilizational collapse and artistic impotence is expressed in possibly even stronger terms by Khodasevich than by the Paris Note poets, his ostensible opponents. In the poem "Repository" ("Khranilishche"), for instance, the lyric persona wanders through a fine arts museum—a repository of carefully selected achievements of Western civilization. Looking at the "succession of Madonnas," he experiences disillusionment with all notions of "truth and beauty," revulsion, fatigue, and even physical malaise, ultimately relying not on the transfigurative potential of art but on "sour Pyramidon" for temporary relief. The language of high culture and creativity is meaningless for one in the grip of existential crisis, and Khodasevich's verse contributes powerfully to this pan-European *topos*. The title of the cycle, playing with the vision of darkness engulfing Europe, resonates with a range of interwar texts that use night as a figure for collapse and degradation, from Céline's *Voyage au bout de la nuit* to Gazdanov's *Night Roads*.

Khodasevich, Ivanov, and the authors of the Paris Note and Russian Montparnasse produced the most innovative writing of Russian Paris. Their challenge of major cultural proscriptions was facilitated by their position outside the metropolitan realm—not only geographically but in many respects conceptually. While Russian Paris ceased to exist as a viable sociocultural network with the outbreak of World War II, it created a generative paradigm of Russian culture beyond metropolitan borders and produced a broad spectrum of extraterritorial identities: from the nearly total exclusion of the non-Russian context (such persistent focus on the affairs of the homeland would be practiced later by Solzhenitsyn in his Vermont exile, for instance) to the gradual evolution away from a strictly national focus toward hybridization and cross-cultural dialogue (as occurred with Joseph Brodsky, Andrei Makine, and a number of Russian Israeli authors, including Boris Zaidman and Nekod Singer) and the exploration of universal themes (as demonstrated by the Third Hour experience, to be discussed in the following case study).

The Third Hour: Universality in the Cold War Era

The cataclysmic events of World War II brought the transformation or disappearance of older centers of Russian cultural activity abroad and the rise of new ones. By 1952, many of the 450,000 ex-Soviet displaced persons in Europe found themselves in Germany. Gradually, the center of gravity began to shift to other continents, most importantly North America. The Russian community in the United States had already been reinforced by first-wave émigrés fleeing the war and Holocaust, and immigration became a truly massive phenomenon later in the 1940s (with 548,000 arriving by 1950). While the United States remained the chief host country for post–World War II Soviet immigrants, other important destinations eventually emerged, including Israel and France (although Russian life in Paris was never again as vibrant as during the interwar decades).

Transcending the traditional division into second and third waves, the Cold War era presents a coherent historical and political background for tracing unifying tendencies that underpinned extraterritorial Russian culture between the late 1940s and early 1980s. Polarization of the world, the Iron Curtain, and reckless competition between the two superpowers resulted in a minimum of communication between metropolitan and diasporic branches. Those leaving the USSR during the second half of the twentieth century assumed that they would be unable ever to return. Indeed, unlike postrevolutionary refugees, they had no desire to do so, having often experienced repressions, the Gulag, or forced confinement in psychiatric wards. While they had no affinity for the Soviet system, their cultural production displayed the marks of the Soviet idiom, which sometimes resulted in the older émigrés' reluctance to embrace this generation. The dissident movement, frequently taking the form of exported texts even before the emigration of their authors through the phenomenon of *tamizdat* (publication of unauthorized works smuggled abroad) defined the politicized reception of Soviet intellectuals once they arrived in the West. Politicians, publishers, media, critics, and the general public were mostly interested in their eyewitness accounts of Soviet atrocities and construed ex-Soviet writers as, in the first instance, an opposition to the Communist regime. Reflecting on the situation of the 1970s–80s, Olga Matich concluded: "More often than not Russian literature today is read for its political content, both in the Soviet Union and abroad. As a result, the apolitical Russian writer is all but trapped in the stranglehold of politics, even in the West. Following the Russian lead, Western critics tend to apply political criteria to Russian literature and judge it for the most part according to its testimonial and propagandistic value" (1984, 182).

A number of émigré intellectuals and ideologically committed journals, such as *Kontinent*, perpetuated this politicized reception by sustaining their focus on Russia and its current condition. Others, who subscribed to a more universal artistic identity, and wished to liberate themselves from the dissident label, published in such periodicals as *Sintaksis*, *Ekho*, *Kovcheg*, *Chast' rechi*, *Novyi amerikanets*, and *Gnozis*. It was harder for the apolitical cohort to obtain publishing contracts and to build a reputation with Western readers, as Russian cultural activities were sometimes financed by Western politicized institutions and states, often covertly. Despite attempts to interpret Joseph Brodsky's persona according to the same dissident model, he became an exceptional case of an ex-Soviet poet who had been arrested, condemned, and expelled from his homeland, yet managed to transcend the émigré frame to become accepted as part of the American intellectual establishment.

The postwar years, unlike the interwar decades, were distinguished by the increased role academic structures assumed in promoting Russian émigré cultural production—as, for instance, in the case of academic publishers such as Ardis, Slavica, and Hermitage, along with periodicals such as *Zapiski russkoi akademicheskoi gruppy v SShA*. There were other important publishing ventures with a Russia focus across Europe and the United States, including YMCA Press and Rifma, the almanac *Mosty*, the journals *Grani*, *Opyty*, and the New York–based *The New Review*, which since its founding in 1942 has been the chief periodical for literary production of the entire global diaspora. The Viktor Kamkin bookstore in Rockville, MD, became the main distribution center for Russian and Soviet books in the United States, as well as a diasporic cultural center. Many literary personalities achieved a high level of integration in their host countries, becoming university professors, editors, publishers, and radio presenters with the Russian Service of Radio Liberty. Alongside the first-wave celebrities Nabokov and Berberova, the likes of Vladimir Markov, Boris Filippov, Igor

Chinnov, Yury Ivask, Lev Loseff, Tomas Venclova, and many others actively shaped the Slavic academic discipline.

Against this background of ideological fault lines and the pull of assimilation, the intellectual community formed in New York around the *Third Hour* journal was remarkable for its inclusive spirit and transcendence of any specifically Russian agenda. Founded by Russian émigrés, it soon outgrew the confines of a diasporic association and obtained a distinctly transnational identity. The society was initiated by the writer, journalist, and translator Elena Izwolsky. The daughter of Alexander Izwolsky, the Czar's Foreign Minister and later ambassador to France, she spent her childhood in Saint Petersburg, Japan, and Europe, and after the Revolution settled in Paris, subsequently moving to New York in 1941. She wrote articles for Anglophone Christian periodicals; authored a biography of Mikhail Bakunin, sketches about Marina Tsvetaeva, and books on Russian spirituality; compiled memoirs; and translated with enviable ease between Russian, English, and French. Izwolsky aspired to create zones of intellectual and spiritual contact between thinkers, irrespective of national origins or political convictions. Herself a convert to Catholicism with a preference for its Eastern branch, she promoted a nondenominational vision of Christianity. Open-mindedness prevented this refined aristocrat from squarely rejecting the Bolshevik regime, and she even visited the USSR after Stalin's death (a rare occurrence among "white Russian" émigrés).

The Third Hour ecumenical society and the eponymous journal occupied a central place in Izwolsky's diverse pursuits. The idea of the journal was discussed in 1944 in the New York home of Irma de Manziarly, who had previously financed cultural projects in Russian Paris, in particular the journal *Chisla*. De Manziarly's past was no less eventful than Izwolsky's. Born in Saint Petersburg to German Protestants, she went on to live in France as well as India, where she studied esoteric teachings and met Mahatma Gandhi. Both women were spiritual seekers who sought an exit from the postwar crisis and wished to contribute to healing and uniting humanity. The wealthy patroness volunteered to fund this ecumenical initiative, and Izwolsky assumed the daunting role of organizer and journal editor. The title of the society and journal was taken from the Acts of the Apostles (2:4–17), in which the apostles prophesy in various tongues to make their message intelligible to all. The editorial policy of universality was clearly stated in the first and subsequent issues: "Against the background of conflicting intellectual trends and tragic world-events, we continue to seek testimonies and expressions of authentic religious and human experiences. We believe that such testimonies in the field of religious life, as well as in literature, poetry and art, exemplify the working of spiritual forces without which the challenge of our time cannot be met. This is the great adventure of dedication and brotherhood to which our generation more than ever seems to be called: a personal call addressed to each, but in the name of all" ("To Our Readers" 1951, 1). The organizers originally intended to publish the journal in English, Russian, and French, but after the first trilingual issue, only English was retained. Between 1946 and 1975, ten issues of the *Third Hour* came out, with the final one a memorial volume dedicated to Izwolsky.

An important aspect of Third Hour activities were regular lectures followed by discussion with a glass of red wine. The society's core members were a colorful collection of personalities, including the composer Arthur Lourié (see Bullock, this volume), the former leader of the *mladorossy* movement Alexander Kazem-Bek, the head of the short-lived Russian Provisional government Alexander Kerensky, the writer Vasily Yanovsky (who became Izwolsky's main editorial associate), and many other authors, thinkers, and public figures who had migrated to New York from all over the world in the post–World War II years, including the poet W. H. Auden, the philosopher Denis de Rougemont, and the art critic and essayist Anne Freemantle. The founders of the Third Hour attracted such an impressive international following because of their cosmopolitan views, their historical experience reflecting the major European catastrophes of the twentieth century, and their considerate rebranding of the classic Russian message of universality (often conceived as "messianic" spiritualization of the rest of the world on Russian terms) into a more equal intellectual exchange and dialogue with global religious and philosophical currents.

Despite the editorial team's Christian orientation, the range and diversity of the journal's publications is impressive: they comprise articles on theology, philosophy, music and the arts, reports on the global ecumenical movement, memoirs, poetry, and fiction. *Third Hour* systematically featured works by Nikolai Berdyaev, Simone Weil, Edith Stein, Alexander Schmemann, and Teilhard de Chardin. De Manziarly shared her impressions of Gandhi, and Wladimir Ryabushinsky contributed an article on Old Believers' icon-painting. Izwolsky wrote about Vladimir Solovyov, Yanovsky about Nikolai Fedorov, and Lourié about the composer Modest Musorgsky. Taken together, these materials reflect the integrity of the group's fundamental beliefs. Several key themes recurred from issue to issue and meeting to meeting: the world is in crisis; the resulting spiritual vacuum may be filled with destructive ideologies; Christianity in its conventional form cannot provide a viable platform for reunification and needs to be reformed; artistic activity requires a commitment to spiritual kinship.

The Third Hour members' perception of a global crisis developed the interwar discourse of the entropic condition of Western civilization. In particular, the journal featured Berdyaev's reflections about "the end of . . . the kingdom of reason" and the advent of a new Middle Ages, when "subconscious and irrational forces have entered history" (Berdyaev 1951, 2). This loss of "forms which were worked out through a long cultural process" (Berdyaev 1976, 81) and reversion to barbarism could result, according to the philosopher, in the rise of totalitarian regimes that seek to solve the social question by destroying freedom of the spirit. Citing Dostoevsky's Grand Inquisitor, Berdyaev claimed that at present the masses were attracted to slavery and ideologies imposed from above. He advocated the creation of "laboratories of spiritual culture" that would work to transform world consciousness, and the Third Hour community heeded this call.

Marrying Berdyaev's belief that "the supreme value is neither the State, nor society, nor civilization, nor culture, but concrete man" (1951, 6) with Emmanuel Mounier's philosophy of Personalism, Izwolsky developed ideas on personal responsibility to humanity and went on to draw parallels with the works of Vladimir Solovyov, whom she considered the precursor of Mounier. She argued that Solovyov's teachings fit the twentieth century better than his own times, as he was "one of the first thinkers who denounced in advance the great sins of the twentieth century: totalitarian ideology, race-hatred, the excesses of nationalism" (Iswolsky 1976b, 75). For Yanovsky, the goal of uniting humanity articulated by the Third Hour was consonant with Fedorov's philosophy of a "common cause"—"the fight against poverty, disease, death" and the resurrection of our forefathers. Yanovsky elaborated on Fedorov's legacy of reconciliation between Church, science, and technology by bringing Henri Bergson into the equation: "Bergson's formula, God created man and man created the machine, is fully acceptable to Fedorov" (1976, 90). Furthermore, defining Proust's *A la recherche du temps perdu* as "an attempt at resurrection" à la Fedorov, Yanovsky urged writers "to cultivate our memory, become fully perceptive of our past, securely fix all the traits of our loved ones, external as well as internal. This is the task that belongs to art" (89). From this perspective, any creative activity is intimately linked to transcendent global spiritual needs. In a certain way, the Third Hour updated the formula of *art engagé*, drawing in part on W. H. Auden's dictum "Art is not enough," which concluded a lecture he gave at the Third Hour soon after joining the group in the 1940s.[11] Izwolsky, in particular, cited Auden's formula to postulate "oblation, a giving up of oneself entirely, instead of a mere intellectual pledge" (Iswolsky 1976a, 127). These examples demonstrate the Third Hour intellectual practice of establishing unexpected resonances between ideas and personalities usually discussed in separate contexts, drawing attention to unifying concerns and the evolution of world intellectual systems and sensibilities.

When considered against the historical context of the Cold War, the arms race, wars of national liberation, the 1960s social movements, rapid technological innovation, and the impact of mass media on radicalization of public discourses, the Third Hour's efforts to promote universal consciousness and reconciliation across deep-running divides stands out as a powerful yet minor countertrend. The main legacy of the group consists in facilitating dialogue across the divides separating Russian and Western philosophical traditions; Russian, European, and American intellectuals; Eastern and Western brands of Christianity; and even Communist ideology and humanist ideals. The ethical, spiritual, and ideological positions of the Third Hour were largely defined by postrevolutionary émigrés, yet they offered a new model of integrating Russian specificity into open-ended global conversations, effectively eliminating the dualistic opposition of Russia and the West that is characteristic of the Russian nationalist narrative. Instead, they mediated the traditional Russian pathos of engagement in the spiritual affairs of the world through Western philosophical and artistic creeds, emphasizing continuity, parallels, and exchanges rather than uniqueness and exclusivity. The Third Hour community transcended their local geography, as well as the Cold War ethos, and cultivated their intrinsic connection to other cultural "islands" across time and space. In doing so, they developed a new approach to constructing Russianness—not in nationalist, spatial, linguistic, or exilic versus metropolitan terms but as a dynamic intellectual identity shaped by diverse global flows and circuits of contact.

The Drifting "Island" of Russian Israel

Along with the United States, Israel received a massive influx of late Soviet-era immigrants. Yet the 160,000 who arrived in the 1970s were later dwarfed by the million-strong *aliyah* (the ingathering of Jews in the Holy Land—literally, the "ascent") of the 1990s, bringing the number of Russian speakers in Israel to its present total of one-fifth of the Israeli population. The nearly fifty-year history of Russian Israeli cultural life in many respects illustrates the transition from the Cold War situation to the contemporary condition of Russian cultural multiplicity, with trends toward intense localization and hybridization of cultural identities competing with global circuits of cultural production. At the same time, formulations of this community's collective identity are based on a dynamic combination of Jewish, Russian, Soviet, and Israeli elements, revealing its fundamental uniqueness among other Russian diasporic formations.

The 1970s *aliyah* included former *refuseniks*, many of whom experienced a Zionist awakening after the Six-Day War of 1967. Their biographical trajectories systematically renegotiated the concepts of "exile," "return," "home," and "abroad," in many respects responding to the fundamental Jewish metanarrative that designates Zion/Israel as the true homeland, life elsewhere as exile, and immigration to Israel as repatriation and redemption (see also Moshkin, this volume). Among those who arrived in Israel during that decade were many writers (David Markish, Leonid Girshovich, Yury Miloslavsky, Ruf Zernova, Eli Luxemburg), poets (Anri Volokhonsky, Mikhail Gendelev, Mikhail Grobman), and literary scholars and critics (Mikhail Weiskopf, Maya Kaganskaya, Ilya Serman). They built a cultural network, created Russian-language journals (*Sion*, *22*, *Zemlia i liudi*, *Vozrozhdenie*, *Menora*, *Ami*, *Vremia i my*), and established the Union of Russian-Israeli Writers. The Russophone community of this initial period had a strong sense of internal coherence and shared cultural values, and given this generation's political circumstances, it is unsurprising that the Zionist theme came to dominate its literary production (as is signaled in the titles of some of the journals just referenced).

Poetry from this period saw a revival of *zionide* (*sionida*), a genre that addresses Eretz-Israel as a sacred locus and projects contemporary situations onto biblical myths, with departure from the USSR often figured as exodus from Egypt.

> Just as at the dawn of time,
> Pharaoh does not let my people go.
>
> **Markish**, "Recitative"
> ("Rechitativ") (1971)

Some poems, such as the "Blue Scream" ("Sinii krik," 1973), by Markish, or Miloslavsky's "Song of the False Dmitrii" ("Pesenka Lzhedmitriia," 1966), highlight motifs of vengeance against the wicked "step-motherland." Prose narratives such as Yulia Shmukler's "We Are Leaving Russia" ("Ukhodim iz Rossii," 1975) and Ruf Zernova's "Our Roads Homeward" ("Nashi dorogi domoi," 1990) are characterized by similar double-coding of exodus from Russia in terms of biblical mythology, and representations of the journey to Israel draw on tropes characteristic of the centuries-long tradition of Jewish writing about pilgrimage to the Holy Land (Ezrahi 2000). Russophone works of this period present thematic and stylistic continuities with Soviet unofficial literature of the 1960s–70s, as a number of writers had been involved in tamizdat or samizdat activities and their first publications in Israel were often works created while still in the Soviet Union.[12] Replacing the "negative communist totality" with "another effective utopian construct," exodus narratives thus serve as a "mirror-image . . . to the canon-forming literature of social [*sic*] realism" (Smola 2015, 98). Mikhail Weiskopf reads the common "plot" of Russophone writing from this period as initiation, with a tripartite structure: symbolic death, liminal stage, and rebirth and acquisition of a new identity. A common sequel to this scenario of initiation is representation of the post-euphoric shock caused by the clash between dreams and reality. Occasionally, texts reflect this negative stage by reversing the previous pattern (picturing Russia as paradise lost, and Israel as a new exile) but more frequently by establishing equivalency between the USSR and Israel. With both homelands exposed as false and unwelcoming, the protagonist is now doomed to eternal migration (Vaiskopf 2001, 246).

David Markish's novel *Dog* (*Pes*, 1984) engages many of these contradictions. It relates the odyssey of an exiled samizdat writer named Vadim Soloviev through Western capitals and Israel. After a series of failed attempts to shake the world with grand spiritual revelations, he becomes deeply disappointed by the "mercantile" West and returns to the USSR, only to be shot by a border guard. On a metaliterary level, the novel revisits fundamental cultural idioms, including the clichéd definition of the Russian national writer as prophet, treating them with extreme ambivalence. Despite the ironic adoption of the Wandering Jew identity, Soloviev is not transformed by his migrations into a hybrid diasporic individual nourished by cross-cultural encounters. His destiny as an author, he believes, is to be a moral authority. In Alice Nakhimovsky's view, this canon needs an oppressive political regime as its prerequisite: "The myth of the Russian writer as 'beggar and prophet,' the moral teacher of an audience who values and needs him, does not work in the West. It is a tradition that is meaningful only in non-freedom. . . . Non-freedom permits certain knowledge of right and wrong. . . . In the comfortable certitude of the totalitarian state, he [Vadim] had a clear identity as a nonconformist writer. . . . In the West all these categories become confused" (1992, 200, 206, 214). The unrealized aspiration of the novel's protagonist to prophetic status, however, also contains a covert comment on the devalued status of high culture in Western/Israeli society. As we have seen in the case of the Third Hour, the paradigm of universal and moral art "exported" by Russian immigrants can find resonance within a broad circle of Western intellectuals but is contingent on specific geocultural conditions, including the writers' ability to convert specifically Russian cultural capital into a more global commodity.

The cultural dynamics of Russian Israel changed dramatically with the end of the Cold War. Perestroika, the sudden opening of Soviet borders and the reestablishment of diplomatic relations with Israel, resulted in massive emigration of Soviet Jews at the end of the 1980s and the start of the 1990s. Many of them were economic migrants who considered Israel a less desirable destination than Germany or the United States yet wound up there as a result of the complexities of the immigration process. One-third of those who did end up in Israel had non-Jewish or part-Jewish origins, and some 90 percent were secular. This "great Aliya" produced new, heterogeneous identities within Israel's Russophone population. It displaced existing cultural networks and created new ones, such as the publisher Gesharim–Mosty kul'tury, the theater Gesher, and the Jerusalem Club, which became a platform for vibrant cultural debates. Compared to the ideologically charged names of older journals, the titles of newly founded periodicals—*Solnechnoe spletenie*, *Ierusalimskii zhurnal*, *Zerkalo*, *Znak vremeni*, *Nota bene*, *I.O.*, *Kedr*, *Chernaia kuritsa*, *Obitaemyi ostrov*, *Dvoetochie*, and so on—suggest the decreased prominence of Zionism. This ideological shift paralleled processes in Israeli society as a whole in these years, such as a partial deconstruction of Zionist ideology, revision of national myths and narratives, and the rise of post-Zionist discourses (Silberstein 1999). Toward the turn of the century, the cynical treatment of national "father figures" became the stuff of popular culture (e.g., the popular TV show *Hartzoufim*) and also left a mark on Hebrew literary production (Bar-Iosef and Kopelman 1999, 31–32).

While still exploring the plot of initiation, 1990s narratives of Russian immigrants transitioned more quickly to a negative representation of Israel (Vaiskopf 2001, 251). In her analysis of works by Efraim Sevela, Iakov Tsigelman, Grigory Kanovich, and Mikhail Baranovsky, Klavdia Smola points to their common motif of disillusionment with the exodus myth. Their protagonists' inability to find spiritual unity with Israel and Judaism renders their geographic relocation senseless and produces a perception of Jewishness as an accident of fate and a burden (Smola 2011). Similar forms of "Zionist dystopia" can be found in the 1990s stories of "failed Aliya" written in Hebrew by Soviet immigrants, including Boris Zaidman. Dominated by nostalgia, these stories project a condescending view of Israeli society fueled by a residual Soviet Orientalist discourse (Tsirkin-Sadan 2014). In concert with the fading of political commitment, since the late twentieth century Russian Israeli literature has participated in the postmodernist trends characteristic of post-Soviet culture in general, deconstructing fundamental myths and engaging in metaliterary experimentation and linguistic play.

An important factor for the development of Russophone cultural activities in Israel in the last decades has been the intensification of physical mobility and economic and virtual interconnection with former Soviet states. This situation mirrored patterns of circulation across the entire diaspora, which was re-energized by free exchange with the metropolitan space after many decades of isolation. Most importantly, for extraterritorial Russian writers, readmission to metropolitan literary life has meant access to larger publishing markets and audiences. Toward the end of the twentieth century, the archipelago of Russian culture began to shift, displaying its multidirectional lateral linkages.

This increased mobility between Israel and the former USSR has even given rise to a new literary genre, mock odyssey, featuring the journey of a Russian Israeli back to the country of origin. Examples include Mikhail Gendelev's *Great (Un)Russian Journey* (*Velikoe [ne]russkoe puteshestvie*, 1993, 2014) and Elena Tolstaya's *West-Eastern Pull-Out-Divan* (*Zapadno-vostochnyi divan-krovat'*, 2003).[13] These travelogues, representing late- and post-Soviet reality with a great deal of irony and estrangement, effectively travesty the tradition of an immigrant's sentimental return to the country of birth. Another strategy of texts addressing Russian reality is the creation of a clash between different codes of memory. Russian Israeli writing routinely challenges the standard discourses of history, offering an alternative perspective, highlighting marginal, silenced, or taboo experiences. This is particularly evident in narratives about World War II or the siege of Leningrad, which explode not only the official epic code of heroism and sacrifice but also the normative Russian lexicon used to articulate memories about the Great Patriotic War, as in Gendelev's *Great (Un)Russian Journey* and Svetlana Shenbrunn's *Happiness Pills* (*Piliuli schast'ia*, 2010).

Among the outcomes of the great mobility of Russian intellectuals since the 1990s has been the phenomenon of the globe-trotting writer who may reside in different locations outside or inside the metropolitan space (see Wanner, this volume). In recent years, the rise of conservative discourses and oppressive measures against nonconformist artistic expression has led a number of prominent intellectuals to leave the Russian Federation. Many leading authors, including Boris Akunin, Ludmila Ulitskaya, and Vladimir Sorokin, now reside primarily abroad yet continue to rely on publishing and media networks in Russia.

Mirroring the cross-border circulation of authors and texts in the contemporary globalized world, this situation has further eroded the "metropolitan" versus "diasporic" dichotomy. Yet in local contexts, such as that of Israel, this new cultural reality has contributed to an even greater plurality in models of Russophone cultural life. The metaphorical title of a short story collection edited by Markish, *On This Bank of the Jordan* (*Po etu storonu Iordana*, 2008), evoking the Jews' passage over the river Jordan into Israel at the conclusion of the Exodus, highlights the distinct status of those Russophone writers whose prose reflects a Jewish frame of reference and continues to gravitate toward the Israeli cultural context. Others, however, like Dina Rubina, articulate a more complex relationship to cultural location. Already a professional writer in the USSR before emigrating in 1990, she wrote prose during the first decade after her arrival in Israel that was saturated with references to the carnivalesque mixture of cultures, languages, and mentalities characteristic of Israeli life. In these works, such as *Here Comes the Messiah* (*Vot idet Messiia*, 1996) and *At Your Gates* (*Vo vratakh tvoikh*, 1992), Russian *olim*, *haredi* Jews, and disguised Arab suicide bombers were depicted as actors in a theater of the absurd. These works were also published by Russian presses and, with their exotic subject matter, appealed to the metropolitan Russian reader. In more recent years, however, Rubina has steadily moved away from an Israeli thematic repertoire and Middle Eastern settings to engage with more "global" plots and themes. A best-selling author in Russia, she is practically unknown in Israel beyond the Russophone community. The protagonists of her latest novels, such as *Leonardo's Handwriting* (*Pocherk Leonardo*, 2008) and the *Russian Canary* (*Russkaia kanareika*, 2014), are defined primarily by their multidirectional migrations across space, time, and memory in narratives featuring rapid shifts between plot lines that mirror the hybrid identity of these deracinated protagonists. These works confront momentous questions of human destiny, the inevitability of fate, and the heavy price exacted upon those endowed with special gifts. While Rubina's vision resonates with aspects of Jewish mysticism, this connection is never quite spelled out. Pulling away from her local setting and cultural institutional frameworks, her authorial position reiterates the aspirations to universal transcendence associated with the Third Hour in another time and place.

Yet in contrast to such broadly cosmopolitan conceptions of identity, Russophone Israeli culture of the past decades has also produced literary voices that explore the local geopoetic modalities of the Middle East. The poet Alexander Barash, in collaboration with prose writer Alexander Goldshtein, articulated the concept of the community of writers living in the region as the "Mediterranean Note," a phrase he used as the title for one of his poetry collections (*Sredizemnomorskaia nota*, 2002). The specificity of this Mediterranean writing, according to Barash, proceeds from a combination of hedonism and apocalyptic vision that recalls late antiquity (Barash 2009). Despite the obvious allusion to the Paris Note, the poet's verse is a far cry from the minimalism of Parisian poets, and numerous toponyms imbue Barash's poems with an intentionally exotic quality. But there is a deeper analogy between the two poetic trends: in both cases, Russian diasporic poetry is informed by the creative potential of a specific place, mediating its character and aesthetics, as in his 1999 poem "Abandoned Syrian military camp . . ." ("Broshennyi siriiskii voennyi lager' . . ."):

> Abandoned Syrian military camp [. . .]
> the Golan is a quiet, empty plateau
> covered with high grass [. . .]

> This place knows two conditions:
> war and interim truce
> And as before sleep or death
> in the yellow evening glow
> a deer glides by, with an adolescent's grace
> disappearing where the gardens used to be
> behind the crumbled basalt walls
> of a Byzantine village.
>
> (**Barash** 2002)

Despite the strategy of localization of Russian culture that links Barash and Goldshtein to their predecessors in Paris, a significant readership of the Israeli authors' works consists of elite metropolitan audiences who value them precisely for their innovative, peripheral poetics.

Certain distinctive features of Russophone Israeli literature predicated on geographical specificity are evident in the poem cited above. Compared to cultural production in other significant centers of Russian dispersion (Berlin, Prague, Paris, London, or New York), it often engages with the landscapes of the whole country rather than the urban contexts alone. From the start, spurred by the providential mission of recovering a specific territory in myths of exodus and return, Russian narratives have reflected on the direct link between land, physical survival, and geopolitics. One of the most productive topics in Russian Israeli literature has been war (as reflected in Gendelev's Lebanese poetic cycle), along with motifs of Arab terrorism and the dangers of everyday existence in the settlements (e.g., Luxemburg's "Settlers" ["Poselentsy," 2008], Yuliya Vudka's *Candle of Memory* [*Svecha pamiati*, 2008], and works by Rubina). In contrast to the conventional construction of Russian territory in the dominant metropolitan tradition as an infinite space with a well-defined "center" and an amorphous periphery (see Kukulin, this volume), Israel is commonly represented through rapid changes of scenery, reflecting the density and diversity of the land.[14]

For some Russophone Israeli authors, a focus on the local landscape serves as a distinguishing trait. For others, a primary marker of difference is the idiosyncratic use of the Russian language. *Simvol "My"*—an anthology of Russophone Jewish literature from Israel, Europe, and America—was conceived to illustrate the decentered condition of Russian culture and to promote translocal conversations, bypassing the metropolitan space. The preface-manifesto states that in the twenty-first century, Russian literature has become international and free from "the hierarchy of 'dominance and subordination,' determined by the geographical location of the text and the author" (Vrubel'-Golubkina 2003, 5–8). It urges diaspora writers to cultivate their "foreignness" in particular by means of linguistic "distancing" from their country of origin.

The poet Mikhail Gendelev decouples language from identity and canon even more forcefully: "I am an Israeli Russophone poet. And a Jewish person. . . . I don't consider . . . a language (Russian in our case) the principle and formational element . . . in a poet's identification" (2003, 519). His poem "To the Arabic Language" ("K arabskoi rechi") thematizes provocatively the rejection of Russian as unfit for an Israeli poet, so long as it remains a proxy for the Russian cultural tradition: "I'd so much like to leave our speech / to leave it painfully and inhumanely." Rewriting his famous intertext, Mandelshtam's "To the German Language" ("K nemetskoi rechi"), Gendelev insists that local challenges, in particular Arab terrorism, require a response in kind; the Russian humanist ethos is, ultimately, inadequate and needs to be recoded. A Middle Eastern poet must "learn" from Arabic an alternative, dehumanized "tongue" of violence: "with your teeth / to spit out into the atmosphere / War desire! [*zhelanie Voina!*]."

Finally, Gali-Dana and Nekod Singer, writers, poets, and editors of bilingual Hebrew-Russian journals, have made even more radical steps toward estranging Russian from its original territory by giving up the commitment to a single language altogether in favor of a linguistic polyphony, effected in complex practices of translation and self-translation. Comparing the nonidentical Russian and Hebrew versions of Singer's prose, Roman Katsman views "the totality of his work" as a "kind of virtual conceptual performance of a multiplicity of languages that play with each other, replace each other, translate, and do not translate each other" (2016, 69).

At the same time as these Russian Israeli intellectuals contribute to a more deeply "diasporic" redaction of the Russian language with regard to the metropolitan circuits, in Israel they represent a resistance to the nation-building strategy of hebraization. Expressing a disappointment with Israeli cultural policies common in Russophone circles, the essayist Anna Isakova laments that two thousand years of diasporic Jewish experience is systematically suppressed in Israel for the sake of a synthetic Hebrew culture based on a reversal of the anti-Semitic stereotype: this "new Jew, the Aryan, is not fond of his past" (2007, 469). In a reflection of this stance, Russophone Israelis often assess their commitment to the Russian language as a sign of cultural superiority in the Israeli context—a link to European culture and an expression of cosmopolitanism. As sociological research demonstrates, Hebrew enjoys low prestige in the eyes of some immigrants inclined to practice "cultural separatism" (Remennick 2002).

The title of Mikhail Baranovsky's story "Izrailovka" reproduces the pejorative Russian nickname for Israel, while the poet Elena Akselrod laments the remoteness of Europe:

> . . . I didn't come full circle. And I ended up—where?
> Europe is not nearby, near me is a Bedouin tent.
>
> (Shklovskaia 2001, 15)

While ambivalence toward Europe, perceived as a cradle of anti-Semitism, has been an important component of the Israeli Zionist ethos, Russian Jews preserve their diasporic habit of assimilating European values as an antidote to what some term the "Asiatic" stream in Russian culture (Marom and Miller 2011, 94).[15] The routes open before the next Russian Israeli literary generation range from writing in a more or less estranged diasporic Russian, integrating a "Russian intonation" in Hebrew, or creolizing both languages and thereby contributing to the further diversification, hybridity, and diasporization of Israeli cultural geography.

Local Global Cultures

In some sense, the history of global Russian cultures offered above unfolds as a spiral, from a moment of open borders linking sites of extraterritorial production with the metropole in the 1920s, through the era of Cold War fragmentation of the Russian world, and back to the present era of even more robust interconnection of sites of cultural life. Yet these sites are themselves more diverse and distinctive than ever before. Shall we speak, then, of "a" Russian language and "a" Russian culture, or should we embrace the notion of Russian languages and Russian cultures as distinct constructs within a polycentric Russian-speaking archipelago? Is there an extraterritorial "world literature in Russian"? The above case studies—Russian Paris, the New York–based Third Hour group, and Russian Israel—problematize any reductive mapping of global cultural dispersion and interconnection. As the Third Hour demonstrates, the aspiration to a truly universal idea of Russian culture may be articulated at a moment of the greatest de facto division of the Russian cultural world. And the case of Russian Israel indicates that the drive toward local hybrid cultural formations may bring success in Moscow.

In our age of massive migrations of intellectuals, virtual connectivity, and proliferation of interstitial identities, nation-states, national canons, languages, and master narratives are insufficient criteria for a taxonomy of global literary outputs. Yet while no one formula may encapsulate global culture, the global may still encapsulate a unity of diversity. Diasporic narratives are nourished by borders and migrations across them, encounters on each side, and interaction between different loci. Remaining in dialogue with metropolitan culture and the national tradition, local cultures simultaneously transcend them, engage in transnational conversations, and create constellations out of diverse aesthetic and ideological vocabularies. Such narratives tend to present specific extraterritorial locations not as peripheral with regard to the metropolitan center but as autonomous and unique. Diasporic authors and communities contest their alleged marginality and assert their hybrid character. Yet diasporic consciousness and patterns of writing inevitably spill over into the metropolitan world, eroding monolithic identities and discourses even as they participate in transnational literary systems.

In the contemporary context, diasporization and hybridity have become conditions for novel ways of "translating" the world. Perhaps they have even become prerequisites for much of today's artistic practices. Contributing alternative possibilities, the open-ended, global diaspora revitalizes a culture obsessed with its own uniqueness, greatness, uniformity, and boundaries. Ultimately, then, geographical fragmentation and unification are revealed as interrelated processes of cultural development that attest to the fecundity of global dispersion as an engine for cultural innovation and collective self-fashioning. The question of whether we should talk about one global Russian culture or many finds an answer only provisionally and, paradoxically, locally.

Notes

1. Marc Raeff's conclusion reflects the optimistic expectations of the late 1980s: "The creation of culture in Russia Abroad is now a closed chapter, for Russia Abroad is no more. Will its culture be reintegrated into the mainstream in the homeland? We believe that the signs of recent years suggest an affirmative answer" (1990, 198).

2. Mikhail Bakhtin defined *chronotope* as "intrinsic connectedness of temporal and spatial relationships that are artistically expressed in literature" (1984, 84).

3. If during most of the Soviet era diasporic production was silenced within Russia, since glasnost it has been celebrated—but not so much for its difference as for its status as a branch of Russian culture now welcomed back to the "fold."

4. On émigré projects of cultural continuity and development of the national agenda, as well as on the reception of émigré literature in turn-of-the-century Russia, see Slobin 2013.

5. On Russian émigré culture, see Struve 1959, 1996; Karlinsky 1973; Raeff 1990; Patterson 1995; Rubins 2005.

6. On Russian émigré life in Berlin, see Volkmann 1966; Williams 1972; Fleishman, Hughes, and Raevskaya-Hughes 1983; Schlögel 1994b, 2007.

7. See Hardeman 1994.

8. See Shlapentokh 2007; Bassin, Glebov, and Laruelle 2015.

9. In the original, the word used for "highbrow," *zaumnyi*, may also be a reference to "trans-sense" words, in the formulations of Russian Futurists.

10. From his anthology *Russian Flowers of Evil* (*Russkie tsvety zla*, 2001) to his more recent works and media appearances, Viktor Erofeev has described a number of metropolitan and émigré writers' shift in recent decades away from the Russian humanist tradition to examine the limits of humanity. This new writing often uses shock therapy to bring the reader face to face with the evil inherent in human beings. The claim to originality of these works, however, can be properly assessed only in the context of earlier precedents, Ivanov's *Disintegration of an Atom* in the first instance.

11. Auden eventually published this lecture in the form of an essay in Auden 1949.

12. As opposed to tamizdat (publishing abroad), samizdat (self-publishing) designates unauthorized printing of texts in the Soviet Union for dissemination within underground circles.

13. Cf. a similar tendency in cinema (e.g., Mikhail Kalik's autobiographical film *And the Wind Returns*, treated in Moshkin, this volume).

14. Even Jerusalem, featured as a sacred center in the earlier Zionist narratives, usually stands for all of Zion (Ezrahi 2000, 237).

15. Furthermore, Russian remains an internal code for a community largely opposed to the leftist intellectual establishment; it thereby provides a zone free of political correctness.

Russophone Writing in Ukraine

Historical Contexts and Post-Euromaidan Changes

Vitaly Chernetsky

Rethinking Identity–Reframing Russophone Culture

Since the events of the winter of 2013–14 in Kyiv, first known as the Euromaidan but soon dubbed by participants the Revolution of Dignity, the significance of Russophone writing in Ukraine has shifted rapidly. Popular protests and political transformations were quickly followed by Russian state interventions to annex Crimea and foment separatist movements in Ukraine's east, ultimately leading to the outbreak of a war around two unrecognized breakaway statelets, the Donetsk and Luhansk "People's Republics." That war is still simmering today and has claimed thousands of lives and displaced 1.7 million people.[1] These events generated a massive cultural response from communities dedicated to Ukrainian political unity (although we should also recognize intense political contestation within that landscape). The Euromaidan's earlier, peaceful phase included public performances, concerts, and art exhibitions; initial gatherings were in large part triggered by social media posts, and various social media platforms and live streaming projects profoundly shaped the narratives of the revolution.[2] Numerous documentary film crews pursued projects ranging from traditional in form to highly experimental and attracting widespread international attention.[3] Literary production has been similarly rich. Although the ongoing conflict has often been described as one between Russian and Ukrainian states and territories, this outpouring of cultural response within Ukrainian society has taken place in both Ukrainian and Russian. This overt collision of political claims and cultural realities has triggered a reevaluation of what, exactly, it is to be a Ukrainian and to write in Russian today.

One key thesis has dominated both scholarly analysis and public discourse about contemporary Ukraine: "the Euromaidan and the subsequent Russian aggression" resulted in "a dramatic change in Ukrainian national identity" (Kulyk 2016b, 588). Commentators have linked this change with a paradigmatic shift in the realm of cultural production. In his recent article "Literary History as Provocation of National Identity, National Identity as Provocation of Literary History: The Case of Ukraine," Marko Pavlyshyn, a leading postcolonial critic writing on Ukraine, identified this change as "the civic turn": "Both research and public commentary detect a major shift in the beliefs and emotions associated with the national identity of citizens of Ukraine during and after the Euromaidan—a shift that had already been presaged in the Orange Revolution of 2004. In short, what has been observed is a transition from an ethno-cultural conception of Ukrainianness to its civic counterpart, where Ukrainianness is understood as an attribute freely chosen by people favorably disposed to the Ukrainian nation-state without regard to ethnicity or cultural orientation" (2016, 76). This process of identity transformation has been beset by many problems and setbacks and is by no means complete. A fundamentally new Ukrainian identity, civic and future-oriented, is being born in the context of ongoing trauma and uncertainty.

This shift contrasts starkly with earlier tendencies, as for the past two hundred years, during the period associated with the formation and development of modern national identities, the Ukrainian national project, similarly to "the nationalisms of other Central and East European nations submerged in dynastic empires . . . , focused on the mobilization of its own ethno-cultural community," even when cultural heterogeneity was acknowledged (Pavlyshyn 2016, 76). National identity was seen as a project of "politicians, writers, and civic activists" (Yekelchyk 2007, 6) to "raise the consciousness" of the masses and reverse the assimilation of educated elites, thereby empowering the ethno-linguistic majority on what is claimed as the nation's ethnographic territory.

However, in the post-1991 context of Ukraine as an independent state, a different project came to the fore—even if its course did not run smoothly. Slowly at first, but with increasing speed in the twenty-first century,

> a collective consciousness began to emerge that observers were prepared to label civic. The Euromaidan of 2013–14, peopled as it was by citizens of Ukraine who in many cases took care to render visible their regional, linguistic and religious diversity, advanced this trend, as did the fact that, except for part of the Donbas, the predominantly Russian-speaking parts of the country rejected secessionist initiatives inspired by the ethno-cultural ideology of the "Russian World," while the volunteers who enlisted in self-organized military formations to combat the Russian-backed separatists were as likely to speak Russian as Ukrainian. (Pavlyshyn 2016, 76–77)

No longer a minority in a multinational empire but now the "titular nationality" of a democratic, ethnically diverse state in its own right, Ukraine has embarked on the replacement of an ethnically based concept of nationhood by a civic one. As this civic identity gains greater relevance and importance in post-Maidan Ukraine, Russophone writing is coming into its own as a form of Ukrainian literature.

Yet we should not draw the line between Ukrainian identity's past and present too sharply, for recent processes have important predecessors in prior periods. In the past, the embrace of a civic Ukrainian identity by cultural producers, as in the cases of Ukrainian-Jewish authors discussed in Yohanan Petrovsky-Shtern's book *The Anti-Imperial Choice*, invariably entailed a switch to Ukrainian language as a means of creative expression. This exchange could also be reversed, as in the case of Raisa Troianker (1908–45), a poet who pioneered the theme of shtetl life in Ukrainian-language writing. After five years of success as a Ukrainian-language author, Troianker abruptly moved to Leningrad, abandoned all ties to Ukrainian and Jewish culture, and reemerged as a conventional Russian-language writer (Petrovsky-Shtern 2009, 111–64). Until recently, the dilemmas of hybrid and split identification faced by cultural producers with ties to Ukraine more often than not remained unresolved, even if history is rich with cases like that of Marko Vovchok (pen name of Maria Vilinskaya, 1833–1907), a Russian noblewoman who fell in love with Ukrainian culture and became the first woman prose writer writing in Ukrainian. In the late 1850s and early 1860s she was a literary star, praised by Shevchenko and Turgenev alike; however, she abandoned her Ukrainian-language literary pursuits after fewer than ten years.

It is this prehistory that underwrites the complex processes of transformation currently underway. Paradoxically, precisely because Russian political and cultural imperialism has for centuries compelled Ukrainian authors to write in Russian, contemporary Ukrainian society possesses a well-developed capacity to accept Russophone linguistic and literary realities as parts of a larger Ukrainian continuum. If Nikolai Gogol's writings are claimed as Ukrainian even if composed in Russian, it follows that exclusionary attitudes toward linguistic practices in contemporary Ukrainian literature are illogical. In order to account for this complex present reality, the relationship between Russian and Ukrainian identities and literature must be traced back to the premodern period. Since the dawn of Slavic cultures, the intertwined yet distinct political and linguistic realities of these communities and territories produced continual shifts and contestation of cultural identities. In the current chapter, I trace the long history of Russian writing in Ukraine and by Ukrainians as a window into the ongoing present articulation of Ukrainian civic identity and literary reality.

Premodern Preludes

If there is a recurring theme that can be traced through the history of Ukrainian culture, it is that of hybridity and overlapping/contested identifications. Even reaching back to the Kyivan Rus' period (tenth–thirteenth centuries), the possibility of speaking of a coherent, unified Rus' identity is not supported by contemporary scholarship (see Plokhy 2006, 10–48). Identity claims remained a prominent topic for cultural discourse in Ukrainian lands in the later Middle Ages, as most of what is now Ukraine and Belarus came under the rule of the Grand Duchy of Lithuania in 1320–63, while another portion of Ukrainian lands came under the Kingdom of Poland in 1345–66. After the Union of Lublin in 1569, these two states merged into the Polish-Lithuanian Commonwealth (with the internal administrative boundary between Poland and Lithuania within it shifting to approximately the present-day border between Belarus and Ukraine).

The Grand Duchy and Commonwealth periods are rich with material for historians studying the worldviews and identities of educated Eastern Slavs in those states (aristocrats, clergy, and burghers). This time period also brought the rise of a unique group of warrior frontiersmen, the Cossacks. Serhii Plokhy and Timothy Snyder have provided comprehensive overviews of regional and ethno-national identity-building projects over the course of several centuries (Snyder 2003; Plokhy 2006); others have zoomed in on some of the details (Sysyn 1981, 1985; Frick 1995; Iakovenko 2002, 2008). In the Grand Duchy before the Union of Lublin, the Eastern Slavic elites were a privileged stratum, and the state's primary official language was Ruthenian, a written East Slavic language that is considered a link between the Old Rus' linguistic continuum (in all of its diversity of regional dialects) and modern Belarusian and Ukrainian.[4] In distinction from the Armenian and the Jewish diasporas, which within the Commonwealth were autonomous and governed by community laws and administration, Ruthenians were only distinguished by their language, culture, and religion, and the end of the sixteenth century saw an acceleration of the pressure on them to assimilate, which arose as a consequence of religious tensions brought about by the Counter-Reformation.

While several prominent noble families fully polonized over the course of just two generations, for others in the educated elite, arriving at an understanding of their identities and allegiances remained far from straightforward. An influential historical narrative asserts that the Commonwealth developed a "civic nation" of the nobility that reached across ethno-linguistic and religious divides, anticipating the rise of civic nationhood elsewhere by several centuries (see Snyder 2003, 1–12). However, acceptance of this theory, postulating the existence of an early modern Polish "nation of nobility," is far from universal (see Frick 1995, 229–45). In fact, a robust debate developed around the formula "*gente Ruthenus, natione Polonus*"—politically a Pole, though ethnically a Ruthenian—most notably associated with the Renaissance-era intellectual Stanisław Orzechowski, a.k.a. Stanislav Orikhovs'kyi (1513–66; see Plokhy 2006, 169–80). As Plokhy sums up, "Orzechowski's narrative indicates that he associated himself first and foremost with the people of Rus', not with the Polish presence in the area. On the other hand, the population of his Rus' was multiethnic and multiconfessional. It was blended into one people by the Polish kings, who allowed intermarriage between representatives of different religions" (2006, 172). This hybrid overlapping identity, however, was only meaningful locally; when traveling abroad, Orzechowski identified himself only as Polish. In other words, his identity politics can be seen as anticipating the rise of the new Ukrainian cultural identity among the local nobility in the Russian-ruled part of Ukraine in the late eighteenth and early nineteenth centuries: for them, too, it was an identity for local use and one that in their minds did not conflict with political allegiance to Russia.

Within the context of Counter-Reformation, the efforts of the Catholic Church in the Commonwealth were also directed at ending the split with Eastern Christianity, leading to the 1596 Union of Brest, which generated an intense polemic among local elites. The lines of this contestation were often far from clear-cut; in fact, several prominent intellectuals reversed their positions, sometimes more than once (Frick 1995). As a corollary, the flowering of Christian polemical literature led to the establishment and growth of Ruthenian educational institutions. The years of polemic also led to the strengthening of the

Cossacks' role in Ukrainian lands; their allegiance to Orthodox Christianity led to their acquisition of a more prominent political and symbolic status.

The end of the sixteenth century through the seventeenth century was thus a time of turmoil that eventually led to violent conflict, but it was also an era marked by a cultural flowering; during this time, Ukrainian literary texts were composed in at least three languages (Ruthenian, Polish, and Latin). Rising political tensions led to the Cossack uprising of 1648, the establishment of the autonomous Cossack state under the leadership of Bohdan Khmelnytsky and the lengthy war that followed (for a reassessment of its legacies from multiple national perspectives, see Glaser 2015). De facto independent but without clear legal status, in its struggle to survive, the Cossack state explored multiple alliances and signed several treaties. One was signed in 1654 with the Muscovite state, changing the status of the Cossack lands into that of a self-governing vassal of Moscow; however, the Cossacks, accustomed to the legal culture of the Commonwealth, saw this treaty as an agreement of equals and therefore interpreted the 1656 peace treaty of Wilno between Moscow and Poland-Lithuania as a violation of that agreement, rendering it void, and instead sought an alternative international coalition. While the Cossacks under Khmelnytsky's successor Ivan Vyhovsky were victorious militarily, Moscow exploited internecine strife within the Cossack leadership that ultimately led to Vyhovsky's downfall and the start of the period known as the Ruin. In 1667 a new border between the Commonwealth and Muscovy, dividing the Ukrainian lands in half mostly along the Dnieper, was established at the Truce of Andrusovo. With the election of Ivan Mazepa as Hetman in 1687, eastern Ukrainian lands began a period of rebuilding in the face of new political realities that were, however, still not fully embraced by elites. Only after Mazepa's disastrous defeat in the 1709 Battle of Poltava, after he formed an alliance with Sweden's King Charles XII, did the status of Russian-ruled Ukraine radically change.

The second half of the seventeenth century was also marked by the rising prominence of educated Ruthenians in the Muscovite state. While some of those intellectuals, such as Danylo Tuptalo (1651–1709), later canonized as St. Dimitrii of Rostov, left Ukraine for Muscovite lands against their will, others actively sought new opportunities. Ukrainian intellectuals such as Stefan Iavorsky (1658–1722) were prominent in articulation and implementation of Peter I's reforms, and Iavorsky's rival Teofan Prokopovych, a.k.a. Feofan Prokopovich (1681–1736), became the new Russian Empire's chief ideologist. As Plokhy notes, "The Kyivans certainly helped Peter if not to formulate his ideas, then at least to articulate them by creating a discourse that popularized and legitimized his policies" (2006, 253). The exodus of ambitious members of the educated elite only accelerated after the Battle of Poltava.

Up until Poltava, we can speak of half a century of strong Ukrainian influence on the literary production of the Russian state, felt not only in aesthetic and scholarly trends but also in linguistic practices. The Ukrainians' reversal of fortunes after 1709 led to an increasing suspicion of their role and linguistic influence. The newly proclaimed Russian Empire pursued a homogenizing project in "Russian" cultural and linguistic space that included Ukraine, at least in the minds of many intellectuals in the capitals—including Ukrainian intellectuals who sought to secure their fortunes in a politically precarious context. In 1720 Peter I prohibited the publication of books in the written standard that had been used in the Ukrainian lands and mandated all future publications to be verified against those printed in Moscow to ensure the absence of linguistic discrepancies—thus reducing Ukrainian to a language of oral culture and manuscript writing. As the autonomy of Ukrainian lands was abolished by Catherine II in 1764, with the Zaporozhian Cossack Host liquidated in 1775 and serfdom introduced in Ukraine in 1783, Ukrainian elites were also finally granted Russian nobility (*dvorianstvo*) status. In consequence, two simultaneous impulses developed: accelerated cooptation of Ukrainian gentry into the Russian imperial structure and exploration of Ukrainian roots in order to substantiate claims to nobility status. In the hybrid identities of local educated elites of Ukrainian lands, Ukrainian orientation was aimed locally and historically, while identification with the Russian Empire was political in nature.[5]

Romantic Vernaculars and Colonial Modernities

At the turn of the nineteenth century, just as Nikolai Karamzin and his allies were revolutionizing the Russian literary language, bringing it closer to the spoken vernacular in a reflection of the pan-European rise of Romantic nationalist thought, the same process began in Ukraine. The 1798 publication of Parts I and II of Ivan Kotliarevsky's travestied *Aeneid* laid the foundation of a new vernacular Ukrainian literature. However, the meaning and role of these vernacular texts were subjects of intense debate.[6] Questions of language use were intertwined with those of implied audience: early nineteenth-century Ukrainian authors wrote in Ukrainian primarily for "home use"—for a restricted internal audience—and frequently chose Russian to address universal themes or a broader audience. Additionally, the success of Kotliarevsky's mock epic spawned imitators who with far less skill sought to use Ukrainian vernacular primarily for comedic purposes. Alongside these Ukrainian-language texts, the early decades of the nineteenth century witnessed the rise of "Ukrainian schools" in both Russian- and Polish-language literature. In the case of Russian, this included such prominent figures as Vasily Narezhny (Vasyl' Narizhnyi, 1780–1825), Orest Somov (1793–1833), and Antony Pogorelsky (pen name of Oleksii Perovs'kyi, 1787–1836).

Even with this expansion of the corpus of literary texts in modern Ukrainian, it was dominated either by the comedic or the folkloric mode (with collections of Ukrainian folk songs published regularly from 1819). Writers often switched to other languages, notably Russian, when exploring other themes. A telling example can be found in Hryhory Kvitka (Hryhorii Kvitka-Osnov'ianenko, 1778–1843), considered to be the father of Ukrainian prose and now mostly remembered for his Ukrainian-language writings. Nevertheless, the volume of writing Kvitka produced in Russian is actually significantly larger. More to the point, while his place in the Ukrainian literary canon is unchallenged, that of his younger contemporary Gogol remains hotly contested. While his father was a Ukrainian-language playwright, Gogol deliberately chose to write in Russian to satisfy his ambition to reach a wider audience. However, as the voluminous bibliography on Gogol demonstrates, his own views on his identity and the later history of the reception of his work preclude an "either-or" approach (see esp. Bojanowska 2007).

The expansion of Ukrainian-language writing beyond these limitations, especially with the publication of Taras Shevchenko's first book in 1840, was greeted with puzzlement and annoyance by many educated Russian elites, as exemplified in a notorious 1841 pronouncement by the father of modern Russian literary criticism, Vissarion Belinsky, that "the literary language of the Little Russians [i.e., Ukrainians] ought to be the language of their educated society, Russian" (Belinskii 1954, 330). Whereas in the 1830s, Ukrainian-language publications were actively encouraged as a manifestation of Count Uvarov's policy of "official nationality," within a few years the imperial censors already considered them dangerous. In subsequent years, leading writers whose place in the Ukrainian canon is indisputable authored, alongside Ukrainian-language texts, a sizable number of works in Russian, Polish, or German. This was the case with Shevchenko, Ukraine's national poet, who wrote both his prose fiction and his post-exile diary in Russian. Other major nineteenth- and early twentieth-century figures with a significant body of work in other languages include Panteleimon Kulish, Ivan Franko, Olha Kobylianska, and Volodymyr Vynnychenko. Such cases commonly constituted strategic temporary switching dictated by political pressures and censorship, including the 1847 crackdown on the Cyrilo-Methodian Brotherhood, the 1863 Valuev Circular, and the 1876 Ems Ukaz, which forbade publication and importation of Ukrainian-language publications in the Russian Empire. This can therefore be compared to the situation of the literary sphere of other nations facing colonial oppression, with writers from a colonized background compelled to write in the language of the colonial master.

In this respect, the status of Ukraine in the Russian Empire and then the Soviet Union has frequently been compared to that of Ireland—a colonized nation whose territory is adjacent to its colonizer and whose population is seen as ethnically different but not racially othered in the same way as that of the European powers' African and Asian colonies. Granting that Russian and Soviet domination over "its own" populations and territories was never, in fact, benign, the cultural status of Ukraine was that of a hybrid between a province and a colony, and substantially different from Russia's so-called internal colonization.[7] As George Grabowicz has observed:

> There is a basic qualitative difference: decrees were passed limiting and prohibiting such languages and literatures as Ukrainian and Lithuanian, not Russian. Beyond that, membership in the dominant nation transcended class distinction: a Russian laborer could feel superior to a Ukrainian intellectual simply because the latter was a "*khokhol*"; by itself this is racial discrimination without actually invoking color of skin (although that, of course, was also a factor in both the Russian and the Soviet empire: one need only to recall the contempt for the "*churki*"). And when this becomes a pattern of behavior in the so-called ethnic territories, it is hardly distinguishable from the behavior and values of classical colonialism.[8] (1995, 678)

As in Ireland, a Ukrainian background did not preclude upward mobility and high imperial office, but only as long as it was accompanied by a "denationalization" of identification.

The implication for local Ukrainian culture, during both the tsarist and the Soviet period, was "a syndrome of dependence and derivativeness," according to which the best and the brightest were either coerced or encouraged to shed attachments to Ukraine. As Grabowicz notes:

> It was entirely normal, for example, that Ukrainian writers or filmmakers or scholars who were very good would be invited to Moscow, where they would become all-Union, i.e., Russian writers, filmmakers or scholars. At times one was simply forced to do so, as was the case with Oleksandr Dovzhenko in the early 1950s; when the Ukrainian poet Vitaly Korotych became an all-Union

> editor at the time of *perestroika*, he was given the option—which one almost always accepted. Regardless, the colonial pattern obtained and its very ordinariness prevented its being seen for what it was. (1995, 679)

Often, especially during the years of Stalinist terror, such flights from Ukraine and distancing from Ukrainian culture by members of the Ukrainian intelligentsia were essentially attempts (often unsuccessful) at physical survival.

(Post-)Soviet Paradoxes

Given these contexts, it is not surprising that in the history of modern literature on Ukraine's territory, instances in which a writer wrote exclusively or mostly in Russian but identified first and foremost with Ukraine were almost nonexistent until recently. The dominant patterns of identification were with the Russian language and culture or with a local—city or regional—identity. The few notable exceptions were associated with the dissident movement, as in the cases of Boris Chichibabin (1923–94) in Kharkiv and Leonid Kiselev (1946–68) in Kyiv. While the Soviet Ukrainian Writers' Union did have an official Russian-language "thick" journal, *Raduga*, it reflected the iron-fisted rule of censorship in Soviet Ukraine and never came close, either thematically or aesthetically, to the boldness of the Riga-based *Rodnik* or the Tashkent-based *Zaria vostoka*.

It is no surprise, then, that during the Soviet period practically no efforts were made by scholars to look at Russian-language literary texts written in Ukraine as a distinct coherent corpus. A rare exception is the Ukrainian-language collective monograph published in 1971, *Rosiis'ka literatura Ukraïny*. Rather than articulate a coherent canon, however, the book presents a soporific roll call comprised of cookie-cutter vignettes of now mostly forgotten writers; even those whose reputation endures, like the deservedly popular children's writer Vladimir Kiselev (1922–95), are drained of all color and character (Mazepa et al. 1971).

That this collective monograph failed to establish and define any specific features that distinguish and unite writers producing literary texts in Russian as a community is symptomatic of a larger problem. For most of them, identification with Ukraine and Ukrainian culture was a low priority. The centralizing forces at work both in imperial Russia and the Soviet Union often meant that horizontal ties between the literary cultures of smaller centers of literary activity were all but nonexistent. Russian-language authors and readers of Donetsk knew little about what was happening in the Russian-language literature of Kharkiv, and vice versa, being focused instead on the all-Union centers of Russian literary life.

Thus, although the Soviet collapse in 1991 created a different context for those in Ukraine who could identify as belonging to a Russophone "beached diaspora" (Laitin 1998), the process of rethinking and reclaiming identities by Ukraine's Russian-language writers in the newly independent Ukraine remained stalled at least until the Orange Revolution of 2004. With the lone exception of Andrei Kurkov, who since his earliest publications in the 1990s insisted that he considered himself a Ukrainian writer writing in Russian as opposed to a Russian writer living in Ukraine, most authors who wrote in Russian but were based in Ukraine remained vague about their self-identification, or separated their status as Ukrainian citizens from their status as Russian-language writers.[9] The tendency among conservative members of the Russian literary establishment to use the word *russkoiazychnyi* ("Russian-language") as an anti-Semitic slur generated a further reason to resist the use of this term.[10]

By the early twenty-first century, however, Ukraine's cultural distinctness from Russia became increasingly evident to both the domestic population and international observers. While the economic crisis of the 1990s took a heavy toll on Ukraine's publishing industry and cultural sphere, to an even greater extent than in most other post-Soviet states, a new generation of Ukrainian citizens was coming of age and becoming culturally and politically active, accelerating processes of identity transformation on a nationwide scale. Famously dubbed an "unexpected nation" by Andrew Wilson (2000), Ukrainian citizens were increasingly forming strong horizontal alliances of the kind that create a meaningful imagined community in Benedict Anderson's sense. Neither attempts to build a high culture in Ukraine's territory exclusively in the language of the former imperial/colonial power nor the spirited attempts to create a robust postcolonial Ukrainian culture that does not incorporate non-Ukrainophone cultural production would ultimately be successful.

Charting a Civic Future

The Orange Revolution of 2004 resonated profoundly both inside and outside of Ukraine. While in Russia it contributed to the development of a political course aimed at stifling social dissent and a more aggressive foreign policy (Umland 2012), internally, the revolution proved that an orientation toward a common future was significantly stronger than any real or perceived ethnic, linguistic, or regional divides (Wilson 2005). The revolution was comfortably bilingual, affirming the unprecedented level of social prestige of the Ukrainian language as it shed centuries of social stigmatization but also the beginning of the development of a stronger and uniquely Ukrainian cultural community in

Russian.[11] What was earlier seen as a sharp divide within Ukrainian society between two groups competing for power and resources, the "creoles" and the "aboriginals"—that is, those members of the educated elites who primarily identify with legacies of the dominant imperial culture and the colonized indigenous ones—was giving way to new configurations.[12] Not surprisingly, Kyiv, Ukraine's capital, provided some of the most influential instances of this newly energized process, notably in two projects spearheaded by the poet Alexander Kabanov, originally from Kherson but based in Kyiv since the mid-1980s. One was the journal *Sho*, founded in 2005, and the other was the poetry festival Kyiv Laurels (Kyïvs'ki lavry/Kievskie lavry), launched in 2006; both became major sites for contact and community-building in Ukraine's literary scene, straddling the language divide.

At the same moment, in Ukraine's second-largest city, Kharkiv, which has a legacy of a strong literary community from its days as the capital of Soviet Ukraine in the 1920s and early 1930s, an attempt by local authors to map the city's rich literary scene across language divides resulted in an influential 2007 article co-authored by the Ukrainian-language poet Rostyslav Melnykiv and his Russian-language peer Yury Tsaplin, "The Northeast of the Southwest" ("Severo-vostok iugo-zapada"; Mel'nikov and Tsaplin 2007). Melnykiv and Tsaplin addressed a general educated audience both inside and outside Ukraine (hence their choice to publish it in a Moscow-based journal), focusing on the language dynamic in the city's cultural scene during the years of Russian imperial and Soviet rule, highlighting both long-term processes of russification and Ukrainian-language literary practices enduring—and at several periods, blossoming—with a remarkable persistence. They provided a comprehensive mapping of the city's contemporary literary community and the ways in which aesthetic, philosophical, political, and other concerns stitched it together across the language divide. While the title chosen by Melnykiv and Tsaplin is an intertextual nod to Viktor Shklovsky's article "The Southwest" ("Iugo-zapad"), published in *Literaturnaia gazeta* on January 5, 1933, and considered perhaps the most influential early attempt to outline the specifics of Russian-language writing from Ukraine as a distinct school, they do not engage in a direct polemic with Shklovsky; rather, a reference to Shklovsky's vague but influential notion of a "southwestern" school of Russian literature serves only as a starting point for their entirely independent cultural analysis.

The processes that slowly but surely began at that time kicked into higher gear after the Euromaidan of 2013–14. The demonstrations in Kyiv's Independence Square emphatically proclaimed Ukraine's unity and its diversity as a source of strength. When a comprehensive anthology of testimonies from the revolution, ranging in genre from social media posts to poetry and essays, *Chronicle of Witnesses: Nine Months of Ukrainian Resistance* (*Litopys samovydtsiv: Dev'iat' misiatsiv ukraïns'koho sprotyvu*), was published in late 2014, it emerged that texts in Ukrainian and Russian were almost equal in proportion within it; indeed, a Russian-language poem, "Who Am I?" ("Kto ia?"), by Evgenia Bilchenko, dated February 21, 2014, and structured as a riff on Andrei Voznesensky's classic poem "Goya" ("Goiia," 1959), became arguably the most famous early literary portrayal of the Euromaidan (Teren 2014, 129–30).[13] This language balance, to many observers both inside and outside of Ukraine who were used to representations of the country as sharply divided by language, was a surprise.

The language situation in post-Soviet Ukraine has attracted significant attention from social scientists (Bilaniuk 2005; Kulyk 2011, 2014a, 2014b, 2015, 2016a, and 2016b) but, until recently, not from literary scholars. Marco Puleri's pioneering inquiry into the self-identification of Russophone writers in post-Soviet Ukraine, based on research conducted immediately prior to the Euromaidan, was published in early 2014; Tanya Zaharchenko's in-depth study of the bilingual literary community of Kharkiv followed two years later (Puleri 2014; Zaharchenko 2016).[14] While Zaharchenko's monograph draws on two theoretical discourses, those of memory studies and borderlands culture, Puleri's approach is explicitly grounded in postcolonial theory. Puleri maintains that Russophone writing in post-Soviet Ukraine is "a genuinely hybrid phenomenon," and he urges readers to hear this voice, which has long been discounted or ignored (Puleri 2014, 368). Building on Tamara Hundorova's model of Ukrainian postcoloniality as a "transit culture" (Hundorova 2013), he asserts that we are dealing with "a moment of productive self-consciousness" (Puleri 2014, 371). Ultimately, Puleri identifies the crux of the problem as the question of whether the authors and texts he analyzes should be approached "as Ukrainian literature in Russian [*ukraïns'ka rosiis'komovna literatura*] or Russian literature of Ukraine [*rosiis'ka literatura Ukraïny*]." As he notes, "The former term describes the phenomenon as integrated in the Ukrainian literary process, while the latter portrays it in the wider context of Russian literature, interpreting its affiliation with Ukraine only in territorial terms" (2014, 375). Although Puleri does not reference this precedent, I would argue that this debate owes much to a similar earlier one among Russian-language Israeli authors, reflected in Mikhail Gendelev's 1991 manifesto:

> What are the distinctive features of Russophone Israeli literature today and what makes it differ from the literature of the Russian diaspora? In contrast to the Russian emigration, which is in exile, or, as Gippius put it, on a mission, we

> are located in our homeland, and this is our main distinction. Our literature is created without an orientation toward Russian realities and a Russian reader; conversely, it addresses Russophone Israeli readers who live in the realities of a different culture. We describe Israeli reality, drawing from our Israeli or Jewish experience, using a language in which (due to a variety of circumstances) we are more proficient, and knowing that we are being read. (1991; see also Gendelev 2017)

Gendelev offers several helpful criteria for approaching Russophone literary production in countries other than Russia; crucially, to advance his argument, he speaks of distinct Anglophone literary traditions that have developed in the former British colonies that cannot be subsumed under the umbrella of English literature. However, Gendelev does not claim that all Russophone Israeli writers accept the designation he proposes; rather, he asserts that we are dealing with at least three distinct groups: Russophone writers who primarily identify as members of a global Russian-speaking diaspora; those who primarily identify with Russian literature of the metropole; and a portion of writers who believe that "Israeli realities demand new means of expression, aesthetic models that did not exist earlier in Russian literature" (1991).

Puleri's respondents, speaking in 2013, right before the start of the Euromaidan, exhibited a similar range of responses. The Kyiv-based author Aleksei Nikitin saw the strengthening of "a real Russian literature of Ukraine" because what he termed the "Moscow vacuum cleaner," the tendency that pushed many of the brightest and most ambitious intellectuals to move to the Soviet—or earlier, imperial—capital, had significantly weakened (although it had not disappeared altogether), while Kabanov still viewed himself as "a Russian poet, a citizen of Ukraine" ("russkii poet, grazhdanin Ukrainy"; Puleri 2014, 379, 381). Puleri considered a crucial step toward a successful integration of Russophone writers into a multilingual Ukrainian literature an openness to accepting Russophone writers as belonging to the larger community of Ukrainian literature by their Ukrainophone peers. This is something many Ukrainian artists had long resisted, for a number of reasons; the Ukrainian poet Serhii Zhadan has been one of the leading figures promoting such engagement (see Zhadan 2016). Puleri's vision for a productive Russophone literature of Ukraine draws on Deleuze and Guattari's concept of "minor literature" as a "minor" practice subverting a "major" language through "stylistic deterritorialization" (for Deleuze and Guattari, this practice is best illustrated by Kafka's work with the German language; for Puleri, it is operational in the Russian of innovative authors like Nikitin and Rafeenko) and an exploration of "interstitial spaces" that he highlights in the poetic practices of Khersonsky (Deleuze and Guattari 1986; Puleri 2014, 382–87). While such "interstitial," hybrid practices are undoubtedly a welcome development in the Ukrainian context, they also merit comparison with similar practices elsewhere, notably the work of the Orbita group in Latvia and the Fergana school in Uzbekistan (Platt, this volume; Kukulin, this volume).

The extent of the paradigm shift within Ukraine's Russophone literature after the Euromaidan and especially after Russia's annexation of Crimea and the outbreak of war in the Donbas is visible in the near-complete absence of Russian-language writers based in Ukraine expressing support for either the annexation of Crimea or Donbas separatists (exceptions include the Crimea-based poet Andrei Poliakov, the Kharkiv-based poet Stanislav Minakov, who has since relocated to Belgorod, and the Donetsk-based poet Igor Bobyrev). On the contrary, leading Russophone authors from both Crimea and Donbas, such as Pavel Goldin, Vladimir Rafeenko, and Elena Stiazhkina, joined the ranks of refugees in Kyiv or elsewhere in central Ukraine, alongside their Ukrainophone peers, the poets Vasyl Holoborodko and Liubov Iakymchuk. The trauma of war brought these Russian- and Ukrainian-language authors into closer contact and dialogue than ever before. In a similarly unprecedented fashion, we now see the emergence of a corpus of Russian-language literary texts that respond to the Russian invasion (notably Rafeenko's novel *The Length of Days* [*Dolgota dnei*], Stiazhkina's novella "In God's Language" ["Na iazyke Boga"], and Khersonsky's recent poetry, including the collections *Missa in Tempore Belli* and *Spaceisours* [*Kosmosnash*]; Uffelmann, this volume).

Collaborative projects between Ukrainophone and Russophone writers that had begun earlier thus received a major new impetus. These projects embraced a wide range of forms and ways of focusing on their shared concerns. An example of a traditional collaboration is the recent *Letters from Ukraine* (*Lysty z Ukraïny*), an anthology bringing together fifty-six contemporary poets who write about the changes in their country in both Ukrainian and Russian. A notable one-on-one collaboration is that of Khersonsky and the Ukrainian-language poet Marianna Kiianovska. More experimental collaborations have included collectively written novels such as the time-traveling family saga *DNA* (*DNK*), which can be described as a Ukrainian response to *Cloud Atlas*. This project brought together seven authors, two of them Russophone (Fozzi and Rafeenko) and the others Ukrainophone, to tell the story of one Ukrainian family from the late nineteenth century up to an imagined mid-twenty-first century.[15] Several cultural projects aiming to create greater mutual understanding between Ukraine's regions—such as the Donkul't (i.e., Donbas culture) festival, which took place in Kyiv and L'viv in 2015, and Halitsiiakul't (Galician culture) in Kharkiv in 2016—provided an important impetus for building a better integrated cultural community across Ukraine.[16] Some authors, including Rafeenko, have called for the creation of a Russian Language Institute in Ukraine and the development of a different local standard of the Russian language.[17] Others who earlier wrote only in Russian, such as Khersonsky and the playwright Natalia Vorozhbit, now also try their pens in Ukrainian, in a gesture reminiscent of Leonid Kiselev, who in the 1960s likewise deliberately chose to switch to writing in Ukrainian as a form of protest. The tendency is not exclusively one-way, though; for instance, the Ukrainian-language literary scene has remained, with few exceptions, less friendly to LGBT authors than the Russian one, which led a prominent gay poet, Vitaly Iukhymenko, to switch from Ukrainian into Russian.

Ultimately, the ongoing transformation of Ukrainian identity and of the place of Russian speakers and Russian cultural activity within it reflects both recent geopolitical shifts and the long history of "cohabitation" of Ukrainians and Russians in shared geographies and intertwined cultural traditions. As long as Ukrainians were a minority in multinational states in which the Russian language and culture were dominant, their identities reflected ethno-national modes of thought. In the post-Soviet context, however, Ukraine is itself a culturally and ethnically diverse—some would even say multinational—state. Aggression from the Russian Federation, legitimated by nationalist rhetoric, may evoke an ethno-nationalist consolidation among some Ukrainians. Yet such a response is a conceptual capitulation to the Russian Federation—one that grants it the continuing status of encroaching empire, and implicitly yields to Russia "authority" over Russian speakers and "Russian territory" everywhere. The articulation of a civic nationality in Ukraine that includes its Russian populations, their language, and their writing contests Russia's claim to the Russian language and culture as its exclusive right.

Russophone Ukrainian literature remains, to use Hundorova's metaphor, in a state of postcolonial transition. The general tendency has been toward developing stronger and more meaningful ties within Ukraine, both among Russophone writers themselves and across language divides. But the outcome of the transition is not yet assured. Russophone Ukrainian writing reflects postcolonial trauma resulting from the unfinished and often painful process of identity shift in the post-imperial context, frequently on a linguistic level as well. Thus Alexander Kabanov's poetry is replete with bi- and multilingual puns, such as the paronymous "*mantry-mandry*" (mantras/wanderings, using the Ukrainian word for the latter in the otherwise Russian-language poem), and peppers the text with references to cultural realia specific to a Ukrainian context. His 2010 collection *Batman Sahaidachny* (*Betmen Sagaidachnyi*) is particularly rich with disturbing hybrid imagery where contemporary Ukrainian daily realities, political discourse, and Western (primarily American) pop culture references clash and fuse in unexpected provocative combinations that reflect the traumas of identification. As a tool for grasping this hybrid new reality, the poet creates a new mythology where one finds, for example, a superhero blend of American pop culture and Ukrainian Cossack history in the book's title character (described in the opening poem), and an ancient yet distinctly Ukrainian dragon. His poetics can be described as post-Brodskian, as he exhibits a strict adherence to syllabotonic forms where any transgression of expectations for rhyme or meter is tightly managed, while his vocabulary casually blends the lofty with the deliberately vulgar. Like classic mythologies of many nations, the new postcolonial myths Kabanov offers frequently contain casual references to violence, which acquire disturbing new relevance after the losses of life and territory Ukraine experienced in 2014. In his post-Euromaidan poetry, Kabanov has continued his practice of mixing deliberate provocation with passionate lyricism. Defiantly, he titled his latest book of poetry *In the Language of the Enemy* (*Na iazyke vraga*), including in it a poem titled "I Dreamt That I Would Die . . . ," dedicated to a deceased friend. The poem closes with the following lines:

> The Ilovaisk curve,[18]
> Memory with a view of the ruin:
> I lived in the language of the enemy,
> I died for Ukraine.
>
> (2017, 6)

The overall mode of Kabanov's poetic reflection remains consistent: his writing is replete with melancholic replayings of trauma resulting from continuing self-identification with the corpus of cultural and political realia associated with Russophone discourse in Ukraine as "creole" or (post-)imperial, and the ideological baggage he sees it as carrying, even if against the poet's wishes, in contemporary Ukraine. Gestures that might signal success in working through this trauma remain unconvincing, as in the following lines:

> I forgive you, blind fools, creators
> of new history, castrated clowns,
> who so long persecuted, so used to doing so,
> my Ukrainian Russian native tongue.
>
> (2017, 132)

Treatment of Ukrainophone culture at an ironic distance and identification of Russophone Ukrainian culture with the speaker's trauma comprise the main drivers of this writing. While one would be hard-pressed to find any praise of current policies of the Russian government in Kabanov's texts, the potential for a Russophone cultural continuum to rupture and fragment is clearly painful to this poet.

Boris Khersonsky's poetry strikes a different balance in placing the poetic persona between Ukrainophone and Russophone worlds. While Khersonsky has not abandoned writing in Russian, he has consistently articulated an affirmation of Ukrainian civic identity and has increasingly turned to the Ukrainian language in both his poetry and essays. Tellingly, he titled a recent book of essays *A Patchwork Quilt* (Khersons'kyi 2016a). Here, he emphatically asserts his bilingualism and places essays in Russian and Ukrainian side by side, arranged not by language but by theme. Still, in his collection *Missa in Tempore Belli*, next to poems articulating hope, life's fragility, and the selflessness of Euromaidan revolutionaries, he presents texts that, echoing Maksimilian Voloshin's writing nearly a century earlier that empathized with both the Whites and the Reds, seek to give insight into the thoughts and emotions of all sides of the conflict, as well as of those who are completely lost and unsure which side they are on. Following the cycle titled "A Geography Lecture" ("Lektsiia po geografii"), which condemns Russia's annexation of Crimea with the famous opening line "Islands are good for vacations. A peninsula is good for an invasion" ("Ostrova khoroshi dlia otdykha. Poluostrov khorosh dlia zakhvata"), one finds a poem warning against attempts to sow ethno-linguistic division in Ukraine, which reinforces the poet's commitment to criticism of those in the pro-Ukrainian camp who still conceive of Ukrainian identity in ethnic-based, exclusionary terms:

> With the help of torches in a dark night
> it is easy to tell a person to shut up.
> You do not belong; you are an alien here, your evil gaze
> appropriates, thief-like, all that is authentically ours.
>
> Stay silent; do not dare repeat our speech,
> lay off our baroque, our Zaporozhian Sich,
> do not listen to the songs we sing.
>
> (2014, 72)

Overall, in contrast to Kabanov's enduring colonial melancholia, Khersonsky offers a postcolonial working through of traumas; his training and academic career as a clinical psychologist are closely linked to his literary aims. For

Khersonsky, all human history is largely traumatic, and the twentieth century in particular, but he retains a disposition of calm confidence. His irony is deeply humanist, as in the poem "Burn Black Tires on a Black Square . . ." ("Na chernoi ploshchadi zhech' chernye avtopokryshki . . ."), included in both *Missa in Tempore Belli* and *Spaceisours*. Composed of two stanzas, it contrasts solemn praise for protesters at Maidan in the first stanza with a searing critique of previous generations of Ukrainians for their passivity in the second, comparing them to a cat rubbing at a tyrant's leg while purring to itself, "God save Ukraine!" "He could have saved it," the poem says, "nothing is difficult for God, / but sadly, God is alone, and we were of no help to him" (2014, 8; 2015a, 233; see also Uffelmann, this volume).

Russian-language Ukrainian writing thus emerges as a rich site for developing a new sociocultural project, exploring its hopes and stumbles, seeking to articulate the pain and the utopian impulse that marked the Euromaidan and the difficult birth of a new Ukraine in the context of ongoing war and crisis. It remains a work in progress, its final contours not yet assured. However, Russophone Ukrainian intellectuals, such as the Crimea-born and Kyiv-based Mikhail Dubiniansky, are increasingly comfortable asserting that

> Russian language in Russia and Russian language in Ukraine steadily grow apart from one another, and with each year this tendency manifests itself with greater clarity. . . . This is not only a matter of linguistic nuances, of the greater pliability of Ukrainian Russian, of its transformation, saturation with local topical neologisms, borrowings from Ukrainian speech, etc. First and foremost, it is a matter of how native speakers perceive the language. The Russian of Russia is "great and mighty"; the Russian of Ukraine is simply convenient, nothing more. The Russian of Russia demonstratively opposes itself to other languages; the Russian of Ukraine calmly coexists with them. The Russian of Russia carries a highly symbolic meaning; the Russian of Ukraine is now perceived as an instrument of communication without additional meanings. This is what the Kremlin failed to understand, when it unexpectedly discovered the existence of Russophone Ukrainian patriots in 2004, and stepped on the same rake in 2014. This is also what many domestic activists, in essence sharing Moscow's retrograde view of the language problem, are incapable of understanding. (**Dubinianskii** 2017)

While some might interpret Dubiniansky's view as far too rosy, recent social science research indicates that "far from successfully mobilizing in defense of their perceived group interests, Ukraine's Russian-speakers have actually lost much of their distinct sociocultural identity which should have informed such mobilization" (Kulyk 2017). Everyday occurrences of nonaccommodating bilingualism, when friends and colleagues carry on a conversation in Ukrainian and Russian or when each interlocutor maintains the language he or she is more comfortable speaking, are common among Ukrainians of the younger generation. An example can be found in the recent award-winning film *Lilac* (2017), directed by Katetyna Hornostai. In it, five twenty-something women gather for a party; throughout, two of the characters speak Ukrainian, the other three speak Russian, yet this does not impede their relaxed camaraderie, and none of the characters is judged for the language she speaks. However, while such bilingual situations are increasingly common, contemporary literature still struggles to represent it, especially when the linguistic preferences of literary characters are not a target of irony.

The current contradictory, transitory state of the Russophone literary scene in Ukraine is confirmed by the first attempt at a comprehensive anthology representing it, compiled by Alexander Krasovitsky and published by Folio, one of Ukraine's leading presses. In preparation for years, the book covers a wide spectrum of literary genres, from experimental poetry to fantasy and science fiction. While it represents the work of two dozen writers, and clocks in at 768 pages, several leading names, such as Anastasiia Afanaseva and Andrei Krasniashchikh, are missing. Ultimately, confusion about the book's title is symptomatic: originally it was to be titled *Russkaia proza i poeziia sovremennoi Ukrainy* (Russian prose and poetry of contemporary Ukraine), but several contributors insisted that the title be changed to *Ukrainskaia proza i poeziia na russkom iazyke* (Ukrainian prose and poetry in Russian). Whether deliberately or as a result of an oversight, both titles are present in the final work: "Ukrainian literature in Russian" adorns the cover, and "Russian literature in Ukraine" is offered in the bibliographic details printed inside the book—which is perhaps only fitting in a snapshot of an incomplete transition (Krasovitskii 2016).

Notes

Research for this chapter was supported by a summer stipend from the National Endowment for the Humanities.

1. Among the most helpful publications on recent conflict in Ukraine and its consequences are Marples and Mills 2014; Stepanenko and Pylynskyi 2015; Wilson 2015; Yekelchyk 2015; Hale and Orttung 2016. On displaced persons, see Internal Displacement Monitoring Centre, www.internal-displacement.org/database/country/?iso3=UKR, accessed March 13, 2017.

2. On the role of live streaming in the Euromaidan events, see Mykhed 2016.

3. The most acclaimed such documentaries include *Maidan*, dir. Sergei Loznitsa (2014); the Babylon '13 collaborative project consisting of short films of varying length (babylon13.com); and the related TV series *The Winter That Changed Us* (*Zyma, shcho nas zminyla*), dir. Volodymyr Tykhyi (2014); *All Things Ablaze*, dir. Oleksandr Techynskyi, Aleksey Solodunov, and Dmitry Stoykov (2014); *Winter on Fire*, dir. Evgeny Afineevsky (2015); and *Freedom or Death!*, dir. Damian Kolodiy (2015).

4. For more on Ruthenian, see Pugh 1996; Verkholantsev 2008.

5. For more on the transformation of Ukrainian elites during the eighteenth century, see Kohut 1981, 1988.

6. Luckyj 1971 is one of the most comprehensive accounts of Ukraine's literary landscape of this era.

7. The thesis of "internal colonization" in Russia received fullest formulation to date in Etkind 2011. While influential, Etkind's theory has also generated a polemical response, most thoroughly articulated in the contributions of Edyta Bojanowska and Robert Geraci to the round table on Etkind's book at the 2013 ASEEES Convention (see also Geraci 2015) as well as in Hundorova 2013.

8. "Khokhol" and "churki" are Russian ethnic slurs for Ukrainians and Central Asians, respectively.

9. Kurkov has articulated this position in numerous interviews and public lectures: see, e.g., Kurkov 2006, 2014, 2016.

10. For one of the most powerful critiques of the anti-Semitic use of the term, see Kherson'skyi 2016a, 289–306.

11. As Oksana Forostyna has noted, "The Orange Revolution spoke both Russian and Ukrainian, but it took another nine years to launch the birth of a new nation, the Ukrainian political nation, in which the use of Russian no longer betrays a pro-Moscow inclination" (2015, 26).

12. The paradigm of "creoles" versus "aboriginals" was most clearly articulated by Mykola Riabchuk (2000).

13. For a detailed analysis of the poem, see Bulkina 2016.

14. Puleri further develops his argument in his 2016 Italian-language monograph.

15. See Semenchuk, Izdryk, and Chernetsky 2016; Khersons'kyi 2016a, which brings together Kiianovska's translations of Khersonsky's poems and his own self-translations into Ukrainian; Zhadan et al. 2016.

16. For more on these festivals, see the website www.dofa.fund, accessed March 13, 2017.

17. See "'Neobkhodimo sozdat' institut russkogo iazyka Ukrainy'—pisatel' Rafeenko," *Hromads'ke radio*, https://hromadskeradio.org/programs/kyiv-donbas/neobhodimo-sozdat-institut-russkogo-yazyka-ukrainy-pisatel-rafeenko, November 12, 2015.

18. A reference to the battle of Ilovais'k in the Donbas in August–September, 2014, between the Ukrainian army and the combined Russian-separatist forces, which resulted in heavy losses of Ukrainian troops.

"Russian Culture" in Central Asia as a Transethnic Phenomenon

Natalya Kosmarskaya and Artyom Kosmarski

Russophone Linguistic and Cultural Space in Central Asia

On a Saturday evening in October 2016, one of the authors of this chapter was walking through the center of Almaty, Kazakhstan's "southern capital," in search of a place to relax and drink coffee.[1] The stroll's endpoint was to be a landmark street locally nicknamed "the Arbat" and "Broadway" (reflecting its connection with the arts)—a pedestrian zone where street merchants sell souvenirs, local artists display their paintings, and street musicians offer performances.[2] Located between Ablai-Khan Prospect (formerly Communist Prospect) and Panfilov Street, which still bears the name of a Soviet war hero, the Arbat boasts a stylized Italian café named "Presso," which on this particular evening was filled with guests, largely Kazakhs, along with a smattering of others of European appearance. Nevertheless, everyone spoke Russian, including the waiters and the children who ran about among the tables. One of several television screens was broadcasting a European football match with the sound muted. To quiet the children, a waiter had turned on a second screen, and the room filled with the familiar strains of a song from a late-Soviet children's animated film. Outside, a street musician continued to produce one well-known melody after another—first "Moscow Windows," a Soviet-era hit forever linked with the name of its original performer, Leonid Utesov, and then "Strangers in the Night," evoking Frank Sinatra, icon of the same era but the other hemisphere.

This one small patch of urban territory brought together in a state of peaceful coexistence a diverse array of cultural expressions: toponyms derived from various epochs and ideologies; exemplars of Western mass culture, canonized in the Socialist era; a smattering of overtly "Soviet" cultural goods, each bearing particular significance for a distinct age group; and standard expressions of cultural globalization. It would be difficult to find a similar scene today in Vilnius, Kyiv, Tbilisi, or Baku. However, such a polyphony of cultural consumption and expression, organically situated in a Russophone social environment—one that would be quite typical for a larger Russian city—continues to be a significant feature of many sizable cities in Central Asia, and most certainly of the capitals and large industrial centers. The portrait offered above of everyday life in Almaty is only one of the many expressions of the phenomenon treated in this chapter, which we will refer to as "Russophone cultural-linguistic space," a term we consider synonymous with the formula "Russian culture in Central Asia" offered in this chapter's title.

This linguistic and cultural space, within which specific cultural norms, knowledge, values, and behavioral modes are circulated and practiced, embraces social actors of various ethnic origins—and crucially, not only Russians proper—as well as formal and informal institutions and cultural networks primarily grounded in the Russian language. The goal of this chapter is to investigate the dynamics of Russophone cultural-linguistic space as experienced by the urban populations of the Central Asian states in the post-Soviet period, as well as to reveal factors contributing to its maintenance or erosion. Additionally, we will consider the historical context for its formation in this region and the specificity of the phenomenon within separate countries. We will also examine the extent to which "Russian culture" in this territory requires continuous external support from the Russian Federation or, alternately, persists as a result of other factors that ensure its self-reproduction on a local, autonomous basis. In distinction from other chapters of this volume, which consider global Russian cultural production by "professionals" in the form of literature, music, or film, our investigation is focused on the expression, engagement, and evaluation of this phenomenon at the level of everyday practices and consciousness.

The empirical data on which this chapter is based derive from extensive fieldwork among ethnic Russians and other Russophones of Kyrgyzstan (1996–2003) and Uzbekistan (2002, 2004); among their urban populations of various ethnic origins (based on six fieldwork trips between 2007 and 2013); and also among urban populations of Kazakhstan (based on three trips in 2016 and 2017). Qualitative sociological methods (in-depth interviews in a life-history and topic-guide format) were the main tools of data collection.[3] Let us offer a few words about our focus on these countries, in particular. Within the Central Asian region, consisting of five countries, our investigation is *prima facie* limited to those states that featured a significant demographic presence of Russians during the imperial and Soviet periods and still host them in large numbers. The first one is Kazakhstan, in which 3.8 million Russians lived in 2009, according to the Second National Census, but only 3.68 million, or 21.1 percent of the total population, in 2015, according to ongoing reporting.[4] The second is Uzbekistan, the only post-Soviet state in which there has been no census since the USSR's collapse. An estimated one million Russians, or approximately 3 percent of the total population, resided there at the end of the millennium's first decade (Vozhdaeva 2008). The third focus of our study is Kyrgyzstan, in which 420 thousand Russians lived in 2009, according to the Second National Census (National Statistical Committee of the Kyrgyz Republic 2009), but only 360 thousand, or 6 percent of the total population, at the start of 2016 (Etnicheskii sostav Kyrgyzstana 2016). If one takes into account the percentage of the population represented by other ethnic groups that are nonnative to these regions, the Russophone populations of these states are slightly higher.

Historical Contexts

As this chapter's title suggests, one of the most important specificities of "Russian culture" in Central Asia is its transethnic character, embracing members of many ethnic groups beyond Russians themselves—an inherited state of affairs that continues up to the present day. How did this situation arise? To answer this question, we must make a brief excursus into the history of the arrival of Russians in this region and, more broadly, of their distinct role in the prerevolutionary and Soviet social-political orders—a role that granted special significance, subsequently, to their culture and language. As we shall see, it was in the process of imperial absorption of variegated territories that Russian language and culture in many ways lost much of their ethnic significance and emotional linkage to Russians as an ethnic group and began "to live their own life."

In the prerevolutionary period, Russians maintained their own identity as the engine of colonization while directing russifying efforts not at ethnic assimilation but rather at the inculcation of feelings of affinity with the Russian state (see Kukulin, this volume). As Andreas Kappeler explains, "Although the imperial patriotism that lay at the foundation of imperial integration did include certain elements tied to Russian ethnic identity (Orthodoxy, a common history and culture), super-national features predominated all the same" (1997, 177). These tendencies were maintained following the 1917 Revolution, in a reflection of certain geopolitical continuities: Russian-Soviet culture was developed as an ideological support for the regime rather than as a vehicle for Russian ethnic consciousness per se (Melvin 1998, 27–34). Furthermore, at the peripheries of Soviet territory, "settler communities," as Neil Melvin refers to them, took shape as multinational and primarily urban-industrial—as the leading edge of Soviet social life; that is why their identity "was defined in sociocultural rather than ethnic terms" (Melvin 1998, 33). Russian language and culture, in this context, came to be seen not as exclusive properties of Russians (nor as their main ethnic markers). The "children of the empire"—Russians and members of other ethnic groups that had been transported to the imperial peripheries, as well as russified autochthones—interpreted them broadly, as fundamental givens of a Sovietized urban lifestyle, with its attendant values and habits, rather than as manifestations of any set of stereotypical "folkloric" features of "Russianness."

Beyond this general historical background, one must also take into consideration the particular character of the integration of the territory under consideration in the imperial and, even more importantly, in the Soviet period. Two features of this process are particularly significant for defining the place of Russian language and culture in today's Central Asia. First of all, the populations transferred to this region in the course of many decades in many waves of migration, from the voluntary to the forced, were themselves extraordinarily variegated in ethno-confessional composition. Besides members of east Slavic peoples, they included Germans, Tatars, Bashkirs, Jews, Armenians, Koreans, and many others. This "non-Russian population, included in migratory relocation, either was already culturally Russian (or at least Russophone), or became such after separating from the native soil" (Vishnevskii 1998, 259).

This "tower of Babel" produced a "melting pot" effect, which over time acted to erode the borders of "Russianness" itself. Indeed, this is unsurprising for polyethnic and polycultural communities, concentrated largely in cities, where the "mixing" of peoples was both physical (through intermarriage) and figural.[5] Moreover, the further a given territory was from the "center"—including the "all-seeing eye" and "punishing fist" of the state—the more attractive it became for a diverse population. This was particularly the case in Tashkent, which gained fame as the most cosmopolitan and "polystylistic" (in both ethno-cultural and social dimensions) city of the "Soviet Orient." Let us emphasize that this is a description of those who arrived in the region from the "north"—those who in both public and scholarly discourse are referred to as "Russophone" or, metaphorically, as "children of the empire" (Kosmarskaya 2006), who in local everyday parlance are called "Europeans"—in distinction from "nationals" ("natsionaly"), members of Central Asia's autochthonic ethnic groups. Take note, too, that in this latter usage, "Europeans" includes not only transplants from the Caucasus or Transcaucasia, for instance, but even Koreans, who might otherwise be classified as "Asian."

The second important feature of the assimilation of these territories to Russian and Soviet space was that, due to specificities of Central Asia and its peoples, Russian and other "Europeans" in the region were cast in the role of social and industrial "kulturtraegers." Soviet social and economic development in peripheral republics, although deriving in part from idealistic conceptions of a socialist "mission civilisatrice," was historically predicated on the more brutal processes of great-power imperial expansion of the tsarist era. Both Russian imperial and Soviet frames of reference reflected a colonial and orientalist geopolitical hierarchy of peoples and territories that designated Central Asia and its populations as "backward" and subject to tutelage (Grant 2009). In consequence, during the twentieth century external intervention was a powerful stimulus to social transformation and modernization for the region's peoples, who were brought into the trajectory of scientific-technical progress and acquired knowledge and practices resonant with modern social life, as well as access to global languages and high culture. Undeniably, the price of this "entry into civilization" was significant: a loss of their distinctive national customs, languages, and traditions.

This was especially the case for the tribes who were the historical basis for the Kyrgyz and Kazakh nationalities. At the start of Russian expansionism in Central Asia, these two groups were distinguished by nomadism and their weak attachment to Islam, as well as their lack of written language and literacy and therefore of literary culture, despite the presence of rich oral traditions. In this, they stood in stark contrast to the peoples who founded the ancient agricultural civilizations and cities of the Fergana Valley, the present-day location of Uzbekistan and Tajikistan. Significantly, in Soviet times, of all of these peoples it was the Kyrgyz and Kazakhs who came into close contact with "Europeans" not only in urban settings but also in rural ones.[6] This ensured an even greater penetration of Russian language and culture into daily life and a far greater extent of russification. Hence, we may observe an ethno-cultural division across the region: on one hand were the originally nomadic peoples—the Kyrgyz and Kazakhs—and on the other were the agricultural peoples of the more southern territories, who were to form the Uzbek and Tajik nationalities. Correspondingly, one may draw a territorial dividing line, placing on one side Kazakhstan and neighboring northern Kyrgyzstan, in which the majority of Russophones of that country reside, and on the other side southern Kyrgyzstan, Uzbekistan, and Tajikistan.

Across the region, the cities—and especially the capital cities—became the main scenes of close interaction between "Europeans" and autochthones. It was here that in the Soviet era, as the previous order of coexistence of "colonists" and "aboriginals" in what were practically parallel worlds was replaced by a total "imperial" penetration into local social life, a special population segment took shape of Kyrgyz, Kazakhs, and Uzbeks who were sharply distinct from their provincial, largely rural co-ethnics in terms of way of life and language preferences. Together with Russians and other "Europeans," they have gradually become the bearers, consumers, critics, and, in some sense, producers of "Russian culture" in Central Asia. In what follows, we will consider the development of this situation.

Cities, Schools, and the Reversals of Soviet Nationalities Policy

Many cities in what is today Kazakhstan and Kyrgyzstan arose in the pre-Soviet period as Russian military outposts. Indeed, it was in this way that the capitals of the two countries arose: the fortress Pishpek, later renamed Frunze and still later Bishkek, and the fortress Vernyi, later renamed Alma-Ata (now Almaty). The stories of their development are in many ways identical. Both outposts sprang up on uninhabited territory, for the nomadic Kyrgyz and the Kazakhs had no traditions of urban settlement.

For many years, the capitals were primarily "Russian" cities, both in a demographic sense—the share of the autochthones grew very slowly—and, more importantly, in a cultural one: they remained zones of Soviet urban culture and life ways. The 1959 Census reports that the population of Frunze was made up of 68.6 percent ethnic Russians, with only 9.3 percent Kyrgyz (Natsional'nyi statisticheskii komitet 1992, 6). The proportion of Kazakhs in Alma-Ata at the end of the 1950s was no greater than 10 percent. In the reminiscences of its residents, the city was "completely 'European' in its architectural layout, ethnic composition, dress code, and language repertoire, at least up to [the] mid-1990s" (Dave 2007, 60). In the late and post-Soviet periods, the mass emigration of Russophones and the influx of members of the titular nationalities transformed the composition of these urban populations. In Bishkek, for instance, the proportion of Kyrgyz had risen to 22.9 percent by 1989, while that of Russophones had dropped to 55.7 percent (Natsional'nyi statisticheskii komitet 1992, 6). According to the First National Census of 1999, the proportion of Kyrgyz in the capital was 52.2 percent and that of Russians only 33.2 percent (Natsional'nyi statisticheskii komitet 2000, 78). The corresponding figures from the Census of 2009 were 58.6 percent and 26 percent.

Yet let us return to the historical conditions behind these processes in earlier years. During the Soviet period, as the Kyrgyz and Kazakhs turned slowly to a settled way of life with the establishment of kolkhoz-sovkhoz agricultural production, the majority of these groups still lived in villages. The principal biographical reason to move to the city was to acquire higher education. In distinction from Russophones, young Kyrgyz and Kazakhs who did not enter university typically returned to rural locations. Following university education, urban Kyrgyz and Kazakh entered the ranks of the intelligentsia and state servitors. Settling in the cities, they intermingled with "Europeans," at first in single-story houses and then in the multi-story apartment buildings that came to dominate the urban landscape.

In the course of time, this mixed urban population gave rise to a particular subsegment of Kyrgyz and Kazakhs—Russophone long-term city residents, often in the second or third generation, who, in contrast to co-ethnics from the *ails*, closely resembled "Europeans" in social status, lifestyle, and cultural norms. In Kyrgyzstan, the term "urban Kyrgyz" came into use, while the equivalent term in Kazakhstan is "asphalt Kazakh." Both terms eventually became key markers of their self-identification. A mandatory aspect of the difficult process of adaptation to urban life was mastery of the Russian language, the dominant urban mode of communication. This experience was often traumatic for newly urbanizing populations. In our view, however, commentators who emphasize the difficulty of linguistic adaptation (compare, for instance, Dave 2007, 62) overlook the circumstance that, in all times and places, provincial people who flock to the "big city lights," even in the absence of linguistic barriers, inevitably confront all manner of challenges in connection with distinctions between rural and urban modes of life, new cultural codes, social norms, etc.

In this period, the distribution and significance of the Russian language in the region was highly uneven. Kyrgyzstan featured a sharp contrast between the more developed zones of the north (including the capital), where a larger population of "Europeans" settled, and its other regions. Consider, for example, the recollections of a respondent who spent her early childhood among "Russians" on the banks of the Issyk-Kul Lake before moving in the early 1970s, as a result of her father's change of employment, to the capital of the mountainous and sparsely populated Naryn oblast, inhabited nearly exclusively by Kyrgyz:

> We began moving into the building, moving the furniture, and my sister and I are sitting in the courtyard. It was an institutional building for bank employees. And there was this huge courtyard and the children of the bank workers were running around, all speaking in Kyrgyz. I had never heard the Kyrgyz language before, or at least I had never paid any special attention to it. I'm six, and I think to myself: what language are they speaking in? I ask my sister, who was two years older, and she answers authoritatively: "In Chinese." (Female, Kyrgyz, b. 1967, higher ed., journalist; Bishkek, 2008)

In addition to demonstrating the differentiation of linguistic-cultural population segments, this account illustrates the adoption of Russian as a "native" first language of socialization in Kyrgyzstan.

Up to this point, we have considered the formation of the Russophone cultural-linguistic space among formerly nomadic peoples. Its establishment to the south followed a somewhat different path. The capital of Uzbekistan, Tashkent, is located on the fertile lands of the oasis that shares its name with the city—the historical basis for a series of agricultural civilizations over many centuries. At the moment of its Russian conquest in 1865 this was a typical ancient Central Asian city, with Mahallah quarters, bazaars, madrasas, and mosques. The new city built by the "Europeans" was sharply distinct from the old one and also geographically separated from it by the Ankhor Canal, a division that persisted for the duration of the Soviet era. To be sure, in time the old city slowly melted into the encroaching new one, for Tashkent was the unofficial capital of the entire Central Asian region and in consequence was subject to continuous industrial and construction initiatives (especially following the 1966 earthquake). Nevertheless, the aura of Uzbek linguistic dominance remained, allowing long-term inhabitants and migrants to preserve knowledge of their native language in a situation of titular-Russian bilingualism. Correspondingly, the adaptation of local populations to urban life was far less traumatic than in Frunze or Alma-Ata.

The distinctions between the formation of the Russophone cultural-linguistic space in Kazakhstan and Kyrgyzstan, on the one hand, and in Uzbekistan, on the other, are also evident in census data regarding language competence. Note that interpretation of such data is a challenge, given the varying wording of polling questions. For our purposes, however, the principle distinctions are striking: "According to the 1989 census, 64 percent of Kazakhs claimed fluency in Russian as a second language, the highest level of proficiency in Russian claimed by a Central Asian nationality. The corresponding figures in 1989 among the Kyrgyz were 37 percent and among the Uzbeks 22 percent" (Dave

2007, 53).[7] Among urban dwellers the level of Russian language competence was undoubtedly higher.[8]

In light of the above, urban Kazakhs and Kyrgyz may undoubtedly be considered "Russian" in the sense proposed by Kevin M. F. Platt in his discussion of Russian culture in Latvia (this volume). The authors' experience of years of fieldwork among Kyrgyz in Bishkek and in other cities of Kyrgyzstan confirms that a majority of titular urban residents possess almost accent-free, grammatically correct Russian—in the manner not of a fluent speaker of a "foreign" language but rather of a native speaker, both in oral and written forms. In the late-Soviet and post-Soviet era this circumstance was often a matter of surprise for outsiders: "A colleague from Moscow, who had never been among us, once came to visit. On the street he saw three girls, two Kyrgyz and one Russian, walking along and all speaking Russian, and says, 'These Kyrgyz are such cultured people!' Then he sees another mixed company speaking in Russian and is surprised again. Finally, I get tired of this and tell him: 'What does being cultured have to do with it? They're just speaking in their own language'" (Male, Kyrgyz, b. 1961, higher education, research worker; Bishkek, 2011). In this situation, we may observe a marked distinction between the language of socialization and communication (in both professional and daily life), and language as a key marker of ethnic belonging. In the main, urban Kazakhs and Kyrgyz consider "their own" languages to be their native tongues in answers on Soviet and (even more so) post-Soviet polls and censuses, while nevertheless relying on Russian in all manner of communication. In distinction from many other former Soviet republics (including, for instance, Uzbekistan), their cultural-linguistic competence should be properly described not as titular-Russian bilingualism of varying degrees but rather as bilingualism featuring the dominance of Russian, the language of their socialization, with often weak (or no) mastery of the "native" everyday language, not to mention its literary version.

To complete the analysis of the situation of Russian language and culture in Central Asia in the Soviet period, let us turn to a factor that is often politely overlooked: the contributions to russification of the party elites of titular nationalities. Scholarly attention has turned to this topic only recently, as a result of a methodological shift in historiography toward consideration of developments in Central Asia not only as the result of the actions of the "center"—that is, Moscow—but in light of the initiatives of local elites in the course of socialist transformations (see, e.g., Abashin 2016a). As is well known, Soviet nationalities policies passed through several moments of radical change. During the 1920s, in the first phase of *korenizatsiia* (promotion of regional social and party leaderships from among local nationalities), a still weak central authority sought to strengthen its role at the peripheries by means of concessions in cultural and linguistic policy. Consequences of this stance included, for instance, the establishment of equivalent status for Russian and Central Asian languages (on the Kazakh case, see Bissenova and Medeuova 2016, 224). Later, in the Stalinist period, the situation was in many ways reversed, as national culture came under strict control and accusations of "nationalism" became a serious offense.

During the Brezhnev period, questions of culture, education, and the like gradually passed to the purview of republican authorities. Yet the results were not what one might have expected. As one historian from Kazakhstan recalls:

> R: Upon inspection, it turns out that Kazakhstan experienced more initiatives in relation to the Kazakh language under the rule of Russians than under Kazakhs. Here's an amusing fact: when the topic of reduction of school instruction in the Kazakh language came up in a meeting with [First Secretary of the Kazakh Communist Party Dinmukhamed] Kunaev, it was proposed by the Kazakh ministers. (I've seen the stenogram.) And the Central Committee responded: "We'll do whatever you decide—it's your language, after all."
>
> I: You mean to say that the reduction was initiated by the Kazakhs themselves?
>
> R: Exactly.
>
> (Male, Kazakh, b. 1968, higher education, historian; Alma-Ata, 2016)

Ironically, the result of increased regional authority was an intensification of russification.

Developments were even more dramatic in the Kyrgyz SSR. In the 1960s, during the extraordinarily long rule of Turdakun Usubaliev as First Secretary of the Republican Communist Party, Kyrgyz language and literature were completely eliminated from the curricula of Russian schools, which constituted the majority of schools, especially in cities, and to which a large proportion of Kyrgyz sent their children.[9] Vladimir Mokrynin, who witnessed these decisions, recalled this shift in detail:

> V.M.: From the start of the 1960s, the policies of the Kyrgyz leadership were aimed at russification of the Kyrgyz. I don't think that they received anything from Moscow. . . . No, this was our own bureaucrats.
>
> N.K.: And how did this come to pass?
>
> V.M.: Our minister of education had been educated in Moscow, at Moscow State University, and was bowled over by Russian culture. He was

an overzealous fellow. Went to theaters, wandered all over the place. . . . He said: I was dressed completely shabbily, but it didn't stop me. The important thing was to get a ticket to this, and then to that. . . . And he came back here with his candidate's degree and started teaching in the History Department. Then a couple of years later he was taken into the Ministry of Education. By the start of the 1960s he was already a minister. . . . And then he went and simply banned the teaching of the Kyrgyz language in the Russian schools.

N.K.: Out of the best intentions, so to say?

V.M.: They were in fact the best of intentions, because it was an abuse of the Kyrgyz language anyway. There were no textbooks, nothing. They would find some Kyrgyz without any pedagogical training at all. . . . They show up and teach any old way. The children laugh at them. He could see that we weren't ready yet in the Russian schools to study. . . . And he took similar steps, unfortunately, with relation to history—the history of the republic. He took it and rammed it into the history of the USSR, where it disappeared. Teachers could teach it or not, as they liked.

As Mokrynin attests, the imbrication of republican elites in the assimilatory mechanisms of the highly centralized Russian educational system and the USSR's hierarchical organization of cultural life, which privileged Russian culture and language, was mirrored in these elites' decisions concerning republican cultural and educational policies. Ultimately, the census figures offered above suggest lower levels of Russian fluency among Kyrgyz than among Kazakhs. Nevertheless, in our view, due to educational policies such as those described here (maintained over three decades—the span of an entire generation), levels of "russophonia" among Kyrgyz have risen considerably higher, especially among urban populations.[10]

Russophone Cultural-Linguistic Space after Independence: Losses, Gains, and Prospects

Russian Language: Current State of Affairs

The collapse of the USSR and start of a new era of independence brought fundamental changes in the status of Russian and the titular languages in Central Asia. The changes were both de jure and de facto. The titular languages gained the status of state languages at the constitutional level and were "rescued from obscurity," in terms of both overall scale and spheres of use (this is especially the case for the Kazakh and Kyrgyz languages). Reborn as the languages of independent nations, they rapidly began to penetrate arenas in which they had only minor presence during the Soviet era: most importantly political life, primary and secondary education, mass media, and book publishing. In the capitals and the large cities, the use of titular languages spread more broadly in daily life as well, as a result of rising numbers of alumni of "national" schools, changes in labor markets (growth of demand for employees with command of the literary versions of titular languages), and, most importantly, the mass arrival in the cities of rural labor migrants.

But the titular languages have also encountered significant challenges in their development, ranging from the linguistic and sociocultural to the organizational and political. Analysis of many of these topics lies beyond the compass of the present investigation (see Kosmarskaya 2006, 166–202, 2015; Altynbekova 2006; Laruelle and Peyrouse 2007, 113–43; Dave 2007, 96–117; Orusbaev et al. 2008; Abdullaev 2009; Schlyter 2011; Sabitova and Alishariyeva 2015). However, we must offer certain observations regarding "politics." From the start of independence, elites tended to comprehend the problem of Russian and the titular languages not so much in terms of culture and communication but rather in relation to the redistribution of power and status—at first between members of the titular nationalities and the "Russians" (an embodiment of the former imperial "Center"), and later—following the legislative establishment of the titular languages' dominance—among the titular elites themselves.

As noted above, in all three of the countries under consideration, the titular elites had assimilated toward Russophone identification. Yet the domestic politics of the three countries were distinct. In Uzbekistan and Kazakhstan, where strong authoritarian leaders suppressed political activity during the 1990s, discussion of language policy and demands for revision of the status of Russian have generally remained confined to the state administrative level. Kyrgyzstan, which has seen two violent transitions of presidential power (frequently termed "revolutions") since 1991, presents a sharp contrast. Here, the language question is deeply imbricated in the long-standing contest between more economically developed and russified "northern" Kyrgyz clans and their "southern" rivals.

Prominent representatives of the latter group, who had little access to power not only during the Soviet period but for a significant period following independence, cherished the hope that "finally, these Russophone Kyrgyz bureaucrats would be swept away or would leave on their own, and our time would come. If they learn the language, then fine and good, but if they don't, we, the Kyrgyz-speaking Kyrgyz, will come to take their place" (interview with sociologist Mira Karybaeva, Bishkek, 2003). The period of "southern" disempowerment seemingly came to an end when the "northern" president Askar Akaev was forced from power and replaced by the "southern" leader Kurmanbek Bakiev in March 2005. Still, Russian did not lose much ground as an instrument of public communication. This strengthened the position of the "northern" Kyrgyz, leading to revanchist aspirations that were partially realized when Bakiev was himself forced to flee the country in April 2010 and replaced by a new representative of the "northern" clans. In this context, Kyrgyzstan regularly witnesses renewed heated public discussions of proposals to diminish the juridical and real status of the Russian language.

Nevertheless, despite all the storms raging "overhead," Russian retains a high official status (at least in two of the three countries) and retains its role as a means of social advancement and a window onto a world of culture, scholarship, and technology. Since 2000, Russian has been constitutionally affirmed as an "official language" of Kyrgyzstan. It is widely used in education and administrative activity at all social levels. In Kazakhstan, Russian has official status as the "language of international communication." In Uzbekistan, in legal terms, Russian has only the status of any foreign language. Yet in terms of social practices, even in this less hospitable sociocultural environment, its function may be described as "without rights, but quite necessary," due to its role in business and education and its importance for professional success and access to the globalized world (Podporenko 2001; Abdullaev 2009).

Post-Soviet census data reflect continued high levels of competence in Russian among titular groups. According to the data of the 2009 Census, 92 percent of Kazakhs understood oral Russian speech, 83.5 percent could write freely, and 79.1 percent were fluent readers (Agentstvo Respubliki Kazakhstan po statistike 2011, 24; see also Morrison 2017). In Kyrgyzstan, according to the 2009 Census, 2,109,393 individuals claimed Russian as a second language, including significant numbers of young people (252,732 for ages 7–15 and 813,966 for 14–28) (National Statistical Committee of the Kyrgyz Republic 2009). Clearly, these figures reflect the language competence not of ethnic Russians (circa 420,000 in the republic) or of other "Europeans" but rather of the Kyrgyz, who numbered approximately 3.8 million, putting the proportion of Russophones among Kyrgyzstan's titular population at roughly 55 percent. Finally, in the assessment of experts, about 5 million residents of Uzbekistan have active knowledge of Russian, while another 10 million have passive knowledge, together making up some 70 percent of the population (recall that Uzbekistan has conducted no census since 1991). The population of students wishing to study Russian has remained quite high in the republic (Abdullaev 2009). At present, according to the field observations of one of the authors of this study in

Tashkent in May and June 2018, between 30 and 40 percent of interpersonal communication in public places (both between Uzbeks and "Europeans" and among Uzbeks themselves) is being conducted in Russian.

The role of Russian as a language of instruction in secondary and higher education also remains high. Since 1991, for obvious reasons, the proportion of titular-language schools relative to Russian-language schools in the region has increased. Nevertheless, schools with Russian instruction are still in demand, especially in Kazakhstan and Kyrgyzstan. In responses collected by the authors over the period 2007–13 in Bishkek and Karakol (the capital of Kyrgyzstan's Issyk-Kul oblast), many "Russian" informants—that is, ethnic Russians and other "Europeans"—recall that during their own schooling during the Soviet years, classrooms included 10–15 percent Kyrgyz children. Currently, in the schools that these informants' children attend or attended after 1991, these proportions are reversed, leaving lower percentages of "Russian" children. Similarly, the demand for Russian teachers, especially native speakers, is stable in the region (see Orusbaev et al. 2008, 488–91).

Despite nationalist rhetoric and the slow yet steady rise of the prevalence of the titular languages, representatives of the titular nationalities from among both elites and the population at large who wish to succeed in life lucidly comprehend the significance of Russian competence for both themselves and their children. In the Soviet era and at the start of independence, choice of school among titular nationalities in Central Asian cities was in large part determined by the high status of Russian and the limited number of schools with instruction in the titular languages (especially in Kyrgyzstan and Kazakhstan). At present, the possibility and complexity of school choice is much greater, but for various reasons Russian schools and kindergartens remain popular. Consider a typical explanation:

> I: And where will your son go to school?
>
> R: To a Russian class. Yes, the process is progressing [of the Kyrgyz language becoming more prevalent], but you know, we still study economics in the university using Russian textbooks. . . . There are no other options. . . . That's why I think: it'll be easier for him if he graduates from a Russian school. His Kyrgyz will be excellent in any case—we speak Kyrgyz at home.
>
> (Male, Kyrgyz, b. 1968, higher ed., bank employee; Bishkek 2011)

Many regional universities offer instruction in Russian and a differentiation between "European" (or "Russian") curricula and "national" ones. In Uzbekistan, just as in the Soviet period, proportions of Russophone students are higher in educational institutions in the capital, especially in the natural sciences and technology disciplines (Abdullaev 2009). In the other two countries, universities throughout the territory also offer Russophone instruction in the social sciences and humanities.[11] Further, students' social lives, both private and professional, are conducted primarily in Russian.[12]

We will conclude this brief overview of the role of Russian in the region with reference to William Fierman's comparative study of Central Asia, the Baltic region, and Transcaucasia, with special attention to the role of Russian in administration, mass media, and education. On the basis of interviews with experts and analysis of public discourse, available statistics, and legislation, his study came to conclusions analogous to our own: although since 1991 Russian competence among the Central Asian titular population has significantly decreased, "even in countries with minute Slavic minorities, Russian continues to be used for many different types of communication, and enjoys a high level of prestige, including in higher education and in top levels of professional, economic, and political spheres. The use of Russian in elite domains and its association with high quality in Central Asia stands in contrast to the situation in the former Soviet republics of the Baltic and South Caucasus" (Fierman 2012, 1077; see also Faranda and Nolle 2011, 639). Extrapolating his findings, Fierman suggests that "Russian will continue to serve certain functions in Central Asia at least for decades to come, and very possibly much longer" (Fierman 2012, 1099).

Cultural and Physical Links across Post-Soviet Space

It is not our intention simply to paint a "rosy picture" of the current situation and prospects of Russian language and culture in Central Asia. The situation is mobile and subject to a great many factors, interacting in a complex manner. Since the start of the twenty-first century, one of the most significant factors supporting the preservation of Russophone linguistic-cultural space in Central Asia has been the rise of labor migration to the Russian Federation, originating primarily in the region's most impoverished countries: Tajikistan, Uzbekistan, and Kyrgyzstan. The demographic growth of titular nationalities, land and employment shortages, and the painful economic transition of the agricultural sector at first elicited an increased flow of migration from rural areas to the region's large cities, and, following the oversaturation of labor markets there, redirection of migrants in search of employment abroad, primarily in Russia. Later, Kazakhstan itself became a significant recipient of migratory flows. The scale of these migrations has meant, in essence, that a significant proportion of the populations of the countries of origin are continuously located in Russophone social situations in the large cities of Russia and Kazakhstan, where they voluntarily or by force of circumstance gain Russian linguistic and cultural competence.

We should, of course, keep in mind that the mode of life, legal status, and occupations of the majority of these migrants markedly differ from those of one particular rural Kyrgyz youth, mentioned above, who fell under the spell of Russian culture in the 1960s at Moscow State University and later became the republican minister of education. Migrants' gray-market economic activity, encounters with xenophobia, and labor without special qualifications in spheres entailing little contact with locals all impede cultural integration—yet do not close it off completely. In our view, over time the cumulative impact of this massive labor migration on the linguistic and cultural profiles of the countries of origin may be substantial. Among the countries under discussion here, this observation is most relevant for Kyrgyzstan, for which the scale of labor migration—from 800 thousand to one million individuals—is equivalent to between one-quarter and one-third of the total adult working population.

From the still sparse research data concerning migrants' everyday life in Russia, the discomfort of displacement may in fact incentivize linguistic and cultural assimilation. Kyrgyz migrants in St. Petersburg, for instance, describe the results of discrimination against their children in Russian schools as follows: "This is one reason why children try to adjust to the local conditions and prefer to affiliate themselves with local Russians rather than with other Central Asians" (Nasritdinov 2016, 263). Furthermore, while still at home, prospective migrants try to improve their linguistic skills voluntarily, in order to improve communication skills or competitiveness in the labor market. Fieldwork in south Kyrgyzstan, the point of origin for many migrants, shows the growth of a pragmatic interest in Russian among locals: "Russian-speaking schools have certainly become popular. Parents want their children to learn Russian because fluency in the language widens job prospects and options for labor migration. . . . Increased levels of labor migration have created a demand for Russian language tuition beyond schools" (Kirmse 2011, 294). Consider the explanation of a "city" Kyrgyz, granddaughter of a well-known Kyrgyz "people's poet," regarding increased demand for Russian in the context of rising migratory turmoil:

> The wild nationalism of the past is no more, because everyone is departing for Russia. I encountered this in a forceful way at the start of the 1990s, when every self-respecting Kyrgyz had to give me a kick: you're the granddaughter of such a person, and you should be ashamed that you don't know your native language, etc. There's none of that now . . . because everyone is heading to Russia and you can't do anything there without language. Courses have appeared for

> Kyrgyz who haven't managed to learn Russian yet. . . . I interviewed a girl for the newspaper who had taken courses to improve her Russian in order to return to Russia in search of a high-paying job.
>
> (Female, Kyrgyz, b. 1963, higher ed., journalist; Bishkek, 2011)

Let us add that successful migrants, upon return to their homeland, often settle in the capitals and large cities, bringing not only newly acquired financial resources but also new cultural-linguistic habits. On the one hand, this reinforces the distinctions between urban and rural settings, to which those with new cultural and economic capital prefer not to return. At the same time, this further supports the long-standing Russophone urban cultural milieu.

Human flows between the Russian Federation and Central Asia are not limited to labor migration alone and involve many other dimensions of contact. Furthermore, cultural products, information, and goods and services circulate within the larger Russophone space, increasing the prominence of Russian as an instrument of communication "over the borders." This circulation is most relevant for countries united with Russia in the Eurasian Economic Union—Kazakhstan and Kyrgyzstan. The dominance of Russia-based media in these countries also serves as a powerful channel of this communication. According to the data of the Eurasian Development Bank's most recent polls, 29 percent of respondents in Kazakhstan and 31 percent in Kyrgyzstan had visited Russia for personal, professional, or tourist purposes during the last five years.[13] Twenty-seven percent of respondents in Kazakhstan and 34 percent in Kyrgyzstan expressed a desire to pursue higher education in Russia, and 48 percent in both countries expressed an interest in Russophone culture—for instance, in imported cultural services or goods from Russia (Eurasian Development Bank 2016, 72, 74, 79).

These figures, significantly greater than the proportions of the "European" populations of the two countries, attest that Russian still plays a significant role as the lingua franca in the exchange of cultural products, ideas, and memories, as well as in the daily and professional communication of people of various nationalities. One respondent expressed the range of emotions and associations, both joyous and sorrowful, tied to Russian:

> All of world culture passes through the Russian language. I recall how once some years back I was sitting at a train station in Crimea. A Georgian was sitting next to me—there are no Georgians who do not know the Georgian language, but there are millions of Kazakhs who do not know Kazakh. . . . I mentioned with anguish that I belong to the generation without language. And he answered:

> but imagine, we could be sitting here unable to say "hello" to one another. And that's all thanks to the Russian language. The Russian language, literature, culture, the past, the war—it's impossible to erase. I just worry about this geopolitics, about this generation that has grown up into skinheads. But everything else is so native to me. . . . Yes, I think in Russian and my son thinks in Russian. That might be a misfortune: I understand Kazakh, and can speak, but my child cannot. Alas, that's how I've raised him.
>
> (Female, Kazakh, born in 1961, higher education, school teacher; Petropavlovsk, Northern-Kazakhstan region, 2016)

Mention here of "the past" and "the war" is highly significant. In this post-Soviet region, the language of the former metropole has been transformed into an object of both emotional and stable pragmatic interest for the titular ethnicities, including their elites. Perhaps surprisingly, in distinction from other former Soviet territories such as the Baltics, the Soviet cultural and historical legacy has not served as provocation, causing titular elites and populations to "see red." Instead, it has reinforced a sense of common past and values, especially in conditions of post-Soviet economic and social turmoil (see, e.g., Florin 2011; Flynn et al. 2014; Umetbaeva 2015; Bissenova 2017). Beyond those other factors explored here, the absence of any large-scale "postcolonial" rejection of the "Soviet," and of Russian language and culture along with it, will sustain the Russophone cultural-linguistic space in this geography for decades to come, as generations pass.

Cities as Linguistic-Cultural "Contested Spaces"

Besides external labor migration, other forms of migration are also significant for Russian language and culture in Central Asia. As indicated above, the excess labor force from agriculture and small cities, in a reflection of the difficult early post-Soviet conditions, flowed first into the capitals and large cities, and only subsequently across national borders. Internal rural-urban migration began in the three countries as early as the end of the 1980s and continues to the present, with equivocal consequences for the urban cultural-linguistic fabric.

In quantitative demographic terms, the inflow of large numbers of rural dwellers, the majority of whom were educated and speak primarily in the titular languages, leads to a "physical" compression of Russophone cultural-linguistic space. On the other hand, depending on the degree of immersion in the new context, some portion of the migrant population acquires the habits of urban life and Russian language competence as a means of social advancement. This process can extend for years for any given individual, but it inevitably affects every new wave of migrants. As the authors' findings testify, even in Bishkek's most marginalized migrant families, adult children are either working in Russia or simultaneously working and studying in Russian at local universities. Parents view this as their most reliable means of upward social mobility to escape the status of impoverished migrant. These processes are most pronounced in Kyrgyzstan and Kazakhstan.

If we examine the consequences of rural-urban migration from a cultural-evaluative perspective, from the point of view of the already established polyethnic urban community and its cultural preferences, the influx of "village" migrants elevates the status of the urban lifestyle, which since the Soviet era has been founded on extensive use of Russian. Russophone cultural-linguistic space is thus reinforced, although only within the confines of a shrinking social-demographic space. Similarly, the social convergence of the "Europeans" with urban Kyrgyz, Kazakhs, and Uzbeks is also reinforced as these groups experience increased solidarity, united in opposition to forces that, in their view, erode the urban life style and threaten to demodernize the city, transforming it into a "huge countryside" or a "chaotic city." Long-term city dwellers pejoratively refer to migrants collectively as "farmers," "mountain folk," or "barbarians." More specific slurs with localized overtones are also in use: in Uzbekistan rural migrants are called "kharypy," in Kazakhstan they are referred to as "mambety," and in Kyrgyzstan they are designated as "myrki."[14] Importantly, "Russian" and titular long-term urban residents have developed a mutual cultural affinity (on Kazakhstan and Kyrgyzstan in this regard, see Faranda and Nolle 2003, 2011). Yet what, exactly, characterizes the Russophone "urban culture" that is defended by these groups and gradually appropriated, intentionally or by force of circumstances, by new migrants? The fate of Russophone cultural-linguistic space in the city is closely linked to the answer to this question.

The Universalism of "Russian Culture" and the Particularities of Globalization

At the start of this chapter we noted that the cultural norms brought to Central Asia by "Russians" in the course of imperial and later Soviet colonization largely lacked "ethnic" connotations. But would it be appropriate to refer to these norms as "Soviet"? Despite the fact that these urban cultural norms existed for more than seventy years in a closed, rigidly ideologically controlled socialist society, to our thinking they partook far more of cosmopolitanism and universalism than one might suspect. This conclusion is supported by memoirs, by scholarly observation, and by the responses of our respondents. Take, for instance, architect Dilora Mardieva's description of her "happy childhood" in the governmental apartment building in Tashkent in the late 1950s:

> There were gatherings around the dining table, May Day outings, trips to concerts and films. The children . . . were taken to all sorts of circuses and theaters. . . . A sports facility had been set up in the basement. . . . There was equipment for tennis and volleyball. . . . It was a highly cultured, healthy life in the center of the city. . . . Our mothers . . . were constantly signing us up for all sorts of activity groups [kruzhki] in the nearby Pioneers' Palace. And the mobile Children's Library of the Republic would come once a week with books—you could order any book you liked: *Neznaika*, *Robinson Crusoe*, or anything else.[15] (Tokhtakhodzhaeva 2008, 101)

Circus, theater, film, tennis, volleyball, accessible children's books including not only well-known Soviet classics but also "permitted" world literature—with a bare minimum of Soviet ideological significance (a May Day outing is, in essence, a springtime picnic), this complex of activities has been preserved to the present as the leisure regime of the average post-Soviet city dweller. Further, if we ignore the names of particular authors, the picture looks similar in any country of the developed world.

Consider the cultural life of Fergana in the 1970s and 1980s from the perspective of city dwellers. In our interviews, that era's replete cultural atmosphere evokes associations with "Europe" ("Fergana was amazing. It was European!"); respondents spoke extensively about the wide array of bookstores, overshadowing even Moscow, as well as about Jazz festivals at the end of the 1970s, when "Fergana became the capital of the USSR—the capital of Jazz." In general, in the late-Soviet years Fergana was culturally and linguistically Russian, often identified as European, but inclusive of the various nationalities making up the urban community at the time (Flynn et al. 2014, 1505–10). Importantly, respondents spoke extensively about "European-ness" in general (as a chief marker of Central Asian urban life) and in particular about "European," "classical" music, and Jazz, commonly evoked together as the privileged cultural preference of city people.[16]

Alima Bissenova has analyzed distinctions in the cultural politics and models of reception of rural migrants in the two "capitals" of Kazakhstan—distinctions linked to these cities' differing locations and processes of population growth. As she explains, in Almaty, with its deep imperial and Soviet history, the influx of rural migrants intensifies the long-term urban dwellers' nostalgia for what they view as a "cosmopolitan Russian-language environment" and "European-oriented informal culture." In particular, as one individual reports in his memoirs, one of the charms of late-Soviet Alma-Ata was its inclusion in a global (meaning American-European) music scene: Jazz ensembles from as far away as New York would visit, while local groups engaged in foreign tours (Bissenova 2017, 653, 655). Similarly, in our interviews in Bishkek regarding changes on the city's central Ala-Too Square, long-term residents frequently expressed displeasure at the typical evening sounds of "Kyrgyz pop," preferring Jazz or "classical music."

David Abramson's ethnographic research conducted in the cities of Kokand and Tashkent during the 1990s and devoted to Uzbekistani sociocultural transition as experienced by several russified (Europeanized) families, primarily urban Uzbeks, sheds light on accepted norms of urban everyday behavior. In the context of a post-Soviet return to "national values," the habits of urban Russophone Uzbeks began to elicit aggressive negative responses from the more nationally oriented population, including rural migrants. As examples of censured behaviors, Abramson describes a woman of twenty-nine who remains unmarried and prefers "European" dress, including short skirts, as well as a younger academic worker who invites friends, including unmarried men and women, to his apartment on the weekends to drink wine, dance, and listen to Jazz and other "European music" (2000, 55–57). The author, assessing somewhat uncritically the emotional stress of his informants—in essence, a typical expression of early post-Soviet social-psychological disorientation—explains it as an outcome of their retention of outmoded, Soviet behaviors, using the terms employed by his informants themselves, who described themselves as "products of the socialist system." For this reason, Abramson titled his article "Socialism's Bastard Children." Nevertheless, one may note that the behaviors in question, habitual for these informants yet rejected by the more traditionally oriented Uzbek context, have little specifically socialist or Soviet content. Similarly, the tacitly accepted norms of behavior in public places, whose violation by rural migrants elicits the condemnation of long-term residents, represent a standard, "universal" array of norms that lack ethnic or ideological connotations. These norms include using crosswalks and refraining from activities such as spitting on the sidewalks, littering, or urinating in public (see Kosmarski 2011; Flynn and Kosmarskaya 2012; Bissenova 2017).

Following the Soviet collapse, the "core" of Central Asian urban culture, in both its elevated and quotidian variants, was liberated from past ideological burdens and expanded exponentially (as occurred also in Russia itself) under the influence of global mass culture. The "absorption" and "reworking" of foreign models became a common phenomenon, but these complex processes do not alter the supernational, universal connotations of this cultural matrix. Although it functions primarily on the basis of the Russian language, this does not render it ethnically "Russian," "Soviet," or representative of the contemporary Russian Federation.[17] It is this universal character, reinforcing globalizing tendencies in local social development, that constitutes one of the chief factors supporting the persistence of the Russophone cultural space of Central Asia.

"Cheshire-Cat Smile": Russian Language and Culture as a Locally-Rooted Phenomenon

The attentive reader will already have noted that, in this extended chapter concerning "Russian culture" in Central Asia, little has been said about Russians per se. Their role in the region is primarily a historical one: in shifting the center of gravity from ethnic to political-ideological values and priorities, it was they who formed the model of cultural-linguistic domination that led to the transformation of "Russian culture" into a transethnic phenomenon, defining the lifestyle, values, and modes of communication of a significant portion of the titular populations in the region (as well as that of the Russians themselves and of other "Europeans") to the present. Our findings in relation to Russian culture in Central Asia support the validity of the principles outlined in the introduction to this volume concerning how the "historically contingent linkage of culture with geography" manifests itself in local contexts.

The historically contingent process by which Russian language and culture became rooted among the titular population, becoming self-reproducing local phenomena, allows one to describe this cultural matrix as a "Cheshire-cat smile": Russophone cultural-linguistic space might continue to function here even without a larger presence of "Russians." In a corollary, one may conclude that the Russian Federation's efforts (which so far have been limited) to support the local Russian cultural milieu are far from determinative, although their energetic pursuit would be beneficial both for Russia itself (considering the presence on its territory of millions of Central Asian migrants) and for the support of cultural diversity in the countries of the region.

The social-demographic dynamics of the post-Soviet years have led to the progressive "compression" of Russophone cultural space in reflection of the decreasing proportions of "Europeans" among the three countries' populations as a result of migration (most intensive in the 1990s) and low birth rates in the context of traditionally higher birth rates among titular ethnic groups. Nevertheless, as demonstrated above, a series of complex, largely unquantifiable counterfactors indicate that it would be reductive to posit the continued existence of the Russophone cultural-linguistic space as dependent only on the demographic prominence of "children of empire."

The rootedness of Russian language and culture in local soil extends also to producers of high culture (considerations of space preclude a detailed account of this topic here). We may note the significant number of recognized authors from among the titular populations who write or wrote in Russian, from well-known figures such as Chingiz Aitmatov, Olzhas Suleimenov, and the members of the Fergana school of poetry to younger authors of the region.

The specificities of Central Asian "Russian culture" have great relevance for ongoing scholarly and political debates on issues such as the following: whether the relations of the USSR to Central Asia should be considered imperial; what the fate of Russian is likely to be in light of the increasing dominance of titular languages in the region; and whether a "completely valid" Russophone culture can exist outside of Russia proper, and if so, to whom it "belongs." In Sergei Abashin's view, when we weigh arguments regarding the identification of "Soviet" as "colonial," we should recall that, regardless of the obvious sins of russification, the cultural products and formations of the region, in contributing to the general Soviet cultural landscape, simultaneously supported the growth of conceptions of particularity among the titular population: "while remaining Soviet, they also belonged to the local population that interpreted them as 'their own,' rather than as externally imposed colonial standards" (2016b, 41, 42).

Alexander Morrison, arguing against political battles over matters of language in Kazakhstan, observes that it would be incorrect to reduce the language situation in that country to a zero-sum game.[18] Based on his experience as a university instructor in Astana, he offers the analogy of the role of English in India, affirming that "Russian is in every sense a Kazakhstani language—Kazakhstanis share in the wider Russian literary heritage, and have developed a distinctive Russophone culture of their own." This is a "Russophone world . . . that extends beyond the boundaries of the Russian Federation, and does not necessarily identify with it, or with ethnic Russianness" (Morrison 2017).

To the range of cultural phenomena analyzed in the present volume (diaspora, national culture, émigré cultures, etc.), our analysis of the specificity of "Russian culture" in Central Asia adds one more significant configuration—that of "indigenized culture." The profound engagement of titular populations both in the production and consumption of "Russian culture" (in the Soviet era as well as today) enriches the polyphony of human global civilization and demonstrates more starkly than any other case the ideological illusoriness, noted in this volume's introduction, of any assumption that "culture is at home in the territory of a nation state."

Notes

1. In June 1998 the capital of the country was moved to the city of Astana.

2. The Arbat is a landmark pedestrian street in central Moscow. Streets with similar "transplanted" local nicknames are located in the capitals of other countries of Central Asia, and in particular in Tashkent and Bishkek (formerly Frunze).

3. The third period of fieldwork was conducted within the framework of the international research project "Perception of Russia across Eurasia: Memory, Identity, Conflict," ERA. Net RUS Plus Research Program (funded by the RFH-RFBR No. 16-21-19003/17-OGON).

4. See TsentrAziia, "Goskomstat Kazakhstana podvel itogi perepisi 2009 goda," February 5, 2010, www.centrasia.ru/newsA.php?st=1265318280.

5. These are not only mixed marriages within the Russian-speaking community but also frequent "third-republic intermarriages" (when no partner is titular in relation to the republic of residence).

6. According to the All-Soviet Census of 1989, Russians made up 30 percent of rural dwellers in Kyrgyzstan and 23 percent in Kazakhstan, whereas in Tajikistan, Uzbekistan, and Turkmenistan they comprised between 3 percent and 6 percent (Arutiunian 1992, 25).

7. Evgeny Abdullaev presents different official figures for Uzbekistan: according to the Census of 1979, between 1970 and 1979 the number of Uzbeks who spoke Russian fluently increased fourfold, to 49.3 percent (Abdullaev 2009).

8. In particular, Olga Naumova's data show that in 1989 nearly ¾ of urban Kazakhs used Russian, rather than Kazakh, in daily life (cit. in Dave 2007, 52).

9. In Frunze, until 1989, there was only one school with Kyrgyz as language of instruction.

10. It was precisely the significant presence of Russophone Kyrgyz among the population (that made up from ¼ to ⅓ of the total at the start of the twenty-first century, by various accounts), as well as their concentration among the intelligentsia and state servitors, that gave rise to an official institution, unique among post-Soviet states—the Linguistic Commission, tasked with examining presidential candidates for literary Kyrgyz language competency.

11. For instance, in the southern oblasts of Kyrgyzstan, in which there have historically been few "Europeans" and presently are almost none, university students begin studying in Uzbek or Kyrgyz and turn to study in Russian during the third year (Orusbaev et al. 2008, 491–92; in particular concerning Russian language use in the south of Kyrgyzstan, see Kirmse 2011).

12. This is confirmed by findings from ten focus groups with students of various higher education institutions in Almaty and eight focus groups with Bishkek students, in research carried out by N. Kosmarskaya and I. Savin in 2016 and 2017. Other studies have reached similar conclusions.

13. These polls are regularly conducted in the seven countries of the Commonwealth of Independent States. Uzbekistan does not participate.

14. For detailed description of new urban sociocultural divisions deriving from internal migration, see Schroeder 2010; Kosmarski 2011; Flynn, Kosmarskaya 2012; Flynn et al. 2014; Bissenova 2017.

15. *Neznaika* ("know-nothing") is the title and the eponymous protagonist of a well-known cycle of Soviet children's fantasy tales of the early 1950s.

16. When respondents speak retrospectively of the urban milieu's "Europeanness," they are envisioning not any real "Europe" (in which very few of them had ever been) but rather a version of the Soviet "imaginary west," in Aleksei Yurchak's terms, tinged with nostalgia and serving as a counterweight to intensifying post-Soviet neo-traditionalism (2006, 158–206).

17. The specificity of cultural globalization in Central Asia and the possible mediating role of Russia in this process has not yet been studied in depth. Stefan Kirmse, in his study of this topic in the context of youth cultural practices in southern Kyrgyzstan, has used rap music as one example of how "global cultural genres are filtered through a Russian lens" (2011, 286, 296–97, 300–304).

18. An upsurge of these battles took place in spring 2017 following Nursultan Nazarbayev's decree concerning the adoption of the Latin alphabet for Kazakh language after 2025.

Distance and Proximity in the Baltic "Near Abroad"

Kevin M. F. Platt

[. . .] In silence we cross Čaka St.
on yellow. We'll ride together for five more minutes. The driver flips on the radio . . .
After the news, I ask Imant, sitting there silently, what he,
as a veteran designer, prefers—PC or Mac? He replies, in pretty good Russian,
that he stopped seeing it in such stark terms a while back, but he only works on a Mac.
"We just don't have any PCs at the agency . . ." ". . . I'll get out by the old Rigas Modas building . . ."
". . . By the way, how do Russians . . . I mean . . ." he wants to ask something
about the peculiarities of PCs, but mixes up computers with my nationality and breaks off . . .
"Funny," from the front seat the student jumps in on the awkward moment,
"I noticed long ago, that when someone names your nationality in a different language
or with an accent, it always sounds sort of insulting, yeah . . . Or when you yourself say, Gypsy,
there's no terminological neutrality, you know? And with Chukchis, forget about it . . .":)
He stops, expecting we'll laugh . . . A familiar song begins in the silence.
But the gang from Tallinas St. can be cheered up only by a huge Jeep,
racing by in the late evening at excessive speed.

Artur Punte, "I know—the only thing that cheers up the gang from Tallinas St.," 2002

Terms of Indistinction

Since 1991, discussions of ethnic identity have been potentially awkward in many places around the former Soviet Union—places where history has reconfigured relationships between languages, cultures, and "nationalities" (to use a Soviet-era category with uneven persistence and increasingly blurry meaning) and cast them together in intimate conversations and confined spaces, such as the car full of commuters described in the above poem, or the city through which it is driving, Riga, Latvia. In Vladimir Putin's description of the recent history of such territories, offered in the wake of the 2014 annexation of Crimea, "millions of Russians went to sleep in one country and woke up in another, as national minorities" (2014a). That transformative moment brought new categories of identity and geography into being. The most significant of these, for my purposes here, is "near abroad" (*blizhnee zarubez'e*), the term that came to be applied in Russia to the band of former Soviet states surrounding the Russian Federation to the west, south, and east, stretching from the Baltics to Central Asia, in which significant populations of Russians and Russophones still reside. When the Soviet Union broke up, these people "emigrated" without leaving the comfort of their own homes from what had seemed, to many, self-evidently "Russian" territory (Laitin 1998; Brubaker 2000). They found themselves in new, or renewed, countries in which Soviet "titular nationalities" had gained the status of legitimate masters of their own nation states. Russians and Russian culture in the near abroad enjoy a sui generis status. They are neither national nor diasporic, neither integrated into "mainland" society in the Russian Federation nor entirely divorced from it. They were never displaced yet nevertheless are out of place. For this reason, Russian culture occupies complex positions in these landscapes. The current chapter describes the Latvian redaction of this peculiar geographical condition through the combined lens of ethnography and discourse analysis, and offers closer analysis of a few prominent examples, including the work of the Riga-based Orbita poetry and multimedia art collective, to which Artur Punte, the author of this chapter's epigraph, belongs.

The near abroad is a heterogeneous category. In consequence of deep distinctions among the histories of the post-Soviet states, along with their differing demographic and cultural-linguistic situations, the status of Russian culture and Russians themselves within them varies greatly. In Latvia, a long and complex history of Russian imperial domination, early twentieth-century independence, cultural and linguistic differentiation, and Soviet occupation and social engineering resulted immediately in fraught relations between ethnic Latvians and Russians in the post-Soviet era. In distinction to the profound interconnection of Ukrainian and Russian cultural, social, and linguistic realities, for instance, Russians and Latvians occupied what were in many ways separate worlds, and continue to do so—with some important exceptions that will be examined below. In distinction to, for instance, Uzbekistan and Kazakhstan, where Russian language enjoys relatively high social status among the non-Russian majority, ethnic Latvians generally privilege their own language and culture and regard that of the Russians as an existentially unnecessary feature of their territory (Kosmarskaya and Kosmarski, this volume). Perhaps most importantly, in distinction to Soviet republics with relatively small proportional populations of Russians in the late Soviet era, such as nearby Lithuania (9.4 percent in 1989) or Georgia (6.3 percent in 1989), some 34 percent of Soviet Latvia's residents were ethnic Russians in 1989, with perhaps another 10 percent of assorted other Russophones, such as Ukrainians and Belarusians ("Vsesoiuznyi perepis' naseleniia"). The case of Estonia is in many respects comparable to Latvia's, although its Russian population is territorially segregated to a greater degree than is the case in Latvia, where most Russians reside in the cities of Rezekne, Daugavpils, and Riga (the republic's capital and largest population center, where fully half of the population resides). In each of these cities the population is divided nearly equally between Russians and Latvians. All of these factors combined have rendered the Russian presence extraordinarily problematic and contested in post-Soviet Latvia—a matter about which there can be "no terminological neutrality," to borrow Punte's formula from the poem.

The implications for the fates of Russians in this region are perhaps most apparent in the history of official categories of citizenship available to them.[1] In 1990–91 the post-Soviet Latvian state was declared legally continuous with the interwar Latvian Republic (1922–40), the constitution of which is therefore still in force. In a clumsy, yet comprehensible response to the near minority status of ethnic Latvians in their own territory, only citizens of the interwar republic and their descendants gained automatic citizenship in its new era, ensuring an ethnic Latvian majority at the polls (Laitin 1998, 95–98; Commercio 2010, 55–57; Kochenov and Dimitrovs 2016). This left all other residents—many of them born and raised in Soviet Latvia, and many of whom had cast votes in support of independence in a landmark 1991 referendum—stripped of many political and economic rights and faced with an initially ill-defined naturalization process. In 1995 a new law on citizenship included a special category of *nepilsoņi*, or "noncitizens," for this large group of former Soviet Latvians—who made up nearly 30 percent of the republic's population in 1995. The majority of these noncitizens self-identify as "Russians," although there are many other ethnicities mixed into this category as well. In the present, noncitizens still make up some 15 percent of the population ("Population Census" 2011). As these numbers perhaps make plain, many noncitizens have refused to naturalize out of disaffection or protest. And while significant numbers emigrated (or repatriated) to the Russian Federation, many have opted not to leave, even though the majority of Russians view policies toward Russian language and culture as state-sanctioned ethnic discrimination (Commercio 2010).

In the 1990s, when the new law on noncitizens was adopted, Russian diplomats complained that the new identity document it brought into being—the purple "noncitizen passport"—had a "halfway" (*polovinchatyi*) character (Stroi 1997b). Yet terms developed for this population in the Russian Federation are no more lucid. Since the late 1990s, a multiply revised law has granted special privileges with regard to travel, emigration, access to medicine and education to "compatriots abroad" (*sootechestvenniki za rubezhom*)—former Soviet citizens in neighboring states who might, in some calculation, "belong" more properly to Russia (Russian Federation 1999). Yet what calculation could determine who might claim these rights? Putin, in his much-cited Address to the Federal Assembly of 2005, announced that with the Soviet collapse—"the greatest geopolitical catastrophe of the century"—"tens of millions of our compatriots and fellow citizens found themselves beyond the borders of Russian territory" (2005). In his address announcing the annexation of Crimea, cited above, he declared that after 1991, "the Russian people became one of the largest, if not the largest, divided people in the world" (2014a). The subtle distinctions between these two formulations point to the categorical complexity of "compatriots abroad"—a temporally confused term that could arguably refer to any former citizen of the Soviet Union or, as seems to be the case in Putin's more recent pronouncement, any ethnic Russian now residing in "non-Russian territory." Yet given the complexity of ethnic Russian identification following centuries of social and cultural assimilation—in which a proud Russian might well be the grandchild of a Pole, Jew, Ossetian, or Ukrainian, or in which an "ethnic Russian" might well consider himself a Ukrainian and take up arms against separatist formations in Donbas—determining which former Soviets are the "real" ethnic Russians is not so easy, either.

Successive revisions of the law on compatriots have attempted to resolve this conceptual incoherence. The current redaction (2013) specifies that "compatriots abroad" are persons living in other states and "relating, as a rule, to the peoples who have historically resided on the territory of the Russian Federation," who have additionally "made a free choice to be spiritually, culturally, and legally linked to the Russian Federation"—a choice demonstrated by "an act of self-identification, reinforced by social or professional activity for the preservation of Russian language, the native languages of the peoples of the Russian Federation, the development of Russian culture abroad, the strengthening of the friendly relations of the states of residence of the compatriots with the Russian Federation, the support of social organizations of compatriots, and the defense of the rights of compatriots or by other evidence of the free choice of the persons in question of spiritual and cultural linkage with the Russian Federation" (Russian Federation 1999, stat'ia 3). Here, we see the collision in the near abroad of complex identity formations inherited from the Soviet and Russian imperial past with contemporary problems of "disaggregation" of citizenship that have been observed as a global phenomenon (Sassen 1996; Benhabib 2004). As the above makes clear, "being Russian" boils down to free choices of "spiritual and cultural" affiliation. To spell out the implications fully: in the post-Soviet near abroad, questions of social belonging and collective identity—questions that, as we have seen following 2014 in Crimea and Eastern Ukraine, have a direct bearing on territorial claims, the establishment of political borders, and the murderous operations of armies—depend on cultural life. Here, histories and states have conspired to render culture and identities unstable, if not openly arbitrary. We might turn in this connection to the poem offered as epigraph above: does writing poems in Russian in Riga automatically render one "Russian" or a "compatriot abroad"?[2] Can one write in Russian without making a "free choice" to be spiritually and culturally linked to the "Russian Federation"? Can one write in free verse? Does the fact that Artur Punte is a Russophone poet of mixed heritage have any bearing on these questions?

This new geographical condition's master term, "near abroad," reflects the uncanny instability of lives lived under its sign. Note that the term itself reflects a view of these territories from Russia—few in Latvia or Georgia, let alone Ukraine, would use it as a primary term of description for their own geographical location. Yet with regard to Russian cultural processes in these places, the term is apt precisely because it bears traces of the Russian imperial gaze. Its common Russian form, *blizhnee zarubezh'e*, deploys not the neutral word connoting close spatial relations *blizkii* but rather the less common form *blizhnii*, which might better be translated as "neighboring." The latter term carries connotations of intimacy and almost personhood—in Russian, the substantivized adjective *blizhnii* means "fellow man" and is familiar from the biblical injunction to "love thy neighbor." Further, one may remark on the term's "oxymoronic" construction, denoting territory at once "close" and "distant"—a suitable location for people who are somehow both compatriots and foreigners. Among the many territories that may be described as "near abroad," Latvia epitomizes this geographical notion in an especially acute manner. From a Russian perspective, it numbers among the most "near" spaces—territorially, historically, linguistically, ethnically, and in terms of economic, social, and familial relationships bridging the border—Russians have resided there for centuries and form a proportionally larger part of the Latvian population than of any other post-Soviet state besides the Russian Federation itself. Yet in other ways, Latvia is among the most "abroad" territories: a member of the European Union and of NATO, geographically positioned in the West, and defined by its non-Slavic titular nation, Latvia and its representatives often have little use for Russians and Russia. In short, from the perspective of the Russian Federation, Latvia maximally combines intimate, almost domestic familiarity with integration into the emphatically (and of late, increasingly) foreign territory of Europe. Latvia is at once "theirs" and "ours," near and far, exotic and homey, in an ironically charged conception of geography correlating precisely with the contested social identities of the region's Russians, who occupy the interstices between societies, languages, and hegemonic formations.

This halfway geographical condition is definitive of the cultural life of Russian Latvians—yet here the word "definitive" takes on ironic overtones. In his seminal study of "identities in formation" in four former Soviet republics in the 1990s, David Laitin envisioned the fate of Russians in Latvia (as well as in Estonia) as hanging between two options—assimilation to Latvian language and social life or a strong "Russian-speaking national revival," with claims for cultural autonomy and political rights (1998, 342; see also Kronenfeld 2004, 2005). Yet two is not enough options, and one is not enough outcomes. Subject to overlapping and porous regimes of identity, and lacking many unifying social institutions as a result of cultural and political disenfranchisement, Russians in Latvia can assume any number of stances toward resolving the contradictions of life in the near abroad across a disunited social scene. And the multiplicity of Russian social experience raises the ante once again on the meaning of cultural activity per se, presenting Russians of the region with the question of what they want to *make* of themselves as Russians. Here, everyone has the opportunity to be a cultural constructivist, in a literal sense.

Yet opportunity does not automatically translate to agency. The halfway situation of Russians in Latvia is in many ways typical of the "in-between" position theorized as fundamental to postcolonial subjectivity. For them, "access to the image of identity is only ever possible in the *negation* of any sense of originality or plenitude; the process of displacement and differentiation (absence/presence, representation/repetition) renders it a liminal reality" (Bhabba 1994, 51). Subjected in the opposed hegemonic public discursive regimes of both Latvia and Russia to conceptions of identity that imply their lack of belonging, excessive presence, or displacement from geographical propriety, the cultural situation of Russians in Latvia may be compared to the "dual domination" that L. Ling-Chi Wang describes as characteristic for Chinese Americans, a state that has recently been extended to apply to Chinese populations in other locations in the Sinophone world, such as Malaysia, by Shu-Mei Shih. As Wang writes: "The conditions for Chinese assimilation are reconceived as racial exclusion or oppression and the demand for loyalty to the homeland as extraterritorial domination. Both are seen as omnipresent and omnipotent powers or forces dominating all aspects of Chinese American life" (1995, 158; see also Shih 2011).[3] In these conditions, cultural self-fashioning must contend with imagined cultural wholes that will never apply in a total, simple, or complete manner.[4]

Example One: Of Wholes and Parts

So how do people go about making something of themselves, as Russians, in Latvia? The remainder of this chapter presents three examples of responses to this complex process of self-fashioning via intentional cultural activity. First, consider the general dynamics of Russian cultural life in Riga as reflected in the conundrums of a successful businessman, an embattled schoolteacher, and other residents of Latvia's capital.[5] Over the course of the past decade, in conversations with Russians in Latvia concerning their lives, I learned that for many of them the term "culture" is a loaded one—and not because they have read the Russian law on compatriots abroad. Given the postcolonial condition I describe above, it might come as a surprise to learn that among these conversations' most common refrains is the claim that the distinguishing feature of Russians in Latvia is that they are "more cultured" than people across the border to the east, in the Russian Federation. The successful Jewish businessman Evgeny Gomberg offered a typical account. For Gomberg, who invited me to his posh cigar club and treated me to a glass of cognac, being "more cultured" means having greater respect for the law, a love of high culture, no tolerance for the absurdities of life in the Russian Federation, and none of the habits needed to survive there, which he lumped together under the term "loutishness," or "boorishness" (*khamstvo*). Two other informants, the younger and less economically privileged brother and sister Evgeniia and Alexander, recoded this distinction as one of personality types: Russians in Russia are "emotional and vulgar" in distinction to those in Latvia, who are "restrained, cultured, and even-tempered." Others, such as the former theater professional Rostislav, told me about the "European" qualities of local Russians' respect for culture. In some respects, this use of the term "culture" activates the concept of "culturedness" (*kul'turnost'*), which primarily references polite behavior in everyday life—greetings to shopkeepers, no public drunkenness or swearing, and so on. Yet in other respects it is high culture that is at stake: as Gomberg elaborated, in Latvia, classic Russian culture is truly valued, as opposed to its debased condition in the Russian Federation. A number of informants told me that a better, "purer" Russian is spoken in Latvia. By any calculation the discussion is inflected with a Soviet pedigree—"culturedness" was first fully articulated in early Soviet social modernization campaigns, while the literature, theater, and ballet evoked by my informants are elements of a modified Soviet high cultural canon. Often, these conversations take on wistful or nostalgic overtones: Russians in Riga know that the culture they cling to belongs to the past—not just in the sense that national canons are always a little dusty but in the sense that the same Russians who take pride in their cultured status also typically explain that Russian culture is under threat in Latvia.

This formulation of local Russian identity, if taken to its logical extreme, results in surprising formulations: as one woman who called in to a radio show I was participating in told me, "Russians in Latvia are more Russian than Russians in Russia." The experience of the schoolteacher Vera fully realizes the contradictions of this formulation. Vera delivered one of the most outspoken articulations of unjust Russian victimhood I have heard in Latvia. We spoke at length about educational policies, which completely eliminated Russian as a language of instruction for higher education and which have successively diminished the place of Russian language and culture in Latvian schools. In her struggle to counteract what she views as an all-out war on Russian culture in Latvia, Vera organizes tours for her pupils to the Russian Federation in order to visit museums and monuments as a way of reconnecting with the homeland. Yet ironically, Vera admitted that going to the Russian Federation was a difficult experience. People in Russia are, in her account, rude, lacking in culture, and unpleasant to deal with. Like Gomberg, Vera described Russia as a land of "boorishness." The paradoxical complexities of this situation are plain: Latvian Russians like Vera are drawn to the Russian Federation in order to experience their authentic cultural heritage; yet at the same time, when they are in Russia, they find themselves surrounded by a lack of culture. Or we can refer back to our master term's oxymoronic potential: Russians in Latvia, because they are abroad, are somehow nearer to the heart of Russian culture than Russians located in the national culture's geographical heart. Russians in Riga experience their home country (Latvia) as a foreign land yet their cultural homeland (Russia) as alien to culture.

Vera's experience exemplifies the "in-between" nature of postcolonial situations, described by Homi Bhabha and other theorists, in which determining the proper cultural identity or location seems nearly impossible. Yet we should note where Vera's experience of cultural dislocation differs from "classic" postcolonial conditions. Bhabha's thought, and much of the work he inspired, is oriented toward cultural hybridity. Similarly, in Partha Chatterjee's influential analysis, anti-colonial articulations of collectivity are characterized by their incorporation of the marginal and the subaltern as definitive of identity. In postcolonial theoretical work, in general, the emphasis has most commonly been on the "fragments" rather than the "whole" of the nation, in its classic constructions in European political theory and philosophy as centered, homogenous, territorially defined and historically continuous. Vera's experience is shaped by her inevitable confrontation with the liminal and fragmentary nature of her position in Latvia, yet for her, and for many others like her, what is at issue is the assembly of this fragmented existence somehow back into the whole of Russian culture. To speak of the "whole of Russian culture" is, of course, a methodological faux pas—as anthropologists have insisted for decades, the cultural should be seen as a fluid, porous, and multifarious set of practices rather than as a terrain of bounded, integral entities (Sewell 1999). Certainly, cultures in actuality are neither bounded nor internally homogeneous or coherent, and this is as much the case in Riga or Moscow as it is anywhere else. Yet for actors across the national and nationalizing spaces of Eastern Europe, the default imaginary of culture inhabits the form of the cultural whole—and this imaginary is possessed of considerable power. In Riga, the Russian Federation looms as a presence that cannot be ignored, extending the gift of belonging to ostensible extraterritorial members. Cultural entrepreneurs like Vera may leverage this potency in their quest to fashion themselves, their students, and their communities as integral to the whole of Russian culture, claiming its power in a struggle for recognition within Latvian society. Yet in so doing, they also subject themselves to institutions, categories, and behaviors originating from elsewhere, such as the terms of the law on compatriots, state institutions that support and define school travel to the Russian Federation, and exposure to Russia's alienating boorishness. They also confront the impossibility of finding a proper place for the Russian whole in a space that, no matter how near it is to Russia, will always remain abroad. This, then, is the reality of dual domination faced by the majority of Russians in Latvia. The situation's stubborn complexity was brought home to me at the end of one of my conversations with Vera, when I belatedly learned that her last name is, in fact, Ozoliņa, which is about the most Latvian name one can have—she is herself of mixed heritage and has as much claim to Latvian belonging as she does to Russian belonging.

Example Two: The Orbita Group and the Folds of Baltic Geography

Yet not all Russians in Latvia aspire to impossible unity with the "mother ship" of Russian culture as a whole. In 2012, if you visited the exhibition spaces of the Cēsis Art Festival, you may have encountered what at first glance appeared to be an exhibit on the history of transistor radios, including some hundred radios attached at various heights to a long, white wall (see figure 4.1). Having walked up to and along the wall, however, you would have found that the radios were turned on, at low volume, each catching a different signal. The radios broadcast a range of offerings: local radio station feed in either Latvian or Russian, poetry recitations in the two languages, and pulses of atonal music. In fact, this was an interactive installation by the Orbita poetry and multimedia collective, which has expressed its fondness for the radio in a variety of projects over the past decade. I will return to this technological passion below, but first, consider the group's practices in general. Orbita is in nearly every way the inverse of Vera's

Figure 4.1. "Radio Wall," The Orbita Group, Cēsis Art Festival, Latvia, 2012.

configuration of culture and identity. The group was founded in 1999 by five poets and artists from Riga, including Punte, with whose poem I began this chapter, and also Semyon Khanin, Vladimir Svetlov, Sergej Timofejev, and Zhorzh Uallik (who in recent years participates only infrequently). Orbita is extraordinarily active, with poetic performances in Latvia; appearances at festivals in Europe, the Russian Federation, and the United States; and multimedia installations such as the Radio Wall, which have been featured in many exhibitions, from Baltic venues including the Cēsis festival to the 2015 Venice Biennale. From the start, Orbita has also been a publisher of prize-winning, beautifully designed books and almanacs offering not only the works of its own members but a range of prose, poetry, and photography from Latvia and Russia.

As the Radio Wall's inventiveness suggests, the members of Orbita view Russian culture in Riga not as a dusty relic enshrined in canonical cultural traditions but as an ongoing process of innovation. Although the group's poets each possess a unique style, they are united by an overall orientation toward free verse—which still strikes ears tuned to the poetic mainstream in Russia as a deviation from the norm of rhymed and metered poetry. Their performances and installations carry their dedication to novel forms over into experiments with multimedia extensions of literature, sculptural materializations, ambient noise, video poetry, and collaborations with musicians and composers in jam sessions or in the production of song lyrics and even operas. The most important feature of Orbita practices, driving a great deal of their experimental activity, is undoubtedly multilingualism. In their publications, presentations, and installations in Latvia, their poetry always appears in Latvian as well as in Russian, projected on screens, offered in parallel, printed in complex interpretations of how a multilingual book can be organized; the group's extensive penumbra of collaborators includes many Latvian-language poets and musicians; their audiences present a cosmopolitan mix of ethnicities; their publishing undertakings include many translation projects from Russian into Latvian and vice versa. We may also note that free verse is a common practice in Latvian poetry, and though this should not be seen as a singular cause for the group's practices, it certainly signals their grounding in local poetic traditions. In sum, Orbita presents one of a very few sites of cultural production to truly bridge between Russian and Latvian languages and audiences, which, as noted above, more typically feel like parallel yet separate universes.

Perhaps we should conclude, therefore, that their activity is intensely localized in Riga—that Orbita has lifted off from the "mainland" traditions of Russia in order to dedicate itself to life in a new location. In contrast to Vera's desire to assert ties to the Russian cultural whole, isn't Orbita something of a rejection of that whole—an assertion of either the dignity of the fragment or the unity of the new entity "Russophone Latvian Culture"? So, by this calculus, Vera represents the near, and Orbita the abroad? Yes and no. Certainly, the Orbita poets' cosmopolitan stance appears alien to dominant trends in Russia—in a more and more pronounced way over the past few years of increasingly isolationist Russian cultural policy and public discourse. Yet they are, in their own manner, also closely affiliated with "mainland" Russian cultural life. Although Timofejev has been the recipient of the "Russian Prize"—a literary honor that aims to foster the Russian world's unity—the Orbita poets are more closely linked to nonstate institutions at some remove from Russian patriotic politics. This includes leading Russian avant-garde and experimental journals such as *Vavilon*, *Vozdukh*, and *TextOnly*, as well as the New Literary Observer publishing house's prestigious contemporary poetry series, which brought out a monolingual volume of Timofejev's poetry. Timofejev has been shortlisted for the highly prestigious Andrei Bely Prize, while Punte's video poetry—in particular his video based on the poem above—was honored at the 2013 Moscow festival Fifth Leg (*Piataia noga*). Finally, the Orbita group is linked by a web of professional relationships with the leading edge of Russian poetic culture.

How should this concatenation of distance and proximity in the near abroad be explained? A return to the topic of radios may shed additional light on this question. Since about 2010, Orbita has been working in a performance format that they refer to as the FM Slow Show—the Radio Wall was a spin-off (see figure 4.2). The venue where you encounter the FM Slow Show might be a theater auditorium, night club, or summer festival. The stage is set with a long table bearing thirty or forty transistor radios of various makes, eras, colors, and sizes, as well as a keyboard synthesizer and a standing microphone. At the back of the stage the Orbita logo is projected on a screen. The four poets, accompanied by the keyboardist, take the stage and unhurriedly turn on the radios one by one, adjusting the devices, which release a tissue of sound composed of white noise, snatches of music, weather and news reports in Latvian or Russian. The musician begins to play slow chords. Then a poet approaches the microphone. The ambient noise grows subtly less audible and the music changes character as the poet reads, slowly and deliberately, a poetic text in Russian, as translations into Latvian and perhaps also English take the place of the logo on the screen, a few lines at a time. Following the recitation, the poet returns to the table. The music shifts again. Another poet approaches the mike to deliver a different poem. The set might last twenty or thirty minutes and include eight or twelve poems. At its conclusion, the poets turn off the radios, to the applause of the audience (rather restrained—in Latvia crowds seldom get riled up).

Figure 4.2. The Orbita Group performing the FM Slow Show, CYCLOP Video Poetry Festival, Kyiv, Ukraine, 2012.

I have seen this show performed multiple times in Latvia and the United States. At times, the musical accompaniment has been prerecorded, and the number of radios has varied. Always, the performance's most overt feature is its interweaving of distinct sound layers. The understated musical accompaniment provides an atmospheric armature, as does a shared amplification system, which brings all acoustical material into equivalence and renders radio signal and poetic utterance comparable parts of a single whole in a mediatic metaphor. This metaphor works via the juxtaposition of diverse languages but also diverse geographic scales—local utterances, in whatever languages show up on the radio dial in the vicinity, are thrown into juxtaposition with poetry in Russian. Note the curious inversion of the typical scalar qualities of radio as a medium: the broadcast signal, which more typically carries communication across great distances, instead carries local messages representative of a specific time and place. The spoken lyric word, in contrast, produced in the here and now, resounds as though it were being translated across space and linguistic barriers on the FM radio waves. When I heard this show in New York, this reversal of scales was at its most extreme—the poets were speaking words that had been transported across an ocean, while the radio signals were, for me, intimately local and recognizable (an NPR news report sounded out at one point). When the Slow Show is performed in Riga, though, we might say that this metaphor communicates an apt representation of the displaced or misplaced voice of Russian culture itself. FM Radio, especially delivered through "vintage" transistor radios, is evocative of other times. This retro quality may remind us that radio has a significant history in the border zone between Europe and Russia, where it once delivered the BBC, Radio Free Europe, and VOA to Soviet citizens who were attuned to what many called "the voices." But FM radio is far from obsolesced in Riga, where, among other things, it now delivers Russian media, often via syndicated broadcasts from Russia that increasingly come across as voices from far away, much as VOA did in the USSR.

The distortion of scale in this mediatic metaphor resonates with a poem by Punte that I have heard performed in this format:

> When all night the wind fondles tin
> while the radio crackles until it pops
> then locks a wavelength, never leaving home
> & you think, look how we've dropped into a fold
> the fabric so crumpled, we've settled in
> set up wobbly chairs, created a sort of order
> as every Saturday: out on the town.
> And what if it's decided to take an iron to it? shake what's loose
> cut the lines . . . mend a lining.
>
> (Timofejev et al. 2015, 112–13)

Like the FM Slow Show itself, the poem meditates on the transience of a microclimate created by crossing transmissions, a "home" shaped by the intersection of radio signals, wind, and landscape. Punte gives us an image of a specific "wavelength," locked onto at random, which shapes itself into a "fold" (I imagine the hollow of a standing wave) and gains material existence. This is a fold that one can drop into and inhabit, at least for a while. Yet it is also a precarious position, with only "wobbly chairs" and "a sort of order": others might "iron out" the fold, "shake" the loose elements out of place, "cut the lines," "mend the lining," and perhaps eliminate this folded reality. In Gilles Deleuze's extended essay on Leibniz, *The Fold*, the figure serves as a master metaphor for the paradoxical relations of soul to material world—the soul is in the world but not of it, and the fold, in an Asian fan or in the folds of a book, presents this odd relationship to space: "the infinite fold separates or moves between matter and soul, the façade and the closed room, the outside and the inside. . . . Conciliation of the two will never be direct, but necessarily harmonic, inspiring a new harmony" (1993, 35). In Punte's poem, the metaphor operates in similar fashion. Especially in the context of the Slow Show, it evokes the space of Orbita cultural activity in Latvia, situated in the fold between Russian and Latvian cultural and mediatic circuits and signals, between local and distant, between near and abroad, in which distance from the origin of Russian culture renders cultural production closest to home in Riga.

Let me be more precise in interpretation of this metaphor. Orbita's success in the multicultural Latvian scene derives from the poets' stance of distance from the patriotic politics of the autarchic Russian cultural whole—and their distance, therefore, from the mainstream of Russian cultural life in Latvia, as represented by Vera, for instance. With regard to their success on Russia's experimental literary scene, one might recall Pascale Casanova's demonstrations of the hegemonic power of nationally organized literary centers, themselves interrelated in a system of unequal transnational competition (Casanova 2004). The Orbita poets remain Russian poets, and their work gains recognition via the Russian literary system's dominant mechanisms of prestige. Yet the motivation for recognition in Moscow, in this case, stands in tension with the centripetal logic of Casanova's analysis: Punte and his colleagues have value at the geographical centers of Russian cultural life in large part *because* of the innovative practices driven by their peripheral location. Their books, inventive and beautiful permutations of the typographical possibilities for combining two languages in one printed object; their performances, elegant meditations on distance and nearness; and their poetry, derived from Latvian and Russian traditions and collaborations—these balancing acts in the cultural intertidal zones drive the avant-garde practice that makes them significant in Russian literary life, acting out the cosmopolitan interconnectedness to which institutions like Moscow's New Literary Observer publishing house aspire. In sum, for these poets, the cultural geography of Russian-language literature of the near abroad reflects in inverted form that of the metropolitan centers of Russian literary life (which itself more and more seems to be an island of "internal emigration"—the abroad near, in other words), in which a cosmopolitan avant-garde balances against a politically legitimated, territorially centered mainstream. In Latvia's Russian literary life, insofar as it coincides with the institutional centers of Latvian society per se, innovative translinguistic poetry occupies center stage because it stands at a distance from canonical Russian cultural traditions, as well as from the cultural politics of those in Latvia, like Vera, who mourn the absence of those traditions. The Orbita poets—situated on "other side" of the literary landscape of the Russian Federation—occupy the fold between Russian and Latvian culture. For them, the slippages in the construction of Russian culture in Latvia, closer to the norm than the norm itself, articulating distinction in terms of sameness, offer an increase in maneuverability that makes possible their unique cultural self-construction.

Example Three: New Arrivals in Riga

The nearness of Orbita's abroad to scenes of experimental culture in Russia proper reflects how cultural space within the Russian Federation is also variegated—as any cultural scene, this is a complex, agonistic, and fragmented system. Yet just as the category of near abroad is unstable, so is its relationship to Russia. As the Russian Federation has shifted from pursuing international influence through soft power to projections of hard power, its internal spaces for cultural and political space have shrunk, pushing opposition-minded Russians out of internal emigration and into an external one in a new wave of political transplants to places like Riga. This wave of transplants constitutes my third and last example. Dmitry Kuzmin, for instance, the founder and editor of the leading avant-garde Russian poetry journal *Vozdukh*, which has published works by Orbita, relocated to Riga in 2015 in order to find a safe haven for his publishing work, which strongly promotes oppositional and minority voices, and for his nonheteronormative family. In a similar trajectory, following the firing of Galina Timchenko from the popular internet news portal Lenta.ru, she and many of her staff relocated from Moscow to Riga and established a new news portal, Meduza.io, with anonymous private backing. Meduza.io is intended to counteract the dominance of Russian state media, not only in Latvia but also in the Russian-speaking world, by offering an objective account of events that escapes the Kremlin's domination of Russian informational space.

When I met with Timchenko in the summer of 2015, she told me that her goal is to provide journalism for "the entire so-called 'Russian world,' which is to say not the 'Russian World' in Putin's sense but rather the normal Russian people who live everywhere in the world and read in Russian." In this competition of media spaces, however, the imbrication of "near" and "abroad" makes itself felt in new ways. When asked whether her portal made an effort to reflect the interests and experiences of Russians across the globe (in Ukraine, London, or Riga, for instance), Timchenko was quick to explain that she "lived according to a business plan" and that the majority of her readers were located in Moscow: "It is not my goal, whether I'm located in Latvia or in Bulgaria, to look at the world from the perspective of a person in Bulgaria." Asked why she located her project in Riga, Timchenko explained that "it's a short train ride away from Moscow and they speak Russian here." This is to say, the Meduza.io project, for all of its oppositional character, represents the rather narrow global vision of Moscow elites in a peculiar mirror of the "imperial" attitudes that inform patriotic conceptions of Russian cultural geography rather than any alternative conception of Russian space as decentered or multi-centered. When I began a sentence "This 'Russian world' is organized around . . ." Timchenko completed the sentence in no uncertain terms with the answer "Russia." Here, we see once again the internal incoherence of the near abroad, engendering an exiled opposition that is uninterested in or incapable of integrating an alternative social or political space in order to provide local Russians like Vera with a new cultural identity or whole and instead remains oriented toward the potent yet distant center that represents the whole of Russian culture "as seen from Moscow."

Distinct Borders

Taken together, the three cases of cultural construction examined above demonstrate something of the specificity of the cultural geography of the near abroad. It is perhaps always true that conditions such as hybridity, liminality, and fragmentary identity depend on the presumed ontological or at least actual definitional priority of the whole. Yet in the case of the Baltic near abroad, as a result of histories of occupation, powerful cross-border projections of media, and sheer scale and size, the question of the status of "Russian culture" as displaced, stretched, or folded into the local scene looms in unavoidable fashion. We might also, in conclusion, speculate that the dynamics of Russian cultural life in the Baltic reveal something essential about the cultural system of the metropole. Russian culture, since Peter I's imposition of Western European institutions at the start of the eighteenth century, has oscillated between a conception of cultural life as an extraterritorial phenomenon "brought from Europe," on the one hand, and a competing conception of the emplacement of national culture in its proper territory, on the other. It might be proposed that, just as Richard Wortman observed how "the animating myths" of Russian "scenarios of power" "associated the ruler and the elite with foreign images of political power," authoritative high culture, too, has preserved the foreign odor of imported institutions and made itself felt variously in various epochs of Russian cultural history (1995–2000, i:5). It is in part this extraterritoriality of Russian culture per se that explains the ease with which Russians in Latvia conclude that Russian culture is more at home in European Riga than it is in Moscow. For similar reasons, culture and opposition within the Russian Federation can take the form of pockets or islands of the abroad, the European, the cosmopolitan, or the global—such as the New Literary Observer or Kuzmin's journal *Vozdukh*, while he was still located in Moscow. Yet just as the late-premodern myth of the ruler as foreign conqueror came, in the era of nationalism, to contend with the countermyth of the national tsar and his relation with the land and people, geographical constructions of Russian culture as European or global have contended with countervailing articulations of cultural rootedness in authentically Russian geography. We might say, therefore, that culture across the Russian Federation is in some sense always both near and abroad—which could allow us to conclude on a higher level of abstraction that in the end, Riga, precisely because of the displaced status of Russian culture there, is one of the most Russian places on earth.

Yet the distinctions between the cases examined above also point to the heterogeneity of near abroad as an uneven overlap of regimes of belonging that create a plethora of divergent opportunities and challenges. Finally, these distinct cases point as well to the historical fragility of the near abroad. Recent geopolitical events have hardened the previously porous and flexible borders between Russian and Latvian cultural zones and between political and cultural regimes in both Latvia and Russia. In the phasic history of Russian cultural geography within the Russian Federation, we are fast departing an era in which the extraterritorial and cosmopolitan features of Russian culture as world culture were celebrated, or at least tolerated, and entering one in which institutional and political life allows only rootedness and boundedness. In the process, the variegated possibilities for Russians in Latvia to participate in a Russian world, conceived as an inclusive framework, are being narrowed down into sharply defined and exclusive choices of loyalty and allegiance to Latvia or Russia (see Gorham, this volume). The members of the Orbita collective tell me that they have been traveling less and less to Russia since the 2014 annexation of Crimea—both because "they have not been inviting us much" and out of an apparent loss of interest among the poets themselves. It seems that, for them at least, the abroad is getting less near, or threatening to detach from Nearness entirely, in which case the near abroad may decompose into its component parts—into more recognizable categories of migration and displacement: emigration or exile for those who chose abroad, and diaspora for those who cling to nearness.

Notes

1. The discussion of official identity and citizenship categories in Latvia and the Russian Federation in the subsequent several pages is a much revised version of my previously published work (Platt 2013a).

2. In this chapter, I refer to any resident of Latvia who speaks Russian with no recognizably foreign accent as a "Russian." This is an intentionally "skewed" use of this term that might well provoke objections by many of the individuals so described. My

use is intended to provoke cognizance of the social fissures concealed beneath standard usages—the same sort of cognizance generated by attempts to imagine who might correctly be defined as a "compatriot abroad" in this territory.

3. My application of postcolonial analytical terms to these populations runs against the grain of their more familiar deployments in post-Soviet and post-Socialist space. Most such studies would identify the "postcolonial" subjects of Latvia as the ethnic Latvians, not the Russians. However, the postcolonial is best conceived not as an exclusive condition but as a set of relations inscribed into the present by a history of empire and domination. It makes little sense to think "these are postcolonial subjects" or "this is a postcolonial territory," in distinction to some other subjects or territory.

4. See Wanner, this volume, for discussion of Michael Idov's fictional exploration of similarities between the cultural positions of Chinese-Americans and (Jewish) former Soviet-Americans.

5. For fuller presentation and analysis of the ethnographic data presented in this and the following paragraph, see Platt 2013b, 2013c.

History, Diaspora, and Geography

The Case of Russian-Israeli Cinema, 1991–2016

Alex Moshkin

The Dual Diasporic Condition

When hundreds of thousands of Russian Jews landed in Ben Gurion Airport in Tel Aviv in the early 1990s—completely disoriented by the new climate, language, culture, smells, and even unfamiliar body language—they confronted the meaning of diaspora in a unique manner. Had they just returned home from the Jewish diaspora? Or had they just entered into a Russian one? If a member of this huge population influx was finally at home in her historic land, was she allowed to also yearn for the place she came from? If she was a writer or a poet, was she to write in her "foreign" native tongue or the "holy" Hebrew that would forever feel awkward in her mouth? Was she allowed to feel nostalgia for her previous diasporic condition? Was she at home, or had she just become doubly alienated?

In the course of the last forty years, Israel has transformed from a predominantly Hebrew-speaking society (with a significant Arabic-speaking minority) to a multiethnic and multilingual one, in which Russian is spoken by 20 percent of the population. During the 1970s and the early 1980s, a critical mass of

150,000 Soviet-Jewish dissidents and refuseniks relocated to Israel, followed by another wave of one million Russian-speaking Jews (and their non-Jewish relatives) that started arriving after the fall of the Berlin Wall in 1989. Today, Israel is not only the world's largest hub of Russophone Jewry (1.2 million)—surpassing the United States (450,000), the Russian Federation (400,000), Germany (250,000), and Canada (200,000)—but in certain areas, such as the cities of Ashdod and Be'er Sheva, or the West Bank settlement of Ariel, Russian is the dominant language (Maltz 2015). In consequence, Israel has fortified itself as a major hub of transnational Russophone Jewish culture and a leading participant in an intercontinental conversation about the Soviet past, the post-Soviet present, and the relevance of Soviet historical experience for Jews everywhere.

It is unsurprising that the massive wave of Russian-speaking immigrants has transformed Israel's social, cultural, and political landscapes, as a recent book by political analysts Lili Galili and Roman Bronfman—*The Million that Changed the Middle East*—attests (2013). In contrast to virtually all preceding waves of Jewish migration to Israel, émigrés from the (former) Soviet Union were the first group to openly refuse integration into the Israeli collective at any cost, instead insisting on integration on their own terms (Smooha 2008). To borrow Nelly Gutina's wry words, "As one enters into the national home, it is customary to leave one's baggage by the door or, better yet, in the trash heap. Rejection of one's previous language, culture, and identification has been prerequisite for joining the Israeli mainstream. . . . When we arrived in Israel the country was already built yet, in our opinion, it was in desperate need of reconstruction [*perestroika*]" (2011).[1] Ultimately, the Russian-speaking newcomers were the first immigrant group to challenge the tenets of Zionist ideology relating to Hebrew's linguistic supremacy, the *halachic* definition of Jewish identification, and what they perceived as the country's overwhelmingly religious character. Motivated by disappointment with Israel, Russian-speaking émigrés went on to establish an alternative cultural and social infrastructure in the Soviet image, consisting of Russian-language bookstores, publishing houses, newspapers, theaters, ethnic restaurants, external educational programs, nonkosher supermarkets, television channels, and even a Union of Russophone Writers of Israel.

One may divide scholarship on Soviet-Jewish émigrés to Israel into three camps. The first comprises distinguished North American and Israeli scholars such as Zvi Gitelman and Yaacov Ro'i, whose wide-ranging scholarship on Jewish identity offers a pessimistic view of the possibility of Jewish life outside of Israel. In Gitelman's view, for instance, the identity of Jews in the diaspora is "eroding because its content is diminishing and its boundaries are blurring" (1998, 112). Elsewhere, he argues that for contingent historical reasons, post-Soviet Jewish identity became especially disaggregated because "for most Russian and Ukrainian Jews sentiment and biology have largely replaced faith, Jewish law and lore, and Jewish customs as the foundation of the Jewish edifice" (2001, 269). In his normative approach to Jewish identity, Gitelman privileges religious observance, language, and geography as markers of true Jewishness and ultimately scolds Soviet prodigal sons and daughters for losing their grandparents' authentic Jewish culture, implicitly advocating for a recovery of Jewishness in Israel. To borrow Margarita Levantovskaya's apt comment, "Gitelman . . . probably intends to be descriptive when he concludes that [Soviet] Jewish identity became thin and without content. However, his terminology is laden with value judgment, reinforcing the Soviet, Western and Israeli history of judging Russian Jews as being either 'too Jewish' or 'not Jewish enough'" (2013, 14).

A second cohort includes Russian-Israeli sociologists and cultural theorists such as Larissa Remennick, Julia Lerner, and Nelly Elias, who grew up in the Soviet Union but were educated and live and work in Israel. These scholars utilize their firsthand experience in academic investigation of Russian-speaking Jews, positioning their object of study within larger conceptual and comparative frames of reference. Larissa Remennick's *Russian Jews on Three Continents* (2007), for instance, focuses on the distinct encounters of Russian Jews with the host countries of Israel, Germany, America, and Canada at the twentieth century's close. In contrast to the normative vision of a Jewish world with Israel as its undisputed center, Remennick proposes a dynamic model of interrelation with multiple centers and various cultural, social, economic, and political exchanges.

Finally, a new generation of Russian-Israeli and American scholars such as Olga Gershenson, David Shneer, Sasha Senderovich, and Dimitry Shumsky urges us to eschew a focus on identity in favor of a more nuanced understanding of how various Russian-Jewish cultural and social experiences may be integrated into a broader analysis of global political life, nationalist projects, and transnational belonging. Gershenson and Shneer's manifesto "Soviet Jewishness and Cultural Studies" (2011) advocates for a cultural approach to the study of Soviet and post-Soviet Jewry that departs from the more "traditional lenses of vanishing diasporas, Soviet anti-Semitism, and the disappearance of Yiddish and Hebrew cultures" and instead conceives of Jewishness as a variable performative and representational category that circulates globally.

Using these theoretical investigations as a point of departure, this chapter focuses on how Russian-speaking Jews in Israel activate certain cultural sites and ideological constructs of memory to adjust to their new geographic reality, in the process claiming a position within cultural and social fields and making sense of ongoing geopolitical transformations in the Middle East and within Israel. While the topics of late- and post-Soviet history, memory, and nostalgia have been meticulously explored in both Russian and Western scholarship (Oushakine 2007; Nadkarni and Shevchenko 2014; Platt 2016), much less has been written on the role and function of Soviet-Jewish history in Russian-Israeli cultural production.[2] In what follows, I investigate the development of Russian-Israeli cinematic explorations of the Soviet past's dark byways in relation to other, conflicting historical narratives derived from Zionist, Western, and Soviet frames of reference. Ultimately, my investigation illuminates the complexities of the Russian-Israeli dual identity that have seemingly fated this population to remain forever in one diaspora or another.

I pay particular attention to important consequences deriving from film's institutional specificity. In the Soviet Union, cinema—"the most important of all the arts," according to Lenin—bore a heavy ideological burden, and in Israel, cinema has been recruited for various cultural and social projects. In both contexts, the capital-intensive cinematic process has relied on substantial state support. Clearly, the involvement of the state in the film industry has raised the stakes for the institutional integration of film directors and has magnified the visibility and effect of national and transnational networks and institutions on the development of Russian-Israeli cinema. My analysis disentangles the complex relationship between cinematic genres, financing, and ideological content as these factors relate to Russian-Israeli cinema over the last twenty-five years.

The Returns of Soviet-Jewish History

A heavily ideologically freighted conception of Jewish diaspora played a fundamental role in the films of the first wave of Russian-Israeli filmmakers, which included Leonid Kelbert, Semyon Vinokur, and Mikhail Kalik. The idea of Jewish return to Palestine is not new—it has deep roots in the Jewish religious tradition in which exile (*galut*) and diaspora (*tfutza*) were chiefly understood as punishment for communal sins that would only be redressed by the ingathering of the chosen people in the divinely ordained Land of Israel. In the last two centuries, the Zionist movement appropriated the religious narrative of diaspora in order to codify political and ethno-nationalist aspirations that developed in response to European Judeophobia and the spread of nationalisms across Europe (Engel 2009, 20–27). As a result, Jewish immigration to Eretz Israel, seen through the prisms of "homecoming" and "ingathering of exiles," became the Zionist movement's core doctrine.

After the establishment of the State of Israel in 1948, the concept of Jewish diaspora, based on the foundational status of the idea of Jewish expulsion and desire to return to Israel, underwent another transformation. In the aftermath of the Holocaust, Israel came to see itself as the only permanent and legitimate spiritual and political center of world Jewry while all other territories were cast as foreign, inhospitable, and temporary. This ideologically laden division of Jewish space into Israel and diaspora made it possible for the State of Israel to align itself with the Jewish population worldwide, accessing their political, social, and economic capital, and excluding non-Jewish populations in these lands—especially the Palestinians—from the national master narrative.

Finally, the narrative of Jewish diaspora was again reformulated during the Cold War, as Soviet Jews struggled to emigrate from the USSR. According to Caryn Aviv and David Shneer, this new vision of diaspora resulted from the interactions of Israel, the United States, and Soviet Jews: "American politicians adopted the cause of Jewish emigration as a new tool in their anti-Soviet campaign," while the State of Israel emphasized anti-Semitism in the USSR "to remind the world why Israel, which saw itself as the place of refuge for world Jewry, was necessary in the first place" (2005, 32; see also Yonah 2007). As Maria Rubins explains in this volume, in the emergent construct, the biblical narrative of Ancient Israelites in Egypt was re-appropriated for the condition of Jews in the Soviet Union: the USSR became a historical efflorescence of the metaphysical Egypt, with Brezhnev as its Pharaoh and the emigration of the 1970s cast as an exodus to a spiritual homeland. Promulgated in dozens of books with titles like *Let My People Go* (Cohen 1971), *To Choose Freedom* (Bukovskii 1987), and *Between a Hammer and a Scythe* (Eliav 1965), this narrative was tremendously important for consolidating and mobilizing nationalist and Zionist identification among Soviet Jews and inspiring 150,000 emigrants in the 1970s and 1980s to pack bags and embark for what they perceived as their historical homeland in Israel.

The majority of the first wave of Russian-Israeli filmmakers who arrived in Israel in the 1970s and 1980s did so out of Zionist conviction and not for lack of other options.[3] After immigration, they made films on Jewish topics that they had been unable to treat in the Soviet Union for reasons of censorship. Leonid Kelbert's *Letters from Leningrad* (*Pis'ma iz Leningrada*, 1989), for instance, focuses on the intricacies of the Soviet-Jewish underground movements in Leningrad in 1970s–80s—clashes with the KGB and heroic battles for the right to participate in and learn about Jewish culture. Similarly, Herz Frank's *Jewish Street* (*Evreiskaia ulitsa*, 1992) looks back on the Holocaust in Latvia, complicated relations between Jews and non-Jews during World War II, and the Jewish religious tradition.

Feature and documentary films shot from the 1980s to mid-1990s by this diverse group of filmmakers are united by their use of Soviet-Jewish history and personal and collective memory as master idioms with which to communicate with local and international audiences. Kalik's *And The Wind Returns* (*I vozvraschaetsia veter*, 1991; hereafter, *The Wind*) may be taken as a representative example of this first phase of Russian-Israeli cinema. Produced between 1989 and 1991, the film emerged as the Soviet Union was opening up to the world and the question of the rightful place of Russians and Jews in geography was of particular importance. Would Jews remain in Russia or leave? Should Soviet-Jewish activism be aimed at the preservation and consolidation of the community or at facilitation of emigration? With the crumbling of the Iron Curtain, what would be the relationship between former Soviet Jews in Israel and those remaining in Russia? In an attempt to answer these questions, *The Wind* explores the intricacies of Soviet-Jewish experience and adjudicates between various possibilities for Jewish identity.

Formally, Kalik's film is a Jewish variation on Andrei Tarkovsky's masterpiece *Mirror* (*Zerkalo*, 1978): a nonlinear autobiographical work that incorporates an array of found footage and historical reenactments. The film is a truly experimental work that casts off—both in form and content—the ideological orthodoxies of state-sanctioned Soviet cinema and socialist realism. Rather, it is a formally stimulating art film that is intentionally difficult and confusing and that requires serious and prolonged contemplation. Like *Mirror*, the temporality of *The Wind* is slowed down to the extreme (both resemble floating dream sequences) to allow the audience to reflect, in a Brechtian manner, on the social reality beyond the cinematic frame. Despite these similarities, however, in contrast to *Mirror*'s resistance to narrative cohesion and complex representation of history, *The Wind*'s interrogation of the Soviet past is didactic (à la Eisenstein) and structured by what Salo W. Baron calls "the lachrymose conception of Jewish history"—its representation as a chain of catastrophes and disasters. In an attempt to come to terms with the Soviet-Jewish past as a history of personal and collective suffering, *The Wind* depicts the major traumatic events in the history of Soviet Jewry—the purges of the 1930s, the Gulag, the murder of Solomon Mikhoels, the Doctors' Plot, varying forms of popular and state-sponsored anti-Semitism—and concludes with underground activities of Jewish dissidents and refuseniks. With the help of reenactments, Kalik even returns to the Gulag camp where he spent two years of his life, reconstructing its horror from the blueprints of his memory.

Preoccupation with the Soviet past, characteristic for Russian-Israeli films of this moment, reflects the interplay of two parallel historical processes. On the one hand, the film articulates the Soviet intelligentsia's larger project at the height of Gorbachev's policies of glasnost and perestroika of recovering previously inaccessible histories and formulating a new, truer narrative of the Soviet past. Therefore, the fact that *The Wind* was the outcome of an official invitation to Kalik by Moscow's Gorky Film Studios to return to the USSR and undertake a project of his choosing is perfectly comprehensible. Indeed, the historical labor of *The Wind* (and of first-wave Russian-Israeli cinema as a whole) can be attributed to the continuing significance of legally and ethically unsettled histories of collective suffering and of artistic efforts "to mourn the losses and face up to what in traumatic memory is not closed and cannot be closed," in the words of Shoshana Felman (2011, 202). On the other hand, there is the larger historical context of the conception, filming, and production of *The Wind*. In this regard, it is important to emphasize that the film—a collaborative financial project between the United States (Benyaev Construction Company) and the Soviet Union (Cinematography Development Fund of the USSR and Gorky Film Studios)—can be seen as an attempt to build a bridge between Israeli and Russian realities and conceptions of history at a moment when the Iron Curtain was coming down and the ideological struggle between capitalism and communism was coming to a close.

The reduction of the Soviet-Jewish experience to a story of heroic Jewish fighters and victims versus a totalitarian Soviet state is perhaps the main historical drawback of the early phase of Russian-Israeli cinema. Indeed, by weaving his individual biography into the collective narrative of Jewish history, Kalik presents a historical portrait of urban political and cultural elites that itself elides the experiences of the overwhelming majority of Soviet Jews. In other words, in casting Jews in the Soviet Union as archetypal outsiders, political dissenters, and passive victims of the regime, Kalik not only ignores the professional, cultural, and political contributions of the Jewish community to the Soviet project (both commendable and less so, as elaborated by Yury Slezkine [2004]) but also does a poor job of explaining Kalik's own remarkable achievements in Soviet professional life—his admission to the prestigious Soviet State Film School, VGIK, and his success as a leading Soviet cinematic practitioner. Focusing on the negative aspects of Soviet-Jewish life and experience, the film reproduces a Zionist master narrative that imagines Jewish life in Europe as necessarily leading to either Hitler's or Stalin's camps and presents Israel as the only escape route. To demonstrate this progression, the film follows Kalik on a trauma-laden return voyage to the USSR and into Soviet history, with a triumphant, final aerial shot that implies Kalik's departure to Israel. As with other Russian-Israeli films, *The Wind* finds stability in the Israeli discourse of "homecoming."

Nevertheless, one cannot fail to observe that *The Wind* primarily addresses a Russian-speaking audience in the Russian language on the subject of the Soviet past, Soviet cinematic tradition, and the history of Jews in the USSR. In the span of one sequence of four minutes, *The Wind* presents fragments from Mikhail Romm's propaganda film *Lenin in 1918* (*Lenin v 1918 godu*, 1939), archival footage of Moscow's 1945 Victory Parade, the iconic censored scene from Grigory Aleksandrov's *Circus* (*Tsirk*, 1936) depicting Solomon Mikhoels singing a lullaby in Yiddish, and found footage intercut with a reenactment of Mikhoels's funeral following his secret murder in 1948. Without analyzing in detail Kalik's montage as a statement on the constructedness of Soviet history in cinema, it is sufficient to say that the abundance of filmic citations that flow past the viewer at moments like this, unaccompanied by explanation or voice-over, makes the film rather challenging for any viewer, let alone those unacquainted with Soviet history and culture. Indeed, Kalik's investment in Russian language, history, and culture unintentionally challenges Israel's dominant cultural regime, in which the nation-state, language, culture, and religion harmoniously coincide to the exclusion of all others. Despite the film's overt Zionist identification, this experimental film in the Russian language that delves into the Soviet past was hardly comprehensible for the majority of the Israeli public and cultural establishment. So, in a bitter twist of fate, when *The Wind*—a film directed by a proud Israeli citizen of twenty-two years—was finally granted a premiere at the Jerusalem Film Festival in 1993, it was presented as a foreign film (Vinokur 2003). This was a terrible blow for Kalik, who never made another film.

The film's affective structure recapitulates its ambivalences over Russian and Israeli ideologies and cultural idioms. For like other Russian-Israeli film projects of this period, *The Wind*, despite its devotion to the Israeli narrative of homecoming, is suffused with nostalgia—with a relentless sense of loss and double alienation. These motifs are articulated most forcefully in a scene in which Kalik meets his old friends and colleagues at a restaurant in Moscow after eighteen years of separation. This is a loving portrayal of Soviet hospitality and one of the film's most touching scenes. The returning director is dumbstruck by the emotions that overwhelm him. First-person camera work captures a picturesque scene of Russian *zastol'e*: the table is overflowing with traditional Russian dishes, "Sovetskoe" brand champagne is poured into frosty crystal glasses, and one of the guests plays guitar and sings these lines from David Samoilov's poem "One Day" (1981) in classic Russian bardic manner:

> One day, I will visit you,
> One day, one day . . .
> When I feel victory,
> When I find a new path.
>
> One day I will find you
> Confused, as always.
> One day you and I will fade together
> Into the years of my past.
>
> (**Samoilov** 1981)

In this scene, Kalik refuses to choose between Russian culture and the land of Israel and instead presents a simultaneous experience of nostalgia and resentment, belonging and homelessness, loss and triumph. This scene inadvertently captures the dual diasporic condition of the Russian-Israeli population in the early 1990s, haunted by the question, "What is homeland, and what is exile?" as Olga Gershenson puts it (2009).

The bardic song beautifully captures the pathos of Kalik's double alienation. Its addressee is not a woman; it is the Soviet Union. After eighteen years of exile, Kalik returns to the place of his lost childhood and artistic vitality in order to reclaim his history, identity, and self, articulating the pain of separation and the deep connection he still feels with his past. Significantly, the director frames his return in a heroic key. He returns to the Soviet Union on his own terms, "When I feel victory/ When I find a new path." Yet his triumphant composure conceals as much as it reveals. Between the two stanzas performed in the film, the singer omits a central stanza of Samoilov's poem:

> One day I will see you,
> One day, one day . . .
> And I will come to hate my life,
> And in tears, I will drop on your bosom.
>
> (1981)

These words, had they been performed, would have subverted the Zionist ethos of repatriation in their lucid enunciation of Kalik's mourning for the Jewish diaspora and longing for the Soviet past. His act of self-censorship discloses the operations of Zionist ideology and the symbolic violence it inflicts on the filmmaker. What this palimpsest reveals is the tragic impossibility of articulating a coherent Soviet-Jewish-Israeli identity within the orthogonal structures of

Israeli and Soviet ideological and cultural projects prior to the dissolution of the Soviet Union and the end of the Cold War. *The Wind*, released at the end of 1991 as the USSR was collapsing, symbolically marks the end of the first phase of Russian-Israeli cinema.

Israel's Friendship of Peoples

The historical situation of Russian-speaking Jews changed rapidly after the collapse of the Soviet Union. When Russian-speaking Jews emigrated from the USSR during the Soviet period, they knew they were leaving permanently, never to return. They could not retain their apartments or their passports, and they were only allowed to take with them just one small suitcase apiece for their personal belongings. This situation drastically changed after the fall of the Iron Curtain. Seemingly overnight, restrictions on movement, residence, and economic activity all but disappeared, triggering the migration of about 1.6 million former Soviet Jews to Israel, the United States, Germany, and Canada (Remennick 2011, 1). This massive flow of people unleashed a twofold process: on the one hand, post-Soviet communities implanted themselves in the social landscapes of host countries, and on the other, they established a complex transnational network of relations between Israel, Russia, North America, and Europe (Gershenson and Shneer 2011; Remennick 2013). Clearly, even prior to the arrival of one million Russian-speaking émigrés, Israel was a multicultural space in which various social, ethnic, and political elements—Ashkenazi and Sephardic, secular and religious, left- and right-wing, Jewish and Arab—competed for dominance and autonomy and negotiated a fraught coexistence. However, the influx of Russian émigrés in the 1990s demanded Israeli recognition of social, cultural, and political diversity as never before and was instrumental, according to some political and social scientists, in triggering the de facto era of multiculturalism in Israel (Remennick 2007, 68).

The story of Israeli social diversity should be seen within the larger narrative of the rise (and perhaps impending fall) of multiculturalism in the Western world, which falls beyond the purview of this chapter. Suffice it to say that since the 1980s, more and more outsiders have "infiltrated" the Israeli screen—Palestinians, women, immigrants, Orthodox Jews, and sexual minorities—as multiculturalism and diversity have become the master plots not only of Israeli society but of Israeli cinema, too. Russian-Israeli filmmakers were quick to join the new trend. In the 1990s and early 2000s, Russian-Israeli cinema underwent a revitalization, with dozens of films about the Russian-speaking community in Israel appearing in just over ten years. The films of this second wave are frequently mixed projects, bringing together Hebrew- and Russian-speaking directors, actors, and technical crews. These films are bilingual, locally sponsored, and intended for mass consumption by both language communities. While their subject matter truly varies—from *Saint Clara* (*Clara Hakdosha*, 1995), the story of a Russian girl with paranormal powers, and *Love & Dance* (*Sipur Hatzi Russi*, 2006), a coming-of-age drama about a boy in conflict with his hard-boiled Israeli father over his ballroom dancing, to *Schwartz Dynasty* (*Shoshelet Schwartz*, 2005), about the battle of two Russian-speaking women with religious burial authorities—these films all indulge in conventional narratives concerning the hardships of immigration and eventual social integration (Wakamiya, this volume).

This was a new and far more commercially successful phase of Russian-Israeli cinema. In distinction to the sense of loss, nostalgia, and double-alienation evidenced in the earlier era, this later stage is comfortable in Israel's multicultural space and with communication aimed at both Israeli and Russophone audiences across the globe, extending to the Russian Federation. Rather than clinging to the Soviet past and conversing with its cultural traditions, these films engage with the contemporary experience of Russophone communities of Israel and often uncritically reflect romanticized and clichéd conceptions of this reality (Gershenson and Hudson 2008). Analysis of the most popular and high-grossing of these films, Alik Kaplun's *Yana's Friends* (*Hahaverim Shel Yana*, 1999)—which collected almost every single prize at the prestigious Ophir Awards and was chosen to represent Israel at the Academy Awards—demonstrates how the new cohort of Russian-Israeli filmmakers has successfully navigated the Israeli cinematic field using the discourse of multiculturalism. Meditating on those elements of Soviet and Russian history and cultural traditions that can be salvaged (music, art, food, war, and quite chauvinistically, women), while condemning others to the dustbin of history (alcoholism, the Russian language, and Soviet models of masculinity), *Yana's Friends* highlights the strategies of more recent Russian-Israeli cultural production to situate Russian-Israeli communities in history and geography. In contrast to the earlier films that tend to summon (in minute detail) the heroic face of Soviet Jewry, these later films tap into the demand for representation of Israeli multiculturalism and in doing so, achieve considerable commercial and critical success.

Yana's Friends focuses on the efforts of two immigrant families from the Soviet Union to integrate into Israeli society during the tumult of the first Gulf War. Yana and Fima, the first couple, are forced because of an apartment shortage and their general lack of funds to share their living space with a local bohemian, Eli. Thus, they ironically return to the mode of life of the typical

Soviet communal apartment. The second family is multigenerational, composed of Alik and Masha; their infant child; and Masha's paralyzed father, Yitzhak. Due to quotidian challenges and economic hardships, both families lose their moral compass. Alik sets his paralyzed father-in-law, a decorated World War II veteran, out on the street to beg for money, while Fima flees Israel with the stipend he and Yana had received from the State of Israel for their initial period in the country. The fates of the film's large cast of characters—old and new arrivals from the Soviet Union—map onto the historical events of the first Gulf War and the bombing of Tel Aviv in the manner of a classic historical novel in which the narrative resolution of personal challenges and assimilation into the social whole is deferred until the historical resolution is achieved. The film reaches its climax during the Iraqi air raid on South Tel Aviv, during which Yana and Eli consummate their love in a sealed room, wearing nothing but gas masks (see figure 5.1). The film concludes with Tel Aviv's celebration of victory over Saddam Hussein, and Yana and Eli's celebration of their romantic liaison.

Yana's Friends achieved tremendous success both with critics and the general public. Many commentators have interpreted the film as an "authentic" representation of the Russian immigrant experience—an expression of the so-called Russian soul and continuation of the classic Russian cultural tradition. In the Israeli press, the film was compared to Maksim Gorky's *The Lower Depths* (*Na dne*, 1902) and Mikhail Bulgakov's *The Master and Margarita* (*Master i Margarita*, 1940; 1967). One review proclaimed, rather bombastically, that the film was "not an Israeli film in almost any way" ("Israel Beiteinu" 1999). Reception in the Russian Federation was less triumphal. Sergei Kuznetsov, one of Russia's leading film critics, called Kaplun "a type of Israeli Ryazanov," in reference to the famous late-Soviet comedic director Eldar Ryazanov (Kuznetsov 1999); Lidia Maslova from *Kommersant* noted Odesa's unique sense of humor that underscores the film (Maslova 2001); and Otar Iosseliani from *Obshchaia gazeta* stated that *Yana's Friends* was "filmed in the best traditions of our former comedies" (Iosseliani 2002). Curiously, none of the reviewers in Israel or Russia placed *Yana's Friends* within Israeli cinematic culture, history, or artistic traditions. The film's Soviet/Russian resonance was a positive feature for some reviewers and a negative one for others, but none of the reviews looked past it.

All critical responses to the film have considered it an expression of the passing of the most difficult phase of Russian immigration to Israel, as immigrants were finally finding their place and voice in Israeli multicultural society. Such a position fails to recognize that what made *Yana's Friends*—a film funded in its entirety by Israeli agencies, including Israel's Broadcasting Authority and

Figure 5.1. Alik Kaplun's *Yana's Friends* (1999): Yana and Eli become intimate wearing gas masks during the bombing of Tel Aviv.

the Israeli Cinema Fund—such a successful *Israeli* film was its ability to package Russianness in a consumable and easily digestible way by adherence to Israeli expectations of what "other" places and people look like. By showing former Soviet immigrants as alcoholics and criminals who disrupt local harmony in Israel, Kaplun—who himself arrived in Israel in 1980—reproduces the local regime of hostility toward Soviet immigrants that characterized popular and official discourses in Israel during the 1990s (Elias 2008, 19–20). Indeed, Kaplun's stereotypical representation of Russian-speaking émigrés sheds light on the representational strategies of the new wave of Russian-Israeli filmmakers regarding Russian culture, history, and identity. By correctly aligning with Israel's multicultural climate and its limits on social acceptability, *Yana's Friends*—together with other films of the same moment such as *Saint Clara* (1995), *Paper Snow* (*Haya o Lo Haya*, 2003), *Love & Dance* (2006), *Children of the USSR* (*Yaldei SSSR*, 2007), and *Schwartz Dynasty* (2005)—demonstrates how historical and cultural capital could be converted into cinematic success and economic gain, even at the risk of capitalizing on communal suffering and selling an easily digested semblance of "authenticity" to the dominant Israeli audience.

In the world of *Yana's Friends*, while many aspects of the Russian social legacy are to be discarded, some elements of the Russian cultural tradition and historical inheritance can and must be assimilated into the Israeli multicultural framework. Among these, the Soviet experience of World War II plays a particularly important role. Historically, there is a strong homology between Soviet and Israeli societies in the realm of militarism, cultivated patriotism, and commemoration of the World War II as a foundational source of national history and collective suffering (Roberman 2005). In this light, it comes as no surprise that of all Soviet historical master narratives, *Yana's Friends* appropriates precisely the (so-called) Great Patriotic War in order to address contemporary issues relevant to Israeli society. This is particularly evident in the scene where Masha and Alik quarrel about forcing the veteran Yitzhak to beg for money. Alik, excited by the business opportunity, proclaims: "All of this, all of this money—he is entitled to it! This is people's recognition of his achievements in battle and on the labor front [*trudovoi i boevoi podvig*]. After all, he saved the world from people like him," he concludes, pointing at the television set showing Saddam Hussein speaking in Arabic.

Despite the scene's ironic treatment of outdated communist rhetoric and Alik's lack of moral fiber, its engagement with the Soviet and Israeli understandings of World War II is dead serious. In this short sequence, Alik sets up Nazi Germany as the common enemy of both Jews and Soviets and reminds the Israeli audience of Soviet Jewish soldiers' heroic contributions to victory. By drawing an equivalence between Nazi Germany and Hussein's regime, the film lines up a series of just wars—the fight against the Nazis, Israel's past wars against the Arab states, and the present struggle of the U.S.-led coalition against the "Iraqi aggressor." Ultimately, the film ends on a moment of historical uplift: Hussein is defeated, East and West are reconciled, and a historic opportunity for the peace process has appeared. Produced in 1999, less than a year before the onset of the Second Intifada, *Yana's Friends* reflects the historical optimism of the 1990s, which Israeli historian Anita Shapira called "the decade of hope," with respect to the integration of all groups in Israel, including the Palestinians and Russian-speaking émigrés (2012, 422).

Yet not all elements of Russian cultural and historical traditions were as "lucky" as the Soviet victory over National Socialism. For the multicultural framework is not only about salvaging and inclusion—it is also about filtering and rejection. *The Wind*'s nostalgia was a structural effect of its historical context: of an inability to imagine a full coincidence of Russianness and Jewishness prior to the collapse of the USSR. Things are different in *Yana's Friends*. The geography of the film is fixed, and therefore nostalgia—which, Svetlana Boym reminds us, is both a temporal and spatial phenomenon—is utterly excluded from its diegetic structure (Boym 2001, 10). Instead of yearning for the past, Kaplun models Israeli-Russianness and presents a manual for the social integration of Russian-speaking immigrants. Kalik's focus on Soviet history, nostalgia, and memory are well-nigh excluded from Kaplun's work. Ironically, it is precisely the period when Kalik was working on *The Wind* (1990–91) that Kaplun represents in *Yana's Friends*—an apt illustration of the drift over those eight years in memory of the earlier moment, which appears in retrospect as free of nostalgia. Although *Yana's Friends* mobilizes "retro" Soviet cultural aesthetics—a heavy dose of Russian *romansy* and tango in the non-diegetic soundtrack—the film's characters give almost no evidence of nostalgic yearning for their lost Soviet home.[4] Even Yana—alone, forsaken, pregnant, and penniless in a new country—experiences very little longing for what she left behind. After a short deliberation, she stands on her own feet, symbolically aborts the baby of her runaway husband, and embarks on a new relationship with the Israeli Eli. Yana shows the audience that no matter how painful immigration is, one must keep going in order to earn a happy ending.

The emotional silences of *Yana's Friends* are a by-product of the multicultural bargain: in return for political allegiance, ethnic groups gain recognition, resources, and license to express some elements of their cultural traditions: ethnic cuisine, music, arts and crafts. Yet they are expected to keep silent regarding much of the real suffering of immigration. As Slavoj Žižek argues, liberal multiculturalism can only accept otherness "deprived of its substance—like the multitude of 'ethnic cuisines' in a contemporary megapolis; however, any 'real' Other is instantly denounced for its 'fundamentalism,' since . . . the 'real Other' is by definition 'patriarchal,' 'violent,' never the Other of ethereal wisdom and charming customs" (1997, 28). Accordingly, liberal multicultural is interested only in cultural difference that can be easily integrated into the workings of global capitalism—all else is excluded as dangerous and harmful. Similarly, rather than expressing the authentic voice of the community, Russian-Israeli films of the new wave convert cultural and historical experience into profit, while obscuring the suffering that takes place behind the scenes and the violence that the multicultural ethos, like the Zionist one, inflicts on immigrants. In contrast to Kalik, who attempted to engage seriously with Russian traditions and produce a film on a par with Tarkovsky's, Kaplun eagerly embraces the Israeli model of commercial, popular filmmaking that caters to its audience with an uncomplicated narrative of love and melodrama. The happy endings of films like *Yana's Friends* obfuscate all negative facets of Russian-Israeli social reality—aspects that would be foregrounded in a third phase of Russian-Israeli cinema.

Kulturkampf, or the Obverse of Multiculturalism

The beginning of the twenty-first century brought a darker chapter in the history of Israel and the Middle East. The stalling of the peace process during the 1990s was accompanied by an increase in terrorist attacks, violent clashes between Israelis and Palestinians, and finally the Second Intifada's outbreak in 2000. As optimism drained away, to be replaced by bitterness, resentment, and disillusionment on both sides of the barricades, Israel's "decade of hope" yielded to a "decade of war," with incessant military operations, terror, and bloodshed. Entrenched military confrontation has given rise to sharp political polarization within Israel, the near total defeat of the Israeli left, and an unprecedented rise of nationalist and far-right parties and ideologies. This new era of social, political, and military upheaval—along with destabilization of the post–Cold War balance of power and brutal ethnic violence—has given rise to the political skepticism characteristic of a third phase of Russian-Israeli cinema.

Starting in 2004, film directors of Israel's Russian-speaking community decisively turned their backs on multicultural social integration and began to examine how immigrants have resisted assimilation and retained cultural and social autonomy. In contrast to the first two stages, which shoehorned the community's history, culture, and experience into dominant Zionist or multicultural scripts in the hope of becoming legible to all segments of an Israeli and global audience, the third stage has largely abandoned these aspirations. In the context of Putin's and Netanyahu's consolidations of power, the aftermath of the Second Intifada, and the disintegration of the Middle East's geopolitical frame, Russian-Israeli filmmakers have embarked on cultural, political, and identitarian projects of particularism and segregation that stand in stark opposition to earlier themes of assimilation in a Zionist or multicultural key.

Both documentary and feature films by Russian-speaking filmmakers that emerged during this period—including *Battalion Aliyah* (*Batalion Aliyah*, 2004), *Generation of Loneliness* (*Dor Habdidut*, 2006), *Married to a Palestinian* (*Zamuzhem za Palestintsem*, 2008), *The Loners* (*Habodedim*, 2009), *Welcome and . . . Our Condolences* (*Bruchim Habayim ve . . . Mishtatfim Betzaarchem*, 2013), *White Panther* (*Panter Lavan*, 2013), *Beyond the Fear* (*Al Saf Hapahad*, 2015), and *Forever Pure* (*Tehora La'ad*, 2016)—depict the polarization of Israeli identity politics and the consolidation of an autonomous Russian-speaking identification. The documentary *Battalion Aliyah*, for instance, tells of former Red Army soldiers who were not incorporated into the Israeli Defense Force after immigration because of advanced age and who, in defiance of Israel's military authorities, formed the grassroots paramilitary organization *Battalion Aliyah*, active in the occupied territories. *White Panther* presents Russian-speaking émigrés in Tiberias as violent skinheads and neo-Nazis who paint swastikas on synagogues, engage in criminal activity, and provoke brutal fights. Finally, Maya Zinshtein's powerful documentary *Forever Pure* describes what happens when the Russian-Israeli oligarch Arkady Gaydamak, at the time the owner of the notorious Israeli soccer team Beitar Jerusalem, which prides itself on never having admitted an Arab player to its ranks, decides to buy two Muslim players from Chechnya for his team. The film depicts probably the most heinous racist campaign in the history of Israeli sports and the heart-breaking struggle of two young Russophone Muslim players against Beitar's ultranationalist fan base, known as La Familia. Common to all these films—regardless of their political stance—is representation of the Russian-speaking community as opposed to official and mainstream Israeli society. Taken together, they express deep disillusionment with Israel's Zionist or multicultural projects and instead portray Israel as split along religious, political, gender, class, and ethnic lines.

Beyond the Fear (2015), the last film of the legendary Latvian-Israeli documentalist Herz Frank, codirected with Maria Kravchenko, is emblematic of this third wave of Russian-Israeli cinema in its dramatic presentation of Israel's political and social fragmentation. Although it portrays the increasing intensity and autonomy of Russian-speaking identification within Israel, it also rises above the themes of these films to suggest a possible reconciliation of Russian speakers with Israeli society in the context of the larger political shifts of the early twenty-first century. *Beyond the Fear* revisits a key moment of recent history—the assassination of Israel's Prime Minister Yitzhak Rabin—yet focuses attention on the love affair between the ultranationalist religious zealot Yigal Amir, who committed the murder, and the Russian-speaking Orthodox Jew Larisa Trembovler, a self-proclaimed "Decembrist's wife," who left her husband for Amir. The film is the logical conclusion of Frank's illustrious career of treatments of controversial subjects and of the inner worlds of individuals in extreme situations. It may be compared, for instance, with *Last Judgment* (*Vysshii sud*, 1987), Frank's documentary about Valery Dolgov, a young convicted murderer on death row with whom Frank engages in prolonged philosophical conversations.

Beyond the Fear, which Frank worked on for more than ten years of his life, was completed by Maria Kravchenko—another Russian-Israeli filmmaker who works primarily in Russia—subsequent to Frank's death in 2013. The film tells how Trembovler's life is turned inside out by her fateful decision to start communication with Amir, who is serving a lifetime term of solitary imprisonment for his crime. Trembovler falls in love with Amir, divorces her first husband, retains custody of her four daughters, and embarks on a judicial battle with the Israeli authorities to gain permission to marry Amir, hold conjugal visits, and have children by him—all of which she achieved (see figure 5.2). In a departure from mainstream Israeli coverage of this story, which treated it as a freakish scandal and a pathological case of hybristophilia, Herz and Kravchenko represent Amir and Trembovler's love affair as a tragedy, showing Trembovler's life as a humiliated outcast in constant fear of social retaliation. Ultimately, the film attempts to comprehend Trembovler's radical decision to sacrifice her marriage, comfortable life, and academic future at Tel Aviv University, bringing upon herself and her children a fate comparable to that of Hester Prynne.

The film, a testament to the fracturing of Israel's political sphere and the abyss between segments of the Russian-speaking community and mainstream Israeli society, generated heated controversy from the earliest stages of production. Unanimously rejected by all Israeli funding institutions (even those dedicated to support of émigré or contentious projects), it was ultimately financed by Latvian and Pan-European grants and Russia's Ministry of Culture (Kravchenko and Tsirkin 2015). When it was announced that *Beyond the Fear* was to appear at the 2015 Jerusalem Film Festival, a passionate campaign to censor the film gathered force. Former Israeli president Shimon Peres, a friend of Yitzhak Rabin, announced: "Under the banner of the freedom of speech and protecting cultural discourse in Israel, we must not permit . . . a movie about Yigal Amir, the murderer of the prime minister Yitzhak Rabin. This is an image movie, rather than an innocent documentary—this is an enterprise meant to legitimize and whiten a heinous murderer" (Lukash and Azulay 2015). Finally, Israel's notorious right-wing minister of culture Miri Regev delivered an ultimatum to the festival: either remove *Beyond the Fear* from the program or lose state funding.

Why did *Beyond the Fear* provoke such extreme reactions? Certainly, the film decisively departs from mainstream representations of Amir as a homicidal monster and Trembovler as a pathological immigrant. By focusing not on the assassination and its political impact but rather on Trembovler's judicial struggle, and by presenting Amir's solitary confinement as a violation of his human rights, Frank produced a startlingly compassionate vision of the murderer and his bride as victims of the Israeli government. By concentrating on Trembovler's point of view and refusing to offer a bird's-eye account capable of reconciling the contradictory voices in Israeli public life, the film models the shattering of Israeli politics and society. Yet perhaps the film's most damning offense was its accurate reproduction of Trembovler's own discursive frames—Kravchenko and Frank even reuse the title of Trembovler's Hebrew-language autobiography,

Figure 5.2. Herz Frank's *Beyond the Fear* (2015): Trembovler and her children visit Amir in prison.

Saf Ha'pahad (*The Threshold of Fear*), which was self-published and distributed unofficially (in samizdat fashion) via the post office. As Sasha Senderovich has argued on the basis of her public writings, Trembovler mobilizes the discourse of Soviet dissidents to legitimize her own and her husband's cause, presenting him as a political prisoner in the Soviet mold, fighting a brave battle for freedom and equality against an oppressive regime (2011). The film reproduces this frame, telling the story of a courageous nonconformist who sacrifices everything—her husband, her job, and social security—to step beyond the façade of state-sponsored ideology. The very title of the film harks back to Natan Sharansky's classic dissident memoir *Fear No Evil* and reproduces a major trope of dissident texts—namely, the need to "[overcome] fear of the authorities" in order to achieve "inner freedom."[5]

Frank's film illustrates the complex and by no means homogeneous condition of the Russian-speaking community in Israel today. Situating Trembovler and Amir in the familiar structures of dissident narratives, Frank and Kravchenko represent the attraction of many Russian-speaking Israelis to ultranationalist and far-right political parties and ideologies (Philippov and Knafelman 2011). Sharansky himself resigned from the Israeli government in 2005 in protest of

Sharon's plan to withdraw Israeli settlements from the Gaza Strip. One might mention other Russian-Israeli nationalist political figures as well, such as Avigdor Lieberman, who has agitated for the deportation of Israeli Arabs and implementation of compulsory "loyalty oaths" to Israel as a Jewish state for Arab citizens of Israel. Yet the film, and these larger contexts, as well, cannot be taken simply as evidence for the social and political isolation of the Russian-speaking community. On the contrary, nationalist mobilization among Russian-Israelis is also a sign of their integration into a political movement that embraces many other segments of Israeli society.

Furthermore, while the portrayal of Trembovler's case in *Beyond the Fear* surely reflects the Russian-speaking community's alienation from the liberal mainstream, the history of the film's production and reception also demonstrates other dimensions of Russian-Israeli political and institutional assimilation. Although he had worked before on topics of Jewish history and experience, *Beyond the Fear* was Frank's first—and unfortunately last—wholly Israeli film in terms of content—focused on Israeli people, topics, and political contexts. The success of his undertaking may be judged by the extent that the film touched a nerve among the Israeli public. Even the Minister of Culture's ultimatum to the Jerusalem Film Festival, in the long run, evidenced the institutionalization, rather than alienation, of Russian-speaking filmmakers. For ultimately, it was met by a united front of Israeli and international filmmakers in protest of Regev's infringement of freedom of expression. Regev was the victor in this confrontation: *Beyond the Fear* was relegated to a single screening in a run-down, private theater a day before the festival's opening, beyond the pale of the official program (an ironic echo of the Festival's decision twenty-two years earlier to screen Kalik's *The Wind* as a foreign film). Nevertheless, the film initiated an important and timely debate on state funding, the limits of cultural expression, and the relationship between art and ideology, galvanizing Israeli artists and public intellectuals in opposition to Regev's campaign "to cut government funding for Israeli artists and institutions that aren't loyal to the state" (Steinberg 2016).

To conclude, the three films I have focused on in this chapter—Mikhail Kalik's *And the Wind Returns* (1991), Arik Kaplun's *Yana's Friends* (1999), and Herz Frank's *Beyond the Fear* (2015)—encapsulate three distinct moments in Russian-Israeli history and cinema. Kalik's *And the Wind Returns*—one of the last Soviet films to be made, just before the dissolution of the USSR in 1991—focuses on the attempt by Russian speakers in Israel to embrace the Zionist project of identity-building yet betrays Kalik's sense of loss of other kinds of identities: those of the Soviet intelligent, esteemed filmmaker, and courageous Jewish dissident struggling against the evil Soviet regime. Despite its ideological allegiances, the film—a Soviet-American coproduction—reflects the reality that many Russian-Israeli filmmakers had limited access to Israeli funding institutions because of the general lack of interest in such films by the Israeli audience. Kaplun's *Yana's Friends*—made eight years after Kalik's film and financed in full by Israeli cultural institutions—revisits this same historical moment of 1990–91, yet from a multicultural perspective of 1999 that celebrates an ideologically flattened diversity and is optimistic about the possibility of peaceful cohabitation of all Jewish groups within Israel. Produced less than a year before the start of the Second Intifada, the film illustrates that moment's historical optimism in its retrospective depiction of 1991 as devoid of nostalgia and suffering. Finally, Frank's *Beyond the Fear*—produced in 2015 as an investigation of the impact of Rabin's 1995 assassination on Israeli politics and society—departs from the hopeful scenario of the previous wave of films and instead foregrounds the polarization of Israeli politics in the run-up to and aftermath of the Second Intifada. The film expresses the fragmentation of the multicultural dreams and the radicalization and nationalization of Israeli society as a whole. Yet the film also suggests that this fragmentation is no longer that of an exclusion of Russian voices from the Israeli mainstream. On the contrary, the accented voices of Frank's former Soviet subjects are in concert with the broader discourse of nationalized Israeli politics—a consonance that matches Avigdor Lieberman's appointment as Israel's defense minister in 2016. Yet the fate of the film—rejection by all Israeli funding institutions and the need to turn to Russian and Western sources to finance it—also hints at countertrends among Israel's cultural elites. Reflecting what is happening with Israeli cultural, political, and nongovernment organizations as a whole, the situation around the production, screening, and reception of *Beyond the Fear* demonstrates how, as Israeli society fragments, the institutional identifications of Israeli cultural elites (both Russian- and Hebrew-speaking) are becoming more diasporic and globally distributed. Ultimately, Frank's film demonstrates, in contradictory ways, that "Russians" have finally become Israelis.

Notes

1. All translations from Russian and Hebrew in this chapter are those of the author, unless otherwise indicated.

2. One notable exception is Olga Gershenson's work on Russian-Israeli theater and cinema (Gershenson 2005, 2009; Gershenson and Hudson 2008).

3. In fact, America was just as popular a destination, attracting about half of all Soviet Jewish emigrants (Tolts 2011, 3).

4. *Romansy* is a popular musical genre in Russia and beyond that combines sentimental melodies with lyrical song, often presenting settings of well-known poetry.

5. On this topic, see Benjamin Nathans's comprehensive study of Soviet and post-Soviet dissident memoirs, where he identifies the "search for inner freedom" and "overcoming fear of the authorities" as central tropes (Nathans 2015).

Tell Me Your Story

Recent Russian-American Writing

Lisa Ryoko Wakamiya

> At first, Mark asked me to say anything at all. For the sake of my accent, I guessed. Then, when the novelty of my accent had faded, he demanded more complicated narratives. And if I couldn't come up with the right narrative at once, he would guide me and prod me, as if tuning a radio in search of a suitable station.
>
> **Lara Vapnyar**, *Memoirs of a Muse*

> Over roast chicken Kornblum told my parents and Genady and Freda what an honor it was to have them at his house. He could only imagine what they had gone through. For years he and Rhoda had been involved with trying to help the Russian Jews. If it wasn't too personal, he wanted to know how bad it really was.
>
> **David Bezmozgis**, "Roman Berman, Massage Therapist"

Breaking the Waves of Russian Immigrant Writing

The first, second, and third waves of Russian emigration, extending across the history of the twentieth century, produced heterogeneous literature in new lands and languages. The catalysts that propelled Russian writers abroad—whether revolution, war, religious persecution, violations of human rights, or the promise of new opportunities—led authors to address directly or indirectly their perceived place in the literary tradition (see Rubins, this volume). Following the 1917 Revolution, convinced that Russian culture was being destroyed in their homeland, many émigré writers of the first wave considered the preservation of that culture their responsibility. They continued the Symbolist and Acmeist movements that they had begun in Russia with the understanding "that we should write as if there would be no more poetry after us, that what we wrote in exile would be the last Russian poetry" (Igor Chinnov, cit. in Glad 1993, 33). This perspective, however, was hardly representative. Vladimir Nabokov, a young writer of the first wave, would begin his career as a Russophone writer in Russian Berlin (like many of his relocated compatriots) before establishing himself as an Anglophone American author. That this wave of emigration could be defined at once by its traditional practitioners and a sui generis giant of modern and postmodern letters is characteristic of its diversity. The second wave, which emerged after World War II, was described by one of its members as "an emigration of individuals" (Fesenko, cit. in Glad 1999, 347). Attempts to survey the third wave, which lasted from the mid-1970s through the end of the Soviet era, came up against similar problems of definition as critics engaged in what has been described as "an exercise in frustration. There is too much of it, by too many authors, in too many different genres" (Woll 1984, 377). The Nobel laureate Alexander Solzhenitsyn and the poet-turned-politician and provocateur Eduard Limonov both belonged to the third wave but epitomize it only to the degree that their work represents vastly divergent interests and agendas. The authors of these waves, each in their own ways, negotiated the balance between preserving Russian literary traditions, creating new ones, and expanding the literary émigré experience as global Russians.

In North America, the most recent, fourth wave of emigration has produced prominent and successful authors who write in English, not Russian. While many contemporary Russian émigré writers write for diasporic audiences in the near abroad, Israel, or the Russian Federation (see Platt; Kosmarskaya and Kosmarski; Moshkin; Rubins—all this volume), fourth wave writers in North America write in English about the experience of emigration and situate their work in relation to the American and Russian literary traditions. This new Russian-American writing—emerging in an era of self-conscious metafiction and following in the wake of earlier waves of global Russian literature and traditions of immigrant writing in America—has taken shape by writing against the frameworks that organize its reception and promotion. This is writing that breaks the waves of Russian-American fiction.

The writers of the fourth wave all belong to a single generation born in the 1970s in the Soviet Union and raised in North America. Their work is largely autobiographical, at once "buoyed by the explosion of literature of immigrant experience in America" fueled by Jhumpa Lahiri, Junot Díaz, Aleksandar Hemon, and others, and shaped by the transition of Vladimir Putin's Russia "back into the semblance of its old Soviet self" (Senderovich 2014). Much of their work explores the desire to belong to an America that is at once their own and a new world seen through the Old World eyes of their parents. Yet the very conception of seeing America "through alien eyes" is, at the end of the twentieth and start of the twenty-first century, a well-worn trope. Responding to this existing frame of reference and its conventions, recent Russian-American writing challenges the exchange between the producer and consumer of the story of immigration. When prompted to talk about themselves, as the protagonists of early works by Shteyngart, Vapnyar, and Bezmozgis are, they often tell stories that fulfill the conventions of the immigrant tale that their listener wants to hear. "And what do your parents do?" the immigrant protagonist of Shteyngart's *The Russian Debutante's Handbook* is asked upon meeting his American girlfriend's parents. When after an uncomfortable pause he reveals their "exclusive professions," the girlfriend and her parents express their relief by toasting "to the foreigners." The listener has a stake in hearing the immigrant's story: whether it fulfills a need to hear about "how bad it really was" or how well the immigrant has assimilated the values and promise of the American Dream, the story satisfies the listener's need to hear a conventional immigrant tale.

Readers would do well to resist treating listener figures as proxies for themselves. Listener figures coerce immigrant narrators into performing stories of assimilation, tasking them with providing a "teachable moment" while fulfilling preconceived notions of what immigrant life is like. Listener figures value difference to the degree that it can be instrumentalized and overcome. They intervene from the start, preconditioning the plot and reception of the immigrant's tale. In response to their demands, immigrant narrators weave conventional narratives about economic hardship or success.

The narrators of Vapnyar's, Bezmozgis's, and Shteyngart's works may depict the listener as an arbiter of immigrant narratives, but they are critical of such exchanges, disparaging both the reductive desires of listeners and the immigrant narrator's own tendency to fulfill expectations. Irony is the instrument of choice for Shteyngart, as when his narrator raises his eyebrows and folds his arms, "a gesture [he] performed reflexively whenever his family was mentioned" as if to measure his listeners' satisfaction with his performance. In

"Roman Berman, Massage Therapist," Bezmozgis responds by depicting two immigrant storytellers in the home of a potential benefactor, each narrator positioned to profit from his story of otherness and suffering. One easily obliges his wealthy host who inquires about Soviet anti-Semitism. He lifts his shirt at the dinner table and shows the scar that remains under his ribs from the time he was stabbed by anti-Semitic coworkers. The display provokes his host's tears and affirmations that indeed it was horrible. The other opts to remain silent, retaining some measure of dignity while refusing to comply with his listeners' demands and likely depriving himself of his wealthy benefactor's support.

Simultaneously trading on the immigrant story and denigrating one's need to tell it is a difficult balancing act. To tell one's story is to partake not only in a fictional economy of exchange but in an actual economy that offers authors publishing contracts for their accommodation of market demand. Shteyngart, Vapnyar, and Bezmozgis all received critical and popular acclaim for works focused on the immigrant identities of their quasi-autobiographical narrators. "Vapnyar reinvented herself from an awkward 23-year-old Russian émigré who lived in Brooklyn and spoke little English to a prize-winning fiction writer," one critic enthused (Ciolkowski 2006), while Bezmozgis "went from literary unknown to next big thing" (2004). The autobiographism of their writing and the quick success that followed made them vulnerable to the accusation that they were performing ethnic identities for their audiences (Emily Gould used the term "Slav-face"). Adam Rovner, in his study of fourth wave authors, suggested that their success stems not merely from "self-assertions of Jewish distinctiveness" but from the hope that their work can nostalgically "fill the reservoirs and exercise the memories of distinctiveness that we feel are waning," concluding that "immigrant writers postulate some Jewish essence grounded in prevalent stereotype and are celebrated for doing so" (2006, 322, 324). Publishers had an interest in facilitating connections between the writers' experiences and those of their narrators, and their acts of distribution and intervention suggest that audiences were unironically positioned as well-meaning listener figures who potentially could be informed and gratified by the authors' performances of identity. Institutional interests helped shape the reception of literature about immigrant identity as well as authorial and readerly practices. The writers' "otherness" was a profitable construction—whether for readers' emotional and ideological needs, publishers' bottom lines, the writers themselves, or for all three. This much can be gleaned from reviewers' delight in recounting the conventional motifs of immigrant achievement and from academic studies that enumerate the writers' Russian, Jewish, and American identities while using tropes of resistance that seem calculated to align the critic with the writer in a challenge to ideologies of oppression.

But one can only generate so much literary energy by responding to convention. Having achieved success by parodying or critiquing the conventions of immigrant stories, each of these authors has moved to reinvigorate immigrant writing by rewriting its boundaries or transcending them altogether. In place of a self-reflexive focus on conventional accounts of immigration and their entanglements in institutional and social expectations, they have turned instead to examine what earlier narratives have repressed or deliberately omitted. For Shteyngart, relinquishing self-parodying narratives occasioned a turn to the memoir. Having selectively mined his past to produce his creative fiction, in the memoir he divulges his past in its entirety to explore the difficulties of communication between generations, communities, and readerships.

Bezmozgis has moved further from his own experience to consider how the pivotal moment of emigration determined Soviet-Jewish history, and how the Soviet past shapes a transnational post-Soviet Jewish present. For Vapnyar the self-described "painful" influence of Russian literature on her writing situates her earlier work within a recognized canon of influence. Her more recent writing takes up the challenge of working outside of this history. These and other developments in Russian-American writing reveal how it breaks with its early conventions for narrating otherness, including its association with institutional claims for how the experience of immigration should be presented to larger audiences. It has developed from "the phenomenon of its appearance" (Rovner 2006, 314) to include narratives in which the immigrant figure no longer speaks from the margins to a putative center but occupies a place in the center itself. From here, its authors debate the social role of literature, from Vapnyar's skepticism about generalizing from literature to anything beyond it to Bezmozgis's appeal to action in the public sphere.

Self-Parody, Self-Promotion, and Sincerity

Shteyngart's first novels, *The Russian Debutante's Handbook* (2002) and *Absurdistan* (2006), feature immigrant protagonists who remain socially circumscribed despite far-ranging adventures and ambitions that play out across globalized landscapes. *The Russian Debutante's Handbook* presents a tale of downward mobility and the impossibility of assimilation, and it explores the stereotypes and self-criticism that beset those who aspire to rise in social and economic status. Vladimir Girshkin, the novel's protagonist, is initially enthusiastic about the global circulation of capital, information, and people, but a series of setbacks and failures makes it apparent that not all immigrants can effortlessly integrate into the flow of transnational relations. His initial attempts to be a larger-than-life cosmopolitan lead to extraordinary wealth, but after enduring a vicious beating at the hands of a hired group of skinheads, he returns to a desk job in his American father-in-law's office. There, a commuter from soot-stained row houses at the "tattered ends of his neighborhood," he receives a weekly dressing-down from "some clean-cut superior" (Shteyngart 2002, 448, 451). Despite his bourgeois aspirations, Girshkin in the end must pin his hopes on his soon-to-be-born son to become "an American in America." In contrast to the ambitious Girshkin, *Absurdistan*'s protagonist Misha Vainberg has wealth and a degree in "multicultural studies," and he is a self-described "sophisticate." The obese, rap-loving Vainberg, for all of his claims to power (he is the son of the 1,238th richest man in Russia), is beset by his "impotence and collusion in everything" (37). He finds himself caught in a civil war between rival ethnic groups and fighting for his life, even though the two sides have fabricated the war in a plot to attract American military intervention. He loses his girlfriend to "Jerry Shteynfarb," an "upper-middle-class phony who came to the States as a kid and is now playing the professional immigrant game" (81). The conclusion of *Absurdistan* sees Vainberg's final and desperate attempt to immigrate to New York on the fateful date of September 10, 2001.

At the launch of his career, Shteyngart's tales of immigrant aspirations, achievements, and loss resonated powerfully with readers. *The Russian Debutante's Handbook* won the Stephen Crane Award for first fiction and the National Jewish Book Award for fiction. *Absurdistan* appeared on the 10 Best Books of 2006 lists at the *New York Times* and *Time* magazine. As one critic notes, "Shteyngart has achieved the American Dream: success" (Lederman 2010). Self-consciousness about the "professional immigrant game" was a part of this success story from the start. In the press photo that appears on the back flap of *The Russian Debutante's Handbook*, Shteyngart poses in a heavy winter coat with a bear cub on a leash. The photo satirizes popular clichés of "Russian identity" and dares readers to take at face value his ironic identification with these essentializing emblems of "Mother Russia." At the same time, the photo functions as tacit acceptance that he must work within the limiting, commoditizing, and essentializing discourses of the market if he hopes for his book to sell. His self-presentation invites misreadings, as he observes in the essay "The New Two-Way Street," when the same coat leads to an encounter with an INS agent at JFK airport. "I dress in a style I like to call Immigrant Chic," Shteyngart writes, but the "belabored irony" of his "retro 1970s coat with an outrageous fake fur collar" is lost on the immigration official. The official's angry "No! No! No!" uttered when she assumes he is standing in the wrong line gives way to a chastened, monosyllabic "Oh" of realization when he reveals his American passport and keeps his place in the queue with his fellow American citizens (2004, 286). "Americans have to assimilate to a new country as well" (292), he concludes, one in which mobility and global culture have led to more, and more complex, manifestations of identity and diversity. Like his narrator who gauges the listener's satisfaction with his performance of immigrant identity, Shteyngart is at once a performer and critic of the need to perform pedagogically. He contrasts his figures such as the JFK immigration agent, who fulfill the function of misreading the immigrant experience, with more discerning audiences who stand in for his targeted readers in their ability to see beyond the conventional boundaries of their own expectations. In keeping with the satirical tradition, his works confront readers with new, and more challenging, reflections of the author, the immigrant experience, and themselves.

Shteyngart's public performances came to occupy an even more prominent place in his creative production with the publication of *Super Sad True Love Story* (2010b) and his memoir *Little Failure* (2014). In the promotional trailer for *Super Sad True Love Story*, Shteyngart plays an illiterate Borat-like barbarian whose renowned writer friends (Jeffrey Eugenides, Jay McInerney, Edmund White, Mary Gaitskill) marvel at his unimaginable literary success. In the trailer for *Little Failure*, his comic persona is multiply disenfranchised. He is delusional, short, a caricature of a gay man, and professionally outmaneuvered when the actor James Franco writes *Fifty Shades of Gary*—an account of the two men's "erotic journey"—and eclipses Shteyngart on the best-seller list. These performances acknowledge a bifurcation in his public persona between the knowing author and the woeful misfit he portrays, and more importantly, they assume an informed audience that has learned how to appreciate invitations to misread the author's identity. In contrast to the ironic multivalence of Immigrant Chic, which dares the naïve reader to confuse the author with the immigrant protagonists who populate his works, this is performance *qua* performance. One of the functions of his comic persona is to acknowledge the position of the potential reader *outside* of the book; it operates on the assumption that a detached reader who laughs from comic pleasure *at* the persona will become a sympathetic reader who strives to understands some facet of the writing, including the authorial self, as it is presented *in* the book. Whether or not potential readers become drawn into the book, as viewers of the trailer they have become a part of the book's promotional mechanism. The trailer attracts prospective readers and ostensibly draws them in, but also instrumentalizes them by providing them with a tool to promote the book on their own social media platforms.

"When you write a book you also have to do a lot to promote it . . . you have to spend a lot of time making sure that it's read," Shteyngart has said. "You're not just a writer anymore, you're a multimedia event" (Tannen 2011, 172). The stakes of this game are heightened if readers remain detached from the act of reading, even as they are attracted to authorial self-presentations such as the trailers and the self-abasing Friars Club–style roast to which Shteyngart subjected himself in 2012. Shteyngart's fears for the future of literature underlie his depiction of the economy of contemporary media and the phenomenon of identity branding in *Super Sad True Love Story*, in which social media all but replaces books, and his expression of these fears extends to his promotional appearances accompanying the novel's release. Anxiety over the increasing obsolescence of fiction drives the paratextual comic performances and their excessive need for enjoyment. While potentially drawing readers in, the performances also create an entrepreneurial *jouissance* underlaid with anxiety, in which the abject image of the writer becomes capital but literature itself risks falling out in the process. Shteyngart acknowledges the effects of media not only on reading but on writing in his essay "Only Disconnect," where he describes the impact of buying his first smartphone: "I am becoming a different person—solitary where I was once gregarious; a content provider where I at least once imagined myself an artist. . . . And, increasingly, irrevocably, I am a stranger to books, to the long-form text, to the pleasures of leaving myself and inhabiting the free-floating consciousness of another" (2010a, B27).

In essays and public interviews, distinct from the performances, Shteyngart speaks candidly, movingly, and hilariously about the difficulties of immigration, his family's history, and his beginnings as a writer. Here, and particularly in *Little Failure*, is where we encounter much of what is repressed in the comic performances and earlier works, including a multilingual Russian-American-Jewish writing, anxiety over successful upward class mobility, and fear of becoming inaccessible and incomprehensible to one's family. "This is how they talk," he notes, as he recounts his parents' "supposedly funny banter" with each other, which comes "with a twist of the knife." "This is how I never learned to talk." Through his father's eyes he sees himself as a stranger, "ordering truffled things from the menu." Shteyngart's earlier assertion that "Americans have to assimilate" takes on new dimensions when in *Little Failure* he describes how, on separate occasions during his Russian childhood, his parents hit him. "'In Russia you could do things like that,' I say, meaning punch a five-year-old child in the nose until he bled. . . . 'You couldn't do that in America?' my mother asks" (344).

With this, and other poignant passages in *Little Failure*, any pretense at creating comic personae and immigrant shtick slips away. The narrator can no longer cross his arms and silently raise an eyebrow as abuse becomes an integral part of shaping authorial identity. The inclusion of Shteyngart's therapist—Richard C. Lacy, MD, PhD—in the acknowledgments to *Little Failure* is not intended as a joke.

In their essay about the rhetorical and other maneuvers that accompany moving from the blue-collar world to academia, Raymond Blanton and Joshua P. Ewalt describe the body "moving between worlds, transforming that body's materiality (what it eats, how it thinks, how it moves, what other bodies it moves with). When the body enters into a new territorialization, it alters that territory" (2014). When that territory is one's adult relationship with one's parents, Shteyngart's memoir suggests, it leads to *razvod*, divorce, "not between my mother and father but between them and me" and a subsequent quest for understanding. For Shteyngart, that quest entails silence. "Silence instead of the yelled rebuttals. . . . Within that silence, the words hang in the air, fluttering in Cyrillic, not entirely painless but without the power to bring back the small, unquestioning child at their mercy" (321). This protective silence has a flip side, an inability to say, "*I love you.* Or, better still, *I am you*" (328). "It is time for me to be silent. It is time for me to listen, not to talk," he writes, as his parents' histories and memories come to the fore toward the memoir's conclusion (344). After writing novels that drew extensively from his experiences, Shteyngart claims that with his memoir he "decided to give away the recipe" (Levintova 2014). Having done so, and unveiled the multiple authorial roles—promotional, public, and intensely personal—that accompanied it, Shteyngart has effectively barred himself from creating future protagonists modeled on his own autobiography. Sasha Senderovich (2014) asks whether "literature written in English by Soviet-born émigré Jewish writers has stories to tell that are still fresh and new, and whether they have the ability to pose questions that haven't been asked before." Shteyngart's purge of his past suggests that he has also considered this question. How he will engage future readers remains to be seen.

From Biography to Fiction: Literary Heritage across Borders and Generations

David Bezmozgis's family originally intended to immigrate to Atlanta from Riga, Latvia. Their last-minute decision to move to Canada was "a decision made in a stairwell" at the Hebrew Immigrant Aid Society after a family friend who worked there suggested it (Bezmozgis 2011b). Moments drawn from lived experience, in which the future hangs in the balance, feature prominently in Bezmozgis's writing, from his first collection of stories, *Natasha* (2004), to his novels *The Free World* (2011a) and *The Betrayers* (2014a). In contrast with Shteyngart, each consecutive work by Bezmozgis has seen him depart further from his own experience to tell the story of earlier generations of Soviet Jews in diaspora. This has entailed a trajectory toward more intertextually embedded fiction. Bezmozgis has stated that parody does not have a place in his literary method (Knox, 2010), and if self-parody provided Shteyngart with opportunities to challenge conventional notions of "Russianness," for Bezmozgis the cultural inheritance of the Russian literary tradition demands to be acknowledged, even in works written about and for the present. Bezmozgis's work taken as a whole may be considered a study of how ethics, events, memories, and ideas can be transmitted across generations. It also addresses how ideas, behaviors, and attitudes fade or change over time, and how these losses leave their traces among the living. Among these traces are those of Russian literature, which, Bezmozgis (2012) claims, continues to engage "great moral questions" much more directly than North American literature does. The urgency of these questions is communicated, in part, by the increasingly confined spaces and time frames of each of his subsequent works. For Bezmozgis, telling the story of immigration, which he both thematizes and performs, is as much about patrimony and how stories are structured as it is about the conditions under which individuals compromise themselves or display integrity.

Bezmozgis acknowledges that chronicles of immigrant family life can seem most bound by convention when they are viewed through the experiences and observations of a child protagonist. As a "more personal" collection of stories that works "more conventionally as a bildungsroman" (Terwilliger 2014), *Natasha* uses shifts in perspective to move from a child's identification with his parents' economic striving to an adult's efforts to be integrated into his family's dynamics and history. Mark Berman's family lives "one respectable block away from the Russian swarm"; they sit on "cheap stools" around the table, their "green and ugly" Pontiac parked outside. Mark dutifully accompanies his father to "seek the help of a certain rabbi . . . looking appropriately forlorn [and] sufficiently aware of [their] predicament to feel the various permutations of shame" (3, 24–25). With his precocity and knowledge of English, Mark often understands more than he is willing to share with his parents, "but there was nothing they would not openly discuss in front of me, often soliciting my opinion." The immigrant child thrust into the role of cultural interpreter, yet socialized to obey his parents and other adults as figures of knowledge and authority, eventually grows into a sixteen-year-old "compromised by everything [he] knew" about his uncle's relationship with his stepdaughter. As an adult, he spends Saturdays at his grandfather's B'nai Brith residence building. Mark's growth accordingly moves the focus from his own living space, body and emotions, and relationship with his parents to his ailing grandmother, widowed grandfather, and a retired sports journalist helping him write a story.

In place of the upward or downward trajectory of the class mobility narrative, *Natasha* associates change with personal responsibility and understanding. Visits to well-placed patrons that are fraught with uncertain potential ("it was unclear whether nothing or everything had changed") give way to a sense of futility and stasis (as when Mark says of his grandfather, "Some people had a talent for making things happen . . . but he was not one of them"). For the reader and Bezmozgis's narrator alike, hope for a change of fortune—a conventional demand placed on the immigrant's story—is exchanged for the continuity of Grandmother's yartzheit or another game of checkers with Grandfather after Saturday morning services. The motivation for the reader and narrative as a whole is "not tradition," which may include narrative conventions associated with the immigrant tale, "but history."

Where *Natasha* expands in time and space, *The Free World* and *The Betrayers* restrict both. *The Free World*, despite the sweeping promise of its title, confines its action to the six months a Soviet Latvian Jewish family must wait in Rome while their immigration papers are processed. *The Betrayers* restricts time and space even more dramatically, depicting one day and one house in which a Soviet dissident turned Israeli politician confronts the Jewish former KGB informant who sent him to the Gulag for thirteen years. *The Free World*, like *Natasha*, is informed by Bezmozgis's family's experience. The novel's temporal and spatial boundaries set it where the characters cannot become settled, their only commitment being to each other. It deliberately does not provide "models of how to overcome constraint . . . or register the difference between our critical freedom and the limits placed on others" (Best and Marcus 2009, 18). Rather, the balanced inclusion of each family member's perspective lends itself to incrementalist readings in which the reader surveys moments suspended in time. For one family friend, preparing an immigration form to America is a simple contingency plan that entails disavowal of the Communist Party. For the family patriarch Samuil Krasnansky, "a breathing archive" of the Soviet past, such a disavowal amounts to apostasy. Whether completing an immigration form or one's memoirs, for him writing must be sincere; it "is always between one's self and one's soul" (106). The novel's egalitarianism and slowly progressing present raise the question of whether authors and readers, and novels and literary criticism more broadly, require the imbalance of melodrama or the intervention of redemptive narratives for their own sake. In place of melodrama and redemption, *The Free World* offers a fragmentary glimpse of immigrants at an impasse that demands writing and reading practices of "minimal critical agency" attuned to observation (Best and Marcus 2009, 17).

The Betrayers considers whether Soviet-era dissidence can provide a model of activism for a younger generation, and unlike *Natasha* and *The Free World*, it promotes action while addressing questions of influence. Historical narratives about dissidents tend to portray solitary heroes in opposition to a monolithic state, but Bezmozgis presents Baruch Kotler, a fallible fictional hero based on the refusenik Natan Sharansky, against an empathetic portrait of his betrayer, now aged and facing indignity every day. The confrontation between the two men, of their public principles and more nuanced private negotiations, plays out as Kotler's son, an IDF soldier, debates whether to disobey the Israeli government's order to dismantle a settlement block in the West Bank. With Kotler realizing that "his time had passed" and his country "desired a different kind of hero" (224), his son challenges both his father and his government with an act that will identify him as a man of principle for his own generation. The theme of sustaining the values of an earlier generation raises the question of literary influence, and Bezmozgis has named Philip Roth's *The Ghost Writer*, J. M. Coetzee's *Disgrace*, Bernard Malamud's *The Fixer*, and Arthur Koestler's *Darkness at Noon* as conceptual models for *The Betrayers*, as well as plays such as Arthur Miller's *Incident at Vichy* and memoirs by Sharansky and other refuseniks (Terwilliger 2014; Bezmozgis n.d.). By looking to these works and present-day Crimea and Israel, *The Betrayers* demonstrates how Bezmozgis's writing has moved from resistance to convention to a literature that depicted the minimal agency of individuals caught in history's sweep, and developed into a literature that engages the ethical question of how to honor one's forebears while being true to oneself.

Loving and Leaving Russian Literature

Lara Vapnyar has described her love of Russian literature as "a one-sided, troubled, humiliating torturous experience." "On the pages of my favorite authors," she writes, "emerged the little, dirty, smelly, devious disgusting people incapable of beauty and grandeur. Those people were Jews. Those people were me" (2005, 295). Vapnyar's early works underscore an uncomfortable relationship between literary influence and self-definition, in which the influence of canon and other institutional narratives are all too representable and overwrite her own. If for Bezmozgis the Russian literary tradition deals with universal questions that have relevance for the present, for Vapnyar it is a repository of stereotypes that demand reconsideration. Writing in English over the course of the last thirteen years about the Russian Jewish immigrant experience in America, Vapnyar has worked to transcend the ideological order that literary canon imposes on her early stories and first novel, opening her later writing to narrators who are not coerced into telling familiar stories or alluding to Russian classics but who are ambivalently engaged with contemporary affairs.

The stories in Vapnyar's first collection, *There Are Jews in My House*, and first novel, *Memoirs of a Muse*, involve a naïve narrator to whom a secret or situation is revealed, with seemingly liberating but often ambivalent consequences. In *Memoirs of a Muse* the protagonist Tanya realizes her dream of upward class mobility when she moves in with a wealthy American writer (see Furman, this volume). Like many Americans, the writer is obsessed with Dostoevsky, although he never seems to read Dostoevsky's work or allude to it in his own writing. When Tanya discovers her lover's copy of a biography of Dostoevsky, his secret is divulged. Dense with highlighted lines and marginal notes, the biography reveals the extent to which the writer has modeled his life after the Russian writer's, even seeing in Tanya echoes of Dostoevsky's "simple and unpretentious" second wife, Anna Grigorievna. While Tanya imagines herself in the role of her namesake, Aleksandr Pushkin's Tatiana, who sees through Eugene Onegin's romantic posturing when she reads his note-riddled volume of Byron, Vapnyar's heroine finds her deficiencies revealed to herself. Next to descriptions of Dostoevsky's second wife, a "none-too-well-developed average girl," she sees her own name ("Tan'a!") written in her lover's hand (2006, 179). She leaves the writer, and with the help of his neighbors, Tanya finds her own place, goes to graduate school, and gets a job. By the novel's conclusion she has married a fellow immigrant and had a child, having "shut the book" of her past to immerse herself in family life.

While the novel's protagonist gains an identity distinct from the hackneyed "Russian" one the American writer imposed on her, her path to liberation, which entails help from neighbors and numerous fortuitous incidents, is paved with conventions, literary allusions, and institutional priorities that are at once the immigrant narrator's trade and the essence by which the narrative voice becomes marginalized. Bruce Robbins identifies chance occurrences and the protagonist's relation with a patron as requisites of the upward mobility story as they can be used to hide the real motives behind social climbing, particularly when the protagonist "finds" love in the end (Robbins 2010, xiii–xv). In *Memoirs of a Muse* Tanya's sympathetic neighbors perform the patron's role as they help her acquire greater independence. At the same time, it is Tanya's serendipitous and unplanned achievements that resolve the loose ends at the novel's conclusion. Tanya's need for a job means that she "had to succumb to teaching" but "surprised her[self]" with how much she enjoyed it. In her free time she makes "random and unwise" tours of her neighborhood based on "whatever fleeting interests" she might have at the moment. It is during one such excursion that she discovers that she had in fact realized her potential as a muse: a recently deceased resident of the American writer's apartment building has immortalized Tanya's thin frame and boots in a series of paintings exhibited in a gallery. Tanya's fulfillment is not the product of ambitious striving but of chance occurrences, the kindness of others, and the lessons of a bad relationship, all archetypal structures and plots that generalize the protagonist's condition for appropriation by a wide readership.

Visible allusions to Russian literature found in Russian immigrant writing, according to Amelia Glaser, provide "a compelling reason for Slavic Studies scholars to take an interest in the[se] writers," to "integrate American fiction into a study of the Russian literary canon in a transnational modernity" (2011, 15, 16). Yet this proposal advances an uncomfortable position for the critic, similar to that of the listener figure inscribed in the works themselves: tell me your story and I'll tell you where it came from. Vapnyar's admission that her early stories were written "the only way I knew how, as a Russian greatly influenced by Russian writers, who are still my painful favorites," and composed "in American, which for me became the language of immigrants, who come from all over the world bringing their stories, their cultures, and their pain" (2005, 299), raises the question of whether Vapnyar's early writing serves as a means of working through and repeating the very conventions that overwrite the narrative voice: the intertwined marginalizing discourses of anti-Semitism, the Russian canon, and immigration.

Vapnyar engages narration as a means of gaining critical distance in her later novels, *The Scent of Pine* (2014) and *Still Here* (2016). In *Still Here* Vapnyar employs a satirical mode and four immigrant protagonists who variously respond to loss and opportunity to address contemporary issues. "Doesn't it feel like we're entering the afterlife?" Sergey exclaims to his wife when they leave Moscow for New York at the beginning of the novel, laying bare his melancholic trajectory. After receiving a posthumously posted letter from his deceased father, Sergey works to develop an app that perpetuates the online presence of the dead as a way to console the living. Sergey has been laid off, and much of the narrative around the app concerns pitching it to potential sponsors, a process of turning memory into capital. Sergey's algorithm for shaping a spectral simulacrum of life parallels the methodical process by which the narrative presents his upward mobility tale.

Two other protagonists provide counterpoints to Sergey's story. One, who works as a literary translator just as her deceased mother did, successfully translates *Humdrum*, a novel that seems to be a mash-up of Alice Munro and Karl Ove Knausgaard, overrun with the sad mundaneness that Vapnyar seems to find emblematic of our time. Her unexpected response to the insistent threat of mortality that hangs over the novel is to adopt a child from Russia. The other protagonist is a nomad, at home everywhere and nowhere, determined to seize the day rather than mourn the past. *Still Here* contrasts Russian citizens subject to political and historical forces, such as a journalist "beaten by pro-Putin thugs," with émigré Russians-turned-Americans who have difficulty knowing what to do with their lives. This ambivalent assessment of contemporary American attitudes to historical and political action also casts a skeptical eye on the institutional significance of literature. For Vapnyar literature is a First World problem. She has definitively broken from the canon of Russian novels in which the discussion of ethical questions is a privilege only afforded to some. In its place she offers a world in which the social, economic, and political have become ordinary, and commitments are discussed at the level of the personal and possible, rather than the social and the ideal. This downsizing correlates with the modest ambitions Vapnyar suggests must accompany writing that addresses the contemporary.

Writing within the World

After fifteen years of consistent creative activity, Shteyngart, Bezmozgis, and Vapnyar have established themselves to the degree that they can no longer write or be read as if on the outside looking in. They write of contemporary concerns and how to honor the past and how to break with it in ways that reflect their changed position and perspectives. The conventions associated with the protagonists' discovery of a cosmopolitan, transnational world and restrictions on their movement within that world due to class or ethnic difference have given way to narrative restrictions of scale. These may be restrictions of time and space and fidelity to facts as required of a historical novel like *The Free World* or Shteyngart's memoir, or the three unities that structure *The Betrayers*, whose ethical dimensions are its primary focus. Narrative restrictions may also be a "mimetic critical reaction to the conditions of the present" (Love 2016, 422) in which any examination of how subjects respond to the "becoming-ordinary of social, political, and environmental crisis" is best registered in "recessive, scaled-down affects" (Ngai 2013). This is especially evident in *The Free World* and *Still Here*, where any consideration of agency or autonomous subjectivity is subject to a metanarrative concern for possible ways of acting in the world rather than the "maximalist claims of transnational and transchronological turns" with which critics align themselves.

Despite these general similarities, Shteyngart, Bezmozgis, and Vapnyar remain fundamentally distinct from one another. Their differences emerge in how they acknowledge their literary influences as a way to situate their work meaningfully within existing traditions, or renounce them as no longer practicable models of marginalizing discourse. The irony Shteyngart abandons to write a truthful memoir is a tool Vapnyar adopts to gain critical distance from literary allusions and conventions. Bezmozgis wrote *The Betrayers* against the backdrop of an unordinary crisis, the Russian occupation of Crimea. Eschewing distance, Bezmozgis argues that the writer and reader, like the protagonists he writes about, must be historical actors: "The novelist who tackles social and political phenomena . . . cannot merely describe—he must anticipate an outcome." After seeing the writer leap without a net, the reader is left to contemplate the possibility "ideally, of leaping with him" (Bezmozgis 2014b). Vapnyar regards such men of action as part of the literary past she has left behind. The women in *Still Here* devote themselves to the continual professional and family obligations that occupy their lives. It is this sort of action that Vapnyar regards as emblematic of our time, when "the reader didn't have time to ponder the philosophy. . . . Perhaps the philosophy [was] so busy and concerned the whole time that you couldn't possible analyze it" (295).

Russian-American writing, globally situated and resolutely historical as it is, is well positioned to reflect upon cultural and political developments. As it continues to develop, so should efforts to assess its new directions, the opportunities and restrictions it encounters as it models new fictional worlds, and its embeddedness in a world that is not exclusively defined by the circulation of commodities or literary and critical conventions associated with immigrant writing. This is literature that responds to its cultural and critical circumstances and contributes to the ongoing work of situating literature, reading, and writing in a globalized world.

Russia as Whole and as Fragments

Ilya Kukulin

> By order of the intelligence services of foreign states antagonistic to the USSR, the accused in the current case organized a conspiratorial group named the "Right Trotskyist Bloc," adopting as their goal the overthrow of the USSR's current socialist social and political order and the reestablishment in the USSR of capitalism and the authority of the bourgeoisie, as well as the dismemberment of the USSR, ripping away Ukraine, Belarus, the Central Asian republics, Georgia, Armenia, Azerbaijan and the Far East.
>
> **Andrei Vishinsky**, Prosecutorial Summary in the "Case of the Anti-Soviet Right-Trotskyist Bloc," 1938

> There are many powers in the world who are afraid of our might or—as one of our sovereigns put it—of "our enormousness." And, as is well known, this is why they try to break us apart. Look what they did with Yugoslavia: cut it into little bits, and now they manipulate anything they like there. . . . In principle, that's what certain people obviously want to do with us.
>
> **Vladimir Putin**, 2014

Fear of Russia Divided

As the authors of this volume posit, all conceptions of culture's place in geography are historically constructed and contingent. Yet Russian emplacements of culture in global geography are also linked together in a web of interrelated traditions and visions of territory. The question of the unity or diversity of

Russian culture within Russia itself is therefore of no little importance for an understanding of our topic. Yet what is "Russia itself"? Forever suspended between imperial, national, "internationalist," and even "global" conceptions of territorial expanse, the linkage between geography and the Russian cultural imagination has long been contested (Bassin, Ely, and Stockdale 2010). The present chapter examines how Russian writers have articulated the relationships between their works and "Russia" as an imaginary, ideological whole, as well as how they have problematized these relationships and how this problematization has developed over time. Ultimately, it sheds light on the political and cultural meanings of the "territorial imagination" in Russian culture—or, to be more precise, on the ways in which the image of Russia's "territorial integrity" has been made and unmade over time.

We may start by observing how moments of ideological crisis have regularly evoked literary works that imagine Russia's territory as divided between two or more antagonistic states. Vasily Aksyonov's *Island of Crimea* (*Ostrov Krym*), for example, responded to the erosion of Soviet ideology in the 1970s. It presents an alternate history and geography, in which alongside the Soviet Union, the "Island of Crimea" (rather than peninsula, as in actuality) prospers up to the present as an autonomous pro-Western enclave. At the novel's conclusion, Crimea reunites with the USSR as a result of a referendum of its residents. Similarly, decades later Andrei Volos's novel *Maskav Mecca* (*Maskavskaia Mekka*) offered a tangential reaction to the early post-Soviet utopian conception of Russia's "return to the civilized world," a conception that was already deeply discredited in the late 1990s, especially after the social fallout following the 1998 financial crisis. In Volos's novel, Aksyonov's scenario is turned inside out. Maskav (the former Russia) is a super-developed, multicultural state that is, however, based on principles of social apartheid. Within it, the small independent Hummunist Land (Gumunistichstkii krai)—in other words, the totalitarian, party-led state—preserves both Soviet ideology and an impoverished, ideologically controlled form of life typical of Russian or Belorusian provinces of the 1950s or 1960s (Kukulin 2004).

More recently, the Russian regime's contemporary crisis of legitimacy has been reflected in Vladimir Sorokin's novel *Telluria* (2013) and Elena Chizhova's novel *The Sinologist* (*Kitaist*, 2017). In Sorokin's work, as a result of Vladimir Putin's reign (the novel states the causal linkage explicitly), Russia breaks apart into grotesque independent states: the Ural Republic, the Principality of Ryazan, the USSR (a dwarf postmodernist state in Western Siberia), Tartaria, and so on (for a map of the novel's geographic reality, see Morozova and Iarova 2013; for analysis, see L'vovskii 2018). Chizhova's novel presents an alternate history of Russia in the twentieth and twenty-first centuries. The novel's plot is based on the premise that Nazi Germany captured Moscow and Petersburg in World War II but could not ultimately defeat the USSR; the German advance was stopped at the Urals and, eventually, the exhausted combatants signed a truce. Shortly thereafter, Germany was itself defeated and occupied by the United States and Great Britain. Paradoxically, however, a moderated form of the Nazi regime, reminiscent of South African apartheid of the 1970s, survives in the USSR's European territory, to which the leaders of the Third Reich fled.[1] The USSR itself persists on the remainder of the USSR's territory—its Asian territories from the Urals to the Far East. Here, Moscow and Leningrad are recreated on the banks of the rivers Ob and Om, respectively, as simulacra perfectly replicating their originals. Both novels project social heterogeneity and the crisis of ideological legitimacy in fantasies of territorial fragmentation. The persistent repetition of this plot can only partially be explained by the influence of the ideology and historical legacy of the Cold War, featuring the superpowers' division of formerly unified states into spheres of influence (as with Germany, Vietnam, Korea, and, to some extent, China).

Sorokin's and Chizhova's novels are clearly derived from a series of post-Soviet science fiction works of based on the premise of Russia's conquest by Nazi Germany. Examples include Andrei Lazarchuk's novella *Inoe nebo* (The other sky, 1993), later reworked into the longer novel *Vse, sposobnye derzhat' oruzhiia* (Everybody able to bear arms, 1997), Sergei Abramov's novel *Tikhii angel proletel* (An angel is passing overhead, 1994), and Sergei Siniakin's *Polukrovka* (Half-blood, 2005). A new wave of interest in such plots began in 2010, when Yury Kharitonov and Mikhail Nesterenko published their novel *Über Alles*. In 2012 Georgy Zotov's book *Moskau* appeared, also with a title mimicking German. In this light, Chizhova's 2017 novel looks peculiar: why would a mainstream author, generally considered somewhat highbrow by critics, resort to a plot specific to alternative-history science fiction? In this connection, the fantasy writer and literary scholar Maria Galina called Chizhova's book an anachronism (Galina 2017). Yet regardless of which previous novels Chizhova actually read, her work reframed and contextualized this plot, rendering it an element of "serious" literature. Furthermore, Chizhova surpasses her popular culture predecessors in her lucid evocation of memory of the Cold War, or, to be more precise, of a complex psychological experience that could not be expressed in Soviet conditions: overt comparison of the USSR and the United States was—for many—covertly juxtaposed with the dangerous comparison of the USSR with Nazi Germany. (This comparison was enacted almost openly in Tatiana Lioznova's enormously popular 1972 TV series *Seventeen Moments of Spring*.)

In light of the durability of the compositional strategy described here, we may propose that Russia's territory has quite commonly been seen as an ideological construct in modern Russian culture. Furthermore, literary investigations of this ideological construct have changed over time, becoming in general increasingly pessimistic. Sorokin's novel ends with the flight of a central character from the degenerating social environment to live in solitude in the forest. In the poet and critic Dmitry Kuzmin's view, this conclusion is "a white flag, raised on behalf of defeated civilization" (Morev 2015). In Chizhova's novel, the "Soviet" (resembling the historical USSR) and Nazi (imaginary) components of Russian geography, as well as the "empire" created by their combination in the finale, are all equally morally repugnant. Both works demonstrate the profound crisis in the current political imaginary and in visions of future historical possibilities.

The literary strategies evident in Sorokin's and Chizhova's works may be traced to the start of the twentieth century. Andrei Bely was likely the first author to inaugurate the theme of the "ideological character" of Russia's territory. Consider the opening of his canonical novel *Petersburg* (1912–1913):

> What is this Russian Empire of ours?
>
> This Russian Empire of ours is a geographical entity, which means: part of a certain planet. And this Russian Empire includes: in the first place—Great, Little, White and Red Rus; in the second place—the Kingdoms of Georgia, Poland, Kazan and Astrakhan; in the third place it includes . . . But—et cetera, et cetera, et cetera. [. . .]
>
> Petersburg, or Saint Petersburg, or Pieter (which are all the same) actually does belong to the Russian Empire. And Tsargrad, Konstantinograd (or, as they say, Constantinople), belongs to it by right of inheritance. And we shall not expatiate on it.
>
> Let us expatiate at greater length on Petersburg [. . .] (1978, 1)[2]

The Russian Empire is presented here as the material and political projection of the Russian emperors' official titles, inverting the "normal" logic whereby the titles reflect the country's various actual territories and its ruling family's territorial aspirations (Etkind, Uffel'mann [Uffelmann], and Kukulin 2012, 8–9).

Ilya Erenburg took the next step following Bely with his dystopian novel *The Trust D.E.* (*Trest D.E.*, 1923), which describes the progressive destruction of Europe. The work recounts the destruction of the great cities of the USSR's European territory as a result of the Soviet-Polish war, their populations eliminated by means of a French bacteriological weapon. All that remains of the USSR are Siberia and the Far East, but within these reduced circumstances the country transforms into an ultramodern, dynamic society: "Irkutsk and Chita could compete with solid American cities. With regard to Vladivostok, for its part, one could with confidence state that in twenty or so years it would be a rival to San Francisco" (Erenburg 1962, 295). Chizhova's 2017 novel, with which we began, "rhymes" interestingly with Erenburg's description of the Siberian secession from a dying Europe: in her version, Siberia remains as a "conservancy" of the Soviet order.

However, although a century-long tradition in literary works has demonstrated that Russian and Soviet territory has been constructed as primarily ideological (rather than geographical) space, academic works studying this phenomenon began to appear only in the early 2000s. As Irina Sandomirskaia and Gasan Guseinov argue, the ideological core of the Soviet geographical imagination was based on a conception of the USSR as simultaneously a universalist project and a besieged fortress (Sandomirskaia 2001; Guseinov 2005). In representations of the USSR, its huge territorial expanse had singular importance: lessons for school children and propaganda texts for adults explained that spatial boundlessness justified the regime's global ambitions (Guseinov 2005, 28–30). For this reason, a state border inscribed through the middle of Russian space, far more than the borders between Russia and the other "union republics," could serve as a potent symbol of the utopian project's failure as well as a sign of the vulnerability of the "fortress" and a blow at territorial nationalism. For authors like Aksyonov, Sorokin, and Chizhova, description of such borders articulates critique of Soviet expansionist ideology.

On the other hand, for more conservative and nationalistic authors, the breakup of the singular national-territorial "body" is a nightmare. Guseinov reproduces multiple caricatures drawn from the nationalist press of the 1990s expressing fear at the prospect of Russia's division into autonomous territories. In description of processes of secession, the conservative science fiction author Viacheslav Rybakov invented the backronym KNDR—Kucha nezavisimykh dereven' Rossii (Pack of Independent Villages of Russia), punning on the identical Russian acronym for the North Korean People's Republic (2003). Continuous crisis in the Caucasus stoked such fears—for Russian propaganda interpreted both Chechen Wars (of 1994 and 1999) as struggles against Chechnya's possible secession from Russia.

Russia as Nation or Empire?

A fuller explanation of the cultural imagination of Russia's territorial integrity and of challenges to it demands an excursus into political history. Many researchers have demonstrated how, beginning with the "era of nationalism" at the turn of the eighteenth and nineteenth centuries, the Russian Empire's status became fundamentally ambivalent in the eyes of both its own elites and foreign observers—although this ambivalence was subject to varied interpretations. The empire was simultaneously declared both a state of "Russians" and a super-national unity (Zorin 2001, 337–73; Zhivov 2008). In this, it was utterly distinct from Austro-Hungary, a neighboring continental empire in which, as in Russia, the metropole was not sharply distinguished from subject territories (or "internal colonies"), yet which pursued, at least in its last decades, national principles in construction of the empire's component ethnic identities. In contrast, Russian imperial ideologies sought to construct "Russians" not simply as a nation in the sense that gained currency in Western Europe but rather as a collectivity of loyal subjects, affectively bonded with the state. As early as Sergei Uvarov's well-studied memorandum to Nicholas I of 1832, one may observe an erasure of the border between ethnicity and loyalty to the state and a proposal to view these categories as interchangeable. For it was in this document that the recently appointed Minister of Education de facto articulated the formula "Orthodoxy, Autocracy, Nationality," which would subsequently become famous as the motto of Russian Official Nationality (Zorin 2001).

This studied equivocation between imperial and national identification had far-reaching implications at the level of the territorial imagination (Bassin 2006). As Stefan Rohdewald explains:

> In spite of their "nonrussian" ethnicities, the western regions, apart from Poland, were considered to be without question part of the internal geography of the Russian Empire. . . . *The integration and assimilation of external territories was intentionally represented and legitimated as an internal consolidation.* . . . A characteristic example is to be found in the insistence, articulated in response to competing claims to autochthonic status by various ethnicities, that Orthodox Russians should nevertheless retain dominance in the western peripheries of the empire. The priority of Orthodox Russians and the necessity to "russify" the region were in this case regarded as faithfulness to long-standing traditions of the newly acquired region. (Rodeval'd 2012, 522–23; see also Dolbilov 2010)

Rendering matters of territorial belonging and ethnicity even more ambivalent, the "Russian" ethnicity was officially defined as inclusive of Ukrainians and Belarusians, as well as Russians proper, all of which were seen as parts of a single and unified people rather than as separate ethnic groups or nations.

At the start of the twentieth century, the socialist revolution led at first to declarations that the new state was multi- and supernational, especially following the creation of the USSR in 1922 (Martin 2001; Hirsch 2005). Equivocation between "Russian" and "imperial" was formally superseded—but, as it turned out, not for long (Brandenberger 2002). Following the ideological transformations of the middle 1930s, the Stalinist USSR was articulated as simultaneously "Russian" and "Internationalist" and Russians were once again proclaimed the cornerstone of state power (Hosking 2006; Aktürk 2012). Unlike the Russian imperial administration, the Soviet Party bureaucracy did not attempt to russify the Soviet and autonomous republics. To the contrary, the goal of Soviet policy was harsh management of national consciousness (Suny 1993; Brandenberger 2002). In territorial terms this meant that people whose native language was Russian considered the entire extent of the Soviet Union more or less as "their own" land. The ethnic identities of non-Russians were promoted as a "natural" attribute of all peoples, yet claims to "national" self-determination were placed "under erasure" with enforced participation in a purportedly "supernational" Russophone Soviet civilization.[3]

Without treating the causes of the Soviet collapse in great detail, we may propose that this momentous outcome was due to a combination of "ideological fatigue" with the generally unexpected reemergence of aspirations for national autonomy (Beissinger 2002). As sociological polling data demonstrate, in 1990 the majority of the USSR's population did not consider its possible collapse a potentially catastrophic outcome (Levinson 2007). However, once this outcome became reality, the secession of former union republics was regarded in widely varying ways. Baltic independence was seen as well-nigh inevitable, whereas many, even among the intelligentsia, viewed Ukraine's transformation into an independent state as a traumatic, or at least strange, turn of events. Besides Joseph Brodsky's controversial poem "On Ukrainian Independence" ("Na nezavisimost' Ukrainy") one may recall a song by the popular guitar poet Timur Shaov, "Transit Train through Ukraine" ("Transitnyi poezd cherez Ukrainu," early 1990s):

> The jaunty fellows enter:
> A customs officer and a border guard.
> [. . .]
> The sergeant rummages through my belongings
> And in his eyes I read:
> "Well, Moscali? You're caught, beasts!"
> It's us, the Moscali, who've eaten his lard;
> And it's us who don't give him his oil and gas.
> [. . .]
> From nervous stress I got all yellow-blue.[4]

In short, for many members of Russian society, the geopolitical transformations of the early 1990s came as an unexpected encounter with ethnic and political demarcations dividing what they had until recently seen as the unified territory of their native land—an unanticipated reckoning with centuries of intentionally blurring the relationship between "Russianness" and the politics of empire.

Immediately after the breakup of the Soviet Union, the term "near abroad" became an active element of the Russian political elite's vocabulary, signaling inclusion of the former union republics in a Russian sphere of influence. At the start of 1994, the conservative political adviser Andranik Migranian and Deputy Minister of Defense Andrei Kokoshin allegedly stated that "the borders of the Russian state . . . cannot yet be considered to be permanent" (Guseinov 2005, 15).[5] During these same years, Vladimir Zhirinovsky called for the (re)conquest of a series of Central Asian and Caucasian territories in his manifesto *Last Drive Southwards* (*Poslednii brosok na iug*, 1993). In intelligentsia circles, Zhirinovsky's screed was at the time seen as absurd to the point of parody, yet today, the politician's assertions that "Abkhazia and South Ossetia can and must be included in Russian territory" (2008 [1993], 10) may be understood as evidence of the long circulation of expansionist aspirations with regard to Georgia among political elites.

In 1997 the political consultants Petr Shchedrovitsky and Efim Ostrovsky published the project "Contours of a Concept of Russian Federation Politics in the CIS" ("Kontury kontseptsii politiki Rossiiskoi Federatsii v SNG"), in which they proposed for the first time in modern history the concept of the "Russian World" as a political unification of the Russophone citizens of Russia and the republics of the former USSR.[6] Shchedrovitsky did not link this concept with aspirations for territorial expansion. He proposed that "the Russian World is . . . a means of the accommodation and adaptation of Russia . . . to globalization" (Shchedrovitskii et al. 2001). Yet with the annexation of Crimea and Russian incursions into Eastern Ukraine, the Russian World concept has been reinterpreted as a program for enlarged borders (Zevelev 2014). Today, enthusiasts of the "Russian World" envision the expansion of Russian territory to incorporate regions of neighboring states that include an ethnic Russian majority, recalling Serbian nationalist dreams of a "Greater Serbia" (see discussion of this comparison in Vujačić 2015, esp. 298–310). The current regime's liberal opponents, in contrast, even before the beginning of the 2013–14 Ukrainian crisis, held that current Russian policies might lead to a state collapse, as luridly described in Sorokin's *Telluria*. Repeatedly, liberal journalists and political scientists have asserted that given the Putin regime's harsh political and economic pressure on regional powers, any weakening of central authority will lead to a rush for autonomy—the regions will "flee" from Russia (compare Gerasimenko 2014). Such a scenario, of course, recalls the history of the Soviet breakup, which, as such commentators suggest, could well repeat itself.

Imperial Prehistories of the Russian Territorial Imagination

Just as the imbrication of empire and cultural identification in Russia are the result of a long history, traditions of literary representation of Russian political space and of its problematization reach back to the modern cultural tradition's beginnings in the eighteenth and nineteenth centuries. Perhaps the only case in which semantic interconnections between Russian literary works and politically marked territory have been studied in detail is that of travelogues, investigated in the last decade within postcolonial critical frames. Another interesting approach is that of "humanistic geography," based on description of the culturally rooted geographic imagination. In particular, Dmitry Zamiatin (2006, 2011; Zamiatin et al. 2008) and Vladimir Kagansky (2001, 2005) have studied this topic, arriving at significant conclusions regarding the Soviet geographical imagination.[7] Yet perhaps the most useful critical support with regard to deeper traditions is found in Viktor Zhivov's classic essay "The Myth of the State in the Age of Enlightenment and Its Destruction in Late Eighteenth-Century Russia," which analyzes the relationship between the poet's image and that of the empire.

Drawing on the work of Lev Pumpiansky, Zhivov explains that originally in Russia, as in other absolute monarchies:

> The state and its outcomes were a motif organic to European classicism. . . . The state was the subject of poetic rapture and philosophical meditation precisely because it was presented as the steward of cosmic harmony on earth. Therefore, the monarch's victories, welfare, alliances, and peace treaties were not only material for visual rendition but also a topic for philosophical and artistic introspection. The progress of the state was perceived as the progress of reason and enlightenment—not the individual progress of a given society but the universal development of a principle, a component part of an all-inclusive achievement. Such was French literature under Louis XIV, German literature in the first half of the eighteenth century, and Russian literature from Feofan Prokopovich to Derzhavin. The constant employment by this politico-philosophical literature, in its efforts to resolve the basic problems of the world system, of the pastoral (as a genre) and of pastoral symbolism points to its deep

> link with the mythology of the Golden Age and with vestigial notions of the monarch as the mediator between good order in the cosmos and good order in the social organism. (2009, 14)

To the end of the eighteenth century the social position of the "man of literature" in Russia was fully inscribed into this cultural and institutional structure, with the exception of a few "anomalous" figures—for example, Antiokh Kantemir—who insisted on their own autonomy based on the autonomy of universal reason.[8] In other words, the Russian poet's task was to represent aesthetically the empire and the emperor's or empress's cosmic role as its guarantor (Ram 2003, 63–120). This task was especially significant in poetry as opposed to prose: the proportion of political odes in Russian literature of the eighteenth century exceeds by a wide margin that of such works in any other European literary tradition.[9]

As Zhivov demonstrates, however, at the century's close the situation began to change as a result of cultural institutions' emancipation from political dictate:

> Catherine [the Great] perceived [the Enlightenment] as one element of a mythology of the state centered on herself. Cultural and historical development therefore appeared to be controllable . . . ; it conveyed no sense of danger. But cultural emancipation implied that cultural development had exceeded mythological bounds, become embedded in the reality of Russian life, and ceased to be controllable. In consequence, the state's cultural policy became conservative. Manifestations of the new approach were the closing of free publishing houses, increased censorship, the arrests of Novikov and Radishchev, and Fonvizin's disgrace. (2009, 23–34)

The period Zhivov considers here coincides with the first moment of problematization of the linkage between literary imagination and empire, understood as a newly ordered cosmos. Revision of this linkage is evident, for instance, in Alexander Radishchev's *A Journey from Petersburg to Moscow* (*Puteshchestvie iz Peterburga v Moskvu*, 1790), which Zhivov does not mention, although he does refer to its author's arrest. One of Radishchev's aesthetic and political discoveries was that imperial space was remarkably heterogeneous, both in social and historical terms. In Radishchev's hands, the sentimental journey became a tool for social subversion—not only because of his critique of serfdom (duly praised in Soviet treatments) but also because the author labored concertedly to articulate a new vision of imperial space, founded not on the wholeness of the cultural-cosmic mission of the state but rather on distinctions between different social groups that he projected into the geographical diversity of places visited by the narrator. In this, *Journey* was perhaps the first work in Russian literary history to problematize the relationship between text, authorship, and politically inscribed territory.

In Zhivov's account, at the start of the nineteenth century the function of establishing order in the world passes from monarch to poet. In light of the systematic suppression in Russia of institutions of civil society and public politics, the figure of emancipated author, possessed of aesthetic autonomy, acquired the function of secular prophet and herald of history's meaning, reflecting the rise of European historicism (Meinecke 1936). In Zhivov's view, Alexander Pushkin's famous poem revising a Horatian ode, "I've raised a monument to myself, not made by human hands . . ." ("Ia pamiatnik sebe vozdvig nerukotvornyi," 1836), demonstrates that "Pushkin, unlike Derzhavin [who authored a previous revision of Horace], openly compares poet and emperor and leaves no doubt as to the poet's supremacy": Pushkin's monument "raises its defiant head higher / Than the Alexandrian Column" (1959–62, 2:4). Pushkin's imagination extended across the empire as a whole in this poem that describes how every language in "great Rus'" would resound with the poet's name, including those of "the proud grandson of the Slavs, the Finn, the still wild / Tungus, and the Kalmyk, friend of the steppe" (1959–62, 2:4). A traditional motif of Russian eighteenth-century odes, praise to the greatness of Empire ("geographical fanfaronades," to use poet and critic Petr Viazemsky's bon mot), is inverted: the empire's diverse ethnic groups become not loyal subjects of the emperor but keepers of the poet's memory. However, as observed above, by the eighteenth century's close anti-imperial conceptions had already surfaced in Russian literature as well—in Radishchev's *Journey* as well as in his ode "Freedom" ("Vol'nost'," 1783). Consider, too, how Pushkin presents the empire in his *Bronze Horseman* (*Mednyi vsadnik*, 1833) as a simultaneously constructive and inhuman force (Pumpianskii 2000 [1939], 159–60).

Parallel to the breakup of the unity of politics, imperial territory, and literature, elements of an independent Russian nationalism arose in the literature of the 1830s to the 1850s and took the form of representations of Russians not as a community of loyal subjects but as victims of imperial power. Nikolai Nekrasov, for example, envisions imperial space's diversity as a variety of sufferings experienced on Russian soil, as in his famous "Meditations in the Entry Hall" ("Razmyshleniia u paradnogo pod"ezda," 1858):

[. . .] O native land!
Can you find me an abode,

For I have never seen such a place,
Where your sower and keeper—
The Russian peasant—does not groan?
He groans in fields, on roads;
Groans in prisons and stockades,
In mines, on an iron chain;
Groans in the drying house, in haystacks,
Beneath a wagon, sleeping in the steppe.
(1949, 1:177)

In Nekrasov's works, ethnically inscribed territory and empire part ways, setting the stage for all later investigations of the "proper" location of Russians in the empire's political and territorial order and their problematic relationship with "non-Russian" imperial possessions.

Two additional factors were of cardinal importance in the rising disunity between the Russian literary imagination and politically organized space: colonial expansion of the Russian empire and the first experiences of Russian political emigration. The "Caucasian" works of Mikhail Lermontov, especially his novel *A Hero of Our Time* (*Geroi nashego vremeni*, 1840), developed the aesthetics of spatial eccentricity in Russian literature, earlier evident in Pushkin's "Oriental" works (Layton 1994; Ram 2003). For Lermontov, the empire could not be conceived as whole in light of its fracturing into the unconquerable space of the Caucasus, on the one hand, and "internal" regions, on the other. A related mode of literary investigation of imperial nonhomogeneity may be observed in the folk exoticism that became fashionable in the 1830s. In his *Evenings on a Farm Near Dikanka* (*Vechera na khutore bliz Dikan'ki*, 1831), Nikolai Gogol represents Ukraine as a region differing in cardinal manner from metropolitan Russia, giving rise to grotesque images and preserving archaic, shocking, or uncanny (in Freud's sense) relationships between people. These images potentially contain seeds of a new form of the sublime, as in the story "A Terrible Vengeance" ("Strashnaia mest'"). At about the same moment, in the 1840s–60s, competing narratives of Russian and Ukrainian history were taking shape (Bojanowska 2007, 14–26; Plokhy 2008; Bilenky 2012; Chernetsky, this volume).

Turning to the second complicating factor in the Russian territorial imagination's development, the emigration of Russian writers from the empire affected their comprehension of imperial space in various ways. Gogol, living in Italy at the end of the 1830s and start of the 1840s, repeatedly emphasized that it was only from outside of Russia that he could see it as a whole. Yet his relationship to Russia during this period was contradictory: Edyta Bojanowska concludes, "It appears Gogol could be Russian only through the act of writing about Russia, as an imaginative exercise" (2007, 213). In the 1840s–50s the revolutionary Alexander Herzen and the aged religious conservative and poet Vasily Zhukovsky arrived independently at the conclusion that experience of Europe allowed them to comprehend the specificity of the European consciousness "in general," which made it possible to understand Russians as important and unique yet also as a subcategory of contemporary Europeans—as is most evident, for instance, in Herzen's essay "From the Other Shore." Certain of Herzen's works written in emigration might be described not as geographically eccentric in relation to Russia but rather as originating from the border. Their imaginary geography is the aggregate of all loci of European revolutionary movements (from the struggle for labor rights in France to the nationalist war for unification of Italy under Garibaldi's leadership). Herzen, in distinction from Zhukovsky, was a devoted critic of the Russian empire, and therefore his problematization of the relationship between text and territory was far more radical and complete. In general, one may conclude that the early experience of Russian emigration or of long-term residence abroad resulted in new forms of geographical imagination and a sharp shift in authors' perspectives. These developments have many times been described in terms of the "dialogue of Russia and the West" or conversations between Russian and Western European cultures (for Herzen's special role in this "dialogue," see Malia 1961; Volodin 1985), and far less frequently in terms of either a transformation in the relationship between literature and politically inscribed territory or a questioning of the propriety of empire.

In a reflection of Russian literary culture's growing cosmopolitanism, a final model for the destabilization of this relationship during the imperial period may be observed in works written from the point of view of a person of a foreign culture—for instance, Nekrasov's *Iz put'evykh zapisok grafa Garanskogo* (From the travel notes of Count Garansky, 1853), in which Russia is presented as though viewed from outside, from a "European" perspective. This is a straightforward but typical example of defamiliarization, as described in Formalist literary theory, used for political satire. The basis for the device in Nekrasov's work is both geographical and cultural: in the author's conceit, Count Garansky, having lived many years in Europe, differs in mindset from typical Russians in such a cardinal manner that his journey though Russia is like that of a complete foreigner. His notes are fictively addressed to a foreign audience, yet it is the actual Russian audience that understands the errors of judgment arising from the count's superficial knowledge. The work's conclusion, when a more informed political orator appears from behind the mask of the naïve narrator, explains that the chief cause of the count's ignorance is the lack of political satire in the Russian press as a result of censorship. In sum, the work employs an extraterritorial point of view on Russia to propose the paradox that Russian literary culture within Russia is devoid of opportunities to criticize political reality, while Russians outside of Russia simply cannot comprehend it. The Russian Empire, in this sense, is rendered as territory that cannot be represented in the cultural imagination.

Soviet Literary Geographies and Their Critique

The Soviet era inaugurated a new period in the articulation of political geography and in the related cultural imagination. Yet ironically, new Soviet cultural traditions resulted in the partial reinvention of a version of the state myth of the Enlightenment era, the destruction of which Zhivov describes in the essay cited above.[10] Soviet writers were once again fixed in a landscape that was ordered by a higher state power—only now, this was the "Party and state leadership." Mayakovsky's works of the 1920s are typical—for instance, his long poem *The Fifth International* (*Piatyi Internatsional*; see Thorsen 2016). Complete return to an imperial state myth such as that of the eighteenth century would have been impossible, of course. Instead, the strategies of representation and comprehension of political territory worked out in the nineteenth and the start of the twentieth century were semantically reconfigured. Exoticism, for instance, became one of the central elements of early Soviet literature—yet now it embodied the variegation of the reconstructed "affirmative action empire" (Martin 2001). The history of this semantic reconfiguration—of the complex intertwining of non-Russian modernist influences giving rise to a new imperial aesthetic that nevertheless renounced modernism in literature—is yet to be written. Such a history could offer an account, for instance, of the surprising influence on Soviet poetry of Rudyard Kipling's colonial poetic works—likely driven by their combination of exoticism, imperial themes, democratic uplift, self-abnegation, and a complex modernist style combined with a superficial illusion of simplicity.

Beginning in the first half of the 1930s, Soviet propaganda revised the dominant mode of representation of the Russians, rendering them the "leading" nationality of the USSR, and indeed the world, and proclaiming Russian culture in its Soviet instantiation to be a universal civilization linking together all other groups (Brandenberger 2002). Soviet nationalities policy promoted national particularism while nevertheless explaining ethnicity not as a cultural phenomenon but rather as a biological one. Ethnic cultures were subject to a secondary ideological "recomposition" (Cadiot 2007; Gatagova et al. 2009;

Cadiot, Zakharova, and Arel 2010) and russification (Zav'ialov 2007). The Russian language was declared the "language of international communication," undermining any possibility of Russian particularism (Slezkine 1994). In sum, Russians were de facto defined once again as a community of loyal subjects while Soviet aesthetic institutions resemanticized the conception of the writer who expresses cosmic harmony in the framework of a reinvented state myth. Nevertheless, in a reflection of the ideological and rhetorical complexity of this new dispensation, Soviet culture was surprisingly flexible, for all its repressive characteristics, making possible articulation of new models of the interrelationship of the literary imaginary and political space.

Among the most important of these models, in connection with the expanded scope of Russian imperial territory, was representation of Russia as an enormous but unified country. Literary works of the 1930s, quickly canonized, renewed the cultural tradition of eulogy for the country's scale and variegation. Yet the point of view from which these qualities of empire were described was that of the private person, completely devoted to state demands, rather than that of the poet who supports or opposes that state. Typical examples include Vasily Lebedev-Kumach's poem "Broad Is My Native Land" ("Shiroka strana moia rodnaia," 1936), the basis of Isaak Dunaevsky's famous song of the same name, or Konstantin Simonov's work "Homeland" ("Rodina," 1940–41, cited here in its 1941 version):

Touching on three great oceans,
It lies, its cities scattered wide,
Crossed by a net of meridians
Unconquerable, broad, and proud.

But in the hour when the last grenade
Has already fallen into your hand
And in a brief instant, you must recall, at once,
Everything that remains far behind,

You recall not the huge country,
That you have travelled over and studied,
You recall your homeland—the one
That you knew in childhood.

A scrap of land, clinging to three birch trees,
The distant road beyond the little forest,

The little river with the creaking ferry,
The sandy shore with the low willow brush. [. . .]
(1990, 98)

Preservation of the balance by which love for the "little homeland" was simultaneously a component of attachment to the "great homeland" and to the ideology legitimating its expanse and political integration was among the central topics of Soviet literature and culture. This rhetoric of sentimental imperialism took final form in the 1940s and achieved canonical status in large part as a result of the codification during World War II of formulae regarding defense of the fatherland from enemies, including defense of one's native hearth. Among Simonov's most passionate poems, for instance, one finds "Kill Him!" ("Ubei ego," 1942), exhorting the killing of German soldiers, which begins with the words "If you value your home . . ."

These poems as songs that relate the individual's perspective to a larger national agenda call to mind one of the most famous American folk songs, Woody Guthrie's "This Land Is Your Land" (1940), which declares that the country's scale cannot justify unfreedom and social inequality. This critical theme counterbalances the patriotic dither expressed, for example, in Irving Berlin's "God Bless America!" of 1918. Analogues of Berlin's song figured in Soviet official literature, yet nothing similar to Guthrie's was possible. Such social critique was articulated only in underground poetry (of Georgy Obolduev or Daniil Andreev, for instance), or in émigré literature such as Vladimir Nabokov's poem of 1943:

No matter in what battle canvases
the sugary Soviet Rus' appears,
no matter what compassion fills my soul,
I will not bow, I will not be reconciled

with all that filth, and cruelty, and boredom
of mute slavery—no, oh no,
I'm still alive in spirit, still not satiated with separation:
pardon me, but I remain a poet.
(2002, 215)

Here, in response to the Soviet recycling of cultural myths dating to the Enlightenment tasking the poet with representation of imperial territory's unity and grandeur, Nabokov returns to the Romantic countermyth of the poet resisting political exigencies.

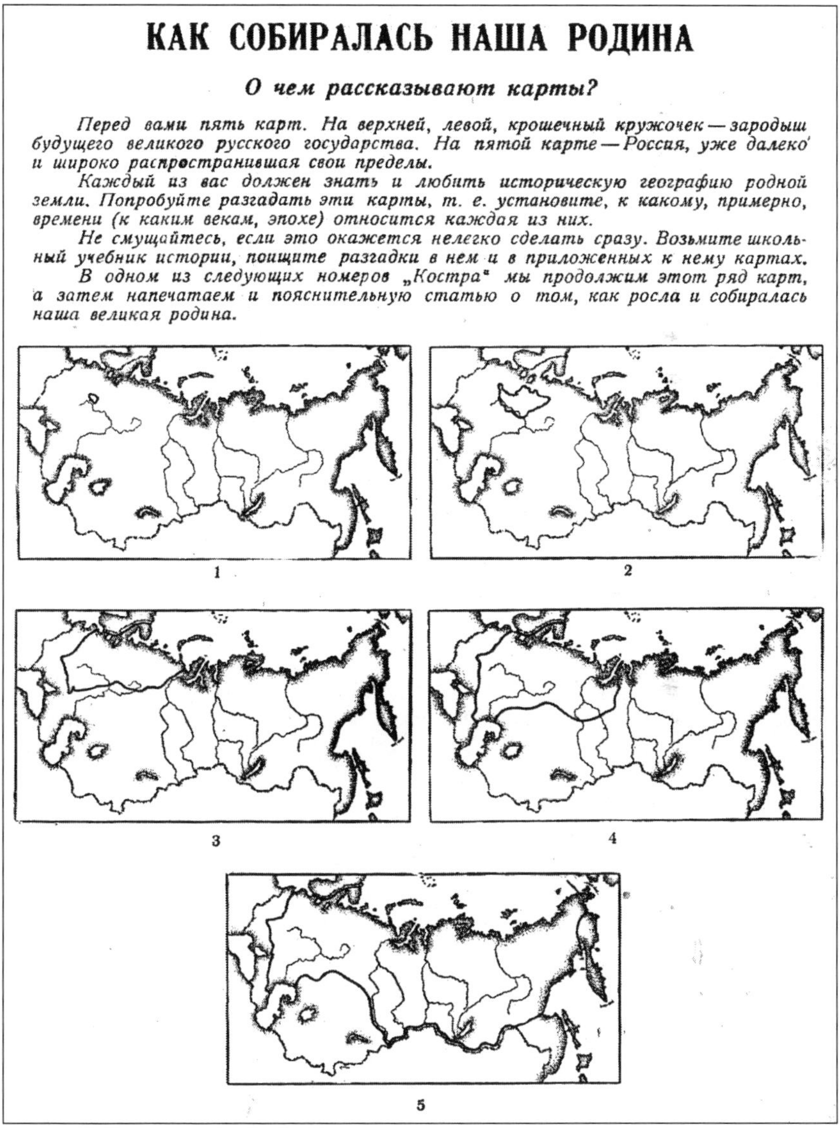

КАК СОБИРАЛАСЬ НАША РОДИНА

О чем рассказывают карты?

Перед вами пять карт. На верхней, левой, крошечный кружочек — зародыш будущего великого русского государства. На пятой карте — Россия, уже далеко и широко распространившая свои пределы.

Каждый из вас должен знать и любить историческую географию родной земли. Попробуйте разгадать эти карты, т. е. установите, к какому, примерно, времени (к каким векам, эпохе) относится каждая из них.

Не смущайтесь, если это окажется нелегко сделать сразу. Возьмите школьный учебник истории, поищите разгадки в нем и в приложенных к нему картах.

В одном из следующих номеров „Костра" мы продолжим этот ряд карт, а затем напечатаем и пояснительную статью о том, как росла и собиралась наша великая родина.

1

2

3

4

5

Figure 7.1. Illustration from the Soviet children's journal *Kostior* (Leningrad, no. 10, 1940), graphically showing "How Our Homeland Was Assembled."

The erosion of Soviet ideology in the 1970s not only evoked radical responses such as Aksyonov's *Island of Crimea* but also new cultural norms in Russian radical nationalist authors' works. In the second half of the 1970s Stanislav Kunyaev was among the leaders of this political-cultural movement (Mitrokhin 2003; Cosgrove 2004, 121–73). Consider his poem of 1980:

> I cast my gaze across the North and the East,
> the sandy and the frozen lands,
> and my rebellious soul is singed
> not by geographical rapture, but by the thought
> that our ancestors progressed unhurriedly
> taking possession of rivers and dialects
> so that the linkage would never wear out
> —half of steel, half made of men
> Let a Mansi man bestow honors upon Ermak,
> and it's time for an Uzbek to praise General Skobelev,
> that there are oil, and forests, and cotton fields,
> and open land on which to place the missiles.[11]
>
> (2017, 74)

Developing Simonov's themes, Kunyaev seemingly intentionally violates the unspoken norm established by the earlier poet, shifting the balance between imperial scale and "little homeland" in favor of empire. Territorial expanse gains independent significance and ceases to be a mode of defense and the matrix in which native hearth and small town are located. Whereas in Simonov's vision the USSR is presented as a great power with no need of further expansion, Kunyaev's work implicitly demands such expansion. Nevertheless, Kunyaev remains within the Soviet geographical frame: for him, the sheer scale of the empire carries primary value. In his poem, the history of conquest and military might gain the status of objects of a quasi-religious cult.

Challenges to this "cult of territory" in the USSR could be mounted only outside of Soviet aesthetics, or at a minimum, outside legally published texts, in unofficial and uncensored literature.[12] In that realm one may observe the Soviet geographical imaginary's deconstruction and the development of alternative approaches to literary representation of political territory, the most striking of which involve representation of the decomposition of Soviet political space. This gesture is characteristic of Soviet-era anti-utopias of the late 1970s and early 1980s. Besides Aksyonov's *Island of Crimea*, discussed above, one may adduce Vladimir Voinovich's *Moscow 2042* (*Moskva 2042*), the action of which takes place in the year referenced in the title. Having traveled to the future, the narrator learns of the existence, at the USSR's center, of Moskorep—the Moscow Communist Republic, consisting of Moscow and its closest suburbs—encircled by a six-meter wall. The remainder of Soviet territory is composed of "filial republics" and lives in even greater poverty than does Moskorep.

A different strategy for deconstruction of Soviet geographical imaginaries that arose in the 1950s–60s involved demonstration of its citational, profoundly discursive nature. Official culture offered "naturalizing" images of the Soviet empire and its geographical position in the world. Disclosure of the discursive, ideological nature of these images was a key subversive response. The first "testing ground" for such strategies was the travelogue—recalling Radishchev's use of that genre to critique dominant conceptions of imperial Russian culture and society—yet in the Soviet context the form's critical use took aim first of all at non-Soviet geographies. Viktor Nekrasov was perhaps the most unusual author of travelogues of the 1950s–60s. The protagonists of his travel essays lucidly understand the literariness and "intertextuality" of their perception of foreign cities. At the start of the essay-sketch "First Acquaintance" ("Pervoe znakomstvo," 1957), Nekrasov throws out a list of phrases characteristic of the conceptual field of Paris in the consciousness of an educated member of the Russian cultural community on the basis of literary (rather than actual) experience:

> . . . Precisely at seven in the morning it was possible to see him in the Bois du Boulogne completing his morning outing on horseback . . .
>
> . . . Every evening, in a fiacre with the curtains drawn on the windows, she would come to him in his bachelor's apartment in the Rue de la Paix . . .
>
> . . . Upon arrival in Paris they rented out three small rooms under the very eaves of the roof, from the windows of which opened out unobstructed views of Saint Sulpice and the Pantheon . . .
>
> [. . .]
>
> What is this? Where did it come from?
>
> From nowhere! I just thought it up. Didn't even think, really, but just dredged it up from somewhere in my memory. It is lodged in there and when it emerges it appears familiar, like postcards of the Eiffel Tower, Notre Dame or the Seine with bridges cutting across it. (2014)

Here Nekrasov demonstrates that the choice of "key objects" of the tourist gaze is not only ideological; it is also predetermined by cultural traditions—a result of cultural and political mythologies.

The transfer of critical insight into the discursive nature of the geographical imaginary to investigation of Russian landscapes was accomplished in Venedikt Erofeev's "poem" (novella) *Moscow-Petushki* (*Moskva-Petushki*, 1970), which might be described as an absurdist travelogue of self-deconstructing Soviet geographies:

> —And where is he now, your Evtiushkin?
> —Who can say where? Either in Siberia or in Central Asia. If he arrived in Rostov and is still alive, that means he is somewhere in Central Asia. And if he didn't make it to Rostov and died, then that means he's in Siberia . . .
> —That's right, I chimed in—in Central Asia you can't die, in Central Asia you can only live. [. . .]
> —And in Siberia? . .
> —In Siberia—no, in Siberia you can't get by. In general, no one lives in Siberia—only blacks live there. They don't ship in any foodstuffs, and there's nothing to drink, let alone "eat." Once a year they bring them embroidered towels from Zhitomir and the blacks hang themselves with them. (2000, 77)

Erofeev's work, as in this example, fragments and deconstructs the USSR's territory into a series of rhetorical figures, laying bare the paradoxical Soviet combination of spatial heterogeneity and banal social and ideological monotony, utilizing geographical toponyms as the basis for absurd metaphors that ironically play on the clichés of everyday discourse.

An additional late Soviet strategy for deconstructing Soviet geographical myths was the "decentralization" of territory, effectively detaching the "little homeland" from the "great" one and making possible reattachment to some other, newly articulated geographical whole in place of Russia or the USSR. Among the first to take such an approach in Russian literature was the poet Gennady Aigi. Beginning in the 1950s, Aigi cultivated an image of a "minor," "unnoticed" life that he declined to link to the grand expanses of the USSR. Instead, his works frequently evoke other highly charged geographical locations and ethno-territorial imaginaries within the USSR or Europe, as in his poem "Kakhab-Roso: The Tomb of Makhmud" ("Kakhab-Roso: Mogila Makhmuda," 1970). Here, he treats his personal relationship with the extraordinary Avar poet Makhmud of Kakhab-Roso (1873–1919) and the place of his burial in his native aul:

> and again it appeared: *Mohammad*'s
> whiteness is so acutely fine here
> from an all-penetrating dream

and he flashed by
flickered flashed by
that weightless island of Kakhab-Roso:

pure grasses of the Holy Spirit!—
the buckwheat's gold *is there*
dusting, insulating it.

(1982, 184)

By unwritten law, the representatives of the "smaller peoples" of the USSR could relate to one another only "via Moscow"—according to the same principle that determined Soviet airplane routes. Aigi rejects this norm and articulates a vision of his own cultural-geographical space that makes possible a dialogue of images above the tomb of Makhmud, uniting Orthodoxy and Islam, both of which were practically excluded from Soviet public discourse in the 1970s. "*Mohammad*'s whiteness" combines references to Mohammad the Prophet and Makhmud from Kakhab-Roso: Makhmud is the Avar form of Mohammad. Bear in mind as well that white is widely associated with purity and holiness in Islam.

This aesthetics of postcolonial "glocalization" was later developed by the poets of the Riga and Fergana poetic schools, which took shape in the 1980s. Both groups conceived their task as poetic interpretation of cultural borderlands. In Riga, that meant the territory between Latvia and Russia and, more generally, between Central Europe and Russia; in Fergana, it meant the zones between Uzbekistan and Russia as well as Central Asian and Russian and Islamic and Christian territories (on the Riga school, see Platt, this volume). In the works of the leader of the Fergana school, Shamshad Abdullaev, references to Sufism are as prominent as those to Italian hermetic poets (Kukulin 2002). Abdullaev's works, although written in Russian, almost never reference Russian locations. They present a web of images relating primarily to Central Asia and Western Europe and evoking both real places and references to films and books, as in his poem "Film" ("Fil'm") of circa 2003:

someone returns with gifts in sandals from the forties,
like father, when he would smile by
the low house—there are no women with bundles on their heads
and even the dogs in the June desert, and a friend
whose left arm lay on your shoulder, were the dry wind
casting sand beneath the burning terrace.
[. . .] . . . the sun is always close, he is still-born, fifty years old [. . .]

one and the same in the mirror, on the bus's running board, in the photo in the yard,
where you imagined in early youth under the crossbeam of the archway
how Swift beat his head against the church wall. You wrote:
"he shot the idyll in a different key,"
motionless silhouettes of a married couple, sitting on floor mats,—
the camera moved only twice (and never above things,
so as not to take account of them) along
the cement barrier leading to the ocean.

(2003, 19–20)

One of the most important features of the Riga and Fergana schools is the absolute absence of references to the Russian Empire or the USSR as a grand, boundless unity and frame for all other geographical visions. Russian culture, in the works of both groups, appears as "younger," and minor—in precisely the sense of "minor literature" articulated by Gilles Deleuze and Félix Guattari (1986 [1975]). In these works, as in Aigi's poem, Russian culture is revealed as centrifugal rather than centripetal. The "periphery" of Russian culture becomes a space for the formation of productive cultural hybrids.

Contemporary Literature between Text and Territory

Contemporary Russian literature has built on the Soviet and imperial traditions, extending their rhetorical and ideological complexity in a new period of contested geographies in culture and politics. One may observe a wide variety of strategies aimed at problematization of Russia's habitual "territorial image," and in consequence, of the relationship between text and territory, which may be divided into four approaches: expansionist, subversive, disjunctive, and marginalizing. In expansionist works, the text evokes a broader geographical and ideological unity than the territory of Russia proper, in a reflection of the Russian politics of national expansion and resurgent great-power aspirations. Such works take up the legacy of late Soviet nationalist authors such as Kunyaev. Perhaps the most overt and radical contemporary representatives of this strategy are Zakhar Prilepin (b. 1975), in particular his journalistic volume *Troubles Not of Others* (*Ne chuzhaia smuta*, 2015), and Eduard Limonov (b. 1943), with his collection of journalistic prose and blog posts *Kiev Kaputt* (2015). Both, in treatment of Russian aggression against Ukraine, treat the Russian border as arbitrary and proclaim that Russian literature speaks for the "Russian world" beyond the boundaries of Russia. In his most recent works, such as his extended essay "Troop" ("Vzvod"), Prilepin overtly presents Russian literature as an element of an imperial expansion project:

> Classic Russian authors went to war left and right, or, if there was no war, served in the military, at the ready to use their weapons at any hour of any day.
>
> Moreover, they participated in each and every war that befell Russia, and wrote about them all as well.
>
> [. . .] "Job vacancy for a poet," we think, "is an absence reflecting the fact that today the poet, who should strive 'for everything,' strives only for himself." (2017, 703, 705)

At this same end of the spectrum one finds authors such as Vadim Negaturov (1959–2014), an amateur poet-lyricist and political activist of the imperial-nationalist movement "Antimaidan," who died in the fire at Odesa's House of Trade Unions on May 2, 2014. His poem "March of Kulikovo Field" rejects present state borders in the name of an imagined Rus', composed of the three east Slavic peoples:

By the Light of Truth, givn' by God in heaven,
The Slavs' Might is reborn
and the three parts of Rus' have been strengthened in unity—
Belarus, Ukraine and Russia . . .

Refrain:
Onward, Sons of Rus'! Onward, Sons of Rus'!
Shatter the horde of infidel scum!
Now Rus' is again in danger! Today it's our turn
to prove our love to the Fatherland!
. . . to prove our love with action!
. . . to prove our love with blood!
. . . to prove our love with our lives!
[. . .]

From overseas skyscrapers, from secret burrows,
Satan's Darkness spreads like venom
to poison Rus', to breed strife
between Slavs united in sacral unity.

> But for the enemy, even surpassing Satan in evil,
> There lies in wait in Rus', with severe patience:
> Stalingrad, and Poltava, and the valor of
> the Borodino and Kulikovo Fields!

Note that not only does Negaturov's "Rus'" exceed the Russian Federation's borders, but it also fails to coincide with the historical USSR, in which, of course, many other territories besides the Slavic republics were included. This innovative reinscription of the cultural borders of Russia may be compared with Alexander Solzhenitsyn's proposals for the partial dissolution of the USSR, expressed in his 1990 political manifesto *How Can We Reconstruct Russia* (Solzhenitsyn 1995–97). However, Solzhenitsyn's ideas, predating the Soviet collapse, were aimed at the liberation of certain non-Slavic Soviet republics ("Empire, get off our back!" he exclaims at one point), whereas Negaturov, in contrast, articulated his religiously grounded Russian nationalism as a justification for imperial expansion and the return of Ukraine to Russian control.

In contrast to these patriotic legitimations of empire, subversive authors propose not a future or necessary expansion of territory but problematization of the very concept of "Russia" as a unified ideological and geographical construct deriving its central meaning from scale and "boundlessness." The works of these authors represent the continuation of the late Soviet traditions that began with Aigi. Perhaps the most impressive contemporary example of this approach is that of Denis Osokin (b. 1975), who became widely known following the critical success of Aleksei Fedorchenko's film *Finches* (*Ovsianki*), based on the author's short novel of that name, which received a number of prizes at the 2010 Venice Film Festival. Osokin himself was honored for best screenplay at the Russian Nika Film Festival.

Osokin's method can be described as a postmodern version of Latin American magical realism. In the Latin American case, the source material for "magical" imagery is in general derived African and Native American myths. Osokin turns instead to the myths and literature of the Finno-Ugric peoples, such as the Mari and Komi. In the late 1990s, the poet Sergei Stratunovsky compared the cultural situation of these peoples with that of the Irish or Native Americans:

> At times, Russian culture's total disregard for its own Irish or native Americans—the Komi, Udmurts, Mari and Mordvins—seems almost paradoxical. In distinction from their brethren in feathers or kilts, our indigenous peoples were too unromantic to inspire a Longfellow or a Cooper from among us and too lacking in sophistication to give rise to a Macpherson or a Yeats of their own. Ethnocide

> and linguicide flattened out Europe's far east with great success: Pushkin in Boldino and Lermontov in Tarkhany [the names of the poets' estates] never even suspected that their ancestral homes were located in Mordvinian lands. (1999)

In Osokin, however, these peoples finally found their Longfellow—albeit a postcolonial one—or perhaps even their own Gerald Vizenor.

The basic elements of Osokin's oeuvre are book-length cycles of poetry and short-form prose. Each is provided with fictive publication data, usually indicating place of origin as a provincial Russian city with an ethnically mixed population (the Russian-Mari city of Vetluga, the capital of the Komi republic Syktyvkar, etc.). Indicated years of publication are at times actual (2013, for example) and at others obviously fictive, such as 1926 or 1919. Some of his works are fictively presented as translations from other languages, typically of "smaller" peoples—Komi or Latvian—and provided with corresponding publication data, such as "Alūksne, 1973" (indicating a small northwestern Latvian city).

Osokin's primary project is the articulation of a geographically and ethnically decentralized representation of Russia. The Russian provinces are understood as a nonimperial yet still maximally multiethnic space of "networked" interrelationships between ethnic and cultural groups. These interrelationships themselves figure as one of Osokin's key objects of representation. The fictive dates and places of publication of Osokin's book cycles are a means to radicalize his gesture of decentralization and to create ironic distance between the author, on the one hand, and the text and its narrator(s), on the other. For him, the provinces' "unnoticed," "quiet" existence does not license their kenotic glorification, as was the case with Fedor Tiutchev, for instance in his classic poem "These poor villages . . ." ("Eti bednye seleniia," 1855). Osokin's works do not represent the non-Russian ethnicities of Russia only or primarily as subaltern. Rather, images derived (or stylized) from the mythology of the smaller ethnic groups allow him to deconstruct conceptions of the unity and homogeneity of Russian culture and territory.

Another author who has worked to reconstruct the relationship between culture and politically inscribed territory in Russia is Sergei Zavyalov (b. 1958), who, in distinction to Osokin, openly proclaims himself a postcolonial writer. His works present the Volga region about which he writes as a palimpsest in which the "Russian" layer is merely the uppermost—an overlay above a Finno-Ugric substrate. Russian territory appears in his poetry as populated by half-assimilated Finno-Ugric peoples—not simply as a heterogeneous space but as one charged with lost, forgotten meanings. Consider two examples from the "Birchbark inscriptions of the Mordvin-Erzya and the Mordvin-Moksha" ("Moksherzian' kir'govon' grammatat / berestianye gramoty mordvy-erzi i mortvy-mokshi," 1997–98):

no place on he
to kiss

how dark he is
with dark spot how hair
twisted as desired

and on he
word like Moscow song
short
like life itself

Vir' kuchkaniasa   pargu kelunia
Priasonza morsi   cinniay narmonnia
Vaj kuva moraj   siiak avardi
Chik-chirik-chirik   morai-kol'gondi

How in the forest   *a downy little birch*
And on it sings   *a throaty bird*
Oh how it sings   *and cries*
Tweet-twee-twee   *cries and mourns*

(1998, 32)

In the excerpt's first half, the Russian language is grammatically and semantically deformed, seemingly by the concealed, half-forgotten presence of other languages at some deeper level (Kukulin 2012). The second half incorporates a fragment from a Mordvinian folk song in the author's translation. In its poetics and imagery, it recalls a Russian folk song, but in the context of the reprinted original it projects more exotic and "authentic" connotations.

The third, disjunctive strategy offers descriptions of the collapse of Russia into separate states, most commonly distinguished not by ethnic but rather by ideological specificities. We may refer here to the works adduced in the introduction to this chapter. To these may be added, for instance, Alexander Delfinov's recent poem, which mirrors the approach of Sorokin's *Telluria*:[13]

—Everything is so complicated now!
—They've destroyed the country.
And we used to live in great Russia!
—And lived in prosperity.
—In prosperity. The entire world
Feared that mighty state! And today
The country's broken up into fragments.
[. . .]
In connection with damage
To the railroad infrastructure
Rail linkages between
The West-European Russian Republic,
The Ural Peoples Republic,
The Siberian Independent Republic,
The Great Buryat Khural,
And the Far Eastern Republic
Have been temporarily interrupted.[14]

The poem's peculiar effect derives from combination of a fantastical environment with a familiar sensibility of nostalgia for a "great state" that "the entire world feared"—a sensibility that during the 1990s was a continuous topos both in everyday discourse and in literary works by conservative figures, such as the following:

Farewell, mighty state,
One sixth of the world's surface
That in making the crossing
We failed to safely carry over.
(**Boris Primerov** [1938–95],
cit. in Guseinov 2005, 33)

Premonitions of collapse, in the case of both Sorokin and Delfinov, evoke the literature of the era of the Civil War, such as Erenburg's novel *The Extraordinary Adventures of Julio Jurenito and His Disciples* (*Neobychainye pokhozhdeniia Khulio Khurenito i ego uchenikov*, 1922), in which the territory of the country gives rise to a multitude of autonomous formations, issuing their own money and organizing regular armies. In general, such direct descriptions of the collapse of the country as an ideological unity stand in opposition to the subversive works, which problematize the concept of Russia as a cultural whole. Schematically, the subversive position in this implicit polemic proposes that whether or not Russia collapses is immaterial, given that it *already* lacks wholeness—Osokin and Zavyalov's stance is that of selective solidarity with one or another element of a constellation of fragments.

Finally, we may close this survey of contemporary literary examinations of Russian geography with consideration of a strategy of destabilization of dominant myths based on the aesthetics of geographical marginality, evident in the works of the contemporary poets Leonid Shvab, Ekaterina Sokolova, and Arseny Rovinsky. These authors, in a manner in some respects analogous to those of the Fergana and Riga poetic schools, partially continue Aigi's aesthetics of geographic imagination. The consistent chronotope of their works, unusual for Russian literature, is organized around or beyond the margins of a large, but somewhat incompetent state—a far-flung existence in a period of imperial crisis, far from the metropolitan center. The state itself is not named, and its image is familiar yet somewhat effaced:

> Not a single airstrip around
> The naked steppe on the map, salt marshes.
>
> (**Shvab** 2005)

> We'll start stomping the empty field
> that we've leased in a neighboring land
> without children or Slavic habits
> maybe something good will come of it:
> a residence permit,
> or an authorization for work.
>
> (**Sokolova** 2017, 46)

After the publication of Shvab's first poetic collections, critics drew comparisons with the indeterminate time and place of action of Dino Buzzati Traverso's novel-fable *The Tatar Steppe* (*Il deserto dei Tartari*, 1940).[15] Indeed, these final examples demonstrate that a passive and more subtle strategy of "benign neglect" of dominant cultural geographies may also be applied to deconstruct and revisit the habitual (for Russian literature) relationships between geography and culture.

In sum, Russia's contemporary letters and political space are sites of contestation between many distinct visions of the proper and likely configuration of Russia's boundaries and influence. These reflections of the instability of Russian political and cultural geography follow the collapse of an empire that still persists in minds and social practices—a collapse that some seek to reverse.

Return, or Departure

In Sorokin's *Telluria*, with which we began, the description of Russia's future collapse is peppered with references to Russian literature of the 1920s, with its "still raw" memories of the Civil War. For instance, the scene in chapter 12 of a "psychological attack" by robots on a passenger train, filled with private traders in foodstuffs (shuttle traders), recalls an episode out of a computer game or a science fiction thriller yet also incorporates a large proportion of language drawn from dialect and conversational speech in a rhythmic prose construction. The narrative overtly evokes the "ornamental style" of Artyom Vesyoly in his novel *Russia, Washed with Blood* (*Rossiia, krov'iu umytaia*, 1927–28) or the stylized speech presented in Alexander Serafimovich's novel *Iron Flood* (*Zheleznyi potok*, 1924). Both authors combine quasi-folkloric neologisms and rare dialectical forms with modernist ellipses and rhythmic prose. For Soviet authors, the fragmentation of the country in the years of the Civil War was a temporary condition and the reassembly of the country's wholeness a progressive historical achievement. In Sorokin's novel, however, the country's lack of wholeness is an established fact, while the conception of historical progress is in principle discredited:

> "Robots!" bawled the engineer Keria so loudly that they heard it in the third car of the train.
>
> They raised their hackles in a flash:
>
> Their hearts jolted and missed a beat.
>
> [. . .]
>
> They raised a clatter.
>
> They raised a natter.
>
> They crushed to the windows, clinging to what have you.
>
> And beyond the windows—the steppe. Heat haze. And a flash on the horizon, as though someone had raised a steel fence: fetters.
>
> Robots.
>
> They step broadly . . . All out. Dragnet. Just because—they are many; no need to economize. (2013)

In addition to its stylistic reference to modernist prose, the episode's plot evokes the "psychological attack" of the Whites in Sergei and Georgy Vasilev's famous film *Chapaev* (1934)—in particular in the phrase "Shiroko idut . . ." ("They step broadly . . ."), a reference to the Vasilevs' "Krasivo idut . . ." ("They step beautifully . . ."). In sum, Sorokin's novel balances between political prognostication of Russia's collapse, a theme that has become so frequent in the 2000s and 2010s, and research into this phenomenon's cultural basis. As the work demonstrates, such prognostication is based in deep Russian political and cultural histories, reaching back to the early twentieth century and beyond. Sorokin's work recalls, along with the many other authors and traditions treated in this chapter, the important contributions of Russian literary culture to both construction and deconstruction of the Russian imperial, Soviet, and post-Soviet Russian geographical imagination. In consideration of these traditions, we gain a lucid vision of the fissures between empire and ethnicity, "small" and "great" homelands, centers and peripheries. We also gain access to countergeographies of the borderland, alternate ethno-territorial visions, and geographies of "minor literature." Here, it is important to note that the discourses of "wholeness" and "unity" are to this day supported by dominant voices and institutions, while their subversion is largely the province of "counterdominant" writing and "minor literatures." While such a conclusion may be unremarkable, in the above I have endeavored to present the diversity of modes in which such subversions and reconstructions of the geographic imagination are carried out.

The transformation of the political and cultural life of Russia in 2014–17 toward a sharp increase in xenophobia, intolerance of nonconformism, "cold civil war," and renewed imperial expansionism is founded on the country's political and cultural development over the preceding decades. The tipping point, in this regard, has been identified variously by various political scientists, who have suggested dates as late as 2000 and as early as 1993 or 1991 as the start of Russia's phasic return to imperial models of geographic imagination and geopolitical action. Be that as it may, this shift in the trajectory of development of Russian society is today more and more apparent and serves as the basis for new cultural conflicts. Yet as I demonstrate in the necessarily general overview above, the last few years' shifts have been elements of complex and bifurcated processes with deep historical roots. For the middle 2010s also witnessed the intensification of processes of cultural diversification that had begun long before and passed through many stages.

The most important innovation in the geographical imagination of contemporary Russian literature is deconstruction of the dichotomy described by Zhivov—the "pendulum swing" between the cult of the emperor or state as demiurge and the cult of the poet who stands in opposition to that state. As we have seen, some contemporary authors, such as Negaturov, have attempted to synthesize these two cultural strategies, transforming the neoromantic poet into a prophet of state exigency. Thankfully, others, like Osokin, have carried out different projects, revealing the territory of Russia as a multilayered palimpsest of many cultures. Such works create a new image of Russian territory—centrifugal, but not expansionist, directed toward attention to the cultural models of the peripheries that subvert authoritative ("central") norms. In this vision of territory, Russia is a space of interaction of various cultural realities, one that is open to the complexity both of the world within and the world outside. As both of these contemporary projects reveal, in an era of regret and anxiety over Russian state collapse and turmoil around its (re)expansion, the cultural problem of Russianness—whether conceived as an overarching matrix of many cultures and peoples, unique ethnic identity, or nation wrapped in an imperial destiny—has yet to be resolved.

Notes

This chapter was prepared within the framework of the Basic Research Program at the National Research University Higher School of Economics (HSE) and supported with a subsidy by the Russian Academic Excellence Project "5–100." The author wishes to thank Natal'ia Poltavtseva and Kevin M. F. Platt for valuable discussions during the work on this chapter.

1. The state's residents are divided into three unequal categories: "blacks" (descendants of Russian Germans and their spouses), "blues" (Slavs), and "yellows" (Turkish peoples). In this Nazified Russia, Jews have been utterly eliminated.

2. All translations in this chapter are by Kevin M. F. Platt, unless otherwise indicated.

3. In a reflection of this state of affairs, external observers during the Cold War not only continued to habitually refer to the USSR as "Russia" but also directed public and scholarly attention almost exclusively to Russians within Soviet space (Hirsch 2005), with the exception of CIA analysts, who periodically compiled rather speculative reports on the potential for protest in Soviet peripheral territories.

4. Lyrics retrieved from http://megalyrics.ru/lyric/timur-shaov/tranzitnyi-poiezd-chieriez-ukrainu.htm (accessed January 12, 2018). "Moskali" is a common anti-Russian slur in Ukraine. "Yellow-blue" ("zhovto-blakitnyi") is a Ukrainianism, referring to the colors of the Ukrainian flag, which has long been used in Russian as a dismissive label for supporters of Ukrainian national consciousness. Note that following the outbreak of Russian aggression in Ukraine in 2014, Shaov was an outspoken critic of Russian interference and the associated wave of Russian propaganda (Sotnik 2015).

5. This phrase, often quoted in research on politics, is in fact not a precise report of Migranian's or Kokoshin's words but rather Guseinov's reconstruction based on texts of the two figures.

6. Absent any political implications, the term "Russian world" has been used in various senses since the early nineteenth century. For more on the post-Soviet "Russian World" project, see Gorham, this volume.

7. See also the works of Kagansky's mentor, distinguished Russian geographer Boris Rodoman, who in the 1970s founded the contemporary study of the "territorial imaginary" of Russian culture. For his current views, see Rodoman 2004.

8. For other exceptions to this cultural institutional structure, see Ospovat 2007.

9. On the cultural semantics of the ode in eighteenth-century Russian literature, see Rogov 2006, 80.

10. Note that previous critics of Socialist Realism have compared it to the aesthetics of the eighteenth century (Siniavskii 1989 [1957]).

11. This jingoist original version was softened (apparently at the insistence of the censorship or editors) in the poem's first publication (in the annual almanac *Day of Poetry*, 1986) and printed only in 2017. However, even in softened form, Kunyaev's poem provoked the indignation of liberal Soviet critics (see Sarnov 1989 [1988], 245).

12. The distinction between unofficial and uncensored literature is that while the former was published, its authors sought to "outmaneuver" Soviet censorship by means of various partial compromises that allowed expression of independent aesthetic or social conceptions. The latter was never published officially and circulated only through informal channels such as samizdat to a smaller readership. Both systems were fully developed during the 1960s–80s.

13. In correspondence with this chapter's author, Delfinov remarked that he had not read *Telluria* and had no knowledge of its subject matter when he composed this poem.

14. The poem was posted on Delfinov's Facebook page on October, 6, 2015, www.facebook.com/alexander.delphinov (accessed January 12, 2018).

15. One may also sense in these works the legacy of the stylistics of Konstantin Vaginov (1899–1934), whose works critiqued the "grand" ideologies and imperial ambitions of his era.

Part Two

Russian Cultures at Large

When Soft Power Hardens

The Formation and Fracturing of Putin's "Russian World"

Michael S. Gorham

> A truly strong diaspora can only exist—I have no doubt about this whatsoever—in connection to a strong state.
>
> **Vladimir Putin**, 2001

> A silent diaspora is not a world, but merely emigration.
>
> **Valery Tishkov**, 2007

The Birth of a New World

On the eve of the 2004 presidential elections, Vladimir Putin's political handlers found themselves looking for core concepts and ideas that could articulate a positive vision of the future. Western models of capitalism and democracy had been tainted by ten years of chaos and mismanagement under Boris Yeltsin during an era that became codified, under Putin, as the "wild '90s" or even "the New Time of Troubles." At the same time, leaders wished to capitalize on the Russian Federation's economic revival (much thanks to petrodollars) and project the state more robustly as a global player. Looking for a more organically "Russian" conceptual anchor to improve global perceptions of a nation resurgent, political technologists turned in part to a loose mixture of language, culture, religion, and history, symbolically unified under the umbrella concept of the "Russian World" (*Russkii mir*). Russian language had long enjoyed special status as a "great and mighty" bulwark of national pride and potent symbol of "Russianness." Not only was it something that Russian nationals had been taught from an early age to regard as sacrosanct: the institution of language had the added ability to expand Russia's geographical borders to a broader, linguistic and cultural nation of global Russians in a manner that unified "compatriots abroad" (*sootechestvenniki za rubezhom*) around a concept that remained largely insulated from political differences.[1] Be they recently "beached" emigrants, washed up on the shores of newly independent countries after the Soviet collapse, or earlier generations of Russian émigrés in Europe, Israel, and the United States, this global Russian community, united by language and culture, presented an opportunity for Putin's resurging Russia to grow its appeal internationally and establish a new, more positive brand in a geopolitical landscape that tended to view Russia as a Cold War relic (if it noticed Russia at all).[2] In June 2007, in conjunction with Russian Language Day and during the Year of the Russian Language, the Putin team institutionalized this attempt to use language and culture as a tool for soft power by establishing the Russkiy Mir Foundation (Fond Russkii Mir).[3] With generous backing from the state, private sector, and Russian Orthodox Church, the foundation rapidly established centers in cities across the near- and distant abroad, distributing instructional materials, hosting conferences and festivals, and generally promoting the use and celebration of Russian language and culture.[4]

With the Russkiy Mir Foundation and the broader notion of "Russian World" at the center of focus, this chapter considers what happens when state ideologues attempt to harness productive traditions of language and culture to create a notion of global identity designed to identify and unite a globally dispersed nation of like-minded "compatriots" inclined, at least, to empathize with that state's fate and interests, and at best, to work actively to promote them. While meeting with greater suspicion among non-Russians from the newly independent states, this undertaking held out promise to promote Russia and Russian globally in a far more fruitful manner than the export of guns or dirty money. In the wake of Russia's 2014 annexation of Crimea, however, when Putin invoked the Russian World and the need to protect it as a main rationale for Russia's military invasion, the concept swiftly transformed from a tool for soft power into one for hard power. Once intertwined with the language of civilizations and their inevitable clashes (Huntington 1996), the Russian World lost much of its innocent association with Russia's celebrated cultural heritage and became, instead, a rhetorical tool for justifying, first, Russian international aggression in Ukraine, and subsequently, the successive closing off of Russian society from the global community. Now imagined as surrounded by enemies whose lifestyles and policies posed an existential threat, the Russian World became transformed, rhetorically, from an instrument for expanding national boundaries beyond geographical borders to a means of rationalizing further isolation, a trend that served to alienate, rather than rally, many of the very target populations it was designed to win over.

Protean Origins of the Concept

Several sources offer thorough accounts of the history of the Russian World concept prior to its adoption by the Putin administration (Gorham 2011; Laruelle 2015). Most important for my purposes here is the term's protean associative arc. Most scholars trace it back to the nineteenth-century tsarist ideologue and Putin favorite, Sergei Uvarov—the architect of the slogan "Orthodoxy, Autocracy, Nationality," which legitimized imperial rule for over a century (Girenko 2014; Abarinov and Sidorova 2015; Laruelle 2015). The fact that none of these studies provides more concrete evidence for this lineage suggests that the association is affective in nature: when thinking of the present-day concept of the Russian World, audiences tend to associate it with a pre-Soviet imperial ideology predicated on the concept of shared cultural and spiritual heritage.[5] As such, this connection evokes associations with a strong central authority, the spiritual and institutional authority of the Orthodox Church, and sensitivity to the needs and beliefs of the people, or *narod*, as the glue that binds (and legitimates) the other two elements of the civilizational triad. "For the Throne and Church to maintain their might," Uvarov wrote in 1848, "they must also support the feeling of nationality (*narodnost'*) that links them."

The term "Russian World" appeared after the Soviet collapse—and particularly in the Putin era—largely thanks to its protean symbolic potential. And it did so among a broad range of ideological voices, not all aligned with the Putin administration's programmatic views. For Russian Orthodox clergy, it became a potent symbol of Slavic unity ("Russia, Ukraine, and Belorussia are the core of the Russian World" [Patriarch Kirill 2009]); for the red-brown coalition of communists and nationalists—a patriotic rallying cry:

> Our misfortune is that our current Russian rulers (*rossiiskie vlasti*) do not need either a strong and mighty Russia or a powerful Russian World. As always in our country, we need to battle with this misfortune all together. Only a change in

> power (*vlast'*) will save Russia. The KPRF must lead this battle and do everything possible so that the Russian World has a reliable core—Russia.[6] (**Nikitin** 2006)

> It would be correct to consider the Russian World a great state (*gosudarstvennost'*) existing on the territory of Eurasia, sometimes getting bigger, sometimes smaller, and the purpose of this state is messianic.[7] (**Prokhanov** 2014)

In contrast to these essentially nationalist views, however, it also served as the impetus for a Western-oriented economic model for Russia's future in the work of the philosopher Petr Shchedrovitsky, among others: "The strategy of forming post-national statehood in Russia can be realized with the support of the resources of the Russian World, professional and trans-professional schools and networks, traditions of innovative thinking and action shaped in the engineering and social-humanities spheres—by and large competitive and on occasion the leading educational technologies" (Shchedrovitskii 2000). Each vision carved out different borders for its own conception of the Russian World—be it pan-Slavic (esp. Russian, Ukrainian, and Belarusian) in the case of the church, evocative of the former Soviet Union for the communists, "Eurasian" for the nationalists, and Western-oriented for the liberal-economic view.[8] The very protean nature of the term accounted for its conceptual vigor: an ideological Rorschach, it was vague enough for advocates from different parts of the political spectrum to see in it what they wished.

Vladimir Putin invoked the term as early as 2001, in an address to the Congress of Compatriots in Moscow, declaring that "the concept of 'Russian World' ha[d] for time immemorial extended far beyond the geographical borders of Russia and even far beyond the borders of the Russian ethnos" (Putin 2001). But it was not until 2004 that the Russian World became a cornerstone of Putin's national policy, thanks to his then chief political technologists, Vladislav Surkov and Gleb Pavlovsky. With a population (and president) turning increasingly sour on Western-style democracy, Surkov and Pavlovsky saw the more historical and national conception of the Russian World as a critical complement to their new policy of "sovereign democracy"—Surkov's vision for a distinctively Russian form of democracy, unencumbered by foreign traditions or meddling. As one participant in the early meetings concerning the initiatives described it, "The concept of sovereign democracy turned out to be key. The gist of it was that the political system of our country, as it developed, must remain under national control and definitely conform to the particularities of the Russian cultural tradition. This turn to the national culture—not in the narrow political sense, but in the broader sense—had to have both an historical and a contemporary rationale. An extrapolation in both space and time. The unifying concept of the Russian World arose as a result" (Visnushenko 2014). While historical and imperial connotations strongly influenced early adoption of the term, according to Surkov the "democratic transformation of the Russian World" was still clearly part of the plan but in a manner building on the "historical foundation of national statehood" (Visnushenko 2014). This delicate dance between past and present, tradition and transformation, civilizational conservation and transnational consolidation (and self-promotion) lay at the core of the Russkiy Mir Foundation project launched two years later in 2007.

Soft Power Emergent: Russian World as International Brand

According to the foundation's executive director, Viacheslav Nikonov, the foundation was modeled after other highly respected institutions for the international promotion of national cultures—such as "the British Council, the Cervantes, Goethe, Dante, and Confucius Institutes, and the Francophonie program" (Sidibe 2007). The initiative's target population, moreover, extended well beyond the Russian Federation's borders and was by no means restricted to ethnic Russians. As the organization's posted "ideology" put it,

> The Russian World is not just Russians (*russkie*), not just citizens of the Russian Federation (*rossiiane*), not just compatriots (*sootechestvenniki*) in the countries of the near and distant abroad, emigrants, natives of Russia and their descendants. It is also foreign citizens who speak Russian, who study or teach it, all those who are sincerely interested in Russia and who are concerned about her future.
>
> All strata of the Russian World—poly-ethnic, multi-denominational, socially and ideologically heterogeneous, multicultural, geographically segmented—are unified through the recognition of a sense of belonging to Russia.
>
> By forming Russkiy Mir as a global project, Russia is discovering a new identity, new opportunities for effective collaboration with the rest of the world and additional impulses for its own development. (quoted in Gorham 2011, 31)

The foundation's stated goals varied little over its first years of operation. The organization's 2010 Annual Report listed the following priorities:

> Promoting Russian language and literature instruction throughout the world;
> Popularizing Russian language and culture;

Supporting scholarly research and projects that advance the study, the preservation, and the development of Russian language, culture, traditions, and the history and philosophy of the Russian World;
Spreading knowledge about Russia;
Cooperating with diasporas, organizations of compatriots, and interest-related associations;
Promoting the creation of and networking among Russian-language social and cultural enlightenment structures overseas;
Promoting expert, scholarly, and educational exchanges;
Supporting Russian-language mass media. (Fond Russkii Mir 2011, 2)

Headlines from the ledger of announcements posted in the foundation's daily briefing largely reflected these priorities, as seen in the following selections from a November 3, 2009, post:

"Russian compatriots discuss cultural and social issues at a conference in Madrid."
"The classic of dramaturgy, Leonid Zorin, marks his 85th birthday."
"Free Russian language courses for children are offered at the Russian cultural center in Tel Aviv."
"The latest congress of the Russian community (*obshchina*) of Azerbaijan to take place on November 8."
"A majority of Russian Federation citizens (*rossiian*) are certain that political repression is unacceptable." ("Novosti Russkogo Mira" 2009)

For the most part, activities in the early years stuck to such "soft" cultural and linguistic initiatives, particularly with regard to the West (e.g., Spain, Israel, and Austria). On occasion, programs related to trade issues might resonate with international relations, particularly within the near abroad. Even at this relatively early stage, however, the foundation also at times operated in a grayer zone, such as that of minority language rights, where, under the right circumstances, soft-power tools could quite easily serve to launch hard-power political battles over geopolitical spheres of interest (cf. Laruelle 2015, 12). Indeed, while the annual Assembly of the Russkiy Mir, even as early as 2008, gushed with celebratory praise for participants' efforts to promote Russian language and culture, it also provided a forum for ardent voices in support of a more robust defense of Russian speakers abroad, particularly in regions where Russian cultural heritage was perceived as under siege. Tucked between reports from Viktor Sadovnichy, rector of Moscow State University, and Liudmilla

Verbitskaya, president of the International Association of Teachers of Russian Language and Literature, the head of the Ukrainian Council for Russian Compatriots argued that "cultural events were insufficient," given the "cultural genocide of the Russian people" taking place in Ukraine ("Kruglyi stol" 2008).

Such appearances of more overt political causes among "softer" cultural programming should come as no surprise, given that the Russkiy Mir Foundation was partially bankrolled by the state. Structurally, while designed on the model of a Western NGO, a good portion of the foundation's administration had links to the government. Its executive director, Viacheslav Nikonov, had been political advisor to Putin, Yeltsin, and Gorbachev, and its board of directors included the ministers of foreign affairs (Lavrov) and education (Fursenko), rubbing shoulders with university presidents and cultural leaders such as the film director Nikita Mikhalkov. Yet in terms of budget, architecture, and mission, Russkiy Mir still stood apart from Rossotrudnichestvo, the larger, more generously funded federal agency with pre-Putin (even Soviet) roots, charged with overseeing Russia's relations with member states of the Commonwealth of Independent States and "compatriots" in general. From its inception in Soviet times (under different names), Rossotrudnichestvo had a more overt orientation on foreign policy. Its focus on compatriots reflected the primacy of birthright and highlighted the potential for citizenship.[9] While Russkiy Mir sought to win over hearts and souls through language and culture, Rossotrudnichestvo focused more on protecting the rights of Russians in the near abroad.[10]

The soft-power tactics of the Russkiy Mir Foundation were designed to appeal to a broader target audience—not just those Russian-language speakers residing in Russia's "sphere of influence" and the near abroad but the estimated 30 million Russian speakers living outside of Russia across the globe—be they heirs of the waves of emigration preceding the Soviet collapse, of the "accidental diaspora" of 1991, or of the more economically motivated wave that followed it (Laruelle 2006; Inozemtsev 2014; Krechetnikov 2015).[11] When the idea of the Russian World became more prominent in Kremlin ideology, language and culture were central in Putin's conception, as was unification—not just of ethnic Russians, as he explained in a speech to intellectuals on the eve of the Year of the Russian Language, but of "all for whom the Russian word and culture are dear, wherever they may live, in Russia or beyond its borders." The centrality of the concept to Putin's agenda is clear from his injunction to his audience to "use this phrase more often—'Russian World'" (quoted in Abarinov and Sidorova 2015).

Putin was quite explicit that the concept should be a unifying force rather than a tool for division or antagonism. Thanks to the common bond of the

Russian language, as he asserted in his annual address to the Federal Assembly in 2007, hatred, xenophobia, and nationalism were inconceivable in the Russian World: "[The Russian language] is not only the guardian for an entire layer of truly global accomplishments, it is a living space (*zhivoe prostranstvo*) for the millions making up the Russian World, which, of course, is significantly broader than Russia itself. For this reason, as the common achievement of many peoples, the Russian language can never become a language of hatred or enmity, xenophobia or nationalism" (Putin 2007). Echoes of this peaceful, inclusive notion of the Russian World, grounded in language and culture, emanated from the pronouncements and literature of the foundation itself. As one early Russkiy Mir promotional video put it: "Russkiy Mir is creating a new global informational and cultural space, because the Russian World is not just a unified people. It is a people living in the world with themselves and with the rest of the world. The key word here is 'peace,' as in the absence of confrontation.[12] The Russian World is Russian reconciliation, concord, Russian harmony, unity, the schisms of the twentieth century surmounted" (quoted in Gorham 2011, 33). The open, harmonious nature of the initiative also stood out in the language of high-ranking politicians such as Duma deputy Aleksei Ostrovsky, then chair of the Duma committee on "Matters concerning the CIS and ties with compatriots," who underscored the absence of borders or ideology: "We have to understand that there are no—and cannot be any—borders of the Russian World. It is important to avoid politicization, that is, the search for deficiencies and possibly enemies as well, since the concept of 'Russian World' is free of ideological and other conflicts" (2008). In the heat of the controversial election season of 2011, the Medvedev presidency's chief ideologist, Igor Iurgens, made a compelling case for a "Russian World without quotation marks" (*Russkii mir bez kavychek*) that served "not as a shield, but a bridge between East and West," "not with the mission of liberator (they are already free)," and "not in the role of big brother," but rather as an "innovative, economic, transportation, and cultural hub that will attract members of the diaspora back to Russia through its actions, not its words" (Iurgens 2011). The key for Iurgens—echoing the 1990s model of Russian World advanced by Shchedrovitsky—was "development of democratic institutions and the framework for civil society" (2011).

Soft Power Hardened: Russian World as Protectorate of a "State-Civilization"

As the examples above illustrate, prior to 2012 one could certainly find expressions of narrower views of a Russian World that represented a Slavic union with Russia at the lead, but these were restricted to the spiritual programs of the Russian Orthodox Church (Father Superior [Igumen] Filipp 2010), to still seemingly marginal nationalists, such as Prokhanov, and to fringe political parties like the "Patriots of Russia," who in their pre-election platform called for the "gathering of the Russian World" and the "reestablishment of the historical unity of the Russian, Belarusian, and Ukrainian peoples as a single great-Russian nation (*edinyi velikorusskii narod*) with the aim of working toward the formation of a single state" ("Patrioty Rossii" 2011). But in the wake of mass protests that accompanied the 2011–12 election cycle, at the onset of Putin's third term, the idea of the Russian World as a means of *consolidation* (that is, strengthening a perceived core by gathering in extenuating parts) entered official formulations and began to eclipse metaphors of union, harmony, bridges, and borderlessness. Language and culture became not so much conduits extending to a greater Russian World but a means of preserving Russian identity in the face of external, existential threats. "For centuries," Putin declared in his first address to the Federal Assembly after his reelection in March 2012, "Russia has developed as a multinational state—that's how it was in the beginning—a state-civilization (*gosudarstvo-tsivilizatsiia*), held together by the Russian people, the Russian language, and Russian culture, which are native for all of us and unify us, preventing us from dissolving into this polymorphic world" (2012).[13]

In contrast to earlier conceptions of the Russian World as living in harmony with the rest of the world, without borders or political ideology, receptive even to dissenters, as long as they were invested in Russia, the view now emanating from officialdom generously employed the discourse of separate civilizations; foregrounded the distinctiveness of the Russian World, its history, values, and even "genetic code"; and underscored the essential antagonism or clash that resulted with respect to competing civilizations (particularly that of Europe). In this scenario, members of the Russian diaspora went from being potential allies in a global promotion of language and culture to becoming potential citizens and foot soldiers of a state-civilization under threat.

Undoubtedly, this sense of civilizational clash and antagonism reached its peak with the annexation of Crimea in February 2014, when public discourse and political rhetoric about the Russian World became overtly belligerent. Putin famously invoked the Russian World and "Russian-language speakers" in his justification of the Crimean invasion and annexation and vowed to "defend both ethnic Russians in Ukraine and that part of the Ukrainian population . . . that feels a direct tie—not only an ethnic, but also a cultural, linguistic, tie—with Russia, that feels itself to be a part of the broader Russian World" (2014c). As the Speaker of the new Crimean Parliament, Vladimir Konstantinov, put it

Figure 8.1. "Russian World—English World" (2015), by Vladimir Kadyrbaev, a reworked version of a famous 1882 painting, *Knight at a Crossroads*, by Viktor Vasnetsov (published in the newspaper *Vremia*, Almaty, Kazakhstan, on August 12).

in his 2015 address at the plenary opening session, Crimea was "on the front line in the battle for the Russian World" ("V Ialte . . ." 2015). And "from a civilizational world view," according to the Communist Party Russian Duma deputy quoted earlier, this "was a war between Western civilization and the Russian World": "The West is aggressively striving by fire and sword to force people in Novorossiia with a Russian world view to abandon their native language and culture. . . . Saving them from genocide is the sacred duty not only of Russia, but of the entire Russian World" (Nikitin 2014).[14]

Underscoring the degree to which ideational borders had shifted from the limitless sphere of the global and the cultural to regional, historical, and geopolitical terms, in his Crimea speech on March 18, 2014, Putin likened the Russian World's "reunification" to the reunification of the two German states after the fall of the Berlin Wall (2014a). In doing so, he rhetorically reduced the reach of the Russian World to the imaginary nation of "historical Russia" ("I'm counting on the fact that citizens of Germany will also support the desire of the

Russian World, historical Russia, toward the restoration of unity" [2014a]). Later that year, in his televised call-in talk show with the Russian people, "Direct Line," Putin went a step further, suggesting that a "person of the Russian World" had "an exceptionally powerful genetic code" by virtue of the mixture of ethnicities and nationalities that shared "a single language in the framework of a single state, living on a common territory" with "common cultural values" and "common history" (2014b). Diversity, in other words, rather than resulting from some sort of outreach to the global community, was already genetically, geographically, and historically built into the Russian nation, which therefore constituted a superethnic national unity.[15] Belonging to this entity was no longer a simple matter of affective inclination: instead, one was included or excluded from the new Russian World by virtue of some combination of ethno-genetic fate and one's willingness to embrace it (and the leaders and state that represented its center). The political scientist and commentator for the state-funded news agency "Rossiia segodnia," Rostislav Ishchenko, echoed this idea and injected it with a more overtly political dimension, writing the following on the pages of the pro-Putin journal *Ekspert*:

> When we talk about the Russian World, it is entirely natural for us to acknowledge Ramzan Kadyrov as a representative (and today in Novorossiia, a defender) of the Russian World, but Movladi Udugov as an enemy of the Russian World. Similarly, Rozenbaum and Kobzon are the Russian World, but Makarevich and Nemtsov are not. Sergei Kuzhugetovich Shoigu is the Russian World, but Kseniia Anatolevna Sobchak is not. The Russian World in this sense is unique in that, in it, people without a drop of Russian blood can be Russians (*russkie*), whereas total Russians who for generations had no one but Russians may not belong. The Russian World is a cultural, ideological [and] political choice—you don't get in by citizenship or birthright. (2014)

By offering contrasts between well-known personages, almost all of whom are of non-Russian ethnic origin, Ishchenko underscores the importance of ideological affiliation as a marker of belonging. Kadyrov is the leader of the Chechen Republic, an ethnic Chechen, and a staunch supporter of Putin; Udugov is also Chechen, but a longtime Chechen separatist activist. Alexander Rozenbaum and Iosif Kobzon are both popular Russian-Jewish singers and former Duma deputies for the United Russia Party; Andrei Makarevich (also of Jewish decent) is a famous rock musician well known for criticism of Putin; Boris Nemtsov (likewise of Jewish heritage) was a former governor of Nizhnii-Novgorod, deputy prime minister under Yeltsin, and leader of the Putin-era political opposition, until his assassination in the Kremlin's shadow in February 2015. Shoigu is the Russian Federation minister of defense and a longtime Putin ally of Tuvan origin; Sobchak, the daughter of the former Petersburg mayor Anatoly Sobchak, is a famous actress and television and media personality as well as a prominent member of the Putin-era political opposition. Most importantly for the author of the cited passage, however, the name or names appearing in the front half of the contrastive pairs have all been outspoken supporters of Putin and his policies—particularly in the wake of the Ukraine conflict—in contrast to those listed second, who have been outspoken critics. The new calculus, as articulated here, clearly prioritizes political correctness over ethnicity and takes citizenship out of the mix altogether.

Reception within Russia and among the Russian-Speaking Diaspora

Commenting on the pages of the official government newspaper *Rossiiskaia gazeta* in March 2014, the political scientist Leonid Polyakov went so far as to claim—dubiously, as shall be shown below—that the Russian World, in its current formulations and expressions in policy, had such popular support that it in fact constituted the elusive "national idea" Russia had been seeking since the Soviet collapse: "Such a mass and unanimous reaction by all Russians . . . can only mean one thing: finally, that unifying 'national idea' has been born. . . . It was born not in the heads of bureaucrats, academics, or PR specialists, but in the hearts and souls of the most common Russians, who are very diverse, but unified in one thing. It was born in that special spiritual space, the name of which is the Russian World" (2014). Upon closer consideration of the actual resonance these key programs and concepts had among their audiences, however, one finds, both inside and outside the Russian Federation, far greater ambiguity and ambivalence than Polyakov's wishful thinking suggests.

Inside Russia, a public opinion survey from December 2014 showed that, when asked if they had ever heard of the Russian World, 71 percent answered "no," with another 13 percent finding the question "difficult to answer" ("'Russkii mir' . . ." 2014). Of the mere 16 percent of respondents who had heard of this concept, 3 percent thought it referred to "all Russian people," another 3 percent understood it as those who were raised in the Russian cultural tradition, and 2 percent had heard the term but could not explain what it was. The remaining options, which all polled at 1 percent or less, included associations with Russian nationalism, "peace for Russians," "Motherland," those who practice Russian Orthodoxy, and the eponymous names of well-known

Russian stores and magazines ("'Russkii mir' . . ." 2014). A study by the Academy of Sciences two months later phrased the question slightly differently, asking "What is the Russian World?" (Gorshkov et al. 2015, slides 39–49). Here, 25 percent answered, "There is no special Russian World," suggesting greater overall recognition of the term. Yet specific conceptions of what it was still varied: 33 percent signed off on the idea that it was "a special civilization that [had] historically taken shape in Russia," 23 percent believed it to consist of "the combination of ethnic Russians in Russia and abroad," and 22 percent thought it referred to "those who [spoke] Russian and [were] interested in Russian culture." Noteworthy likewise was the relatively low number of respondents who associated "Russian World" with Russian Orthodoxy (7 percent) and "the nations that made up the Russian empire and USSR" (12 percent). The main takeaway of most commentators on these surveys was that "Russian World" was, at best, a hazy term among the Russian Federation's population and, at worst, a totally unfamiliar concept. As one commentator wryly put it, "You can hear it among intellectuals, at meetings of highly ranked bureaucrats, and in news broadcasts. But what is concealed behind this term? As it appears, Russian citizens (*rossiiane*) have a hard time answering this question" (Bashkeev 2014).

Given the concept's initial targeting of Russians living outside of Russia, the relative ignorance and ambiguity related to the term within Russia may not be surprising—although it suggests Putin's use of it to justify the defense of Russian-language speakers really could not have had much of an impact beyond intellectuals and the ruling elite. Yet how is the notion understood in the ostensible broader Russian world itself—that is, among populations beyond Russia proper? To get a better sense of both its prevalence and valence, I studied seventeen Russian-language newspapers published in Kazakhstan, Belarus, Latvia, and Germany between 2000 and 2016, looking for mentions of both the abstract concept (*russkii mir*) and the concrete organization it spawned—the Russkiy Mir Foundation.[16] Several trends in the term's recent conceptual history emerge. Prior to the creation of the eponymous foundation, the term "Russian World" appeared seldom if ever in the periodicals. From the time of the foundation's creation in 2007, it began to receive sparse coverage, ranging in content from expressions of suspicion to those of gratitude on the part of local Russophone populations, roughly correlating to the quality of relations between Russia and the Russian expatriate community's host government. Early appearances of the concept in Belarus, for instance, cropped up either in the context of cultural events hosted by the foundation or in news coverage or opinion pieces celebrating Slavic unity through shared spiritual roots in the Orthodox Church.

Sovetskaia Belarus' in January 2011 covered a conference in Moscow sponsored by the Russkiy Mir Foundation and Rossotrudnichestvo, dedicated to using Russian culture to promote "popular diplomacy" (*narodnaia diplomatiia*; Baliakina 2011). One month later, the paper called attention to a Russkiy Mir–sponsored celebration of Yury Gagarin in Mogilev oblast (Kisliak 2011).

In Kazakhstan, aside from an article acknowledging the opening of a Russkiy Mir–sponsored Kazakh-Russian center in Astana 2008 (Smirnova 2008), the weekly *Izvestiia Kazakhstan* failed to mention the foundation or the Russian World concept in any form. Soft-power activities were more on the radar screen of *Kazakhstanskaia pravda*, which featured a series of event notifications from the organization's inception in 2007 straight through to the end of 2013 (e.g., Shevchenko 2009).

The German monthly *Partner* offered relatively measured treatment in the early days of the Russkiy Mir Foundation, reporting on events devoted to cultivating Russian in the home and through television programming (albeit noting that funds for these events were insufficient; Simanovskaia 2009; Obodovskaia 2013). The Berlin weekly *Evropa-Ekspress* offered greater skepticism in critical coverage of topics ranging from the absence of adequate funding for projects the foundation embraced, such as the development of Russian-language schools (Tsipris 2012), to the foundation's tendency to replicate the top-down corruption commonly seen in the Russian Federation's institutions ("Politika . . ." 2008). The dozen-or-so articles that the weekly *Russkaia Germaniia* devoted to Russkiy Mir's early activities likewise projected an image of an organization that was at once underfunded and overly bureaucratic (see Debrer 2008, 2010a).

Latvian press coverage of the Russian World project revealed strain and suspicion from the start. Soon after the announcement of new efforts on the part of the Russkiy Mir Foundation to reach out to compatriots, even sympathetic voices inside the Latvian parliament cautioned that this could only be permissible if it were done in a manner that would not be seen by the Latvian side "as some kind of subversive activity" ("Kreml' reshila zaniat'sia . . ." 2008). A more critical report from December 2009 argued that the Russian World project was a Trojan Horse and simply constituted one instrument in the larger toolbox used by Putin's Russia to impose its political will on neighboring states: "The 'humanitarian dimension' in Russia is not a natural by-product of the activity of society and the state, but rather a conscious and deliberate policy of power aimed at neighboring states. . . . The assortment of its tools includes not just conviction, but also manipulation, propaganda, the creation of the image of the enemy, open confrontation, as well as covert campaigns with secret financing, attempts to control the media, non-governmental organizations, cultural and educational institutions, and churches" ("Latviiskie SMI . . ." 2009). Even in the Medvedev era's relatively benign geopolitical climate, the initiative was written off as a tool for "big politics" under the guise of soft power, primarily geared toward fomenting pro-Russian sentiment in the Baltics: "Providing support for its 'fifth column' in the Baltic countries and not skimping on funds for various PR activities, the Kremlin is least of all concerned about the return of compatriots or the support for Russian culture locally" (Kamel'nikov 2009). According to the same author, Russian "compatriots" in Latvia had themselves grown weary of being used as political pawns in a pointless geopolitical game.

With Putin's 2012 reelection and more pronounced patriotic, nationalist turn, attitudes toward the Russian World project grew further polarized throughout the near abroad. By spring 2012, Russkiy Mir's name was so tainted for some Latvian Russian speakers that one Russian-language school administrator felt compelled to publicly deny accusations that the school was funded by the foundation at all ("Pliner . . ." 2012). Later that year, a representative and defender of Russkiy Mir's work in Latvia expressed an increased feeling of persecution and isolation by invoking the language of division and animosity that would become standard vocabulary during the Ukraine crisis: "It is not a secret to anyone that Russia today is enemy number one for the political powers in Latvia, and the Russian community there is considered a fifth column. That community, moreover, has found itself in a virtual cauldron, surrounded by the enemy, artificially cut off from the rest of the Russian World by borders and harsh border rules. The 'Berlin Wall' was not destroyed, it was transferred to the Eastern borders of Latvia. Only here it has begun to divide the Russian people" ("Nuzhny li segodnia . . ." 2012). Similarly, editors of *Sovetskaia Belarus'* offered defiant, but similarly defensive, support for the newly reelected Putin's "Eurasian Union" on the basis of the Russian World concept: "The Russian World does not presuppose a policy of 'Moscow-centrism.' . . . Ontologically, the Russian World civilization transcends in importance the current special interests of the political elites of Russia, Belarus and Ukraine" ("O konfederativnom soiuze . . ." 2012).[17]

With the onset of conflict in Ukraine, the concept became still more closely associated with Russian hard-power aggression. Mention of the foundation's outreach work waned and attention toward Russia's global belligerence increased. Even observers who invoked the Russian World metaphor in supportive tones reflect the shifting connotations discussed above. After Crimea, the Kazakh paper *Vremia* included a positive reference to Russian World that fused the historical analogy of "gathering of Russian lands" (alluding to the late medieval consolidation of power and territory around Muscovy) with neo–Cold War rhetoric: "The past weekend offered a glaring example of the information war now being waged against Russia by enemies of the gathering of the Russian World and the reintegration of post-Soviet space" ("Vykhodu . . ." 2014). On the other side of the issue, voices ranged from measured skepticism to outright disdain. Illustrative of the former was Russia expert Andis Kudorks's assessment in a report discussed in a September 2014 issue of the Baltic business periodical *Biznes i Baltiia*: "I personally don't believe that a Crimean scenario is possible here. . . . Nevertheless, one has to keep the powder dry, especially in the event of a 'Russian World,' blessed by both President Putin and the residents of Luzda with an automatic rifle in the Donbas, and thereby compromising it as an aggressive concept" (Kabanov 2014). The editorial staff of the German *Partner* went out of its way to declare independence from the Russian governmental policies by formulating an alternative self-definition that bore hallmarks of the soft-power Russian World while avoiding the now-tainted label itself: "We are people of Russian (*russkaia*) culture, of Russian-German (*rossiisko-nemetskie*), European traditions—not in any way of Russian Federation (*rossiiskaia*) politics and not in any way of German-Russian (*germano-rossiiskie*) relations" (Fel'dman 2014; cf. Maertske 2014). And from this relatively defensive perspective the paper viewed events in Crimea and beyond as having had a fracturing effect on the Russian World ("I don't even want to talk about Crimea, which has shattered to splinters the already fragile Russian World of the West" [Kamatozov 2014]). The idea that Putin's actions in Crimea, if anything, drove a wedge through the "Russian World" proved a popular sentiment even in the Russian-language press of Kazakhstan and Belarus, which, by virtue of more restrictive press policies, were more likely than those in Latvia and Germany to reflect official state views. An editorial in the Kazakh *Vremia* echoed this assessment with regret, noting that "the Russian World in the West has been broken down to the molecular level by Crimea and Ukraine" ("Malen'kaia pobedonosnaia" 2014). A 2015 article in *Belarusskaia gazeta* quoted one expert who observed with a tinge of irony and regret, "Some time ago I also got worked up by this idea of a 'Russian World.' But now Putin himself is doing everything possible to ensure that the concept does not spring to life, and in the Donbas the most shattering blow has been brought upon it" ("'Russkii mir' kaput" 2015).

More prominent, however, were expressions of outright contempt for the now tainted term. *Partner* rejected it as a "clerical-nationalist, obscurantist, and xenophobic" concept, which the majority of Russian expatriates living in Germany—despite general support for Vladimir Putin—did not condone (Kochanov 2014; Muchnik 2014). *Kazakhstanskaia pravda* qualified it using buzzwords that conjured up the image of a belligerent army of couch potatoes, zombified by Russian media: "When every God-given day you are harangued by the radio and television, newspapers and magazines, and even certain teachers and invited lecturers at your alma mater about how America is 'the main enemy of humanity,' about 'Ukrainian fascists' and about how the Russian World is the only force capable of standing up to these two 'terrible enemies,' it's hard to resist the temptation to participate" ("Obyvatel' . . ." 2015). In May 2014, the Minsk-based *Belarusskaia gazeta* dismissed proponents of the Russian World as living in an alternative temporal and spatial reality of Soviet and Russian imperial nostalgia ("Zapad . . ." 2014) and portrayed them as "aborigines" infected by the "thermonuclear propaganda gushing" from Russian television ("Vesna . . ." 2014). By April 2015, the once sympathetic *Sovetskaia Belarus'* featured an opinion piece that reframed "Russian World" as an outdated, "pro-Soviet" geopolitical policy, in stark contrast to a "post-Soviet" "Ukrainian world," which, in its embrace of independence, had put an end to the "monopoly on values" once claimed by the Russian World (Kazarin 2015). Perhaps the most widely quoted, dismissive post-Crimea reaction to the Russian World came from President Alexander Lukashenko himself, who, in an August 2015 interview, rejected the notion of the Russian World in general and Belarus's inclusion in it in particular, dismissing the idea as a Russian propaganda tool having no basis in reality: "I asked the [Russian] ambassador in parliament 'What does the gathering of Russian lands mean and what is the Russian World?' No one to this day has explained it. . . . It is nonsense: after the election, some Russian Federation ideologist threw it out and they started to sing its song. And this put our people on their guard. And it's not true—'We are for the Russian World!' I don't understand what the Russian World is. Our people, moreover, do not know what the Russian World is" ("Interv'iu . . ." 2015; cf. Manaspaev 2015). Regardless of any previous affinities to the Russian World, as both Russian political discourse and foreign policy reoriented toward territorial and demographic borders and conflicts following Putin's reelection and the Ukraine crisis, the notion grew increasingly contentious and tended, on the whole, to fracture the very world it was designed to unify. A contested concept from the start grew only more polarizing and problematic and in many cases turned away populations once potentially on board with the project of global Russian cultural exchange.

Russkiy Mir and Russian Worlds

Judging by the coverage it has received in the Russian-language press in the countries discussed here, the Russkiy Mir Foundation has had nominal impact in fostering greater empathy for the Russian brand, suggesting that it has done little to transform Tishkov's "silent diaspora," cited in the epigraph to this chapter, into a vibrant, coherent "world." Part of the problem rests with the foundation's poor funding and overly bureaucratic nature.[18] Part of it may be due to the possibility that, as the political analyst Fedor Lukyanov suggested, "soft power and Russia are not natural bedfellows—it's not in our tradition" (Bai 2015). The primary problem, however, stems from the impossibly mixed tasks the foundation addressed, together with its divergent target audiences. From the outset, it sought to address the needs of at least two Russian Worlds: what one Russian commentator calls "Russian World I," "a community of Russian people who wound up overseas primarily by their own choosing, and have begun to establish themselves in their corresponding societies"; and "Russian World II," "a community the majority of which turned out to be unable to leave the countries that were formed after the collapse of the USSR and became 'professional Russians,' unwilling to establish themselves in the lives of their new countries" (Inozemtsev 2014). By virtue of their distinct circumstances and experiences, the two worlds hold differing attitudes regarding their erstwhile homeland.[19] Where fostering affinity to culture and language may have been a recipe for success with one (Russian World I), the other was likely more receptive to the "citizenship lite" model presented by the discourse of "state-civilization"—although the survey of Russian-language news coverage in the near abroad displays some resistance to this as well. Inozemtsev rightly notes that more recent Russian policy has focused on Russian World II at the expense of Russian World I, which is better educated, strategically situated in leading world capitals, and more influential in terms of social and professional status.[20] Yet even with regard to the "professional Russians" of Russian World II, the policy tends less to improve the situation of compatriots from Russian World II and more to complicate it, as these populations come increasingly to be viewed as a Russian "fifth column" in their countries of residence.

Indeed, a random glance at the post-Crimea daily news briefings sent out by Russkiy Mir clearly reflects the degree to which, by 2015, the foundation's activities and focus had become dominated by hard-power issues relating to Ukraine, Crimea, and Russia's relation to the West, with little regard for the local interests of the diaspora—voluntary or beached—or soft-power initiatives relating to language and culture that dominated the news in its earlier years:

> "A majority of Russians support the idea of refusing to publish religious caricatures"
>
> "The DNR announces that Ukrainian strongmen intend to shoot at public positions"

> "Alexander Lukashenko talked about the deep integration between Russia and Belarus"
> "World-famous writer and founder of the Moscow Art Theater, Anton Chekhov, turns 155"
> "Putin deems it important to remember the possibilities of the Russian language within the framework of the Year of Literature"
> "Residents of the Estonian town of Sillamäe take part in the 'Immortal Regiment' march"
> "Russian citizens (*rossiane*) have come to place greater value on domestically produced goods"
> "The average salary in Crimea has increased by 50 percent"
> "The Federation Council deems the transfer of Crimea to the Ukraine in 1954 illegal" ("Novosti Russkogo mira" 2015)

Rather than bridging the gap between Inozemtsev's "Russian World I" and "Russian World II," the post-Crimean Russkiy Mir seems more intent on projecting the image of a "Russian World III" grounded as much in military strength and anti-Western (and isolationist) values as in culture and language.

In sum, the Ukraine crisis proved problematic for all Russians residing outside of the Russian Federation, raising questions about allegiance in their host societies, splintering diaspora communities, and dooming the original Russian World project, which stood revealed as a relic of a foreign policy and geopolitical outlook of the distant past. What started out as a protean term potentially speaking to a broad swath of global Russians positively disposed toward their native language and culture became so entrenched in a new, fully instrumentalized meaning that it lost the semantic flexibility that originally made it so potent. As the influential editor in chief of the radio station Echo of Moscow, Aleksei Venediktov, pointed out in a recent forum in Latvia, the term is still pliable, but only with regard to its territorial range—it clearly constitutes the "superstructure" of Putin's neo-imperial ambitions; what is less clear is the geographical scope of those ambitions (Sliusareva 2016). Recent events have narrowed the implicit borders of the Russian World to Russia's perceived historical "sphere of influence"—the near abroad. What was once a loose and inclusive metaphorical space has become more actual and contentious—in many cases, palpably so, given the economic and military expenditures required to acquire territory and protect it. Geopolitically, events have shifted the nature of the relationship between Russia and the extraterritorial Russian World from one built on partnership to one between protector-state and aggrieved minority sharing a common genetic code, a common ideology, and a common enemy in a civilizational clash with the Western world. As a result, the Russian World policy, as it has evolved, has brought about the fracturing of the very world it sought to unify. In its current form, it may still be useful as an ideological rationale for internal consumption—although evidence suggests it has not had much resonance beyond the politically engaged intelligentsia and elite—but its prospects for promoting broader appeal for Russia and things Russian globally have been compromised for the foreseeable future.

Notes

1. For a more detailed discussion of the notion of "compatriot," see Grigas 2016; Platt, this volume.

2. The Russian World project examined in this chapter was only one of a number of efforts by the early Putin administration to use "soft power" to project a more positive image of Russia and stake claims in the global arena. Other examples in Putin's first two terms as president include the (re-)creation of RIA Novosti as a serious, Western-oriented, English-language news outlet, the formation of the then soft-power television station "Russia Today" (widely known now as RT), and the culturally rich, off-beat website "Russia Beyond the Headlines." The hard-fought campaign to win the rights to host the 2014 Winter Games in Sochi and the 2018 World Cup can also be understood in this context (Dolinskiy 2015). I use the term "soft power" as discussed by Nye, who first described it as a state's use of culture, education, and the media, among other institutions, to "get what [it] wants through attraction rather than coercion or payments" (Nye 2004, x; cf Nye 2011, 81–109). For other in-depth discussions of Russkiy Mir and related cultural institutions as tools for soft power, see Gorham 2011; Uffelmann 2014; Laruelle 2015; Grigas 2016.

3. Here and throughout I use "Russkiy Mir" to refer to the foundation (in keeping with the transliteration adopted by the foundation itself) and "Russian World" to refer to the more abstract concept or policy rendered in Russian as "*Russkii mir*," "*russkii mir*," or "*Russkii Mir*."

4. For discussion of the term "near abroad," or *blizhnee zarubezh'e*, see Platt, this volume.

5. Laruelle (2015, 3) acknowledges that the term was not used actively in discussions of Russian national identity through the ages, and not nearly as prominently as notions such as "Russian spirit," "Russian idea," and "Russian soul."

6. Vladimir Nikitin is a longtime member of the Russian Federation Communist Party, representing it in the State Duma from 1995 to 2015. His calls for engagement of the Russian World predated Putin's embrace of the concept.

7. Alexander Prokhanov is a Soviet and Russian writer and editor in chief of the nationalist newspaper *Zavtra*.

8. Other names associated with the more recent conceptualization of the Russian World include Vadim Tsymbursky, Sergei Gradirovsky, Efim Ostrovsky, and Sergei Chernyshev.

9. For detailed discussion of Russian policies with regard to compatriots, see Grigas 2016, which argues that soft-power initiatives such as Russkiy Mir are only the first step in a five-stage process of "re-empirialization."

10. This has been especially true since the beginning of Putin's third term in 2012 (Grigas 2016).

11. A 2011 report highlights the sort of cultural activities initiated by the Russkiy Mir Foundation in locales of the distant abroad: "the celebration of Maslenitsa in London, European comedy game shows (*KVN*) in Hamburg, and children's theater productions of 'The Little Scarlet Flower' in the capital of Argentina" (Rokossovskaia 2011).

12. The mention of "peace" here is an intentional play on the original Russian "*mir*," which can mean both "world" and "peace."

13. Cf. the following: "As philosopher Konstantin Leont'ev put it so expressively, Russia has always developed as a 'blossoming complexity,' a state-civilization, held together (*skreplennaia*) by the Russian people (*narod*), the Russian language, Russian culture, the Russian Orthodox Church and other traditional religions of Russia" ("Zasedanie" 2013). For more in-depth discussions of this new, civilizational discourse, see Platt 2008; Gorham 2016.

14. "Novorossiia" is a historicism referring to the region stretching across the northern Mediterranean, including southern Ukraine, acquired by Russia in the eighteenth-century Russo-Turkic wars. The term disappeared from common usage in the Soviet era but reemerged in official Russian discourse when Putin used it in 2014 as a rationale for the annexation of Crimea.

15. Putin's formulation carries echoes of the "greatness and unity" trope that Kukulin, elsewhere in this volume, identifies as a hallmark of imperial Russian imaginaries.

16. Countries were selected based on geopolitical diversity regarding relations with Russia and availability of resources on the Integrum online database (www.integrum.ru). Ukrainian-Russian sources were excluded, as a discourse analysis of this audience's reception of the Russian World notion and Russkiy Mir would require a separate chapter (see Uffelmann, this volume). Papers consulted include the following. Latvia: *Biznes i Baltiia* (1995–2014), *Telegraf* (2005–14), *NovoNews* (Riga, 2006–14), *Vesti Segodnia Plius* (2010–14); Germany: *Evreiskaia gazeta* (2005–14), *Evropa-Ekspress* (2005–14), *Partner* (1997–16), *Russkaia Germaniia* (2000–14); Belarus: *Belorusskaia gazeta* ([*BelGazeta* from 2015] 1997–2016), *Narodnaia gazeta* (1997–2014), *Respublika* (1998–2014), *Sovetskaia Belarus'* (1993–2016); Kazakhstan: *Ekspert-Kazakhstan* (2006–16), *Izvestiia* (2004–16), *Kazakhstanskaia pravda* (1992–2016), *Megapolis* (2005–16), *Vremia* (2000–16). Discourse analysis of newspapers, of course, cannot be understood as a perfect echo of the sentiment of local populations, but in this case it can offer a credible indication of the significance and prevalence of the Russian World concept over time.

17. Grigas points out that Russkiy Mir did not open its first office in Belarus until 2014, since most Belarusians, according to studies, "[did] not consider Russia to be a foreign country" (2016, 229).

18. According to annual budget reports published in *Rossiiskaia gazeta*, the state consistently allocated the modest sum of 500,000 rubles to the Russkiy Mir Foundation

until 2014, when its budget was cut by 10 percent (and then another 5 percent in 2015). Rossotrudnichestvo, as a federal agency, enjoyed budget increases of 20 percent and 21 percent in those same years, increasing to a budget of 3.48 million rubles for the fiscal year 2016–17, and, according to Grigas (2016, 38), projected that it would reach 9.5 billion rubles by the year 2020 (Published Russian Federation budgets obtained through the online portal, "Offitsial'nyi internet-portal pravovoi informatsii," pravo.gov.ru/ [accessed 12 June 2016]).

19. Indeed, as Komarskaya and Komarski (this volume) deftly demonstrate, russification during the Soviet era came as much from republican initiative as it did from federal, to the extent that, with the wholesale embrace of titular languages after the Soviet collapse, Russian became a language "without rights, but quite necessary."

20. For a skeptical discussion of the Russian diaspora's patriotic inclinations and the potential for harnessing it via the internet, see Saunders 2006.

Is There Any Such Thing as "Russophone Russophobia"?

When Russian Speakers Speak Out against Russia(n) in the Ukrainian Internet

Dirk Uffelmann

In memory of Kyrill Dissanayake, † October 21, 2015

Russian-Ukrainian Conflict and the "Russophobia" Allegation

Immediately after the Ukrainian Euromaidan revolution on February 23, 2014, the Ukrainian Rada voted for a law stripping Russian of the status of regional language in Ukraine (Kulyk 2014a). This legislative act was quickly interpreted by Russian officials as an anti-Russian attack of "the most Russophobic among the Rada representatives of the victorious putsch in Kiev" (Bitiutskii 2014). The ostensible need to protect speakers of Russian in Southeastern Ukraine from a "linguistic genocide," a "Russian Holocaust" (Martynov 2016), served as one of the central pretexts for the Russian Federation's annexation of Crimea and its military destabilization of Eastern Ukraine. The Russian state foundation Russkiy Mir (Russian World) rendered this as the defense of a "Russian World from Crimea to Donbass" (Serov 2014).[1] In Russian propagandistic discourse on "Russophobia," however, fault for the military conflict was exclusively attributed to "Ukrainian Russophobes," who allegedly provoked the war: "Russophobes of all stripes who clawed their way to power in Ukraine proposed to prohibit Russian language, culture, history, and Russian identity itself, which led to civil war in Eastern Ukraine" (Valiaev and Zhivov 2015).

Ironically, both the military and propagandistic strategies of Russia in Ukraine drastically reinforced or even brought into being the very anti-Russian sentiments to which they ostensibly responded. As a result, the Russian-Ukrainian military conflict has brought to the fore a collision between two concepts that (in English) differ from each other by just one phoneme: "Russophobia," the fear or derision of Russia and things Russian; and "Russophonia," the global community of Russian language and culture.[2] An intuitive conclusion might be that these concepts are mutually exclusive. Yet are they? The present chapter examines manifold seemingly paradoxical forms of their overlapping, focusing inquiry around a formulation that appears to be intrinsically contradictive in a performative or pragmatic sense: "Russophone Russophobia." As we shall see, this contradictory nexus is a central site of contestation over the fundamental meaning of Russia and Russian culture(s). In what follows, I analyze Russian discourse around the construct of "Russophobia" as a propagandistic assault based on an essentialized and singularized identity of "Russia(nness)." Subsequently, I turn to investigation of performative metalanguage and pragmatic contradictions that provide methodological tools for analysis of anti-Russian sentiments expressed in Russian in Ukraine. My investigation is focused on metalinguistic jokes and poetry culled from the Ukrainian internet—both because this provides a rich source of material and because, as we shall see, the internet, which is identified with fixed locations yet projected globally, is a structural analogue of the kinds of actual relationships that link cultural identities to geographical and political entities. I conclude with the thesis that both the conspiracy theory about "Russophone Russophobes" and the metalinguistic deconstruction of this assumption reveal the multiplicity of Russian political and linguistic cultures as well as the fundamental—although mediated—autonomy of culture(s) from nations, state borders, and geographic fixity. For ultimately, the performative contradiction of Russophone Russophobia is among the most effective tools for critique of patriotic and nationalist formulations of Russian collective identity and political unity.

"Russophobia" as Conspiracy Theory

The discursive and institutional dispositif that Russian propagandists orchestrate around allegations of "Russophobia" is based on the paranoid specter of a conspiracy (Borenstein 2016b).[3] In only a few cases do the authors of this conspiracy theory denounce a distinct group of perpetrators such as "the Jews" (Shafarevich 2005, 71–81). Even fewer contributions attempt rational journalistic or academic argumentation, allowing even the possibility of falsification (Iagun 2015). The majority of interventions are erratic, aggressive, and portentous. They presuppose a singular "Russia as a whole" (Mettan 2017, 33) and an undisputable quality of Russianness (both extending beyond the territory of the Russian Federation) that are under attack. This presupposition excludes internal variation of politically disparate definitions of what is supposed to be "Russian." Whoever criticizes the Russia that this discourse constructs as proper and unique is a "Russophobe" and subsumed under the label "traitors to the Russian world" (Martynov 2016).

From the late 2000s, the "Russophobia" topos began to crop up with great frequency in public discourse whenever Russia engaged in an external military conflict (cf. Kiselev 2008, reacting to critique of the Russian-Georgian war of August 2008; K'esa 2016, 131–32, and Mettan 2017, 11, reacting to criticism of the annexation of Crimea and war in Donbas). The largest wave of internet polemics around "rusofobiia" began in 2014.[4] Yet Russian state-sponsored "research" into the purported phenomenon goes back to the late 2000s: after the failed launch of an "Anti-Russophobic League" in 2008 (Nemenskii 2013, 64), activities sharply increased following 2012 (Darczewska and Żochowski 2015, 12), culminating in the broadly promoted conference "Russophobia and Information War against Russia" (see figure 9.1) in September 2015 (Valiaev and

Figure 9.1. Logotype from the 2015 conference "Russophobia and Information War against Russia" depicting St. George fighting the "dragon of Russophobia."

Zhivov 2015; for critical analysis, see Darczewska and Żochowski 2015, 19–22). In June 2016, the Russian Ministry of Culture issued a call for applications encouraging research in "rossiefobiia" ("Russiaphobia"), offering 1.9 million rubles in funding (Fadeichev 2016).

Among the redundant materials that are copied and pasted from one discursive unit to another in public speech on the topic are the etymological linkage of "phobia" with disease (Nemenskii 2013, 26; K'esa 2016, 76) and the clarification that "Russophobia" is "not merely a critique of Russia but a critique beyond any sense of proportion" (Tsygankov 2009, xiii). Russophobia is described as an almost constant phenomenon extending back at least five hundred years (see Poe 2001; Nemenskii 2013, 60; K'esa 2016, 39; Ruxpert n.d.), if not to the era of Charlemagne [*sic*] (Kara-Murza 2012; Mettan 2017, 103). Hardly any historical overview fails to trace the ostensible phenomenon and its diagnosis to a single quote from a letter Fedor Tiutchev wrote to this daughter Anna in 1867 (Makashin, Pigarev, and Dinesman 1988, 306; see, for example, Ruxpert n.d.). As with much else in contemporary Russian state discourse, the concept of "Russophobia" is buttressed by a transhistorical argumentative strategy that jumps between centuries, between past and present, with a special predilection for quotes from leading Nazis, such as Goebbels, Göring, and Hitler (Kiselev 2008).

Another rhetorical strategy of this discourse consists of quick changes of perspective in enumeration of the victims of the alleged "Russophobia." Given that this is a state-sponsored discourse, the Russian state is the "natural" victim (cf. Borenstein 2016a), yet the arguments identify other targets of critique as well, ranging from the traditional cliché of Russian tyranny and Oriental despotism (Kara-Murza 2012) to present-day Russian politics in general ("The Russophobia I discuss . . . is a fear of Russia's political influence"; Tsygankov 2009, xvi), and President Vladimir Putin in particular (K'esa 2016, 220). The diffuse nature of purported anti-Russian dither is unsurprising. While official discourse generally identifies the president and Kremlin with Russia and Russian culture, a focus on politicians (or one politician), would present the possibility of somebody making a distinction between a "bad state" and a "good people," which for the proponents of a single Russia is to be avoided (Mettan 2017, 32–33). Yet those who raise the specter of an overarching "holistic ideology" (Nemenskii 2013, 27) of "Russophobia" must describe it as directed against the Russian people as a whole (Valiaev and Zhivov 2015; Traditsiia "Rusofobiia" 2016) and extending to all cultural phenomena constructed "as genuinely Russian," such as (a purist understanding of) the Russian language, Orthodox religion (identified with the Moscow Patriarchy), and traditionally understood everyday culture (Il'in 1993, 63). Such claims of generalized "Russophobia" are patently more convincing than railing against, for example, a specialized critique of brutal masculinity as characteristically Russian (Kara-Murza 2012; Armeyskov 2013), or the fantasy that "local Russophobes" hate how Russians smell in metro trains (K'esa 2016, 248).

While both the villains and the victims of "Russophobia" are said to have changed over time, at present "Russophobia" is defined as no less than a Western weapon (K'esa 2016, 271) against all that is constructed as "Russia(n)," identified with the Kremlin and its geopolitical interests beyond the Russian Federation, encompassing the so-called Russian compatriots addressed by the Russkiy Mir Foundation. Colluding with covert Western expansionism, "Russophobes" are reproached for "false claims" that Russia, instead, seeks to expand (K'esa 2016, 128–31). To the contrary, according to this discourse it is "the West" that first unleashed advanced information technologies, especially the internet, as an anti-Russian weapon (K'esa 2016, 191–92, 196–97). Of course, the identification of "Western Russophobia" is less a reaction to any actual attitudes or policies toward Russia, conspiratorial or otherwise, than a justification for Russian aggression. The propagandistic use of "Russophobia" therefore implies a temporal paradox, a *hysteron proteron*: action is posited as a reaction. For this same reason, overt Russian reactions to the "rusofobiia" of others in the form of irony, *steb*, or self-orientalization (Armeyskov 2013) are rarer than simple, aggressive promotion of the need for Russian engagement in a "defensive" hybrid war (see Valiaev and Zhivov 2015).[5] Ultimately, polemics against "Russophobia" are less a diagnosis of any actual Western information war against Russia (K'esa 2016, 271) than a Russian weapon in an information war against the West and Ukraine (for straightforward examples, see the "Rusofobiia" entries of the Russian nationalist online "encyclopedias" *Ruxpert* and *Traditsiia*).

This discursive weapon is of almost universal applicability. According to Eliot Borenstein, "Russophobia" functions as an "all-purpose, blanket explanation for any disapproval of anything done by Russia or Russians" (2016b). The humor of the satirical site Lurkmore's entry on "Rusofobiia" does not diminish the accuracy of its deconstructive definition: "Russophobia is a meme of the patriotic in-crowd of the country [Russia]. It is used against anybody who differs from the views of the aforementioned in-crowd" (Lurkmore n.d.). Andreas Umland describes it as a polemical tool, arguing that the "Russophobia 'club'" is used as a "thought-terminating cliché" for the sake of immunization against any critique of the Putin regime.[6] This same anti-communicative application was already splendidly diagnosed by Dmitry Prigov in 2005:

"'Russophobe' [is] a term in the category of bad names that require no additional definitional effort. Russophobe—that's it. Game over. . . . A sort of expulsion into a zone where you are no longer entitled to any defense of the right to your own opinion or even place of residence" (2005). It comes as no surprise, then, that from Tiutchev's day to the present the primary agents of discourse against "Russophobia" have been representatives of the Russian state. It was only briefly, during the late Soviet period (Shafarevich 2005, first published in samizdat in 1983) and the early post-Soviet period that it was taken over by marginalized right-wing intellectuals (cf. Khazanov 2003, 90–97). Yet those redactions of this discourse have now returned to mainstream politics, advanced by state organizations such as the Russian World Foundation (Martynov 2016).

"Russophone Russophobia" and Ukraine

Even if promoters linked to the Russian state declare "Russophobia" a Western weapon, many of them are no less concerned with what they describe as the internalized "reproduction" of Western Russophobic ideologies (Nemenskii 2013, 54) in the form of "Russophobia among Russians" (K'esa 2016, 243), "Russian Russophobia" (Mettan 2017, 36), the "internal Russophobia" of a "pseudoelite" (Iagun 2015), and "Russian self-hatred" (Nemenskii 2013, 52; cf. Ruxpert n.d.). Since 2013 the open group in the Russian social media network VKontakte "antirusofob_ru," with over 16,000 followers (as of December 27, 2017), has been appealing to "Russia" to "save Donbass" from "Russophobes." This group has also engaged in outing hundreds of purportedly "Russophobic" VKontake groups, other web resources, and Russian opposition figures.[7] The Russian-language Wikipedia article on Russophobia contains a long subchapter titled "Russophobia in Russia" (Wikipedia "Rusofobiia" 2016), supporting Darczewska and Żochowski's suspicion that "the fight against Russophobia is primarily aimed at domestic consumption" (2015, 28) and that the "Russophobia" cliché is being used against any who want a Russia without corruption ("Da ty rusofob" 2015).

Again, Tiutchev's letter (ironically, in Russian translation from a French original) serves as an authoritative reference: "This is the *Russophobia* of some Russian people who, by the way, are highly respected. . . . To the extent to which Russia is achieving greater freedom and asserting itself more and more, dislike of Russia can only become more intense" (Makashin, Pigarev, and Dinesman 1988, 305). The internalization of the "Russophobia" charge, however, performatively concedes something that advocates of a homogeneous "Russian World" seek to avoid. For the existence of internal "Russophone

Russophobes" inscribes a fault line within the Russian community, implying the existence of two distinct cultures, defined more politically than geographically: a healthy one and an infected one. This conceptual knot is telling in the context of the present volume: even those who want to see the "Russian world" united around the Kremlin and President Putin performatively acknowledge a "two-culture thinking in which two traditions and two civilizational identities are joined in an inevitable conflict" (Nemenskii 2013, 53).

This brings us to the crucial significance in this regard of Ukraine, a country internalized by Russian imperialists who deny it the right of sovereign statehood yet also engage in "expanding the notion of 'domestic Russophobia' to Ukraine, i.e. by insisting that Ukraine is and will remain a part of the 'Russian world'" (Darczewska and Żochowski 2015, 16). In the face of this ideological onslaught, Ukrainians strive to defend the "externalized" situation of their country and statehood from that of Russia. Ukrainians were viewed as a fission fungus within an alleged "all-Russian unity" by watchdogs against "Russophobia" as early as the nineteenth century, as the Russian internet encyclopedia *Ruxpert* argues: "Russophobic circles of the intelligentsia in the Russian Empire were reinforced by nationalists of all stripes, including the followers of Ukrainian-ness—a political movement directed toward splitting apart not only the Empire, but the very Russian people itself based on ideas of local identity and the negation of all-Russian unity in combination with Russophobic arguments developed earlier in the West" (Ruxpert n.d.). In 2011 the Kyiv-based Russian-language weekly *Kievskii telegraf* drew attention to the "Russophobia" of Russian-language intellectuals: "A rampant Russophobia, based on overt lies and falsifications, has become so common in Ukraine that frequently . . . not only blatant 'nationally conscious' patriots are getting carried away with it . . ., but even those who by definition should not engage with it—if only for the reason that they earn their bread precisely with the Russian language" (Iakovlev 2011).

It is just those who "earn their bread precisely with the Russian language" who interest me in what follows: what happens to (native) speakers of Russian, of whom there are millions with Ukrainian citizenship at present, when they are targeted as "Russophobes"? What critical tools are available to Russian speakers beyond the Russian Federation to assert their own cultural and linguistic autonomy within the global array of Russian cultures?

Critique of Russia is uttered in millions of Russian-language statements every day. Only a minority of those criticizing Russia or Russianness in Russian do so in a self-reflective way, and even fewer in an ironic or artistically self-undermining manner. To distinguish possible degrees of reflexivity of "Russophone Russophobia," I propose a triangular schematic chart, illustrating

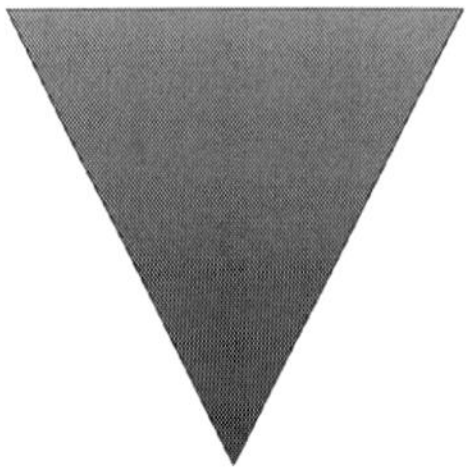

- Occasional critique of Russia in Russian
- Continuous critique of Russia in Russian
- Russian-language critique of Russia with metalinguistic awareness
- Russophone "Russophobia" staging the inherent pragmatic contradiction

Figure 9.2. A typology of Russophone anti-Russian statements.

diminishing frequency, of extensions of anti-Russian statements (see figure 9.2). Only a very small minority of Russophone anti-Russian statements *stage* the performative contradiction inherent in "Russophone Russophobia." This tip of the triangle, which holds the greatest potential for reflection on the political and geographical condition of Russian culture per se, is of special interest in the following investigation of statements critical of Russia on the Ukrainian internet.

As we shall see, critique of all that is constructed as Russia(n)—namely, Russian politics, mentality, culture, and above all language—if expressed in Russian, can collide with the performance of using the Russian language. This collision can redirect the attention of the reader or listener toward matters of language itself, inserting a dimension of reflexivity and performative metalanguage (cf. Jakobson 1985; Verscheuren 2004) into an anti-Russian statement made in Russian. The investigation of such language use demands special attention to performative metalanguage, which, following Ingunn Lunde (2009, 2014, 2017), I define as "metalinguistic comments that take on the form of verbal performance" (Lunde 2014, 149). Regarding the "explicit message" of an utterance, the performative metalinguistic dimension "may reinforce it, help interpreting it, or even contradict it" (Lunde 2017, 201). According to Lunde (2009, 110), implicit metalanguage often combines with explicit reflection on language: "Frequently an explicit, metadiscursive comment and a linguistic practice, or use of a particular linguistic element, combine to give force to the user's argument" (Lunde 2014, 152). Conversely, I argue, an explicit comment on language allows the receiver to detect implicit, performative strategies of metalinguistic evaluation. Explicitly critical evaluations of something Russian can redirect the attention of the receiver to the linguistic performance of this critical utterance in Russian (note that it does not do so necessarily—for example, in the discourse of the domestic opposition in the Russian Federation, where the use of Russian passes unmentioned in the vast majority of cases). If attention is successfully redirected toward the assertion inherent in the performance of an utterance (e.g., the assertion that it is appropriate to make the utterance in the Russian language at all), the receiver stumbles over the performative self-frustration of a Russophone anti-Russian statement.

Of course, the performative tension *theoretically* inherent in "Russophone Russophobia" amounts to a true contradiction only if the critique uttered in Russian is directed against Russian as a language. The recipient might then diagnose a performative or pragmatic contradiction as identified by C. I. Lewis, who defines pragmatic contradiction as "inconsistency between the content of assertion and the act of asserting it." Such an inconsistency surfaces due to the inherent content of the act of assertion itself: "As deliberate, and to be understood as deliberate, this act of assertion conveys the intent that what is said should be believed. But the content of the assertion made . . . is one in which this assertor's assertions are not to be believed *on the evidence of his making them.* This act is self-frustrating of its own ostensive purpose" (1969, 197–98, emphasis added; see also Dayton 1977, 230). Yet although every statement made in the Russian language against the Russian language contains the potential for reflection on performance, there are cases that deliberately *expose* or *stage* the performative contradiction between language practice and message. These are the cases to which I will devote close attention. First, however, we must explore the broader context and range of anti-Russian criticism in the new Ukraine.

Anti-Russian Sentiment in Ukraine

As we have seen, Russian nationalistic propaganda has long accused the West in general, and Ukrainians in particular, of "Russophobia." Among recent events in the new Ukraine that seemed to confirm such accusations were various boycotts of Russian goods and films launched in 2014. Comparable to this are paradoxical "anti-ads" that warn customers not to buy a product displayed in a shop because it is from Russia—a sign, for instance, warning "On these shelves there may be books published in Russia." Such Ukrainian-language slogans seem to confirm the tacit assumption of Russian propaganda that "Russophobia" in Ukraine is Ukrainophone (and that, implicitly, a unified Russian[-speaking] world exists). Certainly, Russian equivalents are far less widespread, although they do exist.

Something similar might be said regarding Ukrainian right-wing parties that seek to trigger anti-Russian sentiments but do so only very occasionally in Russian or with allusions to Russian. One linguistically interesting example is

Figure 9.3. Political advertisement: "In Russia people do not swear with mat [vulgar language] . . . They talk in it."

the metalinguistic ad by the Svoboda Party (see figure 9.3) discouraging Ukrainians from using vulgar language, which the poster associates with Russian (although the linguistic purism evident here is structurally rather similar to purist campaigns in contemporary Russia).[8] From the pragma-linguistic point of view, what is intriguing here is not the Ukrainian anti-Russian slogan but rather the alleged quote in Russian, written in a distorted Ukrainian orthography emphasizing the Muscovite phonetic rule of "akan'e" (when "o" in the syllable before the stress is pronounced as [a]): "V rAsssi matom ne rugaiutsia . . . Na n'om razgAvarivaiut" ("In Russia people do not swear with *mat* [vulgar language] . . . They talk in it"). The Ukrainian framing and "phonetic transcription" of this pseudo-Russian sentence make it clear that we are dealing with an occasionally "Russophone Russophobia" deployed by a predominantly Ukrainian-speaking addressor.

More strategic and continuous than such occasional instances is the use of Russian in political and military blogs, such as the anti-Russian but Russian-language comments on the military campaign in Eastern Ukraine on the Facebook pages of prominent Ukrainian politicians such as Interior Minister Arsen Avakov or military experts such as Dmitryi Tymchuk (Marchenko and Kurbatov 2016). The motivation for using Russian in military blogs is international reach—the functionality of criticizing the Russian Federation in Russian because this postimperial language is understood by many more people abroad than is Ukrainian. This same strategic goal is shared by continuous Russian-only website projects such as OstroV (www.ostro.org) or Radio Vesti (radio.vesti-ukr.com)—Ukrainian web resources that maintain an anti-Russian discourse in Russian.[9]

Screening the entire Russian-language segment of the Ukrainian internet would be far beyond the scope of this chapter's concern with exposed metalinguistic contradictions of anti-Russian statements made in Russian. What is more, tools developed in the field of Digital Humanities are challenged to detect irony, let alone performative contradictions. Following N. Katherine Hayles's recommendation of a tripartite reading strategy that encompasses traditional hermeneutics and tools from the Digital Humanities, an "expanded repertoire of reading strategies that includes close, hyper, and machine reading" (2010, 74), for the present study I first implemented three qualitative selection criteria, based on previous unsystematic hyper-reading, in order to define narrow segments of the Ukrainian internet for further machine search: the relevant sources were (a) to display critical distance to Russia, (b) to express this critique more or less clearly, while (c) applying metareflection on language. These criteria were fulfilled by two prominent caches of Russophone language use in the Ukrainian internet: first, the jokes section of a popular portal for news, videos, photos, and so on (durdom.in.ua); and second, the Facebook entries of the famous Russian-language poet from Odesa Boris Khersonsky, as well as the poems he uploaded to his LiveJournal page between November 1, 2013, and July 5, 2016.[10]

Acknowledging that it would be extremely challenging to automate a search for irony or performative contradictions, initial searches were oriented on the truncated Cyrillic keywords "rusofob*" (plus its variant "russofob*"), "russk*," and "iazy*," the latter being the basis of the Russian word for "language" (which has a—limited—potential for language distinction because the Ukrainian homonym is confined to the meaning "tongue").[11] These automated searches were conducted without the aim of making a quantitative analysis, rather purely in order to detect possibly relevant entries that, in the next step, could be subjected to close reading, enhanced by hyper-reading of users' comments and outgoing links embedded in the relevant entries. The combination of these three modes of reading allowed me to arrive eventually at a set of metalinguistically contradictive entries.

Performative Metalinguistic Contradiction: How Funny Is That?

Durdom and Khersonsky: what a pair! How can such distinct genres as the joke and lyric poetry be comparable with respect to metalinguistically contradictory staging of "Russophone Russophobia"? Yet let us recall that Lunde specifically mentions humor and poetry as modes of reflexive language usage closely related to performative metalanguage: "These are uses of language that draw attention to themselves" (2014, 152). Lunde's discussion of these related genres does not take up the qualitative difference between the degree of metalinguistic reflexivity in jokes, which are often banal, and poetry, with its characteristic sophistication. On the other hand, investigation of these distinct categories of linguistic usage demonstrates that consciousness and metalinguistic critique of the imbrication of language, culture, and geography is by no means the province of sophisticates alone but extends to the most humble, common forms of linguistic activity. And so, with all due apologies for linking one of Ukraine's leading Russian-language poets with a "trivial" entertainment website, the following analysis progresses from the absurd to the sublime, beginning with the jokes from durdom.in.ua.

One must admit at the outset that even if they appear as part of the "anecdotes" section of durdom.in.ua, not all search results based on the above criteria are truly humorous. However, they are frequently quite aggressive. For example: "'The question of Russian as a state language of Ukraine is closed forever,' reports a Russian journalist. 'To force absolutely Russophone Kiev to hate the Russian language and to lose 40 million people who were loyal to the Russian language in just one year—oh yes, for this you have to be a truly great politician. Congratulations!' . . . Let me add for my part: it's beyond the wildest dreams even of the Ukrainian nationalists."[12] This explicit (perhaps even too explicit, for a joke) political comment combines one of the narrowest extensions of objects of Russophobia (it is unmistakably directed against the unmentioned President Putin) with one of the broadest configurations of "Russophone Russophobia"—critique of the Russian language in Russian, even if this critique is limited to "absolutely Russian-speaking Kiev," which, according to the author of the fragment, began to "hate" its own language. The fact that this "joke" fails to lay bare the performativity of Russian language use smacks of sarcasm but not of metalinguistic paradox.

A second example is both explicit in its aggressive critique of Russian politics and performative in its use of word play with Ukrainian phonetics. The play on words centers on the Russian-Ukrainian homograph *geroi* ("hero," pronounced [heroi] in Ukrainian), which here is underpinned with the Russian vulgarism *khernia*, with its associations with a vulgar word for "penis" (*kher*):

> My wish for you, dearest Kremlin well-wishers,
> Is that all the State Dum(b)a should suffer from haemorrhoids,
> And that all your patriotic shit [*khernia*]
> Be buried by hundreds of hero-oids [*kheroi*].[13]

The grammatical errors and low quality of this doggerel suggest that the author only occasionally uses Russian, at least for literary purposes. And, to be sure, this stanza, the first of seven in this vulgar poem, is more performatively ironic about Ukrainian distortions of Russian than about the Russian language per se, although it is of course as explicitly anti-Russian as possible when it comes to political content.

A third metalinguistic joke from Durdom contains a performative illustration of anti-Russian sentiments. The negative Ukrainian ethnonym for Russians, *katsap*, is presented as a reaction to the negative Russian ethnonym for Ukrainians, *khokhol*. Interestingly, the anecdote portrays the latter character as a Russophone writer. The Russian says to the Ukrainian: "Khokhol, why are you writing in Russian? Why not write in Ukrainian?" The Ukrainian answers: "Katsap, you've been fooled again. There is no Russian language. It's just a mixture of Old Slavic, Bulgarian, and Tatar." Here we have a clear performative contradiction in Russian: even if the fictitious Ukrainian writes in Russian and concedes that he does, he denigrates the language he doubly performs in the anecdote by writing and speaking in a nonlanguage. This joke obviously articulates a reactive twist—against the widespread Russian prejudice that Ukrainian is not a proper language but a dialect of Russian.

A fourth example from Durdom brings the greatest authority in Russian language and culture, Alexander Pushkin, into a confrontation with the greatest contemporary authority in Russian politics, Vladimir Putin:

> Even were I Obama
> in my sunset years,
> yet saw Russia's true constitution,

> I'd forget my Russian
> because, my dears,
> it is the language of Putin . . ."
>
> **Aleksandr Pushkin**[14]

Although the reference to Obama is somewhat obscure (perhaps relating to Pushkin's African heritage?) this absurd doggerel presents an essentialization of Russianness and a historicization of the Russian language as discredited by Putin and therefore beyond rehabilitation, even for Pushkin himself. The poem intertextually references Vladimir Mayakovsky's poem "To Our Youth," inverting his appeal: "I would learn Russian / only because // it was spoken / by Lenin" (Maiakovskii 1973, 67). The poem's most complex implication is its irony regarding the impossible "art of oblivion," a kind of meta-ironic comment on anti-Russian attempts at a linguistic *ars oblivionalis* in the face of the postcolonial linguistic reality that, quite simply, you cannot forget Russian if you are Ukrainian.

In the case of the jokes on durdom.in.ua, we are dealing with occasional use of the Russian language from near-native speakers of Russian from outside the Russian Federation who deploy various extensions of Russophobia in metalinguistic critiques of the relationships between political affiliation, geography, and languages: the first and the fourth example above collide language ("Russian-speaking Kiev") and literature (Pushkin) with politics; the vulgar poem of the second example performatively exploits the richness of Russian obscene language and no less performatively infiltrates the Ukrainian accent. The third example confines the performative contradiction to Russian itself: a speaker and writer of Russian refutes the status of Russian as a language. Finally, the impossible *ars oblivionalis* of the final example results in a comprehension that, for the Russian speaker in Ukraine, there is no escape from Russophonia, at least not through "Russophone Russophobia." Taken together, all of the examples act out the *reductio ad absurdum* of a rejection of Russian hegemonic politics, conceived as equivalent to Russian language and culture, carried out in a Russophone utterance. Ultimately, this strategy of performative self-contradiction points most emphatically in each case at the absurdity of assuming equivalence between language use and national or political affiliation. The apparent contradiction is, in the end, revealed to be produced by ideology: Russophone Ukrainians have as much right both to speak in Russian and criticize current Russian politics as anyone else. It is in this connection that the nature of Durdom as an internet platform is particularly relevant. It might be objected that because of the pseudonymity and concealed geolocation of users in Web 2.0, it is often impossible to prove that user posts analyzed above relate to users who are actually located within Ukraine. In any literal sense, we may be certain only that Durdom belongs to the .ua internet zone. Yet we must also recognize that the implications of the performative play deployed in these jokes itself points to the impossibility of confining languages and political affiliations themselves within political borders; "virtual Russians" are not confined to the .ru zone (cf. Uffelmann 2011a, 177). Ukrainian Russophone culture, like "Russian Russophone" culture, rises out of a geonational concept, but, like all other cultural formations, is a global presence that is both everywhere and nowhere in particular.

"Russophone Russophobia" as Reflected in Poetry from Ukraine: Boris Khersonsky

In the wake of the Russian aggression against Ukraine, since early 2014 virtually all of Ukraine's Russian-language writers have turned in part to nonfiction and "become fighters in the information war," adding a "battle shelf" (Kurkov 2015) to the literature of Ukraine, as the Kyiv-based Russian-language novelist Andrei Kurkov puts it (cf. Puleri 2014; Kukulin 2016; Chernetsky, this volume). An especially interesting case is that of Russophone *poets* who utter a critique of Russia because their choice of poetic language might be expected to imply a positive attitude toward Russian as their medium of aesthetic expression. The performative tension in poetic Russophobia in Russian need not necessarily be explicated, as is the case with Anastasiia Dmitruk's lyrical message to Russians, "We Will Never Be Brothers," in her Facebook post from March 10, 2014, which went viral on the Ukrainian internet (Stahl 2015). Alternately, this theoretical tension can be "resolved" by switching to Ukrainian, as we see in Vadim Dubovsky's variation on Dmitruk's poem in a video available on durdom.in.ua, which adds commentary in Ukrainian to circumscribe the performative implication of Russian:

> [in Russian:] We never even *were* brothers.
> The virus of slavery entered your soul.
> You always showered
> Our faith, freedom and language with curses.
>
> [in Ukrainian:] [. . .] I sang in Russian
> So that you could understand me, Muscovite [moskal]. [. . .][15]

Nevertheless, as word-conscious linguistic art, Russian-language poetry from Ukraine is the most fertile category of language use for reflecting, deconstructing or staging the implied performative contradiction of "Russophone Russophobia." In what follows, my focus is on Boris Khersonsky's online presence, because of his pronounced political positions, the explicitness of his prose-like poetry, and the proactive way he addresses the problem of Russophone Russophobia, both in the prose and poems on his Facebook page and his LiveJournal blog since February 2014. Furthermore, Khersonsky, as I explain below, is among the leading practitioners of the fast-growing phenomenon of Russian-language poetry publishing on the internet. His body of work demonstrates forcefully the partial autonomy of cultural life from geographical fixity. Yet Khersonsky should also be viewed as the most prominent example of the larger set of Ukrainian Russophone poets who thematize the problematics of writing in Russian in Ukraine.

Born in Chernivtsi in 1950 into a Jewish family, Boris Grigorevich Khersonsky is an Odesa-based poet and clinical psychologist. Khersonsky converted to Russian Orthodoxy and was a dissident during the 1970s and 1980s, when he published his first Russian-language poems in samizdat. His first official publications appeared in Ukrainian publishing houses in the 1990s. From 2006 his books were also published in Russia (NLO, AGRO-RISK, Limbakh, Sovpadenie), where he was shortlisted for the prestigious Andrei Bely Prize in 2007 for his collection *Family Archive* (*Semeinyi arkhiv*). Sally McGrane argues that his publications in Russia are what made Khersonsky famous (McGrane 2015). In the context of the Ukrainian internet he is relevant as the author of a popular prose-and-poetry blog on Facebook, followed by over 25,000 people, and a LiveJournal diary, offering more poetry (as of December 27, 2017). Both appear under the username "borkhers," often each presenting the same entries, and both are in Russian, although recently the Russian original is sometimes followed by a Ukrainian translation.

In his blogs Khersonsky offers paradoxical gestures with regard to the dichotomy between new and old media. On the one hand, he is highly active in posting (as of December 27, 2017, his LiveJournal blog contained 9,526 entries and 59,026 comments by Khersonsky himself) and replying to followers' comments (of which 131,411 comments have been received). On the other hand, he encourages offline reading almost on a daily basis, using the "cat meme" so typical of internet folklore, posting an endless stream of cute feline images to mitigate his media-anachronistic moralism, encapsulated, for instance, by one of his slogans: "Don't stop reading (and where would we be without kittens?)" (cf. Uffelmann, forthcoming). Khersonsky's use of the trite kitty attractor, however, in no way diminishes the political verve of his writing. Khersonsky's pro-Ukrainian stance in both the internet and his book published in Russia,

Missa in tempore belli (2014), which is devoted to the Euromaidan, the annexation of Crimea, and the war in Eastern Ukraine, earned him severe criticism in Russia (Nepogodin 2014; cf. Kukulin 2016, 171).[16] And reactions to his politics have not been limited to critical reviews: after an interview in which Khersonsky accused the Russian state of orchestrating a series of explosions in Odesa (Khersonskii and Sergatskova 2015), his former flat was the target of a bomb attack on February 10, 2015.

Khersonsky's blogs are full of explicit references to "Russophobia," presented as a negative epithet others apply to him. On May 10, 2014, he defended himself against "comrade web prosecutors, more and more intensively accusing me of Russophobia."[17] Reacting to Boris Nemtsov's murder on February 27, 2015, Khersonsky denounced "Russophobia" as a nationalistic slogan that incites violence: "Where hundreds of thousands with foam on their lips shout about a 'fifth column,' about Russophobia and a new Nazism, you will always find some who decide to put things right with guns in their hands."[18] To him this is a transformation of an old Soviet stereotype: "the anti-Soviet has grown aged/ and transformed into a Russophobe."[19]

Turning to those accused of "Russophobia," Khersonsky declares "Russophobia as a symptom of a disease. But the psychiatrist is always interested in the input of reality to the symptom."[20] Distancing himself from "Russophobia" as a mental attitude, he does not deny the real causes and thus, to a certain degree, the "justness" of anti-Russian sentiments. He even goes so far as to ironically define "Russophobia" as Russia's externalized conscience: "Russian-language literature of Ukraine—this Russophobic, Banderovite literature—nevertheless refers to Russia and, possibly, is an externalized (projected outwards) 'inner experience of Russia'—something like pangs of conscience that one would so like to repress."[21] Yet while displaying his "medical" comprehension of anti-Russian sentiments, Khersonsky calls for appropriate distinctions. Russian nature and religion, he says, must be distinguished from Russian politics: "And I love Russia for its great spaces, its rivers, domes, and plaintive songs. But tanks, the army, the government, that's something entirely different for me." At other moments, he inverts the argument of "Russophobia": "For me the one who wants a strong hand at Russia's throat is the Russophobe."[22] Khersonsky thus proposes a narrow target of anti-Russian critique—President Putin, his present regime, and its supporters, not the Russian mentality or any transhistorical collective being.[23]

The hermeneutic ethos of marking distinctions leads Khersonsky to a differentiation between Russian—and Russian. On the day after the Rada adopted the new language law in February 2014, he called for a distinction between two "dialects" of Russian: "Who can explain to these guys [in the Rada] that the language of Russian bureaucrats and soldiers and the language of the educated, cultured people are different dialects and that we [Russophone intellectuals critical of Russia] are not responsible for the words with which they give orders and write regulations?"[24]

This distinction has taken on a passionate significance for speakers of Russian in Ukraine in the wake of the military conflict since 2014. In 2016 Khersonsky engaged in a multi-portal dispute with Aleksei Tsvetkov (Tsvetkov 2016), carried out on InLiberty, Focus.ua, and Facebook, in which he pointed to the instrumentalization of the Russian language in Ukraine as a geopolitical argument by the Russkiy Mir Foundation (cf. Uffelmann 2016).[25] For Khersonsky this instrumentalization rendered Russian an "enemy language" even for pro-Ukrainian speakers of Russian in Ukraine: "The revolutionary events of 2004 and 2013 and the following war transformed Russian into an 'enemy language' for one part of Ukraine's citizens and into an object of 'defense' for others, which is especially sad because Russian propaganda stubbornly maintains that people are dying in Donbas for the right to 'think and speak in Russian.' So the specter of a 'Russian world' appears behind the backs of Russian-language writers, whatever position they hold about the war" (Khersonskii 2016).

If in his prose commentaries Khersonsky offers a reasoned discursive critique of the weaponized concept of Russophobia, in his poetic texts he adopts a variety of strategies to explode the concept at its most fundamental level. The imposition of the Russian language desired by advocates of an expansive conception of the Russian world, who would, for instance, like Odesa to be declared exclusively Russophone, leads Khersonsky to protest against the Russian language as a compulsory norm in the double poem "Odessa/Odesa" that follows lines in Russian with their translation into Ukrainian:

> they say odessa, russian world—that's not interesting
> others reply if it's not interesting then don't stick your nose in
> no they say we'll turn over all the soil here like a good master
> in somebody else's garden, received as an inheritance
> you'll learn in what language and about what to talk [. . .][26]

Here, Khersonsky's protest comes performatively, demonstrating that dissent can in fact be articulated both in Russian and Ukrainian. And with this performative twist we arrive at the question of how Khersonsky stages performative contradictions inherent in Russian-language critique of Russia. First, he appropriates the Russian nationalist hate word "rusofobskii" (Russophobic) as a kind of ironic genre category in the subtitle of his own poems (recalling Thomas

Bernhard): "An Overtly Russophobic Banderovite Delirium" or "Another Raging Russophobic-Banderovite Invention."[27] Subsequently, the epithet "Russophobe" ("rusofob") even appears in Khersonsky's own sarcastic "Self-Portrait (Summary of a Discussion)," which evokes the mutual accusations of anti-Semitism characteristic of the information conflict in Ukraine, deploying a traditional formula from jokelore, recalling the material studied above:

> There gathered for a meeting once, to let the hatred spew
> All rolled in one a Russophobe, Ukrainianizer, and Jew.[28]

Internalizing the hate word in his "Russophobic mind," Khersonsky signals the ironic intent of his appropriations with an emoji: "We cosmopolite-Russophobe-graphomaniac-Jewbanderovites ☺."[29]

Khersonsky stages a fully fledged pragmatic contradiction in a poem posted on LiveJournal on July 20, 2015, where the speaker performs an utterance in his "native language" that is simultaneously attested to be dead. The performative contradiction is further enhanced by the fact that the "self-burial" of Russian in Russian is accompanied by a Ukrainian version where the dead language is "mova," which thus refers not to Russian but to Ukrainian:

> I also think of my native language [iazyk/ mova]
> that's been buried on the battlefield.[30]

In a five-stanza poem uploaded to Khersonsky's LiveJournal blog on December 4, 2014, and included in the book version of *Open Diary* (*Otkrytyi dnevnik*), which can be read as a reaction to critical attacks from Russia such as that of Vsevolod Nepogodin in *The Literary Newspaper* (*Literaturnaia gazeta*; Nepogodin 2014), Khersonsky defines "a Russophobe" as an "obviously meager, crappy little man," ironically staging the performative tension inherent in Russophobia expressed in Russian:

> Do I hate everything Russian? I do, especially this
> little birch tree and this little church,
> [. . .] Especially frescoes by Dionisii and Rublev
> the raspberry-red sound, the church choir, the twinkling candles,
> especially the sound and meaning of the Russian word.[31]

Not only are Khersonsky's readers acquainted with him as a passionate devotee of Russian religious art (Tallès 2015); in this poem Khersonsky collides the seemingly "Russophobic" object level with the linguistic metalevel of such a discourse: the synesthetic description of the impressions produced in a Russian Orthodox church performatively contradict the hate for the "Russian word" expressed in the very next line.

In order to heighten the sense of contradiction, in other texts Khersonsky deploys the broadest possible conception of objects of Russophobia—the variety encompassing not only statehood ("Russia is a tumor on this planet") but also culture, literature (Tolstoy, Pasternak, Tsvetaeva), religious art, and, finally, nature. By piling up and baring apparent performative contradictions, Khersonsky, the native speaker of Russian from outside the Russian Federation, who gained fame as a poet in Russia, refutes the conceptual coherence of "Russophone Russophobia." Nevertheless, Khersonsky has no illusions about the perlocutionary effectiveness of his staged performative contradictions on readers from the other camp: when the user alfa_delta comments on Khersonsky's LiveJournal poem, "Well, knowing our audience, I am convinced that many might take this seriously," the poet agrees, once again underlining the dilemma inherent in the charge of "Russophobia," which, for all its ideological underpinnings, is difficult to effectively refute in Russian.

Like the jokes found on Durdom, Khersonsky's poetry carries out a performative critique of the conception of Russophobia at its fundamental levels, articulating the multiplicity and independence of Russian cultures from the constraints of political entities and national boundaries. Ultimately, Khersonsky may be considered either a representative of the single, yet politically diverse and contested Russian cultural scene stretching from Moscow to Kyiv, or a representative of a Ukrainian oppositional Russophone culture that itself has resonance within the Russian Federation, or both. His poetry, like all purportedly "national" cultures, and like the internet itself, is identified with specific persons, places (or archipelagos as defined by Masha Rubins in this volume), and (at times) polities. At the same time, that poetry freely moves across the globe to readers in Kyiv, New York, Berlin, Moscow, and Novosibirsk.

In conclusion, it is worth confronting the poet and the jokes with the official anti-Russophobic discourse with which we began. While the latter implies a self-deconstructing knowledge of the abhorred existence of diverse Russian cultures, the former performatively demonstrate the absurdity of applying the notion of "Russophobia" to people who are continuously Russophone and highly aware of language. Critique of Russian state policy and hegemonic cultural norms does indeed coexist with Russian-language use. The performative acts of an ironically staged "Russophone Russophobia" call into question the counterfactual uniqueness and singularity of Russia(nness) as constructed by those advocates of a "Russian World" who accuse other Russian speakers of

"Russophobia." Enactment of the ostensible pragmatic contradictions inherent in anti-Russian statements made in Russian ultimately exposes the ideological underpinnings of these contradictions, affirming in the end the multiplicity and geographical autonomy of Russian cultures that the defenders of a "Russian world"—as an ensemble centered around Russian state territory and the Kremlin—cannot but fail to exorcise with the help of the "thought-terminating cliché" "Russophobia."

Notes

1. For detailed discussion of the Russian World and the annexation of Crimea, see Gorham, this volume.

2. The majority of research uses the spelling "Russophonia," despite some usage of the alternative "Rusophonia" (Gorham 2014, 157).

3. The nationalist instrumentalization of the Russian polemical term "rusofobiia" may be one reason why publications striving for political correctness, like English Wikipedia, have replaced the older English equivalent "Russophobia" (Gleason 1950, and many others) with "anti-Russian sentiment" (Wikipedia "Anti-Russian Sentiment" 2016). This substitution reduces the implication of pathology associated with "phobia" but fails to eliminate the negative evaluative connotations. My use of "Russophobia," consistently in quotation marks, is an overt reference to both the term and its propagandistic nature.

4. A Google search for "rusofob*" in Cyrillic on December 27, 2017, brought more than 623,000 hits.

5. One may also note, in this regard, the infrequency of the use of contemporary postcolonial vocabulary to describe the mechanism of "Russian Orientalization" (Armeyskov 2013; cf. Mettan 2017, 38, 302–3).

6. In the original, the term is "Russophobie-Keule [. . .] Totschlagargument" (Umland 2016a). The English translation by Andrew Kinder in Umland 2016b fails to grasp the brutality of the German terms.

7. See the threads on "antirusofob_ru" new.vk.com/topic-14612220_28404686 and new.vk.com/topic-14612220_28397824.

8. The ad may be viewed at lurkmore.to/Хохлосрач (accessed December 27, 2017), where it is ironically described as a "Social Banderovite ad of a Russophobic character."

9. This category of sites is a good illustration of the need to define the Ukrainian internet not in linguistic terms, as online communication in Ukrainian, but via the top-level domain name ".ua" (cf. Nedashkivska 2010, 409).

10. The beginning of the time span was chosen to coincide with the start of the Euromaidan movement in November 2013. I confine analysis to online material, excluding Khersonsky's published books, even if thematically connected, such as *Kosmonash*

(2015a), or other relevant authors (see Chernetsky, this volume). Where the published version of Khersonsky's 2014 diary *Open Diary* (*Otkrytyi dnevnik*; 2015b) differs from material published online, I add an additional reference. Note that these differences demonstrate the inaccuracy of reviewer Liubov Summ's judgment that the book features the same "spontaneity" and "unfiltered-ness" as the Facebook entries (2015). I owe thanks to Gernot Howanitz, who helped retrieve entries from Khersonsky's Facebook posts.

11. The homonymy is the basis for the Ukrainian Russophobic saying, "Iazykom lizhut'. Movoiu rozmovliaiut'" ("With a tongue [Russian word for language], one licks. One converses with a language [Ukrainian word]").

12. Durdom post, durdom.in.ua/uk/main/anecdot/anecdot_id/27994.phtml, uploaded November 9, 2014, accessed December 27, 2017.

13. Durdom post, durdom.in.ua/uk/main/anecdot/anecdot_id/28085.phtml, uploaded November 13, 2014, accessed December 27, 2017.

14. Durdom post, durdom.in.ua/uk/main/photo/photo_id/49916.phtml, uploaded May 4, 2014, accessed December 27, 2017.

15. Previously available on YouTube, www.youtube.com/watch?v=vzKp-YjchQ, uploaded August 24, 2016, accessed December 27, 2017.

16. To be sure, Khersonsky tends to shock both ideological camps (Tallès 2015); he is also critical of attempts at the linguistic Ukrainization of Russian-speaking Ukrainian territories (Khersonskii and Volodarskii 2014), and his spontaneous reaction to the language law mentioned above, as expressed on his LiveJournal blog on February 24, 2014, was extremely negative (borkhers.livejournal.com/2014/02/24, accessed December 2017, 2017; omitted in Khersonskii 2015b).

17. Khersonskii, Facebook post, May 10, 2014, www.facebook.com/borkhers/posts/792211080813720, accessed December 27, 2017; moved to May 11, 2014, in Khersonskii 2015b, 117.

18. Khersonskii, Facebook post, February 27, 2015, www.facebook.com/borkhers/posts/967548786613281, accessed December 27, 2017.

19. Khersonskii, Facebook post, June 14, 2016, www.facebook.com/borkhers/posts/1236217169746440, accessed December 27, 2017.

20. Khersonskii, Facebook post, March 17, 2015, www.facebook.com/borkhers/posts/977836235584536, accessed December 27, 2017.

21. Khersonskii, Facebook post, May 11, 2016, www.facebook.com/borkhers/posts/1215155521852605, accessed December 27, 2017.

22. Khersonskii, Facebook post, May 1, 2014, www.facebook.com/borkhers/posts/787193094648852, accessed December 27, 2017; omitted in Khersonskii 2015b.

23. Khersonskii, Livejournal post, February 28, 2015, borkhers.livejournal.com/2015/02/28, accessed December 27, 2017.

24. Khersonskii, Livejournal post, February 25, 2014, borkhers.livejournal.com/2014/02/25, accessed December 27, 2017; omitted in Khersonskii 2015b.

25. Khersonskii, Facebook post, June 17, 2016, www.facebook.com/borkhers/posts/1238198542881636, accessed December 27, 2017.

26. Khersonskii, Livejournal post, August 25, 2015, borkhers.livejournal.com/2015/08/25, accessed December 27, 2017.

27. The quotations are from Khersonsky, Facebook post, August 2, 2014, www.facebook.com/borkhers/posts/841529012548593, accessed December 27, 2017; omitted in Khersonskii 2015b; Khersonsky, Facebook post, August 2, 2014, www.facebook.com/borkhers/posts/841868542514640, accessed December 27, 2017; omitted in Khersonskii 2015b. The appropriation of negative heterostereotypes is a popular device in the new Ukraine, especially on the Ukrainian internet, with regard to many denigrating hate words such as *ukrop* (the Russian word for "dill," that partially rhymes with the word Ukrainian), *banderovets* (referring the purported attachment of Ukrainian patriots to the World War II Ukrainian nationalist and sometime Nazi collaborator Stephan Bandera), and so on. This device can be compared to what Henry Louis Gates Jr. describes as the black colonizing of a white sign (1988, 47) and what I have proposed calling self-orientalization (Uffelmann 2011b).

28. Khersonskii, Facebook post, February 2, 2015, www.facebook.com/borkhers/posts/954010451300448, accessed December 27, 2017.

29. Khersonskii, Facebook post, May 24, 2015, www.facebook.com/borkhers/posts/1013737315327761, accessed December 27, 2017.

30. Khersonskii, Livejournal post, July 20, 2015, borkhers.livejournal.com/2015/07/20, accessed December 27, 2017.

31. Khersonskii, Livejournal post, December 4, 2014, borkhers.livejournal.com/2014/12/04, accessed December 27, 2017; Khersonskii 2015b, 261.

The Most Global Russian of All

Michael Idov's Cosmopolitan Oeuvre

Adrian Wanner

Cosmopolitanism: Constructed and Contested

What does it take to be a truly global Russian author? As a Soviet-born and U.S.-educated journalist, editor, novelist, and screenwriter, Michael Idov (b. 1976) seems to belong—at least at first sight—to the group of "hybrid" Russian immigrant writers discussed by other contributors to this volume (see esp. Furman and Wakamiya). Upon second consideration, however, several distinctions come to mind that set Idov apart from the growing cohort of so-called Russian-American authors. First of all, Idov has vociferously distanced himself from any association with the genre of immigrant fiction. In a post on his Russian Facebook page, he talks about having to fight off a multitude of American teachers, and later editors and agents, who urged him to write about his experience as an immigrant—a literary practice he provocatively equates with competing in the Paralympic Games.[1] Idov also differs from most other post-Soviet émigrés in that he writes in both English and Russian and self-translates between the two languages. If we want to use the terminology proposed by Steven Kellman (2000, 12), Idov is an "ambilingual" author rather than a "monolingual translingual" (an example of the latter would be Gary Shteyngart, who, although a native speaker of Russian, writes exclusively in English).[2]

Born and raised in Riga, where he graduated from a Russian-language high school, Idov moved with his parents to Cleveland in 1992 as part of the "fourth wave" of emigration. After graduating from the University of Michigan with a degree in theater and film studies, he settled in New York City, where he began to publish in the *Village Voice*, *TimeOut*, and *New York* magazine. Eventually he became a contributing editor at *New York* while also writing for elite Russian journals and newspapers such as *Bol'shoi gorod*, *Kommersant*, and *Snob*. In 2012 Idov moved to Moscow to assume the job of editor in chief of the Russian edition of *GQ* magazine, a position from which he resigned in 2014 to become the creative director of the Russian film and television studio Art Pictures.

Idov's bouncing back and forth between continents and languages is paradigmatic of a new phase in the history of Russian migration—one that has produced the population of privileged and mobile individuals that Michael Gorham (drawing on Inozemtsev 2014) refers to in his contribution to this volume as "Russian World I." If during the Soviet period, emigration from the USSR was either by choice or necessity a one-way street, Idov's example shows to what extent a more fluid existence has become possible for a particular category of relatively economically privileged individuals with cosmopolitan inclinations. Rather than a permanent change of residence, emigration has become a reversible process allowing for geographically and culturally bipolar or multipolar modes of existence.

Should we look at Idov as an American expat in Russia or as a "diasporic Russian" who has drifted back to the metropolis? As I argue in what follows, he is none of these things, but rather an example of an individual cosmopolitan who constructs himself out of curated fragments of various cultures and locations. To some extent, his position resembles the "lyrical cosmopolitanism" of the Orbita group in Riga—Idov's hometown—as described by Kevin M. F. Platt (2015, and this volume). Building on Latvia's precarious geopolitical position between conflicting hegemonic worlds, this group of bilingual Russophone poets has forged a "constructivist" identity that seems inspired by Bruno Latour's critique of the universalist assumptions underlying traditional concepts of cosmopolitan globalism (see Latour 2004). Similar to the poets of the Orbita group, Idov's cosmopolitanism becomes a matter of artistic practice. While reflecting the cosmopolitan self-fashioning and multicultural and multilingual orientation that one can find among other global Russians (and which, in fact, has been a feature of Russian elites since the eighteenth century), Idov goes further than most in his embrace of a cosmopolitanism that transcends any circumscribed national belonging.

In the context of Russian (or Soviet) culture, the word "cosmopolitan," often accompanied with the qualifier "rootless" (bezrodnyi), evokes inevitable associations with Jewishness. Idov does not deny his Jewish descent, but he considers his Jewish origins a purely "racial" matter with no cultural or religious impact, as he explained in an interview with Elena Polyakovskaya (2010) on the Russian-Jewish website Booknik. One could argue, though, that Idov represents a perfect example of the "urban, mobile, literate, articulate, intellectually intricate, physically fastidious, and occupationally flexible" Jew that Yuri Slezkine has described as a key actor of modernity in Russia and elsewhere (2004, 1). Not surprisingly, some audiences in Russia respond well to Idov's construction of a cosmopolitan selfhood, while others reproduce the position of the anti-cosmopolitans.

A cursory assessment of Idov's reception in Russia reveals that there is some contention over his "Russianness." Fedor Bondarchuk, the founder and director of the Art Pictures studio in Moscow, gave the following characterization of Idov in a press release in 2014: "Born in Latvia and having lived in America for 20 years, it would seem that [Idov] has to be a man of the world—but for me he is a very Russian writer, who has never stopped exploring the Russian character."[3] To be sure, not everybody in Moscow shares this assessment of Idov as a bona fide "Russian writer," which makes one wonder whether Bondarchuk's endorsement was perhaps meant as a defensive gesture. A 2010 review of Idov's self-translated novel *Kofemolka* on a website associated with the right-wing Russian National-Democratic Party introduced Idov as a "Jew from Riga" who expresses himself in a sort of Anglo-Russian "surzhik"—"the language so near and dear to our half-educated emigrants" (surzhik is a creole of Ukrainian and Russian). The reviewer, Vasily Chapaer (2010), claims that Idov's novel slanders and smears Russia and its culture. He suggests that "Mister Idov" should consider translating his book into Latvian, Yiddish, or Hebrew and advises him to "clear out of the Russian language."

Idov's Transcultural Self-Fashioning

How does Idov position himself within the field of global Russian culture? I propose to approach this question through the lens of Idov's own creative oeuvre as a novelist and screenwriter by focusing on his representation of global Russian culture, his own participation in this endeavor, and the reception of the transcultural aspects of his work. Of course, no straightforward one-to-one correspondences between literary works and Idov's self-construction can be made. Rather, Idov uses his characters and their identities, sometimes even their non-Russian emigrant identities, as foils, setting himself up as the master manipulator of cultural attachments. This distinguishes him from many currently fashionable Russian-American immigrant writers who have built their careers by constructing themselves as "Russians" in their various fictional self-representations (see Wanner 2011). They have no doubt been encouraged to do so by agents and publishers who see "Russianness" as a commodity in the current fiction market (see Wakamiya, this volume). By contrast, Idov has pursued a different professional strategy, largely eschewing the label of "Russian-American" writer (as I have argued in Wanner 2014).

Thus far Idov has published two books of fiction, with one of them appearing in both English and Russian versions and the second one in Russian only. His first novel, *Ground Up*, was published by Farrar, Straus and Giroux in 2009 and shortly thereafter appeared in Moscow in Idov's own Russian self-translation, published by Corpus under the title *Kofemolka*.[4] In 2013 the same Russian press brought out a second book of his fiction, titled *Chës*, consisting of a novella with the same title and eight short stories. Four of the stories were originally written in English but never appeared in that language; two are published in Idov's own Russian self-translation; two more were translated by the husband-and-wife team of Viktor Sonkin and Alexandra Borisenko.

The novel *Ground Up* and the novella *Chës* both have an autobiographical kernel. The plot of *Ground Up* revolves around the unsuccessful attempt of a hip New York couple to run a Viennese-style café in a gentrifying neighborhood of Manhattan's Lower East Side. In part, the story is based on Idov's own experience of running a café together with his wife for six months in 2005, which he recounted that same year in the *Slate* article "Bitter Brew." *Chës*, which follows the tour of a second-rate rock band called "Hysteresis" through the American Midwest, harkens back to Idov's own career as a rock musician. The word "chës," in Russian slang, denotes a tour of performing artists, usually with the connotation of deficient professional and artistic competence. In his younger years, Idov performed as a guitarist and singer in several bands, including the group "Spielerfrau," but he eventually concluded that he had greater talent for writing than music.

The depiction of "Russianness" in *Ground Up* and *Chës* is of particular relevance regarding Idov's self-positioning within the Russian-speaking diaspora. Yet it should also be said that Idov's characters cannot be taken as direct representations of his own situation in Russian cultural life. Mark Scharf, the Indiana-born protagonist and first-person narrator of *Ground Up*, is the son of

Soviet-Jewish immigrants but with fading Russian cultural and linguistic credentials. Rather than a first-generation immigrant who achieves an impressive degree of literacy in both his first language and in that of his new homeland, like Idov himself, Scharf is an assimilated upper-middle-class hipster embedded in a bourgeois-bohemian multicultural milieu. His wife, Nina, hails from the Malayan-Chinese diaspora. Having grown up in the United States, she is at home neither in China nor in Malaysia. As a descendant of Russian Jews, Scharf shares with his wife what one could call an alienated "doubly diasporic" identity. He identifies with neither Russia nor Israel. The only other Russian-Jewish character in the novel is a repulsive lecher, whose attempts at fraternizing provoke revulsion in Scharf, while his Israeli landlord and contractor make it clear to Scharf that "their definition of their own kind didn't include me" (74).

The hero of the novella *Chës*, Eddie Yu, has a similarly conflicted multicultural pedigree. A third-generation Chinese-American and socially awkward graduate student in economics at the University of Michigan, he is torn between the exigencies of a conventional middle-class career and yearning for the artistic creativity and self-expression offered by the itinerant life of a rock musician. Vaguely foreign in the eyes of white Americans, Yu resists and resents all attempts to orientalize him. The fact that he eventually ends up in a relationship with an ultra-blonde American woman of Swedish descent appears to parody a typical arriviste immigrant plot. One wonders whether Yu's Asianness does not serve as a stand-in for Jewishness, given that the two ethnicities, with their reputation as brainy and vertically mobile "model minorities," at times share similar connotations in the American popular imagination. Asian and Jewish tropes are also mixed up in *Ground Up*, which is infused with staples of Asian-American fiction such as the difficult relationship and power struggle between Scharf's Chinese wife and her domineering mother. Furthermore, there is an analogy between the situation of the Chinese diaspora in Malaysia and that of the Russian population of the "near abroad" in terms of its peripherality in the Chinese world and conflicted place in the local ethnic matrix.[5] Making Scharf's wife a Malayan Chinese can thus be read as an oblique comment on Idov's own diasporic status. His artistic strategy consists in setting himself up as a sort of "super-cosmopolitan" who can manage other people's identities and recombine them to fashion or represent his own.

Russian characters only play a subordinate role in Idov's fiction. There is no mention of anything Russian in *Chës* until about halfway through the novella, when we are unexpectedly introduced to Slava Dikushin, a "mysterious Russian immigrant" who deals in Moscow conceptualist art and supplies the leader of Yu's band with nuggets of occult wisdom. Dikushin's colorful past, by his account, included shady deals at the Leningrad Hotel Astoria with the "young friends of young Putin" as well as amicable relations with the likes of the Soviet-Russian rock star Boris Grebenshchikov, Madonna, Philip Roth, Andy Warhol, and Joseph Brodsky, who allegedly borrowed a line from Dikushin for one of his poems (Idov 2013, 51–52). Dikushin's claims are overblown to the point of absurdity. And as his name signals ("dikusha," known in English as "the sickle-winged grouse," is a rare exotic bird living in Siberia), his main function as a character consists in holding up to ridicule the cliché of the "mysterious Russian immigrant" who is endowed with boundless spiritual power and cultural capital.

By downplaying his own Soviet origin and deriding the Russian immigrant mystique, Idov resists the temptation of self-orientalization. He displaces the immigrant experience in various ways by turning his authorial perspective into a superior position of insight and transcendence of immigrant, diasporic modes of construction of selfhood. As an individual he rides above these matrices. In that sense, Idov occupies the opposite position of Gary Shteyngart, who has commoditized his immigrant identity in a self-ironic performance by assuming the personae of the clumsy "Russian bear" and neurotic Jewish schlemiel (see Wakamiya, this volume).

At the same time, by self-consciously distancing himself from the constraints of any given cultural formation—diasporic or national—Idov at times floats so freely above geography that he risks becoming incomprehensible to readers. The fact that he wrote *Chës* in Russian and published it in Russia would suggest a Russian target audience familiar with cultural figures like the rock star Grebenshchikov or the Moscow conceptualists. The story's American setting may be a selling point for Russian readers eager to learn about life in the United States. However, it is hard to believe that the numerous allusions to a specifically American cultural context would be understandable to an average Russian reader (and, unlike *Kofemolka*, *Chës* does not come equipped with explanatory notes). For example, a Russian with no U.S. experience would probably have difficulty locating the "murderers from Columbine" (28), or even understanding the meaning of such words as *Tripl Ei* (44) or *redneki* (77), Cyrillic transliterations of "Triple A" and "rednecks." Furthermore, some of the story's insider jokes seem directed at an American rather than a Russian audience. We are told, for example, that the original drummer of "Hysteresis" decided not to move with the other band members from Ann Arbor to New York in 2008 because he was unwilling to quit his promising job as a junior sales manager in the corporate headquarters of Borders Books (57–58). A Russian reader is unlikely to be aware that Borders went bankrupt three years later.

The implied reader of *Chës*, then, seems to be someone much like Idov himself—a cosmopolitan Russian conversant with cultural life on both sides of the Atlantic. For such a person, the choice of language—Russian or English—seems of secondary importance, since they are functionally interchangeable. The eight short stories that follow *Chës* take place across a wide spectrum of global locations, ranging from godforsaken provinces in the Russian and Soviet periphery to Japan and Hawaii, Malaysia and Switzerland, Venice, Mexico, Detroit, and St. Petersburg. The themes of travel and migration form a common thread among many of these stories. Everybody is constantly on the move from one country to another, whether for business, linguistic research, defection, creative inspiration, or musical performance. The "global village" emerging from the book is a large-scale projection of the multicultural milieu depicted in *Ground Up*.

Who are the actual readers of this kind of fiction? There is some indication that Russian society includes a segment of people who aspire to be like Idov. It was precisely its cosmopolitan, upscale New York "coolness" that made the Russian translation of *Ground Up* a success with Muscovite readers. Idov himself commented on the fate of his novel in Russia as follows: "It only sold a few thousand copies, but they seemed to have been the *right* few thousand copies. There is a certain kind of Muscovite, mostly young, mostly employed in mass media, that eats and breathes New York; they glommed onto the book, which details a yuppie couple's misfortunes on the Lower East Side, like it was *Sex & the City*—a guide in the guise of a novel. Given the demographic, the ratio of readers to reviews was close to one" (Idov 2011). *Chës* did not receive the same enthusiastic reception, however. A reviewer on the Livejournal blog "Bookriot" (2014) faulted the book for its lack of a clear target audience. He characterizes the author as "seemingly some sort of American" ("omerikanets") and adds: "It is hard to understand for whom this is written. . . . Is the author looking at Russia from behind the border, or is he looking from Russia across the border?" The need for national "clarity" is something that distinguishes Idov's reception in Russia from that in the United States, where nobody seems to be particularly bothered by the idea that a writer can be American, Jewish, and Russian all at once.

The "Bookriot" reviewer singled out the volume's final story, "Proshchal'naia simfoniia" (The farewell symphony), for special opprobrium in view of its alleged lack of a defined national point of view. "Proshchal'naia simfoniia" harkens back to the novella *Chës* in that the main hero is again a musician on tour. Oskar Lunquist, a young viola player in the St. Paul Symphony, travels to St. Petersburg to perform Haydn's "Farewell Symphony" on New Year's

Eve 1999, the night when Boris Yeltsin unexpectedly resigned as president of Russia and handed power over to Vladimir Putin. Like Eddie Yu, Lunquist is socially awkward and shy with women, but he gets lucky with Olya, a young translator who invites him to a midnight walk after the performance. Just as the virginal Lunquist finally musters up the courage to kiss Olya, he is accosted by two drunk militiamen who unexpectedly appear out of the darkness. Having determined that Lunquist has no money, they take him to a police precinct, where they proceed to brutalize him. Not knowing any Russian (the sound of the language reminds him of the words "cash transaction" [247]), Lunquist desperately tries to communicate with his torturers in German in order to prevent them from breaking his hands, but they mistake the word "Bratsche" (viola) for "brattsy" ("pals") and "ich spiele" ("I play") for "izbili" ("they have beaten [me] up"). When Lunquist is finally released on the morning of January 1, 2000, the radio in the car bringing him back to his hotel resounds with the announcement "*Cashtransaction* Yeltsin *cashtransaction* Putin" (270).

As becomes clear, Idov's conceit consists in showing Russian reality through the eyes of an uninitiated American. It is also evident that bilingual Idov has to struggle to fit his linguistic consciousness into one alphabet or language. Translation of the story, originally written in English, presented him with some challenges. Russian phrases, inasmuch as they are filtered through Lunquist's consciousness, are spelled with Latin letters, while English words spoken by the Russian policemen are printed in Cyrillic ("Но мани?" [260], meaning "no money?"). In other instances, the broken English of Russian speakers is rendered with grammatically incorrect Russian, as when Olya tries to calm Lunquist with "Ne volnovuisia!" ("Don't worry" [261]).[6] For a Russian reader, the result of this double perspective is a sort of dramatic irony. "Proshchal'naia simfoniia" is in many respects a typical St. Petersburg tale. The virginal hero led astray by an alluring female and punished for yielding to sexual temptation by having his "bride" snatched away is reminiscent of Gogol's "Nevsky Prospect" and "The Overcoat" (as are the corrupt policemen). St. Petersburg's iconic architectural landmarks all appear filtered through the eyes of Lunquist and thus acquire an "estranged" quality, as in this depiction of the Hermitage: "To the right stood a mint-green palace, on the roof of which crowded, like hesitant suicides, dozens of disproportionally large statues" (254).

Only one member of the St. Paul Symphony has seen all this before. The clarinetist Yasha Slutzker, we are told, is "the only Russian in the orchestra" (235). When his colleagues tease him with "welcome home" after the plane lands at Pulkovo airport, Slutzker reacts with a vulgar expletive. Clearly, he does not care to be pegged as a Russian immigrant (and, judging from his name, as well as from the alleged "Klezmer" quality of his solos [236], he is not really a "Russian" to begin with). The Russian translation again complicates the issue. While the English word "Russian" could conceivably refer to a person originating from Russia or the Soviet Union regardless of ethnicity, the term "russkii" clearly (mis)identifies Slutzker as an ethnic Russian. Even though he distances himself from his country of origin, Slutzker enjoys displaying insider knowledge of his former homeland. In particular, he warns Lunquist to stay away from Russian policemen, about whom he has some very unflattering anecdotes to tell. Although Slutzker is a minor character, his informed cynicism plays an important function, providing a corrective to Lunquist's naïveté.

The story thus provides both an American view of Russia and, indirectly, a Russian view of America, given that the American's perception of Russia is presented through the filter of a Russian narrator, who contrasts the American's naïve perspective with the views of an Americanized Russian character who has temporarily returned to Russia. While this multiple mirror effect may sound complicated, it seems hard to agree with the "Bookriot" reviewer that it constitutes an artistic shortcoming. One could argue that the double perspective engenders a "stereoscopic" view that allows a sharper focus. Even though the story was originally written in English, the translation into Russian actually enhances its effect. Had Idov published it in English, it would have been little more than an orientalizing account of Russia for American consumption.

The Constructivist Cosmopolitanism of "Global Russians"

Idov's own answers to questions about his national identity have varied over the years and seem to shift according to who is asking. To Russian journalists he tends to present himself as an American. When questioned about his "patriotism" during the Sochi Olympic Winter Games, he declared that he mainly roots for the United States, adding: "As far as Russia is concerned, my Moscow friends are very dear to me, the Russian language, in which I am lucky enough to be able to talk and write, is very dear to me. This is basically all that I morally have the right to say" (Degai 2014). As we can see, Idov defines his Russian identity as essentially linguistic and literary in nature. He stresses the fact that he *writes* in Russian—in other words, it is an identity that he is able to craft himself. To be sure, language is a powerful marker of identity, and it goes without saying that a native language carries important cultural and emotional baggage. Nevertheless, even though Russian is Idov's native idiom, it seems doubtful that Moscow could be his natural or permanent "home." As a Baltic Jew, Idov is well aware that his linguistic and cultural Russianness is the historic consequence of Russian and Soviet imperialism and colonialism. Mark Scharf, his fictional alter ego in the novel *Ground Up*, experiences pangs of "imperial guilt" in the presence of Inara, his Latvian cleaning lady, whom he greets with a Latvian "*Labrit*" (Good morning) to atone for the fact that "her compatriots [were] long forced to say '*Dobroe utro*' to mine" (Idov 2009a, 37). With regard to Slavs, however, Scharf assumes an attitude of breezy Russo-centric Panslavism. He has no qualms translating the deposition of a "frail Slovenian émigré" in court, explaining: "I don't happen to speak Slovenian, but figured its hisses and whistles ran close enough to Russian" (25). At the New York marathon, where he volunteers as a translator, he declares Russian and Polish to be his languages of expertise. As he explains, this was "not because I knew Polish but because Poles should know Russian" (27). Later in the story, seized by imperial *and* class guilt, he tries to chat up the two Polish workers in the construction crew who renovate his café, but it turns out that "they didn't care about the Molotov-Ribbentrop pact, or actress Barbara Brylska" (76).[7]

Ultimately, then, Idov's Russianness is an imperial (post-)Soviet phenomenon facilitated by the Molotov-Ribbentrop pact. Tellingly, Idov begins the preface to a volume of essays on Soviet design that he edited in 2010 in the following way: "I belong to the last generation that can reasonably call itself 'Soviet'" (Idov 2010b, 6). The fact that he titled his book "Made in Russia" rather than "Made in the USSR" shows to what extent the two identities have become entangled. It is also a self-conscious avoidance of the nostalgia industry of the late 1990s, when "Made in the USSR" became a popular song and slogan. After Russia's "independence" from the Soviet Union, an attempt was made to distinguish between ethnic Russian identity (denoted by means of the word "russkii") and civic Russian identity pertaining to all citizens of the Russian Federation (denoted by means of "rossiiskii"), but as an ethnic Jew from Riga and U.S. citizen, Idov qualifies for neither label. He can only be considered Russian in his capacity as a former Soviet citizen and as a projection of the host society culture. The linguistically russified and culturally Sovietized Jewish population of the Soviet Union, the majority of which now resides in Israel, the United States, and Germany rather than in the Russian Federation, provided a seemingly perfect example for the ideal of a supranational, Russophone Soviet ethnos (except that the Jews, despite their assimilation to the prevalent culture, still were denigrated as "rootless cosmopolitans" and singled out for governmental and grass-roots stigmatization).

Perhaps it was this experience of acculturation to a dominant ethnicity that facilitated the assumption of a new identity in emigration. At least that is what Idov seems to suggest when his fictional character Mark Nicolas Scharf muses about his middle name: "The only thing I hated more than my family name was the middle one, shamefacedly fashioned Ellis Island-style from my father's Nikolai, itself a scaredy-cat Slavic gloss on the Jewish name Nakhim. A two-step of *passing*" (2009a, 226). Idov seems to condemn melting-pot style assimilation if it means the abandonment or concealment of one's ethnic roots, even though he himself (in another "scaredy-cat Slavic gloss"?) changed his last name from Zilberman to Idov, which was his mother's maiden name.

What, then, is Idov's own self-assigned identity? In a 2010 article for *New York* magazine titled "Klub Prokhorov," Idov discussed a group he called "Global Russians," and in which he included himself. The term was apparently coined by Vladimir Yakovlev, the former editor of the weekly *Kommersant*, who also takes credit for having created the term "New Russians" in the 1990s. From 2008 to 2011 Yakovlev served as the first editor of the glossy magazine *Snob*, a project financed by the billionaire and one-time presidential candidate Mikhail Prokhorov. According to Yakovlev, "Global Russians" are *Snob*'s target demography (Kharitonova 2008; see also Iakovlev 2011).[8] How does Idov define this notion? As he explains in his *New York* magazine article, "the term indicates a combination of Russian culture and language with Western education, a well-stamped passport, and liberal Western views. . . . They're not interested in the Russian ghetto of Brighton Beach or the Russian assimilated culture in Fair Lawn, New Jersey. They're dismissive of the nouveau riche shoppers and clubbers. They think they're better than those others are. They're consumed by cosmopolitanism and all it entails" (2010a).

Idov's notion of cosmopolitanism posits thus a kind of immigrant identity that eschews both assimilation and parochial ethnicity, and also opposes the capitalist ethos of the New Russian plutocrats. Nevertheless, there is a distinct overtone of stratification and elitism. Not everyone can afford to belong to the exclusive global Russian club, and *Snob*'s creators never pretended otherwise. Idov seems to have no problem with the socioeconomic privileges attached to this concept and with what Kwame Anthony Appiah, in his book on cosmopolitanism, has called "an unpleasant posture of superiority toward the putative provincial" (2006, xii). At the same time, the category of global Russians needs to be broken down into two substrata: there is obviously a vast difference between oligarchs like Mikhail Prokhorov and middle-class "cultural producers" like Idov, who fulfill a service function in the global Russian ecology.

The components Idov lists as key ingredients of the global Russian worldview—progressive politics, an international orientation, contempt for the trappings of bourgeois materialism, a high validation of language and culture, and a feeling of superiority vis-à-vis the less enlightened—are reminiscent of the classic values of the Russian intelligentsia. The Russian critic Varvara Babitskaya, in her review of Idov's *Kofemolka*, also draws a connection with the old notion of the intelligentsia—"a major Russian brand no worse than vodka or balalaika," as she calls it—that became defunct in the economic turmoil of the 1990s. In her opinion, Idov's success among global Russians can be explained by the fact that they recognized him as one of their own. As she reasons: "The current educated class has lost its identity and wishes very much that someone would call it by its name. Perhaps the answer to that request is a *global intelligentsia* [English in the original], which has lost its national allegiance and even the 'fifth line' [in the passport asking for nationality] and which exists beyond the borders of the Russian Federation in a much purer version than within. In the same manner, the Russian language, preserved in the mouth of emigrants, often sounds purer to a sensitive ear than the language of the contemporary Russian press" (2009). The preferred habitat of Idov's global Russians is a multicultural, multilingual, secular, hedonistic, and culturally sophisticated urban environment. This is represented by the bilingual, "quasi-European" city of Idov's birth, Riga, and by New York, the place where he launched his career and which he called "the only city where I can live" and the only place about which he has "any kind of sentimental feelings" (according to his 2010 interview with Elena Polyakovskaya).[9] An additional habitat for Idov's global Russians is among the cosmopolitan Muscovites who identify with publications like *Snob* or *GQ*.

It is interesting to note that Idov chiefly claims the "global Russian" label when he is addressing an American audience (as he did in his *New York* magazine article). When asked by a Russian journalist whether he belongs to the category of global Russians, Idov responded: "The phenomenon exists. The problem is that there are about a hundred people, and seventy of them write about the other thirty. But I am an American, after all (or rather, a New Yorker—during the Bush years this was a very important distinction, now somewhat less)" (Bavil'skii 2009). As we see, Idov seems to cherish the idea of shifting his identity according to his interlocutor by assuming the position of the respective Other—to Americans he is a global Russian, to Russians he is an American, and to American provincials he is a cosmopolitan New Yorker. His positioning could be described as the opposite of (post)colonial mimicry. By disassociating himself from any given context, he assumes the role of a cosmopolitan who is always at home "everywhere else."

Ultimately, Idov's constructivist cosmopolitanism also explains his relationship to his fictional characters. Unlike straightforward self-portraits, they are based on parts of Idov's own identity but also reflect his transcendence of those parts. In the same way as he is an American to the Russians, and a Russian to the Americans, when he shows those parts of himself to his readers, he signals to both audiences that they are components of his implied authorial identity that he has overcome in assuming the persona of a self-constructed cosmopolitan.[10]

Londongrad and the Russian Culture Industry

A particularly informative illustration of Idov's brand of cosmopolitanism can be found in the TV series *Londongrad*, one of the first creative projects that he undertook after quitting his job at Russian *GQ*. Commissioned by the Russian channel STS, *Londongrad* was the first Russian TV series filmed in London, the capital of global Russians. Idov served as the main screenwriter for the sixteen installments of Season One, which aired in September 2015. The premiere was the most watched program on Russian television in its timeslot, with a viewer share of over 20 percent according to an STS press release. The original impetus for *Londongrad* came from Vyacheslav Murugov, the director of STS and co-owner of Art Pictures Studio, who was interested in creating a series featuring the life of the Russian community in London. As a cosmopolitan Russian-American, Idov seemed to Murugov the ideal person to tackle this project. In several interviews, Idov has stated that, when tasked with developing a scenario about "Russians in London," he wanted to avoid the usual clichés—oligarchs, organized crime, decadent luxury—that inevitably arise with this theme (see Nikitin 2015 and Sitkovskii 2015). Nevertheless, these topics come up constantly in *Londongrad*. Misha Kulikov, the main hero (played by the actor Nikita Efremov) is a cynical Oxford University dropout who runs an agency called "Londongrad," which provides a variety of services to (mostly rich) Russians. His two partners are Alisa Zagorskaya (played by Ingrid Olerinskaya), the estranged daughter of a Moscow oligarch, and Stepan Sysoev (played by Pavel Ilin), a mysterious cabbie and former cop who speaks no English and, in a touch of surrealism, drives around town in a battered Soviet-era Lada.

This set-up of characters allows Idov to have it both ways, as it were: his heroes occupy an economic niche in the plutocratic world of Russian London, but they are not really of this world. Misha and Alisa, similar to the characters of *Ground Up*, are clever, middle-class hipsters, while Stepan mimes a tough Russian provincial *muzhik* who lacks cosmopolitan polish. All of this distances them from the Russian moneyed elite, on which they at the same time depend for their livelihood. The distance between Kulikov and his clients may be seen as a representation of the stratification of the global Russians into wealthy power brokers and an intelligentsia "service class," discussed above, to which

Idov himself belongs. As Idov explained to the journalist Gleb Sitkovsky (2015), "because of the nature of his occupation, [Kulikov] constantly comes in contact with Russian oligarchs, but he himself cannot stand them. This means that we look at them through the eyes of Misha Kulikov."

The various modalities of Russian life in London are reflected in carefully staged interior designs. The opulent mansions of the nouveau riche elite (see figure 10.1) contrast with the slick modernist look of the Londongrad corporate office (see figure 10.2), which features reproductions of avant-garde paintings by Kuzma Petrov-Vodkin and Kazimir Malevich. Meanwhile, the somber cabinet of the Secret Service station chief at the Russian Embassy (see figure 10.3) sports an illuminated portrait of Putin and a picture of Stalin's never-built Palace of Soviets.

Apparently, Idov felt a need to control the narrative of *Londongrad* and its reception beyond the TV screen. Simultaneously with the first season's airing, he kept a blog on the website of the journal *Afisha Daily* providing background information about each installment and responding to viewer comments (Idov 2015). A common denominator of Idov's pronouncements is his attempt to de-politicize the series. According to Idov, his intention was simply to tell a well-crafted story while at the same time parodying a variety of cinematic genres and paying homage to models such as Richard Curtis's *Love Actually*, Guy

Figure 10.1. Michael Idov's *Londongrad* (2015): Boris Brinkman (played by Sergei Rost), Misha Kulikov's attorney, exemplifies the opulent lifestyle of the Russian nouveau riche elite.

Figure 10.2. Michael Idov's *Londongrad* (2015): Stepan Sysoev and Alisa Zagorskaya at the "Londongrad" corporate office. The walls are decorated with reproductions of Kuzma Petrov-Vodkin's "Red Horse" (*left*) and Kazimir Malevich's "Red Cavalry" (*center*).

Figure 10.3. Michael Idov's *Londongrad* (2015): The FSB station chief at the Russian Embassy in London, framed by a portrait of Putin and an image of Stalin's unrealized Palace of Soviets.

Ritchie's *Snatch*, or Aleksei Balabanov's *Brat 2*. As Idov asserts more than once, the milieu of Russian London was of secondary importance to him—as far as he is concerned, the story could be set anywhere in the world.

Idov's statements are clearly at variance with the comments made by STS studio executive Vyacheslav Murugov, who sees the exotic, touristy location as a key element of *Londongrad*'s appeal. In Murugov's opinion, "even the most banal dialogues, with the background of Piccadilly or the Millennium Bridge, look striking, they give a completely unexpected new vision: you seemingly watch a Western series, but they speak Russian" (2015). It seems hard to imagine that Idov would not cringe at such a characterization of his screenplay. Remarkably, although numerous smaller roles are played by British actors, very little English can actually be heard in *Londongrad*. Following a long-established practice in the Russian film industry, English dialogues are all drowned out by a Russian voice-over, apparently because the Russian TV viewers cannot be expected to cope with actual English. This linguistic uniformity makes the seemingly cosmopolitan show strangely parochial.

Ultimately, however, the predominance of the Russian language corresponds to Murugov's intention. As he explains, for him the series is not about England or the clash between Russian and British mentalities, but about the immutable nature of the Russian character. What attracted him to the theme of the Russian diaspora in the first place was that "a Russian remains a Russian everywhere, bringing with him a piece of the motherland" (2015). The promotional material released by STS takes a similar tack, presenting the content of the show as "the difficult fate of Russians who, by a whim of destiny, find themselves far away from the motherland, beyond the sea, in London. In order to remain themselves, to preserve their soul and their ribs whole and safe, they have to stick together."[11]

The discrepancy between Idov's and Murugov's approaches illustrates the binary between "cosmopolitan" and "provincial" mentalities of Russian tourists in Britain discussed by Ryazanova-Clarke (this volume). The evident disconnect between Idov's vision for the series and the marketing campaign around it maps onto the rapid shift of Russian public discourse about the West in the years it was produced and aired, when, as Gorham explains in his contribution to this volume, the "Russian World" project transformed from one of outreach to the cosmopolitan diaspora to consolidation of Russian populations abroad behind Russia's "unique" civilization. Perhaps partially out of political necessity, STS promoted the show not as a portrait of cosmopolitan global Russians but as a celebration of Russian patriotism. The promotional slogan for the series became *uznai svoikh* (literally "recognize your own people"). Resurgent anti-Western xenophobia in the wake of the Ukrainian conflict presented its own challenges for the release of a Russian TV series based in London. The Union Jack, originally featured in the show's promotional material, had to be replaced with a less offensive double-decker bus, as Idov later reported in a *New York Times* article (2016). Perhaps it was the inherent clash between Murugov's and Idov's views that eventually led to Idov's dismissal from the project after the first season (a second season was filmed without Idov's participation). Idov's termination also demonstrates the power differential between the two classes of global Russians that the show itself portrays—those who hold the purse strings and those who fulfill the function of hired "creative minds."

The conflict over *Londongrad* highlights Idov's own uneasy position with regard to class and national allegiance. Like his hero Misha Kulikov (with whom he shares the same first name), Idov is an intellectual whose livelihood depends on the Russian moneyed elite but who does not necessarily share its values and worldview. As we have seen, he tries to dodge the political pressures of present-day Russia by stressing the nonpolitical, "l'art pour l'art" nature of his work. For a creative artist, especially one working in Russian film and television, this means a constant tightrope walk. Here is Idov's both evasive and revealing response to a Russian journalist who asked how, as a "global person," he deals with the "patriotism that has unexpectedly seized the whole country": "I usually hide from such questions behind my American passport—who cares about my opinion of a country of which I am not a citizen. And, overall, I am a rootless cosmopolitan. But only in the sense that genuine patriotism for me is not connected to a state, but to culture and language. I am a great fan of Russia. Most of all, I would like the country to be a leader in world culture, to produce books that everybody reads and music that everybody listens to" (Nikitin 2015). Idov's ironic embrace of the term "rootless cosmopolitan" turns the anti-Semitic slur into a proudly accepted badge of honor, or a shield. As Margarita Levantovskaya (2013, 190) has observed, "'Rootless cosmopolitan,' the phrase that reminds us of false accusations directed at Jewish intellectuals under Stalinism, now stands for a new, aspirational identity that threatens nationalist narratives." At the same time, Idov's somewhat quixotic, or perhaps nostalgic, vision of Russia as a leading producer of world culture reflects the position of a cosmopolitan intelligentsia that is becoming increasingly marginalized amid the paroxysm of present-day Russian "patriotism." The apolitical ideal of disinterested artistic production with a worldwide resonance, as admirable as it may sound, does not mesh well with the issues of economics and military expansion that underline Russia's current quest for geopolitical power.

An article that Idov published in the January 10, 2016, issue of the *New York Times Magazine* looks like an attempt to come clean about his role as an "American writer who writes Russian films." He mentions that he moved to Moscow at a relatively hopeful moment, when hundreds of thousands of people were protesting in the streets for a "Russia without Putin," but he has no illusions about the direction that the country has taken in the meantime. While the pursuit of independent journalism, in the form practiced by *GQ* magazine and other organizations like it, has become increasingly perilous, Idov claims that show business has been more or less left alone by the regime. This presents creative opportunities, especially for a TV channel like STS that "wisely refrain[s] from news content altogether." Idov's summary of his role in the Russian culture industry draws once again on his status as a transnational outsider:

> So far, the only way I was able to make it in the Russian culture was to ignore the facts. Just like I blithely pretended that I was editing GQ, not GQ Russia, I would write my scripts as if they would end up at CBS or Channel 4 in Britain. I didn't force myself to inhabit the Russian point of view, even if my characters were ostensibly Russian, and instead wrote them from a remove—and I think that's precisely what worked, because the Russians themselves are tired of their centuries of self-examination. (2016)

Whether this approach will be sustainable remains in doubt—Idov himself, by using the past tense, hints at the precariousness of the situation. A larger issue raised by his cosmopolitan liberalism is the conflict between idealism and power, given that a creative artist can easily be coopted by the agenda of financial backers. This includes not only the pillars of the Putinist regime in Russia but also, more generally, the forces of global capitalism. As we learn from his recent memoir *Dressed Up for a Riot*, Idov's attempt to turn the Russian *GQ* from a glossy lifestyle magazine for the moneyed elite into a vehicle of serious journalism was frustrated not so much by government censorship as by the opposition of the big advertisers. As he explains, "The last thing a luxury advertiser wanted to see was their product opposite something unexpected" (2018, 80). In order to survive, the witty, cosmopolitan culture of the *Snob* variety depends on the financial largesse of oligarchs and billionaires like Mikhail Prokhorov. An illustration of this conundrum can be found in the very plot of Idov's novel *Ground Up*. Mark Scharf sees his Viennese café in the Lower East Side of New York not primarily as a moneymaking enterprise but as a sort of cultural statement, an emblem of sophistication and authenticity in a world of stultifying corporate chain outlets. Not until the end of the novel does he realize that his venture was only able to exist because, unbeknownst to him, his dreaded mother-in-law—a hard-nosed corporate lawyer, bully, and philistine—had been paying the bills.

Cosmopolitans No More?

It seems unlikely that the global intelligentsia that Idov represents will triumph in Russia anytime soon. Rather, the opposite will probably occur. Since the Ukrainian conflict, it has become harder and harder to be a global Russian, as Vladimir Putin has been reeling Russians into Russia and "claiming" populations that live abroad in various ways. This is hardly compatible with Idov's notion of global Russianness. Other bilingual cosmopolitan intellectuals such as the Russian-American journalist Masha Gessen have fled Moscow for the United States, and Idov himself now resides in Berlin. The exodus of intellectual and artistic luminaries (which also includes the economist Sergei Guriev, now residing in Paris, or the writer Boris Akunin, who has moved to England) raises the question whether the era of open borders and Russian cosmopolitanism was just a temporary fluke of the early Putin years, when life in Russia was prosperous and stable enough to support global Russian wealth and transnational cultural and intellectual integration after the instability, poverty, and cultural confusion of the 1990s and before the chauvinism and xenophobia of more recent years. One wonders whether the phenomenon of the versatile transnational Russian intellectual will now be replaced once again by the previous Cold War model of writers and artists in "exile."

As a countermodel to Russian nationalist cultural isolationism, Idov's cosmopolitan brand of culturally sophisticated global Russians, funded by transnational moneyed elites, presents its own pitfalls and contradictions. As has been pointed out more than once, cosmopolitanism as an emancipatory project is marred by its entanglement with the forces of neoliberal global capitalism, which makes the pursuit of a "'Third Way' between rampant corporate globalization and traditionalism or nationalism" (as described by Calhoun 2002, 874) a fraught enterprise. While engaging in a seemingly disinterested project of artistic excellence, Idov nevertheless fulfills a "service" function in a system based on hierarchic hegemonic power. In self-fashioning a cosmopolitan persona out of the shards of discrete languages and ethnicities, Idov strives to avoid capture within a repressive circumscribed identity, and, as we have seen, he takes care to distance himself from the materialistic values of "the nouveau riche shoppers and clubbers." Nevertheless, his vision of a Russian cultural revival detached from economic and nationalist realities may ultimately be revealed as the utopian project of a brief historical interlude.

Notes

1. Michael Idov, Facebook post, June 14, 2014, https://www.facebook.com/michaelidov/posts/10152474616132988.

2. The most prominent Russian "ambilingual" writer of the past century was Vladimir Nabokov. Ambilingualism can also be found among the current generation of Russian-American poets (see Wanner 2018), but Idov appears to be the only ambilingual Russian-American novelist active today.

3. Michael Idov, Facebook post, April 21, 2014, https://www.facebook.com/michaelidov/posts/10152351014637988. All English translations of Russian quotes are my own.

4. For a comparison of *Ground Up* with its Russian self-translation, see Wanner 2013.

5. See Platt's contribution to this volume for comparative discussion of the cultural position of extraterritorial Chinese and Russian populations.

6. The correct form would be "ne volnuisia."

7. Brylska, the Polish-born star of the 1975 Soviet hit movie *Ironiia sud'by*, is probably better known in Russia than in her country of birth.

8. Interestingly, "Global Russian" seems to have no Russian equivalent. In Russian texts, the term always appears in English and is spelled in Latin rather than Cyrillic characters.

9. Idov made this statement before his move to Moscow. He now resides mainly in Berlin, another "cool" global city.

10. Idov's latest pronouncement on his identity comes at the end of his recent memoir *Dressed Up for a Riot*. He claims that his three years in Moscow "resoundingly failed to answer" the question of his own Russianness, but, given that his daughter is now undeniably a Russian native speaker, he has "successfully kicked the identity can down the road to the next generation" (2018, 261–62).

11. See http://londongrad.org.

The "Globe-Trotting Russian" in Scotland

Discourses of Russian Cultural Tourism

Lara Ryazanova-Clarke

Russians at Large

Most of the chapters in this book consider the relationship of Russian culture to geography in light of literary and other cultural production by Russian communities across the globe. What happens, however, if we examine the relationship of culture to geography from the reverse perspective—from that of the consumption of other cultures by Russians on the move? How do Russians make sense of themselves in relation to other territories and cultures? Until the fall of the Soviet Union, very few Russians could lay claim to the sobriquet "globe-trotter." Visits abroad were available to an extremely small group of Soviet citizens who held a place of privilege in the Soviet social hierarchy or were being rewarded for political loyalty. Tourism in the Soviet era was constructed in a distinct manner that differs greatly from Western and current global practices. In contrast to bourgeois tourism, designed to satisfy the vulgar urges of pleasure-seeking, passive consumers, Soviet tourism promoted travel as a purposeful, patriotic journey for intellectual and cultural exploration, but even more for bodily self-improvement through walking, hiking, cycling, and the like (Koenker 2003, 2013; Gorsuch and Koenker 2006).

Furthermore, the notion of *turist* in the Soviet Union related predominantly to domestic travelers: the communist regime cultivated ignorance about foreign countries among its citizens (Gorsuch 2003, 761) and promoted phantasmatic political geographies of its own design. Readers of the Soviet press were invited to compare the accounts of the healing, restorative, and educational properties of Soviet spaces to visions of Western depravity, decadence, and poverty. Anne Gorsuch provides examples from *Pravda* articles of the 1950s written by Soviet correspondents in New York, who describe that city as dangerous, "dirty and neglected," and "full of rotting, messy, discarded goods, scraps of newspaper, cigarette butts and such waste" (Gorsuch 2003, 779). Travel abroad was permitted from 1955 on, but political control was kept tight, including the requirement of an exit visa, for which the application form included questions about family and work history, relatives living abroad, and family members interned during the war (Gorsuch 2011, 112). In addition, the applicant was obliged to pass an interview with the "ideological committee." Traveling to Western countries occurred in groups organized by the official state travel agencies (Intourist and the Komsomol agency Sputnik) and organizations (such as trade unions or the All-Union Society for Friendship with Foreign Countries), or in delegations of participants in cultural, sporting, and academic events.

The primary official role of Soviet travelers abroad was to serve as envoys of peaceful coexistence between socialism and capitalism while promoting the Kremlin's political messages. At the same time, "exposure to the foreign was supposed to help [tourists] to become 'more Soviet' and, as the Intourist guidebook for Soviet tourists instructed, 'to love their homeland even more strongly'" (Gorsuch 2011, 16). In contrast, less privileged members of Soviet consumer society, who had little chance of seeing "decaying" capitalism with their own eyes, generated their own myths of life in the West (*zapad*) or abroad (*zagranitsa*). For more and more Soviet people in the last decades of the USSR, the West was the absent wonder of lives led elsewhere, in the desired land of plenty symbolized by jeans, the Beatles, and colorful neon signs. This imaginary West was produced locally by imitation and symbolic replacements that had little to do with real geographies (Yurchak 2006, 158–206).

The cultural history of the Soviet and imperial *imaginaire* has been the main perspective from which Russian tourism has received growing scholarly attention in recent years (Ely 2003; Gorsuch 2003, 2011; Hirsch 2003; Offord 2005; Gorsuch and Koenker 2006; 2013; Layton 2009; Peteri 2010; Snow 2012; Koenker 2013). These valuable studies aside, the role of international tourism in shaping and narrating the Russian geographical imaginary since the end of the Soviet era has received little attention. Some aspects of post-Soviet tourism have been addressed in a series of publications on the commodification of the Russian language (Pavlenko 2012; Muth and Ryazanova-Clarke 2017). But the question of how contemporary tourism informs the self-identification of traveling Russians—the question that lies at the core of understanding the geographical imaginary of post-Soviet Russia—still remains to be addressed. This chapter focuses on the above question, exploring identity construction of Russian tourists from a discursive perspective.

The fall of the Iron Curtain, followed by the crumbling of the Financial Curtain, which continued to separate formally liberated but poor Russians from the rest of the world throughout the 1990s, coincided with intensified globalization processes across the world, contributing to the reconfiguration of post-Communist world geographies. Today, foreign tourism has become a favorite Russian pastime. First arriving as an activity of the new middle and wealthy classes, foreign travel for leisure subsequently spread to lower income groups as, with an expansion of low-cost flights and package tours to the Russian market, cheaper ways of traveling and experiencing foreign countries and cultures emerged. Of course, as Russians have become able to see previously inaccessible locations for themselves, the political and cultural narratives of the Soviet era have given way to new forms of geographical imagination. Yet we would be wrong to claim that the visions of the past have completely dissipated.

As studies of tourism have argued, tourists and tourist industries are the sites for the production of particular conceptions of place and culture, linked to the socioculturally framed "tourist gaze." According to John Urry and Jonas Larsen, looking at a place does not occur in a cultural vacuum. In fact, every act of looking is a "learnt way of seeing": "People gaze upon the world through a particular filter of ideas, skills, desires and expectations, framed by social class, gender, nationality, age and education. Gazing is a performance that orders, shapes and classifies, rather than reflects the world" (2011, 2). The tourist gaze is an embodied, performative practice of interaction with the local environment that has both a visual and a linguistic articulation. Examination of how language articulates foreign travel experiences may demonstrate how the tourist gaze is conditioned by contemporary forms of cultural, social, and economic life and by dynamic processes by which they change. This chapter provides a case study of Russian tourist discourses in order to offer insight into how globalization of Russian sociocultural practices has created a set of geographical meanings and imaginaries that train the post-Soviet gaze. The study draws on twelve hours of recorded data in the form of twenty oral narratives, obtained from Russian visitors in Scotland, collected during ethnographic fieldwork that took place in Edinburgh from March to November 2015.[1] Using this material as a basis, the chapter addresses the following questions: How do Russian tourists imagine foreign places? What set of contexts affects their tourist gaze? How is the self of the Russian globe-trotter constructed and performed in tourist discourse? And finally, what does this new liberty in global mobility *mean* for the Russians who choose to undertake a trip to Scotland?

Russian Tourism in the UK

Truly mass Russian foreign tourism dates to approximately the mid-2000s (Furmanov et al. 2012). Within a decade, it grew into a well-established economic sector, involving thousands of operators and a myriad of destinations across the globe. The growing demand for foreign travel was created by a sustained period of economic growth, which led to markedly increased spending power and the emergence of a relatively affluent and culturally inquisitive middle class in Russia (Ryazanova-Clarke 2014a). Over the last decade, Russian overseas tourism grew annually at an impressive 15 percent rate (Tiurina 2012), while in 2013, the year before the outbreak of conflict in Ukraine, the increase was as high as 32 percent (Tiurina 2015).

The rupture between Russia and the West over the Ukrainian crisis, Western sanctions against Russia, low oil prices, and depreciation of the ruble have had a negative effect on the outward flow of Russian tourists. According to a Levada Centre poll, in summer 2016, the number of Russians planning a holiday abroad decreased from the previous year by half, from 6 percent to 3 percent of the population (Interfax 2016). In real terms, though, in a massive country like Russia, this still amounts to over 8 million people who were able to participate in the international tourist market. From the outset, the UK has been a favorite Russian tourist destination. Since the beginning of the millennium, when the annual number of Russians visiting the UK was 110,000, the numbers more than tripled by 2014 to around 343,300 per year, including 318,000 coming to Britain as tourists.[2] This created a basis for optimistic forecasts that, provided there were no major unexpected contingencies, the figure in question would reach 370,000 by 2021 (VisitBritain 2014, 32).

The commonplace image of Russians abroad has a notorious track record of producing ironic and derogatory attitudes in host countries ("Russkie turisty . . ." 2009; Maksimova 2013). But by the time of this study, the image of Russian tourists abroad was improving—as their capacity for spending rose they increasingly appeared to be attractive and desirable customers. The year 2013 saw an increase in Russian spending in the UK by 16 percent, and despite a recorded drop of 17 percent from that figure in 2015, Russians are still bracketed within the highest spending group (BMI 2015, 16)—leaving at the till £1,057 per visit, twice the amount spent by the average international tourist (Bearne 2014; VisitBritain 2014, 36). Scotland is a major beneficiary of this dynamic, occupying second place after London among destinations for Russian international tourism and Edinburgh—the second most visited destination after London (VisitBritain 2014, 40). Until recently, Russians presented the fastest growing and highest spending category of international visitors to Scotland overall—thus, in summer 2014, a record number—11,000 Russian tourists—visited Scotland, surpassing visitors from China, India, and Brazil (Williams 2014).

The rapid growth of tourist travel among Russians serves as an expression of foreign tourism's ever-increasing importance as a highly valued aspect of post-Soviet cultural life and leisure. As we shall see below, for Russians, tourism functions not only as a recreational and educational activity but, more importantly, as a tool of identity construction and a marker of social, economic, and cultural differentiation. Ultimately, it is a means to enhance one's cultural capital. In 2014 VisitBritain, a UK government-funded national tourist agency, published a detailed study on Russia as a tourist supplier for Britain. The research findings of this study are attributed to a variety of academic, public, and independent market research bodies. The surveys quoted in the document show that Russians perceive foreign travel as a matter of prestige, taking priority over domestic holidays—and, according to Russian Statistics, 33 percent of Russians "dream of going abroad" for a vacation (VisitBritain 2014, 15). In another survey, conducted by Arkenford Market Research for VisitBritain, advice from family members, friends, and colleagues is listed as the main factor affecting the choice of Russians' travel destination (VisitBritain 2014, 22). Hence the stories of visits shared within these groups become especially important in shaping and propagating the patterns of perception of the foreign world, including the tourist gaze.

As the world has opened up before Russians, the geographical imaginaries embedded in generations of Russians have been remapped and redefined. The mass fantasy of sultry, "exotic" geographies has moved from Soviet tourist destinations in the Caucasus and Crimea to the beaches of Thailand and the Caribbean, while the "civilized" West has been reconfigured from a location of consumerist forbidden fruits and Cold War rivals into a "normalized" place in which one might set up a second home, educate children, or conduct banking. Moreover, foreign tourism has become a means for the globalization of Russian cultural forms and practices as travel creates spaces and contingences for articulating "global Russianness" (see Wanner, this volume).

Today, international tourism has firmly settled in Russian public culture, where narratives of Russian tourist imaginaries are mass mediated and reproduced. A plethora of television and radio travel programs have joined the industry of "worldmaking" (Hollinshead et al. 2009) that conjures up certain images and rhetoric to create favored representations of people, cultures, and places. The list of television and radio travel programs that fire the imagination of millions of potential travelers include the Ukrainian travel show "Orel i reshka" (Heads and tails), available on Russian TV channel "Piatnitsa" (Friday); Dmitry Krylov's "Neputevye zametki" (Wayward notes) and Vladmir Pozner and Ivan Urgant's "Puteshestviia Poznera i Urganta" (Pozner and Urgant's traveling adventures) both on Channel 1; and the radio show "Poekhali" ("Out of here," 2008–14), presented by Marina Koroleva on the Echo of Moscow Radio station. In addition, the range of travel magazines has also become broad, including *GEO* (currently closing down), *Vokrug sveta* (Around the world), *Turizm i otdykh* (Tourism and leisure), *Voiazh* (Voyage), *Puteshestvie vokrug sveta* (Round-the-world journey), *Turizm—praktika, problemy, perspektivy* (Tourism: Practice, problems and perspectives), and so on. All of these media institutions contribute to formatting future global tourists, forming textual and visual expectations, shaping imaginary frames, and training the gaze.

Tourism: Imagination, Identity and Discourse

Contemporary tourism is both a product and a manifestation of globalization. Following Arjun Appadurai's pioneering work on globalization, mass tourism has been discussed through the metaphor of flow, in which movements of people (ethnoscapes) are interlinked with other-scapes, consisting of movements of technologies, finance, images, and information and ideologies (Appadurai 1996; see also Jaworski and Lawson 2005; Salazar 2012; Salazar and Graburn 2014, Herrero and Roseman 2015). Anthony Giddens (1991) describes travel as a "fateful moment" in life when the experience of movement across space and cultural matrices may contribute to the re-imagining of the self. From the early pilgrims' creation of moral geographies and sacred topographies to eighteenth-century European grand tours, nineteenth-century sentimental journeys, and twentieth-century adventure tourism, travel has been seen as a means for personal discovery and transformation (Cunningham 1994; Offord 2005; Layton 2009). With the removal from familiar space and its associated habitus, tourism drives subjects through a liminal experience, a passage through a "little death," as they are thrown into the unknown and tasked with acquiring new behavioral dispositions and reassembling a new habitus that combines the elements of both the original and the new cultural locales (Jack and Phipps 2005).

The key essence of tourism resides in an imaginary, which, according to Paul Ricoeur, achieves its forceful materiality in discourse (2004, 268) and is both a function and a product of meaning construction (1994). Working within this frame of explanation, the anthropologist of mobility Noel Salazar conceptualizes tourist imaginaries as "socially transmitted representational assemblages that interact with people's personal imaginings and are used as meaning-making and world-shaping devices" (2012, 864). Like the gaze, imaginaries are socioculturally situated. They are explained as "complex systems of presumption—patterns of forgetfulness and attentiveness" (Vogler 2002, 625) and "implicit schemas of interpretation" (Strauss 2006, 329). Rather than being idiosyncratic, imaginaries are shared both within a society and across borders (Salazar and Graburn 2014). In the formation of tourist identities, imaginaries work as integral components (Adams 2004). These practices of self-imagination and self-fashioning are complemented by interrelated processes of engagement with—and representation and consumption of—the other. In the cultural economy of tourism, individuals and groups re-imagine themselves and construct their own social and cultural identities via consumption of a foreign and prima facie distinct culture.

However, the total system of such cultural consumption has received various interpretations. Some, such as Hollinshead, stress that tourism produces mediated uniform images that today have become an aspect of global business (1998, 121). Consumption of the other, with its power to renarrativize and spectacularize the place, homogenizes "the world," producing universal sets of imaginaries, disseminated as representations of globally known locations (Hollinshead et al. 2009). Others argue that the cultural flows of transnational imaginaries are far from uniform and homogeneous; instead, they produce ruptures, disjunctions, and inequalities (Appadurai 1990; 1996). Jack and Phipps also dismiss claims for the homogeneity of tourist practices and suggest that these practices should rather be conceived as a "participatory set of interactions-in-the-world" (2005, 5) in which the culture of the traveler and the host culture interact and engage in unique cross-cultural dialogues, in a unique exchange of linguistic, emotive, and material nature.

The tourist imagination is not directly observable, yet it generates certain material manifestations, including, most importantly, discourse. Mobility is inherently discursive: when processing their experiences, tourists turn into "mobile story-tellers" (Jack and Phipps 2005, 64). They shift into high semiotic gear and, using the tourist gaze, systematically produce, order, and narrate their experience (Urry 2002, 2005; Urry and Larsen 2011). Travel and narration are closely linked: movement becomes a kernel around which discourse is created and meanings are constructed (Jaworski and Pritchard 2005). In what follows, I conceptualize globalized tourism practices as conflicted in nature—as a discursive negotiation between sameness and difference, the global and the local, familiarization and defamiliarization. Tourism is first of all a relationship and, as Ingold notes on the relational model of a human being, "the self is constituted as a centre of agency and awareness in the process of its active engagement within an environment. Feeling, remembering, intending and speaking are all aspects of that engagement, and through it the self continually comes into being" (2000, 103). How, then, do Russian tourists come into being in Scotland?

To answer this question, in what follows I consider the anthropological views expressed by Appadurai, Hollinshead, and Salazar on the flows of the tourist imaginary as a cultural globalization process. I triangulate these views with Jack and Phipps's notion of tourism as cross-cultural interaction and with a broadly conceived perspective that apprehends sociocultural meanings, imaginaries, and, identities as inscribed in discourses (Thurlow and Jaworski 2003, 2010, 2011; Jaworski and Lawson 2005; Heller et al. 2014). I comprehend the tools of these discursively constructed imaginaries and the meanings they consist of as "frames of imagination" (a notion I derive from the concept of "knowledge frames" developed by Teun van Dijk [2003]).[3] Frames of imagination manifest themselves in various argumentation strategies and rhetorical topoi, which assume specific linguistic forms of articulation as outlined by Wodak and Chilton (2006) and Wodak et al. (2009), as well as van Leeuwen (1996, 2008) and others. My analysis of these frames of imagination aims to identify specific discursive elements, mechanisms, and strategies employed by Russian tourists in the process of gazing at, interacting with, and consuming Scottish cultural sites, which in turn are repurposed in performances of a "global Russian identity."

Salazar defines the relations between the traveler and the local environment in terms of two distinct "logics": the first is a "cosmopolitan logic of equivalence" that usually ignores local differences and homogenizes traveling experiences, and the second is a "provincial logic of differentiation" that creates divisions and differences (2012, 875). The section below presents an analysis of Russian tourist discourses that takes Salazar's two positions as a point of departure and examines what the patterns discovered by Salazar say about Russian culturally conditioned frames of imagination. I will argue that in contrast to two clear-cut "logics," what we observe in the Russian material are trends and orientations rather than clearly defined types: the discourse shows complex and often hybrid assemblages in which the elements of the cosmopolitan and the provincial are produced inconsistently and sometimes superimposed.

Data Analysis: The Cosmopolitan-Oriented Frame of Imagination

I begin with discussion of the cosmopolitan-oriented frame of imagination, and in particular, with a subcategory that may be termed "Scotland is the West (Europe / the wider world)." When talking about Scotland, many Russian respondents employ a strategy of generalization and deemphasis of cultural and geographical nuance. Whatever effort Russian tourists might have taken to select Scotland out of all possible tourist destinations, they often convey that this country is for them just a sample of the West, perceived as a homogenous unity. Scotland is therefore imagined through metonymy as a part of a larger Western whole, while the notions of "Europe" and "the West" are often used synonymously. This pattern may be observed in Example 1:

(1) Магазины закрываются рано. Ну это как бы общеевропейская тема (D-1)

The shops close early. But this is a common European theme, so to speak.

As seen from this example, the amalgamation of Scotland to a larger Western imaginary other entails the subject position of a knower: the tourist displays a presupposition of familiarity with how things are or should be in Europe, while the tourist gaze betrays a blind spot with regard to locality, as it picks out these "common European" features in Scotland and ignores others. Possibly, this frame of imagination goes back to Russian cultural matrices in which the West has traditionally been a significant category of otherness in Russian constructions of identity (Tolz 2001, Ryazanova-Clarke 2012).

A variant of this subframe may be called "Scotland is part of the familiar wider world." It relates to situations in which tourists legitimize their claims of having a "correct" perception of Scotland by referring to their larger experience as world travelers and performing their global awareness. Tourists applying this subframe typically narrate their experience as a homogenized imaginary of foreign places in general, extrapolated to their consumption of Scotland. This can be seen in Example 2, in which the tourist D-5 explains her ability to appreciate Scotland by the fact that she is an avid traveler.

> (2) Я была много где на шарике, и у меня острое ощущение красоты. (D-5)
>
> I have been many places around the globe and I [therefore] have an acute sense of beauty.

Russian tourists displaying this subframe of imagination highlight their cosmopolitan aspirations and discursively mark their worldliness and ability and eagerness to experience a foreign place. In these situations, tourists imagine transculturally, often using the tropes of comparison and sourcing images from globally mediated representation and stereotypes of spaces, as in Example 3:

> (3) Если сравнить с Америкой, я не обратила внимания, чтобы в Эдинбурге были бы серии ресторанов, таких как Старбакс, и тоже отсутствие пробок. Свободное движение. По сравнению с другими европейскими городами, здесь не так много велосипедистов. Чувствуется, что это другая культура, много ресторанчиков, кафешек, что присуще европейским городам. (A-1)
>
> If we compare [Scotland] with America, I have not noticed that there are restaurant chains in Edinburgh such as Starbucks. Also, there are no traffic jams. Free flow of traffic. In comparison with other European cities, there aren't so many cyclists. One feels that this is a different culture, there are many restaurants, little cafes, which is typical for European cities.

Here, the cosmopolitan frame projects worldly knowledge of other landscapes and cultures that heightens the status of the tourist as a knowing and sophisticated individual.

Yet the cosmopolitan frame of imagination does not necessarily imply a uniform group of Russian cosmopolitans who embrace the world. The same frame may be expressed in combination with negative judgments of non-Russian cultures and may open a space for display of a globalized version of post-Soviet ressentiment—the psychological state resulting from the suppressed feeling of envy and hatred and from the impossibility of satisfying these feelings. Liah Greenfeld (1990) discussed the conditions for ressentiment as being (1) belief on the part of the subject of the parity and interchangeability between the subject and object of envy and (2) suppression of actual inequality. In the case of the "Scotland is the West" subframe of imagination, tourists use the strategy of homogeneity to create equivalence between themselves and the object of their imagination and from this position may make disparaging remarks regarding the West and, metonymically, Scotland, as shown in Example 4:

(4) T-1: Ну мне кажется, что так по всей Европе: построена классика, неоклассика, и даже минимализм, который присутствует в лучших образцах современной архитектуры, там, начиная с Корбюзье, да? и тут человек, который сейчас населяет Европу—он какой-то очень . . . легкомысленный. Он какой-то очень несерьезный. Он какой-то . . . Я смотрю на своего зятя, который [работает] в Гугле, я никак не понимаю, за что ему деньги платят. [. . .] он постоянно ходит в каких-то таких майках, что мне просто страшно, понимаете? Он какой-то несолидный человек, какая там тросточка! И вот теперь эти все несолидные люди генерируют какие-то сумасшедшие идеи,

T-2: да, и всему миру их диктуют.

T-1: [. . .] какие-то одуванчики!

T-1: Well, I think it's like this all over Europe: they've built these classical, neoclassical and even minimalist buildings, which can be seen in the best examples of contemporary architecture, well, starting from Corbusier, right? And here's the guy who populates Europe—he's, how should we describe him . . . frivolous. He's, like, not serious at all. He's like . . . I look at my son-in-law, who is [working] in Google, I don't understand what they pay him for. [. . .] He perennially wears some kind of T-shirts, it shocks me, you see what I mean? He's, like, an insubstantial person, very far removed from [carrying] the [traditional British] cane! And now all these insubstantial people generate some kind of crazy ideas . . .

T-2: yes, and dictate them to the rest of the world.

T-1: some kind of weathervanes!

In Example 4, the two tourists talk about their impressions of Scotland via generalizations, bringing into conversation European architectural landmarks and names such as Corbusier. This imaginary of homogenization triggers the narrative of othering of the West, described through strategies of dissociation and negative attribution. The first traveler (T-1) uses a flurry of adjectives characterizing those who live in Europe as *frivolous*, *not serious at all*, and *insubstantial* before finally summarizing their collective character with the botanical metaphor *oduvanchik* (dandelion), which encapsulates in the image of the fluffy flower the idea of a light-minded and changeable personality, attributing negative connotations to this personality. Moreover, T-1 refers to the Western person as someone with *crazy ideas*; with which T-2 is fully in agreement. The second participant in the joint narrative seems to follow a dominant Russian official narrative when she represents people in Europe as those who "dictate to the world," meaning that they are intolerant of Russians' values and way of life, and they lack the democratic tendency of tolerance toward others. As Greenfeld argues, ressentiment leads to the transvaluation or rescaling of values. The passage above shows such transvaluation in which the values of "Europeanism," and linked to those, the values of Scottishness, are denigrated.

For some Russian tourists, consumption of a "Scottish lifestyle" presents an opportunity to imagine themselves fitting into the local environment, blending in and accepting the new Scottish habitus. In this subframe, which I refer to as "Going native," respondents display their knowledge of Scotland, not from a position of otherness but as individuals who have become naturalized to the new environment and perform their possession of local qualities, as expressed in Example 5.

(5) Скоттиш брекфаст с беконом! Меня люди не могут [. . .] понять—в России нет настоящего бекона, после этого начинаешь страдать на всю оставшуюся жизнь. (S-2)

Scottish breakfast [Eng.] with bacon! People can't understand me—in Russia there is no real bacon; after that you begin to suffer for the rest of your life.

Here, Russia is othered and denormalized through a description of it as a place lacking a characteristic and treasured feature of Scotland—Scottish bacon, the allegiance to which is marked through use of English. The speaker performs affect in a description of her sufferings back in Russia, for the rest of her life, without this desired token of Scottishness.

A story frequently produced by respondents describes being taken for a local, behaving like a local, or expressing tastes that coincide with the preferences of locals. One such story is narrated by two girls in their twenties in Example 6. It relates to their experience of visiting the Royal Edinburgh Military Tattoo:

(6) D-1: А у меня довольно забавная история. . . . Собственно говоря, когда мы ходили на Эдинбуру милитари тату, и мы сидели на трибунах, соответственно когда играет шотландский оркестр различные как бы знакомые нам шотландские мелодии, так слова песен, которые мы знали . . .

D-2: А мы знали практически все [*laughs*].

D-1: Мы сидим на фестивале, нас четверо или пятеро, в общем мы сидим и поем все эти песенки хором.

D-2: Ну да, так тихонечко.

D-1: Да, и так между делом между собой так тихонечко разговариваем, понятное дело, по-русски . . . А за нами сидят люди, ну как бы англичане—разговор просто между собой . . . Потом какая-то была пауза, и мы слышали, что, типа, посмотрите на этих перед нами сидящих. Такие, типа, молодые ребята, а уже такие шотландские националисты! [*laughs*]

D-1: And here is quite a funny story . . . Actually, when we went to the Edinburu Militari Tatu [accented Eng.] and we were sitting in the stands, when actually the Scottish orchestra played, like, the various tunes that we knew and the words that we knew.

D-2: And we knew practically all of them [*laughs*].

D-1: So, we sit at the Festival, four or five of us; so we, like, sit there and we sing all these little songs together.

D-2: Yeah, we are, like, singing quietly . . .

D-1: Yeah, and speak quietly between ourselves, naturally, in Russian. And behind us these, like, Englishmen sat, and simply chatted among themselves . . . Then there was some kind of a pause, and we heard, like, "look at them sitting in front of us: like, they are so young and are already such Scottish nationalists!" [*laughs*]

We see in Example 6 that the speakers D-1 and D-2 align themselves with Scots through multiple discursive elements. First, consider the structure of the story, in which the culmination is that the Englishmen took the Russian girls for Scottish nationalists. The end of the girls' story, presented in free indirect speech, conveys a strong positive emotion marked by emphatic prosody and laughter. Other salient strategies of self-presentation are the two speakers' metacultural and metalinguistic commentaries—the girls construct the meaning of "being local" through overlexicalization of their knowledge of both the tunes and words of the Scottish songs played at the Military Tattoo (which, ironically, is a maximally tourist-directed Scottish event): "the tunes that we knew and the words that we knew—and we knew practically all of them."

As in the earlier example of the Scottish breakfast, the girls at the Tattoo mark their acceptance of the new Scottish habitus by *languaging*—that is, by stylizing the local language. By switching to English in referring to Edinburgh Tattoo, the two speakers, to use Pierre Bourdieu's words, "position themselves within the repertory of customary practices of a local culture" (Bourdieu 1991, 194). Moreover, the girls perform a local level of metalinguistic awareness as they highlight their aural ability to distinguish the English people sitting behind them by the way they speak.

Provincial-Oriented Frames of Imagination

The provincial-oriented frame of imagination is represented in discursive passages in which Russian visitors seek visions and representations of otherness against a background of the familiar. Its first subframe, in which reference to Russian geography becomes a typical feature of the tourist narrative, may be termed "Scotland is unlike Russia." Discourses deploying this subframe assume the tourist gaze situated in Russia as a constant against which all other cultural and social locations are measured, allowing that which is not part of Russian everyday experience to be noticed and foregrounded while similarities are obfuscated. Thus, against a Russian background, many Russian respondents remark on the politeness and nonaggressive behavior they encounter in Scotland. Scottish people are imagined as friendly, kind, humane, and attentive to the needs of the visitors, as seen in Example 7.

> (7) Главное отличие в принципе почти всех стран от России это то, что люди гораздо более приветливые—ну, в Шотландии это гораздо сильнее заметно. То есть, тут люди просто на каждом углу здороваются и извиняются даже когда ты вроде ничего не сделала . . . и соответственно это очень приятно видеть это огромное отличие в устройстве жизни . . . в России, в частности, в Москве все всегда куда-то спешат, бегут и не замечают других людей. А здесь вроде бы все работают, все занимаются чем-то, но при этом у всех всегда находится время остановиться и поговорить. (S-3)
>
> In principle, the main difference of almost all countries from Russia is that people are much friendlier, but in Scotland it is much more noticeable. That is, here people say hello and sorry at every step, when you haven't even done anything wrong . . . So, it's very pleasant to see an enormous difference in the organization of life . . . In Russia, specifically in Moscow, people are always in a hurry, rush and don't notice other people. But here, it seems . . . everybody works, does something, but at the same time all of them always find time to stop and chat.

As we can see from Example 7, this subframe typically displays strategies of intensification, generalization, and assimilation—people are again stereotyped, but this time positive qualities of being polite, friendly, and welcoming are uniformly attributed to the Scots. These qualities are imagined through tropes of comparison, *locus amoenus* (a lovely, idyllic place), and hyperbole—manifested in superlative forms and other means of exaggeration: "much friendlier, much more noticeable, an enormous difference, at every step."

The rootedness of the tourist gaze in Russian geography is especially apparent in discourse fragments in which Scotland is described through Russian linguo-cultural references. In other words, tourists transfer Russian culturally specific realia, references to the Russian habitus, often manifested by set phrases and quotes, to the new environment. Such cross-cultural transfer may be seen in Example 8, capturing the tourist using the strategy of evoking a predication from Soviet holiday-making practices (*dikarem*), in which having a holiday independently without booking a guided tour or getting a place in a holiday resort was an unusual and risky matter, and applying it to their Scottish experience.

(8) Мы много наездили дикарем. (D-4)

We traveled in the "wild" style [independently] a lot.

Another speaker imagines his group wandering in the Scottish hills by evoking the characters of the Soviet cult animation film *Hedgehog in the Fog* by director Yury Norshtein (1975) (Example 9):

(9) Спустилось облако—мы такие как ежики в тумане. (S-6)

A cloud descended—and we are like "hedgehogs in the fog."

The story of Norshtein's hedgehog is one of becoming lost in an unknown, foggy landscape, charged with wonder and majesty but also potentially frightening and dangerous, and subsequently returning to a homey and familiar hearth and friends. Similarly, this first variant of the provincial-oriented frame casts the tourist encounter as one of disorientation that enriches, yet most importantly allows clear vision of one's familiar environment and identity via contrast with the partially known other.

A second subframe of the provincial-oriented frame may be termed "Marking social distinction." It is manifested in wealthy tourists' narratives that transfer to global contexts the social stratification and self-positioning established within Russia's social hierarchy. Integral to this subframe is a perception of Scotland as primarily a service provider, which is narrated from the subject position of a "first class" international traveler. Thus, the discourse passage produced by tourist W-1 in Example 10 reveals a clash between assumptions and expectations that she associates with her superior social standing and the lack of proper attention paid to her status in Scotland.

(10) Немножко бросилось в плане сервиса. Даже не сервиса, а отношения. Мы сюда приезжаем, мы вам рады. Но . . . работайте сами. Нет портье, который отнесет чемодан в номер. . . . И несешь сам! (*laughs*). Это сравнить там, скажем, с Италией, с Францией . . . там конечно этого больше. (W-1)

It struck me a bit in terms of the service provision. Even perhaps not the service but the attitude. We come here—"we are happy to see you. But . . . do the work yourselves." There's no porter to carry your suitcase to your room. . . . And you carry it yourself! [*laughs*]. If you compare this to, say, Italy or France, there is much more of that there.

In both presuppositions as well as articulated statements, Example 10 demonstrates expectations reflective of the Russian moneyed class. In particular, tourist W-1 expects to have the service of a porter at her hotel and to experience subservience on the part of service personnel, along with a high level of attention from the hosts and relief from onerous chores. To mark her dissatisfaction, the speaker applies irony toward Scotland through her strategy of a shift in footing—she assumes the voice of what she imagines as the generalized Scots: "we are happy to see you. But . . . do the work yourselves." A sense of entitlement is articulated by the slightly mitigated but, nevertheless, still emphatic expression of cultural shock: "It struck me a bit." Although this subframe of the imagination includes some cosmopolitan elements (Scotland is compared with other European places), the tourist also localizes and exoticizes the shortcomings of the Scottish service sector by describing those as a colorful Scottish trait, an "attitude" rather than a true failing of "service," which, as she explains later in her narrative, relates in her imagination to a marker of down-to-earth, modest, and industrious Scottish Presbyterianism. The other side of such exoticization seems to be W-1's effort to create a contrast and project herself as a globally aware cosmopolitan while making Scots look backward and provincial.

A third variant of the provincial-oriented frame may be termed the "Search for cultural otherness." This subframe manifests in discursive moves in which Russian visitors seek signs of Scottish cultural distinction. Such frames are especially frequent in descriptions of first contact with Scotland, which regularly contain marked emotiveness and expressive representations of the other:

(11) Другой мир, и наконец я до него добралась! (S-1)

Another world! And at last I've arrived here!

(12) Первое впечатление у меня было: залезли в автобус, на второй этаж, думаем, блин, а вот сейчас поедем по другой стороне дороги! (D-6)

My first impression was: we climbed into a bus, up to the second deck, and we're thinking, darn, now we'll drive on the other side of the road!

In Examples 11 and 12, stress on the new environment's alien nature is indicated in S-1's use of the phrase *drugoi mir* ("another world") in qualifying Scotland, the marker *nakonets* ("at last"), which expresses impatience to experience this different world, and the use by D-6 of the emotive quasi-obscenity *blin!* ("darn!") and emphatic prosody.

In the discursive representations of this subframe, as demonstrated in Examples 13 and 14, Scotland is frequently exoticized. Some perceptions follow an orientalist pattern, according to which tourists say they expect to see savage highlanders and wild aborigines or describe Scots in gendered and sexualized terms as hardy masculine men. Conflating space and time, the tourist gaze shaping these narratives imagines Scotland as a land of fairy tales, a dark historical past, and bloody and violent legends:

(13) Сейчас по дороге встретила несколько лиц, вы знаете, это Хэмингуэй в Шотландии! Настолько яркие, настолько вот мужественные лица, очевидно, что это вот аборигены, потому что судя по вашей природе, по вашему этому климату, по тем ветрам, которые мы со вчерашнего дня на себе испытываем, конечно, здесь люди должны быть очень сильные, крепкие, да? . . . вот такие настоящие мужчины. (T-3)

Right now, on my way I met several faces—you know, this is Hemingway in Scotland! Such vivid, masculine faces—it's clear that these are aboriginals because judging by your nature, by this climate, by all these winds that we have endured since yesterday, of course, people here must be very strong, robust, right? Such real men.

(14) D-7: Вообще очень сказочное ощущение отсюда, от Шотландии, как будто в сказку вообще попала. Вот . . . эти древние легенды о всех этих волшебствах, там героях, о мифических этих всяких местах Шотландии—они реально вот ощутимы. Идешь по Хайленду и думаешь: сейчас из-за холма вылезут феи,

D-5: да, и дикие горцы!

D-7: In fact, there's a real magical feeling here, in Scotland, as if you've landed in a fairy tale. All these old legends about all this magic, heroes, all these mythical Scottish places—they are really palpable. You are walking in the Highlands and thinking—now fairies will come out from behind the hill.
D-5: yeah, and wild highlanders!

Many testimonials such as those in Examples 13 and 14 demonstrate the speakers' desperate search for authenticity. The emotional content of these stories displays a nostalgia that is not actually based on lived experiences but is rather what Appadurai defines as "armchair" or "imagined nostalgia" (1996, 76). Much of the imagined nostalgia produced by Russian globe-trotters is informed by the interdiscursively evoked media texts and visuals the tourists were exposed to before their trips—such as the film *Highlander* or an episode about Scotland in Krylov's "Neputevye zametki," both shown on Russian television. In the Russian tourist imagination, Scottish history is embedded in universal, clichéd tourist images, as discussed by Hollinshead. Places such as Edinburgh's Royal Mile, narrow lanes—"closes"—of the Old Town, the Edinburgh and Stirling Castles, and the Holyrood Palace are consumed as borrowed narratives, while photographs and souvenirs are taken for tokens of authentic Scottishness. Illustrating another of Hollinshead's points—that tourism is a form of desire (2009, 429)—these Russian globe-trotters, through the act of consuming these clichés, express their yearning for an imagined authentic Scottishness that would allow them to enter into dream worlds that grant them access to experiences of the past. The popularity of this subframe of the imagination within the collected data tallies with VisitBritain findings that Russians more frequently than other tourists relate to the UK as a romantic, educational, and spiritual place (VisitBritain 2014, 27).

The urge to enter into the past in Scottish locales thought to be authentic and pure is sometimes so strong and vivid that tourist narratives display irritation with and rejection of signs of contemporary life that intrude on the imagination. Example 15 shows how the strategy of contrast is implemented by a tourist to counterpose her dream to reality. The speaker's privileging of the dream and attribution of authenticity to it are marked by reference to the signs of the city's contemporary evening life as "dissonance" and negative evaluation of young people enjoying themselves, calling them *podvypivshie guliaki* ("tipsy revelers") and *prazdnoshataiushchiesia liudi* ("loiterers"). The tourist gaze zooms in on somebody's golden sandals picked out from the crowd, making footwear into a symbol of contemporary Scots' emptiness and unworthiness of the dramatic Scottish past:

(15) Мне вот вчера [. . .] казалось, что здесь есть некое противоречие между городом, старым, хранящим средневековые тайны, всякие истории с нечистью, с суровой архитектурой, с жестким, очевидно, населением, которому очень непросто давалось в жизни, очень трудно—и веселящейся [. . .], вполне европейской толпой на улицах. В таких блестящих босоножках, таких, ну, подвыпивших гуляк, но уже не того, морского, пошиба, а вполне европейских, вполне французских, вполне лондонских, таких праздношатающихся людей, которые любят проводить время вместе. [. . .] В общем, был некий диссонанс. (T-1)

Well, yesterday it seemed to me that there was some contradiction between the town, which is old, which harbors medieval mysteries and all kinds of stories about fiends. A town with stern architecture and a hardened, it seems, population for whom life was never easy, very hard—and this jolly, [. . .] completely European crowd in the streets. This sort of tipsy revelers walking in these glittery sandals. But they are not of that sea-faring cut, but fully European, fully French, fully Londoners, these loiterers who like spending time together. [. . .] In general, there was a certain dissonance.

As in the case of some of the earlier examples, this one demonstrates how within one discursive passage tourists may mix elements of both major frames of imagination. While the narrative has clear exoticizing strategies that relate to Scottish historic and mythical themes and the theme of people's "authenticity," the contrasting segment, in which the speaker constructs homogeneity between Scottish youth and the European and London street crowds, is narrated within the cosmopolitan-oriented frame.

Russian Tourists between Cosmopolitanism and Parochialism

Twenty-five years after the world opened up for Russians to explore, many Russian tourists have turned into seasoned travelers who feel at ease hopping borders. An encounter with Scotland refreshes and excites their gaze, providing an opportunity for some to sample an experience of the civilized Western "abroad," and for others—to play out desires to visit exotic distant places. Tourists' stories of cultural engagement with Scotland reveal a variety of patterns of imagination generally tending toward the two types of "logic" defined by Salazar—that is, the cosmopolitan-oriented and the provincial-oriented types. Within these tendencies, Russian tourist narratives demonstrate a number of subframes, each with their own characteristic discursive strategies, means of articulation, and performances of self. Some are more clearly distinguished, while others display an instability of imaginaries, frame-shifting, and hybridity of vision.

Moreover, Russian tourist narratives manifest the entanglement and complexity of the many iterations of the "global Russian" subjectivity. As tourists consume Scotland and breathe the air of the "Western" world, their stories, in one way or another, negotiate the age-old, vexed dilemma of Russia's place in European civilization. It is received knowledge that Europe has been "the main 'Other' against which the idea of Russia has been defined" (Neumann 1996, 1), and that Russian identity discourses have for centuries included a comparison with the "West" (Tolz 2001; Ryazanova-Clarke 2012). Since publication of Petr Chaadaev's *Philosophical Letters* (1836), in which he fashioned Western Europe as a model of "normal" history and blamed Russians for backwardness and a lack of originality vis à vis the enlightenment of "l'homme de l'Europe," debate over Russian belonging has never ceased. Our tourist material vividly demonstrates that the emergence of the geographically mobile class in Russia has failed to frustrate existing master narratives about Russia's place in the world. On the contrary, these narratives continue to be internalized and reproduced by Russian "globe-trotters," forming a recursive background motif in the palimpsestic patterns of their tourist imaginations. With freedom obtained and their assumption of a place in a global landscape, contemporary Russian travelers use discursive strategies of comparison and contrast to mark linguistically whether they belong to the European world or represent a completely different entity. Oriented to the "Russian question," many testimonies are inevitably yoked, in one way or the other, to sociocultural spaces back in Russia, and some transcend the temporal boundary to Soviet practices and experiences. From the perspective of these spaces, many tourists conduct their dialogue with Scotland employing comparing and contrasting discursive strategies. Tourists displaying a "cosmopolitan" imagination attach themselves to Scotland, seeing in it a member of the European civilization to which they strive, and discursively performing their acceptance, belonging, and pride. For others, integration of their Russian selves into Scottish Europeanism is problematic—as they express in discursive demonstrations of contempt for the West and a sense of ressentiment, expanded from Russian-specific to global contexts.

For another group of tourists with predominance of the "provincial" imagination, a comparison between Russia and the West leads to an understanding that Russia is perhaps "not European enough." This is demonstrated in narratives showing speakers' insecurity at Russian "backwardness," embarrassment, and sense of inferiority. Still others imagine Scotland as an unfamiliar exotic province, worlds apart from metropolitan Russia. The difference they draw between the Russian self and the significant Scottish other triggers a variety of sentiments—from tourists' expression of feelings of their own superiority over Scottish provinciality to a humbling escapist admiration for the Scottish cultural sublime. The latter—tourist escapism and an imagined nostalgia—is perhaps the most globalized, mediatized, and clichéd frame of imagination. However, as VisitBritain asserts, Russians are ahead of other national groups in searching for the romantic in tourism, which explains the frequency with which Russian visitors color their Scottish imaginary in an exotic light.

In sum, Russian tourists' narratives of Scotland yield an array of meanings that show Russians' deeply conflicted relationship to their place in the world. On the one hand, while the "provincial" and "cosmopolitan" visions of Russian "globe-trotters" appear as extreme binaries, these frames of imagination are nevertheless unstable and often collide within the space of a single speaker's discourse, as many examples demonstrate. On the other hand, taken together, the two categories of imagination point to the deeply rooted and complex ideological knot of the antinomies of Russian modernization. The ambiguities of the tourist imagination have implications for the variability of cultural capital stockpiled by "globe-trotters" for presentation back at home. What will a carefully selected Scottish tartan souvenir indicate at our tourists' house parties, which are thrown upon their return? For Russian "patriots," it will perhaps mean a reaffirmed need to ward off the European other. For "Russian Europeans" it will signify the value of their owners' desire to remain attached to their European dream, or will demonstrate their superiority to Russian provincialism and to those unable to travel. Lastly are the numerous escaping romantics—who, looking at a token of Scotland, will probably continue dreaming of walks with the fairies.

Notes

This chapter reports the findings of the project "Travelling Cultures: Discourses of Russian Tourism in Scotland" (2015), funded by the British Academy and Learned Professional Societies. The grant was awarded by the CRCEES Consortium.

1. The data consist of transcripts of one-to-one and small group semi-structured discussions led by a moderator. All participants were from the Russian Federation touring Scotland and represented various age groups (from 19 to 60) and various social groups and professions (students, schoolteachers, performers, and business men and women). The visitors took a variety of tourist pathways—a general guided bus tour of Scottish

sites, a whiskey tour, and individual visits without accompanying guides. Tourists were asked to talk about their tourist experiences and impressions of Scotland.

2. See Federal'noe agentstvo po turizmu, "Vyezd rossiiskikh grazhdan za rubezh po naibolee populiarnym napravleniiam," 2014, https://www.russiatourism.ru/contents/statistika/statisticheskie-pokazateli-vzaimnykh-poezdok-grazhdan-rossiyskoy-federatsii-i-grazhdan-inostrannykh-gosudarstv/vyborochnaya-statisticheskaya-informatsiya-rasschitannaya-v-sootvetstvii-s-ofitsialnoy-statisticheskoy-metodologiey-otsenki-chisla-vezdnykh-i-vyezdnykh-turistskikh-poezdok/; Federal'noe agentstvo po turizmu, "Informatsiia o chisle turistskikh poezdok grazhdan Rossii v zarubezhnye strany za 2014 god, soglasno ofitsial'noi statisticheskoi metodologii otsenki chisla v"ezdnykh i vyezdnykh turistskikh poezdok, utverzhdennoi ukazom Rosstata ot 12 avgusta 2014 No. 510," https://www.russiatourism.ru/contents/statistika/statisticheskie-pokazateli-vzaimnykh-poezdok-grazhdan-rossiyskoy-federatsii-i-grazhdan-inostrannykh-gosudarstv/vyborochnaya-statisticheskaya-informatsiya-rasschitannaya-v-sootvetstvii-s-ofitsialnoy-statisticheskoy-metodologiey-otsenki-chisla-vezdnykh-i-vyezdnykh-turistskikh-poezdok/.

3. By "knowledge frame," van Dijk means generalized schemata that represent socially shared knowledge and other forms of social cognition such as attitudes, values, norms, and ideologies (2003, 92). For a more detailed account of the discursive organization of knowledge, see Goffman 1974; van Dijk 1998, 2008, 2010; Fairclough 1992. For discussion of how this relates to the post-Soviet situation, see Ryazanova-Clarke 2014b.

Rewriting Gender

Russian-American Women Writers and the Challenge to Russian Femininity

Yelena Furman

Immigrant Identities and Gender Trouble

Sasha Goldberg, the protagonist of Anya Ulinich's *Petropolis* (2007), secures a life in the United States by becoming a mail-order bride with the Kupid's Korner agency in Moscow. Her profile, put together by a cynically savvy matchmaker familiar with the demands of male American clients, turns a slovenly teenager into a traditional Russian woman who "love[s] to clean" (123). As Sasha's sardonic assessment of her eventual fiancé's beliefs about Russian women reveals—"Who the fuck *loves* to clean?" (123)—she fully recognizes that the profile represents a role that she must play in order to get to America. This projection of the image of a submissive, domestically inclined Russian wife as a role recalls Judith Butler's declaration that "gender is an 'act'" (1990, 146). Butler's framework grants insight not only into Sasha's subjugation to traditional gender roles but also her eventual transcendence of them. As feminist theorists have pointed out, "gender, as a construct, mediates the relation between bodies . . . and social meanings about them. It is a symbolic system by which bodies enter into sociality" (Verdery 1994, 226). The workings of this system, according to Butler, hinge on the repetition of norms. For this theorist, gender is neither biologically determined nor culturally inscribed on bodies but rather emerges by repeated performances of (hetero)normative scripts that regulate culturally sanctioned masculine and feminine roles. Yet precisely because the stability of gender categories depends on repetition, it becomes possible to subvert normative formations since there is always the possibility of a failure to repeat. Butler's theory highlights the potential for gender's alterability: if it can be performed differently as a result of a failure to repeat the norm, intentional or not, then gender is neither innate nor immutable. Sasha's trajectory realizes the possibility of "troubling" gender that Butler identified. Furthermore, it demonstrates the special conditions for gender trouble that arise from immigration.

Butler's conceptions are a useful framework for discussions of not only gender but also hybrid cultural identities, which have become central to the self-perception of many different kinds of communities and individuals in recent decades and which have been theorized in important recent studies (Kellman 2000; Singh and Schmidt 2000; Lim et al. 2006; Raab and Butler 2008; Guignery et al. 2011; Cheyette 2013). To be sure, contemporary analyses of hybridity do not conceptualize identity as an "act." Yet the cornerstone of these scholarly discussions has been a conception of identity as fluid rather than static: hybrid identities come about precisely as a result of historically and biographically contingent combinations of national, cultural, and linguistic affiliations. Indeed, as some scholars have argued, as an analytical category, "identity" often runs the risk of reifying what are always constructed and shifting categories of social being (Brubaker and Cooper 2000). Attention to the performative character of identity makes it possible to grasp the fluidity of identification.

This performative understanding of both gender and hybrid identities proves indispensable in analysis of Russian-American fiction, which has evoked a growing body of scholarship in the last several years (see, for example, Wanner 2011, 2012; Furman 2011, 2016; Klots 2011; Senderovich 2015b).[1] In academic and popular discourse, the term "Russian-American" is used to describe Soviet and post-Soviet, mostly Jewish, immigrants: those of the third wave, from the 1970s to the early 1980s, and of the fourth wave, from the *perestroika* reform period through the early 1990s, respectively.[2] "Russian-American" is only one of many other "hyphenated" identifications that arose as a result of the extraordinarily large numbers of Russian-speaking immigrants who dispersed across the globe in these years to become Russian-Canadians, Russian-Israelis, or Russian-Germans (Kishinevsky 2004; Remennick 2007; Gitelman 2016).[3] Since the beginning of the twenty-first century, there has been a flowering of literature by writers who either emigrated as adults or came of age in immigration and who identify, in varying degrees, as "hyphenated Russians" yet write in a language other than Russian. The majority of these writers of "translingual Russian fiction" (Wanner 2011) live in the United States and work in English, including Gary Shteyngart, Lara Vapnyar, Anya Ulinich, Irina Reyn, Ellen Litman, and others. Their works commonly focus on the experience of Russian Jewish immigrants in America and the hybrid cultural and linguistic identities that result from the interplay of Russian, Jewish, and American cultural affiliations; but as Lisa Wakamiya points out in this volume, several of these writers have "moved to reinvigorate immigrant writing by rewriting its boundaries or transcending them altogether," while at least one (as Adrian Wanner discusses in his own chapter in this volume) stands "apart from the growing cohort of so-called Russian-American authors" due to differing textual concerns.

Some scholars have begun looking at representations of new gender identities in this fiction. Karen Ryan argues that Russian-American women writers reject traditional conceptions of gender by renegotiating their protagonists' relationship to the domestic sphere, leading "to the productive formation of new identities" composed of Russian and American elements (2011, 66; see also Ryan 2013). In a recent special issue of *East European Jewish Affairs* devoted to "The New Wave of Russian Jewish American Culture," Margarita Levantovskaya analyzes the ways in which Lara Vapnyar's *Memoirs of a Muse* (2006), Irina Reyn's *What Happened to Anna K.* (2008), and Anya Ulinich's *Lena Finkle's Magic Barrel* (2014) rework gender identity in the context of intertextual play with Russian and Jewish-American male authors through "disidentification," which Levantovskaya (2016, 313) identifies as "the minority artist's way of engaging with old scripts and negative stereotypes, and using them to create new texts that destabilize established norms."[4] In the same issue, Karolina Krasuska (2016, 299) discusses the treatment of gender in Nadia Kalman's *The Cosmopolitans* (2010), involving "queering genealogy," by which she means producing an "interethnic/racial network of dependences and a counterpart to insular Jewish heteronormativity." Nevertheless, many texts by Russian-American women writers, including some cited by these scholars, exhibit varying degrees of acceptance of conventional gender roles, reflecting more traditional views of gender that have been imported by Russian immigrants to America. Still, the significant number of Russian-American women writers who have by now come on the literary scene, many of whom produce texts about female experiences featuring strong female protagonists, have established a distinct female—and to a significant degree feminist—presence in Russian-American fiction.

The present chapter begins with a discussion of how Russian-American women writers' treatment of gender both reflects and repudiates Russian cultural attitudes, ultimately carving out a women-centered space in Russian translingual literature. A close analysis of two texts, Vapnyar's *Memoirs of a Muse* and Ulinich's *Petropolis*, focuses on how these two authors reflect some Russian gender norms but for the most part trouble them. In both novels, this troubling occurs in the context of the protagonists' move to America, whereby reconfiguration of gender identity proceeds alongside reconfiguration of cultural identity. *Memoirs of a Muse* spotlights the protagonist's move from Russian muse to Russian-American author, thereby regendering the traditionally male sphere of artistic production to claim it as a female space in immigration; Ulinich's *Petropolis* asserts a nonconventional female body whose expulsion from Russia for sexual (mis)behavior becomes the catalyst for the creation of new, hybridized forms of cultural and gender identity in America. As such, these two texts sanction new performances of Russian-American womanhood.

The Feminization of Russian-American Fiction

Works by Russian-American women writers exhibit a push-pull dynamic of displaying conventional versus convention-breaking conceptualizations of gender, sometimes in the same text. Given the overwhelmingly negative and/or dismissive attitudes of most post- and ex-Soviet men and women toward any critical examination of gender, it is hardly surprising that treatments of gender in some works by Russian-American women writers bear traces of such a "resistance to gender theory." In general, Soviet and to this day post-Soviet conceptions of gender are rooted in "the assumption of natural sexual difference" (Ashwin 2000, 11), which determines distinct social roles for men and women. This kind of assumption is widespread in the Russian Federation and persists as well in the Russian immigrant community in America, where, as one study of Russian immigrant women showed, in terms of "the work-family divide, juggling multiple roles was a typical situation for most former Soviet women, and this did not change in the U.S. . . . No one expected their male partners to sacrifice their careers or incomes for the sake of childcare" (Remennick 2007, 253 and 267). Understanding gender as a matter of biology rather than as a cultural construct, the vast majority of post- and ex-Soviets might find Butler's conception of gender as performance utterly foreign in both senses of the word.

On the one hand, the fact that Russian-American women writers do not passionately advance particular views on gender is in itself significant as a (perhaps unintentional) move away from these attitudes. On the other hand, most of these writers also eschew gender as a category of self-definition and analysis. Whereas their interviews, essays, fiction, and websites highlight their status as immigrants and their hybrid identities, they include virtually no references to gender, suggesting that, for them, as for most post- and ex-Soviet women, this question holds little significance. In the absence of focused considerations of gender as such, Russian-American fiction often reflects traditionalist conceptualizations of femininity revolving around marriage, maternity, and caregiving. A small but telling example is Sana Krasikov's "There Will Be No Fourth Rome," part of her *One More Year* collection of stories (2009), in which the protagonist's remark "if you get more than two women in one room . . . the talk invariably turns to fertility" (223) illustrates an unquestioning alignment of women with their role as mothers and presupposes an understanding of gender as rooted in biological givens. Two of the texts in Levantovskaya's excellent discussion of challenges to gender norms—Reyn's *What Happened to Anna K.* and Ulinich's *Lena Finkle's Magic Barrel*—are also susceptible to quite contrary readings as well. In *What Happened to Anna K.*, a reworking of Tolstoy's *Anna Karenina* set in Russian immigrant New York, Reyn's choice to remain within the source novel's parameters results in a representation of women that conforms to, rather than undermines, traditional conceptions of gender. In Ulinich's *Lena Finkle's Magic Barrel*, normative gender roles seem to be the default mode: specifically, women are positioned as nurturing, self-sacrificing helpmates (the kind of role that undergirds Lena's relationship with the commitment-phobic Orphan).

Yet while some Russian-American writers reinforce traditional conceptions of gender, others diverge from them, describing strong female characters who do not conform to gender expectations. A case in point is Masha, the protagonist of Ellen Litman's *The Last Chicken in America*, who ends the novel-in-stories as an unmarried graduate student at Harvard. More broadly, the now considerable number of Russian-American women writers whose prose overwhelmingly features sexually independent female protagonists and focuses on women's experiences has effected a renegotiation of the gender dynamics of this body of literature as a whole. As one scholar writing about the different context of African and African-American literature notes, the preponderance of male voices representing and theorizing the African diaspora resulted in the fact that "diaspora people have been masculinized, and the diaspora has been claimed as an especially male place," a situation subsequently challenged by women writers whose production of women-centric works has inserted female voices into the conversation (Gourdine 2003, 1). Russian-American women writers perform a similar gesture in a different framework. The most prominent figure in Russian-American fiction is Gary Shteyngart, whose *The Russian Debutante's Handbook* (2002) is widely acknowledged as founding this literary trend. Shteyngart's oeuvre is a decidedly male endeavor: his in-your-face novelistic narratives feature male protagonists and markedly "masculine" shooting/exploding/chasing scenes, while his memoir, *Little Failure* (2014), is an account of a Russian Jewish immigrant boy's journey to manhood. Shteyngart remains the face of this form of literature due as much to the volubility of his public persona as to his writing itself. He therefore tends to overshadow many other members of this cohort. Russian-American women writers can be seen as redressing this imbalance by carving out a women-centered textual space. And, like New Women's Prose in Russia in the late 1980s and 1990s, fiction by Russian-American women writers challenges the male-dominated Russian canon and, arguably, also the American one.[5]

In this context, Vapnyar's endeavor is especially noteworthy as she directly addresses questions of gender and presents feminism in a positive light. In the absence of any organized feminist movement in the USSR, the only version of emancipatory rhetoric available to Soviet women was that of the state, which "exhorted women to be both producers and *re*producers," with the result that "they bore the double load of full-time work and all domestic responsibilities."[6] This rhetoric elicited a wary reaction from many Soviet-era women (Goscilo 1996, 8). In the last years of the USSR and the early post-Soviet period—when Vapnyar and Ulinich emigrated—broad mobilization for the fundamental reevaluation of Russian society stimulated a reconsideration of women's roles and the appearance of a nascent feminist movement, which nevertheless did not take root.[7] To this day, feminism in Russia carries overwhelmingly negative associations not only for men and social conservatives, but for many women and progressives as well: "Russians harbor deep suspicions regarding any and all aspects of its contemporary instantiation because of its Western provenance and because the unrealized promises of emancipation under socialism remain sedimented in collective memory" (Goscilo and Lanoux 2006, 20). This outlook also largely characterizes Russian immigrant women: the "line of ideological attributions" of feminism's negative qualities "has been repeatedly voiced by former Soviet women when asked to describe how they understand feminism and why even the most educated, independent, and successful of them would never call themselves feminists" (Remennick 2007, 269).[8]

Vapnyar's essay "Hillary's Underpants: The Sad Tale of 'Clintonsha,' or She-Clinton" (2008b), written during Clinton's first run for president, is possibly the only piece by a Russian-American writer that openly challenges such views.

Vapnyar notes how deeply sexism is ingrained in Russian society, calls out the traditional gender assumptions underpinning both negative and positive perceptions of Clinton, and calls for her to become the first female president of the United States. Vapnyar is similarly forthcoming in treating gender identity in *Memoirs of a Muse*, which, given its focus on a Russian woman's journey to adulthood in America, forms a (chronologically prior) counterpoint to Shteyngart's male-centric memoir, similar to the way that Ulinich's *Petropolis*, in highlighting the sexual adventures of its female protagonist, forms a counterpoint to the male protagonists' prominent (mis)adventures in Shteyngart's novels.[9] The fact that *Memoirs of a Muse*, like *Petropolis*, still partially reproduces traditional gender formulations complicates but does not negate the innovative feminist significance of this writing.

Regendering Authorship: Vapnyar's *Memoirs of a Muse*

Vapnyar is the author of five volumes of fiction: the short story collections *There Are Jews in My House* (2003) and *Broccoli and Other Tales of Food and Love* (2008a) and the novels *Memoirs of a Muse* (2006), *The Scent of Pine* (2014), and *Still Here* (2016). *Memoirs of a Muse* presents her most explicit contestation of traditional conceptions of womanhood. The novel is based on extensive literary play with the diary of Dostoevsky's mistress, Apollinaria (Polina) Suslova, in whose footsteps the protagonist, the Russian immigrant Tanya (Tatiana) Rumer, (rather implausibly) decides to follow in an attempt to inspire her American boyfriend Mark's creative literary efforts. Given that this text is concerned with the theme of immigration, the discovery of a self-sufficient and independent female identity proceeds in tandem with the articulation of a viable hybrid cultural identity: Vapnyar's protagonist learns not only how to be a Russian-American but also how to be a Russian-American woman. Specifically, Vapnyar links this process of self-fashioning in immigration with the protagonist's transformation from Russian muse to Russian-American author, a change that entails a regendering of the conventionally male sphere of artistic production to claim it as a female space in immigration.

Recently arrived in the alien environment of the United States, Tanya manifests a sense of selfhood that is in flux: as she laments on her first night in New York, "Where had I come? What was I doing here?" (78). A crucial factor in her disorientation is a lack of competence in English; on her first date with Mark, she is "ashamed of the rough, awkward sounds of [her] English" (94) compared to his fluent speech. Tanya's decision to become his muse is thus partially explained by her efforts to find a place for herself in a new and disorienting society and her desire to participate in some way in the production of literature. Yet her choice is undergirded by unquestioning acceptance of normative gender roles derived from her life in Russia, entwined with hallowed notions regarding artistic creativity. In Moscow, the male schoolteacher she is in love with tells her that her goal in life should be to become "the companion to a great man" (47). Taking this dubious career advice seriously, Tanya demonstrates how her identity is structured by traditional Russian conceptions of gender that underlie cultural notions of authorship: literary creativity is decidedly the province of men, whereas women, endowed with lesser abilities but greater emotional capacity, are assigned the role of helpmate and nurturer.

Tanya's story may be seen as a comically exaggerated illustration of Butler's idea of gender performance: whereas Butler maintains that individuals generally perform gender roles unintentionally, Tanya consciously takes on the role of Mark's literary companion. Tanya feels that becoming his muse is her destiny: as she puts it, "My whole life prior to meeting Mark was a series of . . . steps all leading me to this inevitable high point—becoming a writer's muse" (97). Modeling her behavior on Suslova's, she reads the latter's diary "to search for answers or to apply the ones I'd already found" (97) and subsequently begins to keep her own diary, titling it "Memoirs of a Muse" (106) and shaping it as a chronicle of Mark's writing process. Yet *Memoirs of a Muse* presents a caricature of Russian literary gender roles. Whereas Suslova inspired a genuinely talented writer (which, to be sure, does not mitigate the patriarchal character of the relationship), Tanya chooses one who is neither gifted nor even committed to writing. Mark spends most of his time "between novels" (131) and is preoccupied with material comforts. Dedicated to Mark's writing process, Tanya's diary remains comically lacking in substance: "He sometimes sits, perched on a chair, with one leg bent and serving as a prop for his elbow, and the other folded under his butt" (175). Eventually, the diary's form begins to reflect its banal content, its entries becoming "shorter, scarcer, boasting more and more abbreviations and neglected misspellings" (175). Subordinating one's life and writing to a man's is inherently problematic, yet Mark's pathetic lack of talent makes Tanya's vocation as muse all the more absurd.

Beyond lampooning traditional gender roles, Vapnyar's novel demonstrates the possibility of other performances of female identity, which goes hand in hand with the acquisition of a hybrid Russian-American identity. Like other Russian-American protagonists, Tanya progresses from feeling like a Russian foreigner to a new sense of social belonging, beginning with her acquisition of English (with the help of a neighbor's romance novels). The novel's last chapter, which brings the story up to the present, completes Tanya's account of finding her way in American life. The room her neighbor finds for her after she leaves Mark becomes "the first place in America where I . . . felt at home" (209), and as she walks around New York, she reflects, "I was . . . learning to see the crowd as a group of distinct individuals rather than a hostile mass, learning how to feel a part of the crowd myself" (209). Eventually, she completes a graduate degree in Russian history and becomes a college instructor. She retains links to her cultural origins through teaching Russian history, continuing to speak Russian, and maintaining close ties with relatives, while becoming an American academic settled in suburban New Jersey. Like many other protagonists of Russian-American fiction, Tanya makes the transition from disoriented Russian immigrant to hybrid Russian-American.

Likewise, Tanya's gender identity undergoes a shift catalyzed by her acquisition of English. While still with Mark, Tanya finds a biography of Dostoevsky in English in which Mark has inscribed her name not beside descriptions of Suslova but in passages devoted to Dostoevsky's relationship with his wife, Anna Grigorievna. Reading Mark's notes reveals some unpleasant truths about how Mark regarded their relationship: "And finally the gem of gems came: 'He could do with her what he willed . . . because in her great love for him she was ready to endure everything, to bear anything submissively'" (179). Tanya ruefully admits, "This was me. I couldn't argue with that" (179) as she accepts the realization that, contrary to her desire to emulate the strong-willed Suslova, she has accepted the role of inferior partner in an unequal relationship.[10] Her alienation from her role as muse is amplified by her discovery, now that she can read Mark's work, that his novel "was a bad book. Completely, hopelessly bad" (200). In *Memoirs of a Muse*, learning English not only grants Tanya entry into American life but also motivates her disassociation from Russian gender norms, an act of emancipation that ultimately makes it possible for her to write her own story—the larger *Memoirs of a Muse* that constitutes the novel itself.

To be sure, for much of the novel, Vapnyar's text relies on traditional notions of gender in terms of its refraction of literary history. Like Suslova herself in Russian literary culture, her fictional counterpart in *Memoirs of a Muse* is exclusively identified with her role as Dostoevsky's lover and literary inspiration rather than as an individual with her own needs and aspirations. Tanya assumes the same kind of role in her relationship with Mark. Yet ultimately Vapnyar's novel upends this configuration on various levels, most notably by regendering the traditionally male authorial sphere as female. Despite the many Russian women writers active from the nineteenth century on, and with some notable exceptions, such as Akhmatova and Tsvetaeva, the Russian literary canon is overwhelmingly defined by male authors. In this context, for women to assume the authorial position enacts what one scholar refers to as "claiming a male model" (Gourdine 2003, 89).[11] Yet moving to a "masculine" position does not in itself undo the fact of that position being considered masculine in the first place. Vapnyar's feminist maneuver consists in reclaiming the "male model" for women by presenting authorship as a decidedly female enterprise while relegating acts of male writing to the background. Whereas she both paraphrases and cites Suslova's diary directly, she almost entirely passes over Dostoevsky's oeuvre, despite some reference to his texts and his appearance as a character. Entering into dialogue with Suslova's writing rather than Dostoevsky's, Vapnyar asserts and privileges the authority of female writers. Moreover, Tanya's neighbor Vera is an artist who, as Tanya discovers after Vera's death, launches a comeback through a series of paintings titled *A Girl in the Elevator* (211), for which Tanya served as an unwitting model. In this final instance, Vapnyar reconfigures both sides of the muse/author binary as female.

The most prominent instance of female authorship in the novel belongs to Tanya herself, whose prodigious literary efforts ultimately far outweigh Mark's "hopelessly bad" writing. *Memoirs of a Muse* alternates between two plot lines: Tanya's retroactive narration of her life with Mark and her own rendition of Dostoevsky and Suslova's relationship, based on her reading of Suslova's diary. As first-person narrator, Tanya is the fictional author of both the autobiographical and the imagined biographical texts; and she also, of course, metatextually reflects the identity of Vapnyar herself. The link between authorship and reconfigured gender identity is foregrounded in the final chapter's account of Tanya's life after leaving Mark: marrying a man "drastically different from [Mark]" (207), she achieves a balanced relationship with her husband in which they each have professional careers and are equally involved in care for their daughter. In this last chapter, narrated from the vantage of the present, Tanya completes the trajectory of the narrative by producing a text that chronicles her own transformation from subordination based on Russian gender norms to independence achieved in a less rigidly gendered social context.

The ending of *Memoirs of a Muse* both upholds and undercuts the narrative's feminist momentum, an ambiguity arising from Tanya's turn to a new metaliterary reference: Tolstoy. Although, as an independent Russian-American woman, she ultimately rejects the Dostoevsky-Suslova prototype, substituting another male author (and a misogynist to boot) is not much of an improvement. Looking through her now-abandoned diary before she has to pick up her daughter, Tanya writes in the novel's final sentence, "Just one last tiny peek at the diary before I shut the book . . . to return to family life" (212), underscoring her break both with her former role as muse and, by extension, her model in

Suslova. In describing her current life, Tanya announces that her proudest professional achievement is her role as "historical consultant for yet another movie version of *Anna Karenina*" (208). The progression from Tanya's problematic relationship with Mark to the domestic tranquility of her present married life is paralleled, then, by a progression from Suslova and Dostoevsky to Tolstoy, who famously valorized family life predicated on retrograde conceptions of women's roles, particularly in *Anna Karenina*. At the same time, in a final instance of privileging female authorship, Vapnyar not only invokes but also rewrites her famous predecessor. Whereas Tolstoy depicts family life based on rigidly delineated gender roles, Vapnyar presents Tanya not only as a wife and mother but also as an intellectual professional. Responding to Suslova, Dostoevsky, Tolstoy, and the Russian tradition in toto, Vapnyar's protagonist and novel transcend women's gender roles as mandated by traditional Russian culture and assert instead Russian-American women's agency, creativity, and freedom to write their own identities.

Rewriting the Female Body: Ulinich's *Petropolis*

Anya Ulinich is the author of two works, *Petropolis* and the graphic novel *Lena Finkle's Magic Barrel*; of the two, *Petropolis* undertakes a significant reconfiguration of Russian femininity.[12] Unlike *Memoirs of a Muse*, in which Tanya's negotiations of cultural and gender identities proceed simultaneously, these processes do not carry equal narrative weight in Ulinich's text, which foregrounds the issue of cultural hybridity. Nevertheless, gender remains a fundamental theme in *Petropolis*: similar to texts by practitioners of New Women's Prose, this novel focuses on the female body and female sexuality, subverting normative conceptualizations. Ulinich presents an alternate configuration of a nontraditional female body, whose expulsion from Russia for sexual (mis)behavior becomes the catalyst for finding a place in America, legitimating new performances of both gender and cultural identity.

Whereas *Memoirs of a Muse* recounts the process of learning to perform cultural and gender identity differently, *Petropolis* presents from the outset an alternate performance in which the body itself is the source of difference. Born and raised in Siberia by her Russian mother, Lubov, and speaking Russian as her native tongue, Sasha is, in this sense, a white, ethnically Russian body. As indicated by her last name, Goldberg, she is also a Jewish body, as her father, Victor, was adopted by a Jewish family. Lastly, and uniquely in Russian-American fiction, Sasha is also a partially black body since Victor was the product of a Russian woman's tryst with an African student during the 1957 Thaw-era

Moscow Youth Festival. In Russia, her Jewish last name and especially her dark skin mark her as other, as the reaction of a shocked passerby indicates: "*Negritianka*!" (Negress!), the citizen exclaims upon seeing someone so far from the cultural norm (281). Yet while Russians see her as other, she sees herself as part of this culture. When Marina, another Russian-Jewish immigrant she meets in an ESL class in the United States, remarks that Sasha does not "look Russian" (93), she playfully responds, "Meet me: Sasha Goldberg, a real-life Russian *negritianka*" (93), also answering in the affirmative when Marina asks, "You're Jewish, right?" (94). With Sasha's body, inscribed as an intersection of Russian, Jewish, and black, *Petropolis* insists on a new performance of Russianness that accommodates rather than excludes hybrid combinations of identities.

Sasha's body is also the basis for a different performance of gender in that it eschews normative prescriptions for female physical appearance. After decades of a generally prudish public culture regarding sexuality in the USSR, Western-influenced gender norms have become dominant in post-Soviet Russia, as women are exhorted to strive for unreal standards of sexualized feminine beauty by an array of fashion magazines that "emphasise the idea that beauty labour is a duty—a key component of performing femininity for Russian women" (Porteous 2013, 133). In contrast, Sasha's body defies conventional female attractiveness. She is "overweight and uncoordinated" (4), sloppy in physical appearance, and awkward in bearing, earning the nickname "Hippo" (65). At the same time, this body is very much recognizable as a woman's and is associated in the novel with traditionally conceived feminine functions, such as pregnancy and giving birth, and with the roles of mail-order bride and domestic laborer. In severing the association of woman with beauty, Ulinich reconfigures gender norms.

Moreover, Ulinich subverts the dictum that sexuality is the exclusive province of conventionally attractive bodies. Regardless of her defiance of normative standards of beauty, Sasha nevertheless readily engages in sex, both as a teenager in Asbestos 2, with the handsome lowlife Alexey, and in the United States, with her major love interest, the quadriplegic Jake, who is the son of her unhinged Chicago employers. If Shteyngart's novels lend Russian-American fiction a markedly masculine tone through prominent presentations of their protagonists' erotic conquests, Ulinich makes the opposite gesture of "inserting female sexual desire into narratives of diaspora politic" (Gourdine 2003, 87). Although Sasha's acceptance of the role of mail-order bride could be read as submission to patriarchal norms, it soon becomes clear that this undertaking is a performance par excellence intended to coopt those norms. Sasha knows all along that this is a farce, engineered for American consumption by the Kupid's Korner matchmaker, who writes Sasha's profile as a "Passionate Dark Beauty" (109) with a love of cleaning to project a version of an exotic, domestically inclined, and sexually available body. Soon after arriving in Arizona with her fiancé, Neal, she rejects this role altogether: she picks the lock of the bedroom containing her passport and leaves for Chicago to start a new life; search for her father, Victor; and enter into a sexual relationship of equals with Jake. Sasha moves from playing a subservient, sexualized Russian woman toward being an independent one who owns her sexuality in an America that includes space for both the performance of nostalgic patriarchal norms (by traditionalists like Neal) and non-normative performances of identity.[13]

It is precisely Sasha's sexual activity that makes possible a different performance of gender in immigration. Sasha's succumbing to her sexual desire for Alexey results in an out-of-wedlock pregnancy and the birth of her daughter, Nadia, which ultimately precipitates Sasha's departure for America. Sasha's banishment stems from her mother's well-intentioned yet cruel actions—Lubov insists on raising Nadia as Sasha's sister and sends Sasha away to Moscow to study art in order to give her a chance at her own life; Sasha leaves Moscow for the United States as a mail-order bride in an initially fruitless attempt to bring Nadia to live with her. It is thus Sasha's transgression of sexual codes of behavior for young women, particularly from the type of intelligentsia family to which Lubov aspires, that ultimately results in her removal from Russia. As such, Sasha is an example of what some diaspora studies scholars refer to as a "sexile": she is forced to leave her country of origin due to sexual practices that conflict with social norms (Martínez-San Miguel 2014).[14] Being a sexile is inextricably linked with dominant notions of cultural identity—banishing sexual "deviants" upholds a nation's "patriarchal, heteronormative discourses of collective identity formation"—but at the same time has the potential to produce "alternative communal identities" for those thus (s)exiled (Martínez-San Miguel 2014, 165). In just this way, Sasha's expulsion from Russia ultimately leads to her production of an alternative gender and cultural identity in America.

This new identity develops as a move away from Russian norms of female sexual subservience, reinforced by American projections of Russian patriarchal traditionalism, such as those reflected in the mail-order bride transaction that brings Sasha to the United States. *Petropolis* presents Sasha's sexuality as the force through which she most powerfully asserts herself in immigration. Economically disenfranchised and culturally lost upon her arrival, Sasha controls at least one element of her life: her sexuality. Although Neal and the mail-order bride industry treat her body as an object, she is in fact an active sexual subject who unapologetically engages in sex for her own pleasure. If in Asbestos 2, the more experienced Alexey guides the relationship with the virgin Sasha, in her ultimate relationship with Jake she is the driving force. Their pairing reverses the traditional gender binary of male activity and female passivity: Jake is physically passive, not only because it is now he who is at first a virgin but also because of his disability. When they become lovers in New York, she is literally the powerhouse of their lovemaking, physically maneuvering Jake by "pull[ing] him up" from his wheelchair and showing him what needs to be done by "bringing his hands together and slipping them under her sweater" (306). Whereas her first sexual experience with Alexey is marked by youthful hesitancy, her first coupling with Jake shows her as a body actively seeking fulfillment: "Closer to the edge of ecstasy with every tiny movement of his fingertips, Sasha waited until he was hard again, guided him in, and came" (307). Sasha's assertively sexual and pleasure-seeking female body constitutes a new, nonnormative gender performance in immigration.

At the end of *Petropolis*, the themes of reconfigured gender and cultural identity converge: Sasha's sexile leads to an "alternative communal identit[y]" as her nontraditional female sexual body finds its place in a newly constructed family in New York. For the majority of the novel, Sasha is an outsider—first as a Jewish black body in Russia and subsequently as a Russian body in an alien United States. In Arizona, she is wryly bemused by Neal's banal world of discount shopping and complaints about "taxpayer dollars" (125). In New York, she is dumbfounded by her stepmother Heidi's all-permissive childrearing techniques that leave Sasha wondering whether "Heidi *like[d]* being hit" by her child (257), as well as by her insistence that Victor's and Sasha's problems can be solved by "talk[ing] to Dr. Phillips" (257). As is the case for Vapnyar's Tanya, Sasha's alienation from American culture is linked with her poor command of English: "After six years in the U.S., English still felt almost alchemical, impossible" (291). In contrast to Tanya's case, Sasha's transformation from cultural outsider to someone with a sense of belonging does not resolve itself smoothly. At the conclusion of the novel, when she brings the young Nadia to New York after Lubov's death, Sasha muses that Asbestos 2 will be "a curious footnote to her [daughter's] American life" (318), whereas "Sasha herself is made of it" (318), a phrase that attests to her continued sense of Russianness and displacement. Nevertheless, *Petropolis* ends with the narrator's statement that, as she walks to her New York apartment, "Sasha takes wider and wider steps, waiting to trip, but the sidewalk is strangely uniform, un-Brooklyn-like, and she makes it home without falling" (324). This description acts as a metaphor for Sasha's life in America. Reuniting with Nadia and Jake, and growing close to Heidi despite their differences, Sasha creates her own nontraditional family and becomes rooted in a new place. Whereas English may still feel foreign, the narrator observes that she now "thinks in an in-between language" (324). In this way, Sasha performs a new cultural and gender identity in immigration: that of a Russian-Jewish-black-American nontraditional woman who, appropriately, finds a home in a pluralistic, multiply varied New York.

Nevertheless, while championing alternative performances of cultural and gender identity, Ulinich still appears to retain traditional conceptions of gender in connection with maternity, reflecting, perhaps, the persistence of Soviet and Russian views. Regardless of women's long-standing participation in the workforce and the many public debates on the "woman question," the idea that female identity is inextricable from motherhood is perhaps the most deeply embedded element of Russian conceptions of "natural" gender characteristics and has remained unchallenged from the Soviet to the post-Soviet era.[15] One study of Russian students' life strategies found that, with only one exception, "the most important life purpose declared by young women is motherhood" (Baraulina and Khanzin 1996, 110). In America, the continuing prevalence of such attitudes is summed up by one female immigrant's declaration: "'You are not a complete woman as long as you don't have a child'" (Remennick 2007, 267). In a seeming echo of such views, all of *Petropolis*'s major female characters are mothers. The psychologically unbalanced and overbearing Lubov is Sasha's mother and Nadia's adoptive mother. Victor's American wife Heidi, despite her graduate work in Russian history, is until the end of the novel primarily a frustrated stay-at-home mom. Sasha's teenaged maternity identifies her with motherhood early on. Of course, physical distance from Nadia, combined with Nadia's belief that Sasha is her sister, attenuates her role as a mother. For all that, her daughter is a constant emotional presence. Sasha's pining for her child is highlighted through several italicized passages of internal addresses to Nadia, in one of which Sasha explains that while she originally had not wanted her baby, eventually "*I realized that I had no future away from you*" (102). Certainly, Sasha's unique life story reconfigures typical conceptions of motherhood: neither her broken birth family nor the complex network of relationships she assembles by the end of the novel conforms to patriarchal or traditional conceptions of family life, and her combination of unabashed sexuality with maternity defies deeply ingrained Russian conceptions of mothers as asexual and pure. Nevertheless, Ulinich's insistence that Sasha and all the other major female characters in *Petropolis* must be mothers in the first place appears to reflect deeply held Russian beliefs concerning womanhood, producing an unresolved tension between conventional versus convention-breaking attitudes toward gender.

In conclusion, both *Petropolis* and *Memoirs of a Muse* demonstrate that the process of articulating a new, hybrid identity in immigration is potentially a scene for the creation of new gender identities as well. Each of these novels may be read as a series of failures to repeat the norm that, as Butler theorized, opens a space for change. In the last fifteen years, as the phenomenon of Russian-American fiction has taken off, its many female authors have created a women-centered textual space, producing works centered on female protagonists and women's experiences. Of these, Vapnyar's *Memoirs of a Muse* and Ulinich's *Petropolis* stand out by directly engaging with the topic of gender, challenging Russian and Russian-American norms by means of faulty repetition and rescripting—focused experiments in gender trouble. In *Memoirs of a Muse*, Tanya literally writes her own new gender identity by stepping from Russian muse to Russian-American author and regendering the act of authorship; in *Petropolis*, Ulinich shows how Sasha, lacking conventional feminine attributes, articulates her own conceptions of assertive and unapologetic sexuality, which while forcing her out of Russia, ultimately allows her to build a nontraditional family structure and find a place for herself in immigration. Taken together, these novels show how new performances of gender identity become possible in the hybrid space between different understandings of what it means to be a woman. It is an open question whether, given the continually expanding list of Russian-American writers, gender will emerge more forcefully as a topic in other texts. Consciousness of feminism—other than in a negative sense and without a genuine understanding of its concepts—is not characteristic of Russian culture or the Russian immigrant community in America. Nevertheless, Vapnyar's and Ulinich's novels are examples of a small but visible shift. Just as New Women's Prose signaled a redefinition of femininity in Russia, these texts present new variants of Russian-American womanhood, offering alternate possibilities for performing gender roles.

Notes

1. These discussions often evoke Homi Bhabha's idea of the "Third Space" (1994) that emerges in an encounter between two (or more) cultures. Russian-American hybridity exists precisely as such a newly constituted third space, which privileges neither of the terms surrounding the hyphen but is instead their amalgamation.

2. This chapter uses the terms "Russian" and "Russian-American" to refer to place of birth and linguistic and cultural ties rather than ethnicity, following a practice common among members of the Russian-American community itself. Given the Jewish affiliations of the majority of this group's members, the term "Russian-American" should often be understood as shorthand for Russian-Jewish-American.

3. The third wave brought 250,000 Jews from the Soviet Union, while more than 1.6 million immigrated in the fourth wave, mostly to the United States and Israel, but also to Canada, Germany, and Australia (Remennick 2007, 4).

4. The theory of disidentification comes from José Esteban Muñoz, whom Levantovskaya quotes (Levantovskaya 2016). While both Levantovskaya's discussion and the present chapter view *Memoirs of a Muse* as challenging Russian conceptions of femininity, Levantovskaya stresses the protagonist's Jewishness. In distinction, this chapter considers Jewishness—represented only in scant references, such as the protagonist's aunt's and uncle's bottles of Manischewitz and the yarmulke her uncle wears to the Jewish center to get free food (77–78)—as less central for Vapnyar's novel.

5. New Women's Prose (Novaia zhenskaia proza) designates a category of late- and post-Soviet writing by women built around an open depiction of the female body. The group is typically described as including Liudmilla Petrushevskaya, Svetlana Vasilenko, Valeriia Narbikova, Marina Palei, and Nina Sadur, among others. Like Russian-American women writers, the authors of New Women's Prose had an equivocal relationship to feminism: some, like Vasilenko, embraced it; others, like Petrushevskaya and Palei, rejected identification with it (Goscilo 1993; Goscilo 1996, 87–116).

6. One exception was a feminist group founded in the late 1970s by Tatiana Mamonova, the writer Yulia Voznesenkaya, and two others, who came to feminism via political dissidence. Their activity precipitated KGB reprisals and eventual expulsion from the Soviet Union. Yet even they adhered to a biological model of gender, bolstered by their predominantly Russian Orthodox beliefs (Holt 1985; on Voznesenskaya, see Furman 2009).

7. Valerie Sperling, whose work describes post-Soviet Russian women's movements in detail, writes that feminist mobilization "thrived briefly in the 1990s and then declined in the first decade of Putin's rule before a new wave of feminist organizing began in 2010" (2015, 48).

8. To be sure, some of Remennick's interview subjects' conceptions of feminism had become more positive in the United States: "Entering American society with strong negative attitudes towards Western feminist ideology, many immigrants came to appreciate over time the gains it brought to women, especially in the workplace" (2007, 276). However, feminism's positive aspect for these women remained largely confined to this sphere.

9. Vapnyar's "Slicing Sautéed Spinach," from the collection *Broccoli and Other Tales of Food and Love*, features Ružena, a doctoral student in Women's Studies, one of the few instances in Russian-American fiction of such an overt feminist sensibility.

10. In another resonance with Butler's concepts of gender performativity and its iterability, Mark's relationships with women appear to be repeated performances: noting several other names written in the margins of the Dostoevsky biography, Tanya observes, "Mark must have been auditioning women for a long time" (179–80).

11. While Gourdine uses this term in relation to female protagonists becoming involved in lesbian relationships, it is also applicable to Vapnyar's heterosexual protagonist.

12. Like Vapnyar, Ulinich structures both of her novels around plays with the Russian literary canon. *Petropolis* reworks Mandelshtam's poem from his *Tristia* cycle, "At a terrifying height a wandering fire" ("Na strashnoi vysote bluzhdaiushchii ogon'"), while

Lena Finkle's Magic Barrel rewrites Bernard Malamud's "The Magic Barrel." Like Vapnyar's work, although in a more restrained manner, both revise male-authored texts from the perspective of women. On intertextuality in Russian-American fiction, see Finkelstein 2016; Furman 2016; Levantovskaya 2016.

13. To be sure, even after leaving Neal, Sasha is cast into gendered roles. In Chicago, she becomes a maid for a rich family, while in New York she runs a cleaning business. Yet just as her performance of a patriarchal gender identity with Neal is a conscious strategy, in these subsequent episodes Sasha pursues her own goals, making the most of the options available to immigrant women as a result of patriarchal associations of women with the domestic sphere.

14. As Martínez-San Miguel notes, while the term conventionally refers to "the expulsion of queer subjects" (2014, 166), she is expanding its use in relation to any censured sexual behavior, such as adultery and mixed-race relations.

15. In the Soviet Union/Russia, the highest echelons of power have regularly offered pronouncements on women's "natural" childbearing duty. In the last years of the Soviet Union, Mikhail Gorbachev sought to help women achieve this "truly female destiny" (Buckley 1989, 194). Soviet official concern regarding maternity was largely driven by late Soviet demographic crises (Buckley 1989, 179–82). Under Putin, similar concerns, magnified by a Russian nationalist agenda, have prompted a return to pronatalist policies (Chandler 2013, 107–32).

Song in a Strange Land

The Russian Musical Lyric beyond the Nation

Philip Ross Bullock

Between and Beyond

Writing in the Viennese newspaper *Blätter für Musik, Theater und Kunst* in 1855, the Russian composer and pianist Anton Rubinstein argued that "song is the only musical genre to have a fatherland" (1855, 145). The present chapter tests this claim by exploring how song is, and is not, connected with national culture, and by suggesting how diverse musical genres interact with global culture. In particular, it proposes two contrasting case studies of chamber vocal works composed outside of the "fatherland." The first and most important case study focuses on the Russian-born émigré composer Arthur Vincent Lourié. Here, the emphasis is on how song's perceived association with national culture facilitates a nostalgic relationship with the past through memory. By contrast, settings of Russian poetry by the British composers Benjamin Britten and John Tavener illustrate very different attitudes to and institutional experiences of Russian and Soviet culture. Throughout, this chapter interrogates the connection between poetry, music, and situation, asking whether the national identity of song is a product of a composer's ethnicity, his or her geographical whereabouts, the language of a song's poetic text, or the contexts of a song's performance and reception. As we shall see, Rubinstein was entirely correct, yet simultaneously utterly mistaken, for song is at once the most intimately national and also the most portable unit of cultural life.

Rubinstein's view rests on a close, even exclusive identification between song repertoires and their corresponding national literatures. Yet such a definition overlooks the large amount of foreign poetry set by composers, as well as the extensive circulation of song outside of its national borders. The development of the French *mélodie* is unthinkable without Adolphe Nourrit's performances of Franz Schubert's *Lieder* in Paris in the 1830s (Tunley 2002, 89–101). More generally, the canonicity of German song ensures its central role in the repertoire of singers of almost all nationalities, even at times of geopolitical tension (Tunbridge 2013). National song traditions have often incorporated foreign poetry, whether in translation or the original language (Galushko-Jäckel 2015, 335–66; Weaver 2015; Bullock 2016). Rubinstein was as drawn to German poetry as he was to Russian, just as his musical language betrays the influence of Felix Mendelsohn and Robert Schumann. Does this mean that his German-language songs should not be considered part of the Russian tradition? Or should such works be counted alongside the substantial number of settings of German poetry, particularly that of Johann Wolfgang von Goethe or Heinrich Heine, by other nineteenth-century Russian composers?

It is worth dwelling on Rubinstein's claim, since it offers a number of ways of thinking about the circulation of music in global culture, and it usefully breaks down a single art form into a number of discrete genres, each with its own patterns of performance and reception. Opera, for example, has long been embedded in networks that facilitate its cross-border circulation. For a large part of its history, it has been composed and performed in the musical *lingua franca* of Italian, the language in which Rubinstein's *Demon* was first heard in London in 1881 (Taylor 2007, 179). By contrast, orchestral, chamber, and instrumental genres do without text altogether (even if works occasionally allude to literary plots and characters), and hence seem to cross borders without any need of "translation" (which is not to say that they are not sometimes perceived as "foreign" or "national"). The career of the virtuoso instrumentalist, like that of the prima donna, is one that takes place within an international circuit of performing venues (Cowgill and Poriss 2012). Rubinstein himself owed his reputation as a musician to both his extensive foreign tours and his anthological concerts "covering the entire history of European piano music from the English virginalists to contemporary Russian composers" (Taylor 2007, 194). By comparison, song seems to be more narrowly confined within the national context. Associated with domestic performance in the salon, intimately bound up with national canons of poetry, and—in Rubinstein's analysis at least—originating in rural folklore, song might well be the musical genre most closely linked to its "fatherland," and hence resistant to global circulation.

Yet Rubinstein also argued that song was the Russian genre most likely to become known in the West. Partly, this stemmed from his belief that the other genres of Russian music were still underdeveloped in comparison to European traditions. But his belief that song could spread the reputation of Russian music abroad reveals an awareness of how translation and publishing could facilitate the international circulation of culture: "It would be desirable if foreign music publishers could acquaint the public at least with songs (by publishing them in two languages), and in this way the public would be offered much that was new, artists would be exposed to a fruitful field for consideration, and in general the horizon of their artistic tastes would be usefully expanded" (Rubinstein 1855, 146). Although opera and orchestral music have dominated studies of the reception of Russian music in the West (Thomas 2005; Fairclough 2007; Bullock 2009; Alexander 2012, 2015a, 2015b; Muir 2013; du Quenoy 2015), there is an important story to be told about the discovery of Russian song. Transcription of Russian songs for piano solo enjoyed considerable popularity in the nineteenth century, as in the case of Franz Liszt's 1842 arrangement of Alexander Alyabev's "Nightingale" ("Solovei"). Later, songs were printed in bilingual editions that facilitated performance by singers with no command of Russian, as attested by the popularity of Petr Chaikovsky's "None but the Lonely Heart." Performers, too, introduced Russian music to European audiences. Pauline Viardot established the habit of interpolating Alyabev's "Nightingale" in the music-lesson scene in Gioachino Rossini's *Il barbiere di Siviglia*, and around the turn of the twentieth century, Maria Olenina d'Alheim brought the songs of Modest Musorgsky to the attention of French musicians at a time when he was still little appreciated in Russia (Tumanov 2000).

A further factor in the dissemination of Russian song was the publication of literary anthologies. Paul Collin's *Trente poésies russes* (1894) includes French versions of poems by Aleksei Apukhtin, Nikolai Grekov, Mikhail Lermontov, Dmitry Merezhkovsky, Nikolai Nekrasov, Aleksei Pleshcheev, Yakov Polonsky, Pushkin, Ivan Surikov, Aleksei Tolstoy, and Fedor Tiutchev, all of which had previously been set to music by Chaikovsky. In part, Collin's enterprise can be seen as a tribute to the Russian composer, who set four of Collin's own poems as part of his *Six Romances*, opus 65 (1888). More importantly, however, it constitutes a response to the predominance of prose works in the French reception of Russian literature, and in particular, to claims about the untranslatability of verse, made by Eugène-Melchior de Vogüé in his influential study *Le Roman russe* (1886): "The Russian poets have never been and never will be translated. The life and beauty of a lyric poem is in its arrangement of words and its rhythm; this beauty cannot be transferred into a foreign form. I once read a very admirable and exact Russian translation of Alfred de Musset's '*Nights*'; it produced the same sensation as when we look upon a beautiful corpse; the soul had fled, like the divine essence which was the life of those charming verses" (de Vogüé 1886, xi–xii, translated in de Vogüé 1887, 8). In disputing de Vogüé's pronouncement, Collin's anthology also attests to the importance of music in shaping patterns of literary reception; tellingly, its subtitle describes it as a series of imitations of various songs ("mélodies imitées par Paul Collin"). A similar point can be made about Rosa Newmarch's *Poetry and Progress in Russia* (1907). The first survey of Russian poetry to appear in English, it included historical and critical essays, as well as a number of Newmarch's own translations. Significantly, some of these had first appeared in 1900, in a brochure published by the Steinway Hall to accompany a lecture-recital given by Olga and Henry Wood and Newmarch herself, and which was later published in the journal of the International Musicological Society (Newmarch 1900, 1902).

But what happens to song when the link between music, language, and creativity is reframed as a result of migration or exile (a topic considered from the perspective of literature by Maria Rubins in this volume)? Although ethnomusicologists and historians of popular music have been assiduous in analyzing the power of song to create affective communities outside of political, national, and ethic borders (Baily and Collyer 2006; Biddle and Knights 2007; Kiwan and Meinhof 2011; Toynbee and Dueck 2011; Krüger and Trandafoiu 2014), there has been less consideration of this phenomenon with respect to the Western art-song repertoire. This question is even more acute within Russian studies, where it is only recently that music's place within the context of emigration has been examined systematically. This situation is related, in part, to a widespread belief that music functions as a kind of "universal language." Marc Raeff's classic study of "Russia Abroad," for instance, operates on the assumption that "music, as a language that knows no national barriers, was easily absorbed by and integrated into the host environments" (1990, 99). A further factor is the presence of Igor Stravinsky, whose chameleon-like ability to engage with the artistic debates of his host environments, as well as his claim to a kind of aesthetic formalism, has shaped discussion of musical acculturation. Here, Hermann Danuser's account is typical: "Stravinsky . . . can serve as an example of a composer bound to an ideal of autonomy, one that grounded him artistically throughout the various periods, countries, and stylistic phases of his life: Russian, French, America; or Russian folk-like, (neo)classical, serial" (1999, 161).

Yet recent reevaluations of Stravinsky's career have inflected the narrative of his ability to assimilate new local vernaculars within a spirit of cosmopolitan internationalism, adding a deeper understanding of his enduring connections to his homeland. Stephen Walsh has painted a more complex biographical portrait of the vicissitudes faced by the composer in the years following his removal to the United States (2006), and Jonathan Cross has delineated themes of alienation that run throughout his career, arguing that these can be traced directly to his experience of exile (2012, 2013, 2015). The greatest challenge to Stravinsky's carefully nurtured myth of "autonomy" has come from Richard Taruskin, whose voluminously detailed study of the composer's works up to and including *Mavra* (1922) has ramifications not just for the works of the early French period but for his entire oeuvre.

Taruskin's five theses are worth citing in full, as they illustrate how Stravinsky's "global" career was rooted in an enduring relationship with the Russia he had left behind (at least until his brief return in 1962):

> That Stravinsky achieved artistic maturity and his modernist technique by deliberately playing the traditions of Russian folk music against those of the provincial denationalized Russian art music in which he had been reared, which he had at first accepted uncritically, and in toto.
>
> That he came to his knowledge of folklore, and his attitudes concerning its creative utilization, not from his musical training, but from his association with the artists of the "World of Art" circle.
>
> That he deliberately retained that which was most characteristically and exclusively Russian in his musical training and combined it with stylistic elements abstracted from Russian folklore in a conscious effort to excrete from his style all that was "European."
>
> That the stylistic synthesis thus achieved formed him as a composer for life, whatever his professed stylistic and esthetic allegiances.
>
> That for all these reasons Stravinsky was the most completely Russian composer of art music that ever there was and, if present trends continue, that ever will be. (1996, 18)

As Taruskin demonstrates, Stravinsky's career was indebted to lessons learned in Russia and subsequently applied to the cultural contexts of his adopted homelands. In the competition for worldwide recognition, Stravinsky astutely marketed himself as Russian enough to be authentic, yet international enough to be modern. Like those writers whose international status is marked by extensive translation and the award of prestigious prizes (Casanova 2004; English 2005), he found a means to represent his homeland, even as he was exiled from it, simultaneously inhabiting and eventually dominating the transnational cultural fields that bestow artistic value.

Revisionist accounts of Stravinsky's life in exile have been accompanied by widespread interest in the musical life of "Russia Abroad" (Flamm, Keazor, and Marti 2013), as well as in the work of composers such as Alexander Tcherepnin and Nicolas Nabokov, whose experience of emigration unfolded along very different lines (Korabelnikova 2008; Giroud 2015). The complexity of Sergei Prokofiev's career in Western Europe and America has also come in for more nuanced analysis, as have the reasons behind his eventual return to the Soviet Union (Morrison 2009). More broadly, attention has been paid to the role played by music within the Eurasianist movement (Taruskin 1996, 1126–36; Vishnevetskii 2005; Dufour 2006; Levidou 2008). Described by Marc Raeff as "the only truly novel (in spite of its syncretism) philosophy of history to emerge in Russia Abroad" (1990, 107), Eurasianism derived its intellectual underpinnings from nineteenth-century Slavophile thought and was associated with a commitment to Orthodox spirituality and the belief that Western notions of rationalism, individualism, and progress were ill-suited to Russian society. While rejecting the Bolsheviks' interest in class-based revolution and the dictatorship of the proletariat, Eurasianism nonetheless interpreted the October Revolution as a crucial turning point in world history and the first step in a global geopolitical reorientation away from a "decaying" Western civilization. Significantly, Eurasianism paid considerable attention to the arts, and to the way in which music in particular was ideally placed to restore a lost unity and wholeness to a broken world. The movement's importance can thus be seen in its attempt to make sense of emigration in world historical terms—to theorize a form of émigré identity that rejected both assimilation in the host environment and nostalgic belief in the émigré mission to preserve the best of Russian culture. Politically naïve it may have been, but in its ardent philosophical idealism, Eurasianism offered a vision of exile that looked not back but forward, and with explicitly global aspirations. It is to one of the leading cultural representatives of Eurasianist thought that the discussion now turns.

The Cosmopolitan Muse

Naum Izrailevich Lur'ia was born in the Mogilev province in modern-day Belarus in 1891 or 1892. Substituting St. Petersburg for the original place of his birth, he reinvented himself as Arthur Vincent Lourié, studying at the capital's conservatory and establishing himself as a leading member of the city's artistic elite. He remained in Soviet Russia after the October Revolution, heading the music section of the Commissariat of Enlightenment under Anatoly Lunacharsky. In November 1922, he moved to Berlin, never to see his homeland again. He relocated briefly to Paris in the spring of 1923, only to return to Germany (this time to Wiesbaden) while the French authorities examined his relations with the Bolsheviks. He received permission to settle in Paris in October 1924, taking French citizenship in April 1926. In France, he was closely associated with Stravinsky until the two men became estranged in the mid-1930s. As a result of his Jewish roots, Lourié moved again in 1941, this time to the United States, eventually settling in Princeton, where he died in 1966 (Bobrik 2014).

A noted figure within the Russian emigration during his lifetime and a composer with a substantial output, Lourié has only recently come in for scholarly reevaluation. Studies have been published on his opera *The Blackamoor of Peter the Great*, written in America between 1948 and 1961 (Emerson 2006; Móricz 2008a; Emerson and Móricz 2009–10), but an earlier stage work, a setting of Pushkin's *Feast in Time of Plague* that dates from his Paris period, has figured less prominently in criticism. A number of orchestral and choral works—the *Concerto spirituale* of 1928–29, the *Sinfonia dialectica* of 1930, and his second symphony, the so-called *Kormchaia*, of 1936–39—have also been studied (Levidou 2008, 154–99; Taruskin 2014). There has, though, been less discussion of the genre in which Lourié worked most consistently throughout his life: song (although see Móricz 2008b and 2014, 17–18; Morrison 2014, 280–85). Song represents a fascinating prism through which to consider the fate of Russian culture in emigration, not least because through its fusion of literature and music it brings together the linguistically bound medium of poetry and the supposedly universal language of music. Lourié's songs exemplify the link between language and national identity but also illustrate what happens to this link when creative artists live and work in exile. Just as language can create affective communities through attachment to a shared cultural heritage, it can equally constitute a barrier, whether to performers outside a particular linguistic community, or to audiences unfamiliar with both a foreign culture and its artistic conventions.

The careers of other composers who left Russia after the October Revolution give some sense of the ways in which exile has shaped their treatment of song. A prolific composer of songs before 1916, Sergei Rachmaninov produced no more works in this genre after his emigration (Sylvester 2014). Although he continued to compose in Europe and America (as attested by his Fourth Piano Concerto, Third Symphony, the Symphonic Dances, the Rhapsody on a

Theme of Paganini, and the Corelli variations for solo piano), his silence as a song composer is indicative of the loss of his native language and culture in emigration. The career of Nikolai Medtner suggests that such silence was not inevitable; before 1917, he set a substantial number of poems by Pushkin, Tiutchev, and Afanasy Fet, in addition to the large corpus of texts by Goethe, Heine, and Friedrich Nietzsche that testified to the importance of German Romanticism in turn-of-the-century Russia (Mitchell 2016). This pattern continued after Medtner moved to Western Europe in 1921, settling first in Germany, before eventually taking up residence in England in 1935; it also suggests that despite his deracination, song could express a nostalgic affinity with the past. Sergei Prokofiev's songs offer another response to emigration. Before 1917, he set a number of Silver Age poets, such as Konstantin Balmont, Zinaida Gippius, and Anna Akhmatova. Residing in Western Europe, however, he returned to song only once, setting five poems by Balmont that were prompted by their friendship in the early 1920s. Prokofiev returned to song after settling permanently in the Soviet Union in the mid-1930s, when his work reflected the revolutionary culture he encountered there (Bullock 2006). Stravinsky's output as a song composer offers yet another configuration of the relationship between music, language, and location. In fact, song was only a tangential aspect of his oeuvre in his Russian period, and his "rejoicing discovery" of the irregularities of Russian folk prosody meant that even before emigration he abandoned the principles of faithful text-setting that were central to the Russian art-song tradition, thereby taking an important step toward severing the connection between language and national identity (Taruskin 1987). Although he would go on to set texts in French and English (as well as in Latin), it would be with a blatant disregard for "correct" placement of accent and stress. In attending to the musicality of poetry, he liberated it from its national contexts, weaving it instead into his own transnational, exilic aesthetic.

Lourié's songs fall into a number of discrete groups and illustrate precisely how song adapts to the effects of migration.[1] The songs written before Lourié's emigration in 1922 show a wide range of literary influences (see table 13.1). For all his reputation as a musical "futurist" (Gojowy 1993), there is little avant-garde poetry here, other than individual settings of Alexander Blok and Vladimir Mayakovsky elicited by the October Revolution. Rather, Lourié's predilection is for his Silver Age contemporaries, such as Mikhail Kuzmin, Fedor Sologub, and especially Akhmatova, with whom he was then romantically involved (Kralin 2000). His Pushkin settings of 1920–21 suggest that had he stayed in the Soviet Union, Lourié's choice of texts might have become more conservative. Lourié's taste in Russian poetry was accompanied by an almost equal interest in

French verse, especially that of Paul Verlaine, yet this does not indicate that his songs aspire to a place in the French tradition. Rather, they illustrate the prominence of translation within modernist poetry, here represented by Innokenty Annensky, Valery Briusov, and Sologub. Such poets conceived of translation as part of a broader Silver Age renaissance of Russian culture, something that is especially true of the work of Viacheslav Ivanov (Davidson 1989), whose versions of Sappho form the basis of one of Lourié's most significant early works.

Table 13.1 Arthur Lourié's settings of poetry, 1912–1922 ("Russian" period)

Year	Title	Poet	Translator	Notes
1912	*Deux poèmes* (1. "Le piano qui baise," 2. "Je devine, à travers")	Verlaine	Briusov (1.) and Annensky (2.)	Published in Russian in St. Petersburg as Op. 5, and later incorporated in the cycle *Verlaine*
1914	*Quasi valse*	Kuzmin		Published in Petrograd in 1922
	Grecheksie pesni	Sappho	Ivanov	Twelve songs in two books, published in Petrograd in 1918
	Chetki	Akhmatova		Five songs, published in Petrograd in 1919
	"Dal ty mne molodost' trudnuiu," "Iiul' 1914," and "Plotno somknuty guby sukhie"	Akhmatova		
1915	*La dame chante doulcement*	Christine de Pisan		Subtitled *Cinq rondeaux*, score registered with the French society of authors, composers, and music publishers in January 1939
	Suite japonaise	Akihito and anon.	Aleksandra Brandt	4 songs, published in Paris in 1926
	Triolety	Sologub		2 songs, published in Petrograd in 1920
	Rozhdestvo Bogoroditsy	Kuzmin		A version of an apocryphal text
	Plach Bogoroditsy	Anon.		Published in Petrograd in 1918
	Corona Carminum Sacrorum			Settings of the *Ave Maria* (1915), *Salve Regina* (1917), and *Inviolata* (unrealized), published in Petrograd in 1920
1916	*Tri svetlykh tsaria*	Heine	Blok	Published in Petrograd in 1919

continued on next page

Table 13.1—*continued*

Year	Title	Poet	Translator	Notes
1917	*Rondel*	Mallarmé		Published in Moscow and Petrograd in 1923
	"Un grand sommeil noir," "Dans l'interminable . . . ," and "Vendanges"	Verlaine	Briusov and Sologub ("Vendanges")	Later incorporated in the cycle *Verlaine*
	Azbuka	Lev Tolstoy		Two children's songs, published in Petrograd in 1920
1918	*Nash marsh*	Mayakovsky		Declamation with piano accompaniment, published in Petrograd in 1918
	"Tak poshli nashi rebiata"	Blok		From *Dvenadtsat'*, projected settings of the rest of which were never composed. Published in Petrograd in 1920
1919	"J'ai peur d'un baiser comme d'une abeille . . ."	Verlaine	Sologub	Later incorporated in the cycle *Verlaine*
	Verlaine	Verlaine		Published in Petrograd in French without Russian translations
	Bolotnyi popik	Blok		Published in Petrograd in 1920
1920	*Shagi komadora*	Blok		
	Quatre chansons populaires de Basse Bretagne			
	Dorozhen'ka			Based on a folksong, photostated score prepared by Durand, Paris
1920–21	*Elisium*	Pushkin		Four of a project set of eight settings, published in Petrograd in 1921
	Dve kolybel'nye	Akhmatova		Second song dedicated to the memory of Lev Gumilev
1922	*Nishchenki*	Akhmatova		

French disappeared almost entirely from Lourié's output once he took up residence in Paris (see table 13.2) and began to embrace devotional poetry from the Catholic tradition (prefigured by his earlier settings of Christine de Pisan). This decision can be traced to his own spiritual convictions; he had converted to Catholicism in 1913 and became close to the neo-Thomist philosopher

Table 13.2 Arthur Lourié's settings of poetry, 1924–1938 ("French" period)

Year	Title	Poet	Notes
1924	*Regina Coeli*		A Marian antiphon from the Catholic rite
1926	*Inproperium*		Text taken from Psalm 68
	Sonnet	Dante	From the *Vita Nuova* ("Tutti li miei penseir parlan d'amore"), also included as the fourth movement of Third String Quartet
	Obriadovaia		Tradition wedding lamentation
	Two Songs	Anon. and Ilya Selvinsky	Published in Paris
1928	*2me Tzigane (Sérénade)*		Revised 1951 as *The Song of Mitya Karamazov*
1934	*Procession*	Raissa Maritain	Published in Berlin and Paris in 1936
1934–38	*Délie*	Maurice Scève	
1938	*A Cristo crucificado ante el mar*	José Bergamin	Published in New York in 1946

Table 13.3 Arthur Lourié's settings of poetry, 1941–1962 ("American" period)

Year	Title	Poet	Notes
1941	*Two Poems* (1. *Ecce puer,* 2. *Alone*)	James Joyce	
1945	*Sonnet*	Mallarmé	*Dame sans trop d'ardeur . . .*
1941–48	*Ave atque value*	Nietzsche	Subtitled *Drei Dionysus-Dithyramben*
1945–48	*Little Gidding*	T. S. Eliot	
1958	*Paysage de sons*	Van Gogh	
	Iva	Akhmatova	
1959	*Zaklinaniia*	Akhmatova	Settings of four extracts from *Poema bez geroia*
	Erste Stunde	Rilke	
	Vocalise		Also referred to as "Pesen'ka krotkoi" (Song of the meek one)
1962	*Ten'*	Akhmatova	

Jacques Maritain and his Russian-born wife, Raisa, in the 1920s (Emerson 2014). Yet Lourié's settings of religious verse in Italian, Latin, and Spanish also illustrate how his exilic Russian identity interacted with a transnational religious identity that cut across ethnic, linguistic, and cultural boundaries. Moreover, there are no texts set in translation; the linguistic border-crossing that was so characteristic of the Russian period is replaced by the simultaneous coexistence of a number of individual literary traditions.

In America, Lourié returned to the poetry of Akhmatova, but he also drew inspiration from a small body of poetry in English, as well as from works by Nietzsche, Rainer Maria Rilke, and even an extract from a letter by Vincent Van Gogh (see table 13.3). As with the French period, texts are not set in translation; instead, their polyglot polyphony represents the hybrid influences that Lourié had assimilated both before and after his emigration.

The Voicing of Exile

One work stands out as Lourié's most profound attempt to come to terms with the condition of exile and to exploit the medium of song as a vehicle for representing, and potentially even overcoming, loss. Composed over a nearly three decades between 1920 and 1948, *The Slender Lyre* (*Uzkaia lira*) began life as a short cycle with the title *Recollections of Petersburg* (*Vospominaniia o Peterburge*). Initially, it comprised three songs written in the early 1920s, to which a fourth was added a few years later. The cycle evolved throughout the 1930s and 1940s, and by 1941, it had gained two more songs and a text for a planned seventh whose music was partially drafted in Port Kent in August 1943. Lourié continued to ponder the cycle for a few more years, even considering new poems that could be added. By the summer of 1948 the work's conception was finalized. Diary entries for August 21 and 31 of that year show Lourié refining the arrangement of the individual numbers, as well as contemplating whether the cycle could ever be published:

> Yesterday I began work on sorting out the notebook of songs, *Recollections of Petersburg*, written in various years of wandering. The notebook was begun in Moscow in 1920 and is now being completed in New York. The whole collection will be entitled *The Slender Lyre* and dedicated to the memory of Olga.[2]

> At home all day. No telephone calls or visits. Work on the lyric songs. Six pieces have already been sorted out and copied into a new notebook. Three still remain. It is barely likely that a publisher can be found for *The Slender Lyre*. Who needs

> this now? And then there's the whole question of a translation, into French, into English. It requires someone really interested in this task, so that the notebook might see the light of day.[3]

Lourié's forebodings proved to be correct. The cycle remains unpublished, surviving only in a number of manuscript and holograph copies in the possession of the Paul Sacher Stiftung in Basel, the New York Public Library, and the Amherst College Center for Russian Culture.

The slow, almost obsessive evolution of *The Slender Lyre* traces Lourié's emigration from Russia, through Western Europe, and eventually to the United States (table 13.4). Equally important is his choice of poetry. Lourié had always been drawn to Blok, whom he knew in Petersburg and whose poetry structures *The Slender Lyre*, standing as a metonymic representation of the city's Silver Age. As Olesya Bobrik observes, "In the first, Russian period of his life, this was the real world in which he lived. In emigration, especially in America, the poetry of the Silver Age became for him a necessary milieu, re-created within him and in his works" (2008, 444). Notable too is the cycle's lack of interest in émigré

Table 13.4 The composition of Arthur Lourié's *The Slender Lyre*

	Original Russian title	Lourié's French title	Poet	Place of composition	Date of composition	Notes
1	"Govoriat cherty"	"Ce sont les diables qui parlent"	Blok	Moscow	December 1920–January 1921	
2	"Slovo miloi"	"La parole de l'aimée"	Pushkin	Berlin	1922	Originally placed third
3	"Grafine Rostopchinoi"	"A la comtesse Rastopchine"	Lermontov	Wiesbaden	1924	Originally placed second
4	"Posviashchenie"	"Dédicace"	Pushkin	Paris	Christmas 1927	From Pushkin's *Poltava*
5	"Cherez dvenadtsat' let"	"Après douze ans"	Blok	Paris	1932	
6	"Toska vospominaniia"		Lermontov	New York	1941	
7		"Pour vous à déchifrer toute seule"	Tiutchev	Port Kent	August 1943	Drafted, but unrealized
8	[unknown]		Blok			Unrealized
9	"I dolgo l' mne smotret'"		Blok			Also titled "Epilogue," unrealized

literature. Lourié was, generally speaking, circumspect in his relationships with his fellow émigrés—an attitude reciprocated by those critical of his early Bolshevik associations. The composer made no attempt to voice the experience of exile through the words of those who shared his fate. By contrast, Lourié's settings of Pushkin, Lermontov, and Tiutchev attest to a newly found interest in the poetry of the nineteenth century, which seldom figured in his earlier output. The Petersburg theme thus becomes a means of representing—in its double sense of both "depicting" and "making present"—a city to which Lourié could only ever return in imagination.

Exilic themes and a return to the past can be found in other works written in America. His operatic version of Pushkin's *Blackamoor of Peter the Great*, for instance, has been interpreted by Klára Móricz as "a personalised monument to Russian culture, which, by the evocative power of music, re-creates a lost world preserved in memory as a shadowy, fragmentary existence" (Móricz 2008a, 213). Like *The Slender Lyre*, it was composed over an extended period (between 1948 and 1961). And like *The Slender Lyre*, it juxtaposes a variety of literary sources to create a thematically coherent yet stylistically heterogeneous whole. Alongside Pushkin's novella, there are lines from Catullus, Vasily Trediakovsky, Alexander Griboedov, Lermontov, Fet, Tiutchev, and Evgeny Baratynsky. And the opera ranges, as Móricz notes, "from Ancient Rome to modern Russia by way of medieval France, Renaissance Italy, Enlightenment France, Romantic England, Decadent France, and eighteenth and nineteenth-century Russia" (2008a, 190). Yet there are important differences between the opera and the song cycle. *Blackamoor* presents an episode from Petersburg's history as understood by one of its most famous literary sons. *The Slender Lyre* certainly sets verses by poets associated with the imperial capital, yet there are few references to the city itself. Instead, its themes are the passing of time, the contemplation of lost youth from the perspective of maturity, and the poet's relationship to a series of interlocutors (including readers, muses, fellow creative artists, and even posterity itself).

A work by Lourié with closer parallels to *The Slender Lyre* is his *Incantations* (*Zaklinaniia*), a setting of four fragments from Akhmatova's own late masterpiece *Poem without a Hero* (*Poema bez geroia*), which itself reflects on the lost culture of the Silver Age. Lourié's songs represent a continuation of the themes first explored in *The Slender Lyre*; as Móricz notes, they reflect on the Silver Age and represent "not only traces of the past but also a conscious effort to follow these traces backwards and thus to reconnect with a lost time" (2008b, 93). Although *The Slender Lyre* mirrors the mosaic-like, fragmented structure of *Poem without a Hero*, its conception of Petersburg differs from Akhmatova's, as Móricz observes:

"What distinguishes the aging Akhmatova and the aging Lourié is their relationship to their past and its eccentric masks; for Akhmatova, in retrospect, these masks turned into repellent, demonic devices, while for Lourié they remained cherished relics of a bygone time that had never lost its grip on the composer" (2008b, 81). Composed and collated over nearly three decades and juxtaposing poets from the nineteenth century with verses by Blok, *The Slender Lyre* is nonetheless partly analogous to Akhmatova's exploration of time and memory in *Poem without a Hero*. It also suggests that Lourié's nostalgic evocation of Russia's imperial capital predates the years of his American exile and began even as he prepared to leave Soviet Russia.

Writing in the 1930s, Lourié had optimistically subscribed to the view of music as a universal language, which, unlike literature, could survive the trauma of exile: "A rupture with the national territory is almost a rupture with the national language upon which literature subsists. This is not so with music, since the language of music is not necessarily connected with any country" (1932, 527). Such views were shaped by Lourié's Eurasianist politics, yet as emigration shaded into exile, and then into a fragmented diasporic existence (not least as he was forced to trade his prominent place within "Russia Abroad" in France for a more unsettled life in North America), his attitude became increasingly tinged with nostalgia and melancholy. *A Slender Lyre* suggests a return to the linguistically bounded medium of poetry, and hence a seeming rejection of music's internationalist, cosmopolitan aspirations. If Rubinstein was right in arguing that "song is the only musical genre to have a fatherland," then *A Slender Lyre* testifies to Lourié's attempt to reconnect with both a time and space from which history and politics had separated him.

Perhaps unsurprisingly, Lourié's exploration of song's power to voice and possibly even heal the experience of exile found few listeners, either in his lifetime or thereafter. As he confided in his diary (citing Kierkegaard) on January 17, 1946:

> "Write!"—"For whom?"
> "Write for the dead, for them thou lovest
> In a time that is past."—
> "Will they read me?"—"Nay!" (cited in Bobrik 2012, 167)

Without access to networks of patronage, he struggled to have his compositions published or performed. The support of the leading émigré conductor Serge Koussevitsky meant that some of his orchestral works were heard in the immediate postwar period, yet Lourié knew nothing of the success of his one-time friend Stravinsky. Lourié's songs seem to have been rarely programmed, either in America or in Europe, not least because of his lack of connections with performers who might advocate his works in concert. Prokofiev's first wife, Lina Codina, often included her husband's songs in recitals (as well as those of other Russian composers). Nina Koshets was closely associated with both Prokofiev and Rachmaninov, and Medtner's settings of German poetry were eventually taken up after World War II by the soprano Elizabeth Schwarzkopf (who also recorded some of his Pushkin settings in English translation). By contrast, Lourié's songs found little response. Cynthia Davril performed some of his *Greek Songs* in English translation at a concert in Copenhagen's Odd Fellows' Hall in November 1923, and Lourié's diary records a performance of an unnamed setting of a poem by Lermontov (possibly one of the two included in *The Slender Lyre*) given as part of a concert of French and Russian music in March 1944. Lourié's setting of a Mallarmé sonnet was premiered in New York in March 1946 in an eclectic concert given by the Odessa-born soprano Valentina Vishnevska (and accompanied by Vladimir Dukelsky, who was to become better known as an American popular songwriter, Vernon Duke). Including songs and arias by Wolfgang Amadeus Mozart, Claude Debussy, Gabriel Pierné, Reynaldo Hahn, and Richard Strauss, it also featured a large number of songs, many of them receiving their North American premieres, by modern Russian composers, whether Soviet (Anatoly Aleksandrov, Marian Koval, Alexander Spendiarov), or émigré (Dukelsky, Nikolai Lopatnikov, Rachmaninov, Stravinsky, and Lourié himself). Yet Vishnevska's choice of Lourié's Mallarmé sonnet is striking. A French poem, set to music by a Russian émigré composer resident in the United States, and included in a heterogeneous, multilingual program performed by a Russian émigré singer, its "fatherland" is far from clear.

Russia Imagined from Without

One way to think about the relationship between song and national identity is through the prism of language and how it shapes the circulation of culture. Whereas German, Italian, and French constitute the "global" languages required of singers aspiring to international careers, Russian remains the preserve either of native speakers, or of a small group of performers who have acquired sufficient command of the language to give an impression of fluency. For singers without such skills, translation remains the only option, and it is significant that Lourié assumed that the texts of *The Slender Lyre* would have to be published in French and English as well as in Russian. Yet a very different set of issues is raised when composers set texts in foreign languages, especially ones they do not understand with any degree of fluency or cultural intimacy (the question of how nonnative speakers engage with the Russian literary canon is treated by Miriam Finkelstein in the final chapter of this volume). Two works by British composers—Britten's *The Poet's Echo* (1965) and Tavener's *Akhmatova Songs* (1992)—illustrate contrasting configurations of the relationship between poetry, music, and national identity. Here, song ceases to be the preserve of composers working with their native language, whether in their homeland or in emigration, and becomes instead an instance of a transnational cultural encounter whose nature is determined as much by institutional factors as by artistic ones.

Consisting of six settings of poetry by Pushkin, *The Poet's Echo* was composed in August 1965 while Britten—and his partner, Peter Pears—were guests of the Armenian Composers' Union. Their visit to the Soviet Union—the third of five that they made between 1963 and 1971—was in part the result of Britten's lifelong engagement with Russian music (Pyke 2016). By the 1960s, he had established close creative friendships not only with the soprano Galina Vishnevskaya and the cellist Mstislav Rostropovich (the dedicatees of *The Poet's Echo*) but also with Dmitry Shostakovich. Pears's published accounts of the trips that he and Britten made to the Soviet Union in 1965 and 1966–67 emphasize their personal, social, and creative aspects (Reed 1995, 98–134, 135–52), yet they would have been impossible without the official approval of the Soviet state (and, indeed, the close involvement of the British government, too). Britten and Shostakovich first met in London in 1960, when Rostropovich gave the British premiere of the Soviet composer's First Cello Concerto. Subsequently, Rostropovich and Vishnevskaya became regular visitors to Britten's Aldeburgh Festival, where their repertoire often included Russian works. Although Vishnevskaya was prevented from singing in the premiere of Britten's *War Requiem* at Coventry Cathedral in May 1962 by the Soviet Minister of Culture Ekaterina Furtseva, she was allowed to record the work in London the following year.

Foreign tours by leading Soviet performers served to advertise Soviet esteem for the arts and acted as a form of "soft power" that complemented more traditional forms of diplomacy and political engagement, especially in the context of the Cold War. Vishnevskaya and Rostropovich served as Soviet cultural ambassadors on the world stage (at least until they were expelled from the Soviet Union and stripped of citizenship for their support of Alexander Solzhenitsyn). Vishnevskaya's memoirs paint a picture of the couple as victims of the Soviet system (Vishnevskaia 1985), yet she and her husband were nonetheless able to take on prestigious (and well-paid) foreign engagements, recording extensively, receiving substantial state honors, and enjoying a lifestyle that most Soviets would have deemed highly privileged. Soviet interest in Britten was of a different order. Not only was he a leading figure of the British musical establishment, but he had long been associated with left-wing politics. Moreover, his musical language was legible within the aesthetic framework of Socialist Realism inasmuch as it adhered to traditional tonal norms and was hence far more acceptable than the European avant-garde that proved so alluring to younger composers during the so-called Thaw (Schmelz 2009). When Britten and Pears first visited the Soviet Union in March 1963, it was to take part in a festival of British music resulting from bilateral cultural agreements between Britain and the Soviet Union. It was in Moscow that Britten's Symphony for Cello and Orchestra (one of a number of works written for Rostropovich) was premiered in March 1964, and by the mid-1960s, Britten's involvement with Soviet cultural politics had become so close that there was talk of an official commission from Moscow's Bolshoi Theatre for an opera based on Tolstoy's *Anna Karenina* (with Vishnevskaya as Anna and Pears as Karenin); in the end, the British Foreign Office put an end to the project as a result of the Soviet invasion of Czechoslovakia in August 1968 (Kildea 2013, 478–79).

The Poet's Echo embodies the personal, political, and institutional connections that bound Britten to official Soviet culture. The work illustrates how song can transcend borders when supported by the infrastructure of the state. Although prompted by a volume of English translations (Fennell 1964), Britten's choice of Pushkin was consonant with the promotion of nineteenth-century classical literature during the Soviet period. Moreover, its composition was facilitated by resources provided by the Union of Soviet Composers, and its earliest performances were strongly associated with two of the country's leading artists. Although the cycle's first publication was in three languages (the original Russian, plus singing translations in English and German explicitly designed to facilitate international circulation), its first commercial recording by Vishnevskaya and Rostropovich was alongside romances by Chaikovsky, reinforcing its organic connection to the Russian vocal tradition. *The Poet's Echo* enjoys, therefore, a double identity as both a work by a world-renowned British composer (who also set texts in French, German, and Italian), and as one of the most significant Russian-language song cycles of the second half of the twentieth century. Paradoxically, the extent to which Britten's reputation was supported through concerts, recordings, and publications (Kildea 2002) means that *The Poet's Echo* has become one of the best known and most widely recorded of all Russian-language vocal works of the second half of the twentieth century, eclipsing many others by "native" Russian composers, whether Soviet or émigré.[4]

Tavener's settings of Akhmatova contrast with Britten's songs in several key points. Whereas Pushkin's canonical status meant that he was accessible for

Russian composers to set to music, much of Akhmatova's poetry was, for a large part of the Soviet period, banned, censored, or available only in part (other than for readers of samizdat). Interest in Akhmatova was, in fact, widespread amongst Russian composers in the late Soviet and immediate post-Soviet periods, when settings of her poetry formed part of a broader rediscovery of early twentieth-century modernist culture (Rozenfel'd 2003). That Prokofiev had produced a famous cycle of Akhmatova settings in 1916 meant that when a later generation of composers turned to her work, they were effectively reestablishing a musical and literary tradition whose continuity had been interrupted. If Russian composers tended to view Akhmatova as part of the legacy of modernism, then Tavener's engagement with her poetry was more directly influenced by his conversion to Orthodoxy in 1977, as a result of which "I concerned myself with all things Russian" (1999, 37). An early consequence of this interest was his setting of Akhmatova's *Requiem* for soprano, tenor, and orchestra in 1979. Tavener consulted the scholar and Orthodox priest Sergei Hackel for advice about Akhmatova's original Russian (just as Britten had worked with Rostropovich and Vishnevskaya on Pushkin's prosody); nonetheless, his *Requiem* is decidedly the product of an outsider's interest in an aspect of Russian culture that was ignored within the then Soviet Union but preserved in exile (it is telling, for instance, that anxieties about religious sentiment always bedeviled Soviet attitudes to Britten's *War Requiem*). Tavener was well aware that Akhmatova's poetry was treated with caution within official Soviet discourse, although his claim that "Akhmatova's poetry was not allowed to be published in Russia at that time" is an overstatement (1999, 40). Consequently, his setting serves to preserve and canonize a literary work that was excluded from official circulation in its homeland, at least until the years of glasnost and perestroika. The first performances of *Requiem* were given in Edinburgh and London in 1981, conducted by Gennady Rozhdestvensky. On his return to the Soviet Union, Rozhdestvensky was questioned by border guards, who were anxious that the concert program contained prohibited material. The work would not be heard in Moscow until 1989 (Haydon 1995, 151, 222–26).

Tavener returned to Akhmatova in 1992 with a short cycle of six songs for soprano and solo cello (there is a later version for soprano and string quartet). Although the Soviet Union was no more and Akhmatova's poetry could be said to have returned to its homeland, no longer requiring the intervention of foreign and exilic communities to preserve it for posterity, Tavener's *Akhmatova Songs* emphasize themes of exile and alienation central to the Russian poetic tradition. The first song—a setting of Akhmatova's "Dante" (1936)—sees the Florentine poet exiled from the city of his birth, even after his death. The second song imagines the Caucasian settings to which Pushkin and Lermontov were banished, and the third praises Boris Pasternak as a poet unbounded by national traditions ("the whole earth was his heritage"). In the final song ("Death"), Akhmatova conceptualizes her own death as "the dread moment of the parting with my native land," and as an act of crossing "the border of something which has no certain name."

Vishnevskaya has suggested that in *The Poet's Echo*, Britten evoked the sound world of Russian song, especially the music of Mikhail Glinka (Pyke 2016, 321). By contrast, Tavener's *Akhmatova Songs* make no attempt at imitating Russian models; for all his interest in Orthodox spirituality as a marker of Russianness, his musical language is profoundly, even naïvely syncretic. His vocal lines are often melismatic and redolent of both Byzantine church music and quasi-oriental modes, and one song also includes material derived from an Indian raga, in homage to the cycle's first performer, the Indian soprano Patricia Rosario (the cello part was taken by Steven Isserlis, whose Russian origins influenced the conception of another of Tavener's Orthodox-inspired works, *The Protecting Veil* [1987] for cello and orchestra [Pyke 2016, 278]). Yet certain features of the cycle do suggest intertextual dialogue both with the Russian song tradition and with foreign responses to Russian poetry. The timbral combination of soprano and cello inevitably conjures up the partnership of Vishnevskaya and Rostropovich. In particular, the opening song of Shostakovich's *Seven Romances to Words by Alexandr Blok* (1967)—a setting of Blok's "Song of Ophelia" for soprano and solo cello—constitutes a sonic backdrop to Tavener's *Akhmatova Songs*. Structurally speaking, the *Akhmatova Songs*—six poems by a single poet—mirror the form of *The Poet's Echo*, a work that also bridges the Russian and Western musical worlds. It is not just language, then, that can shape the perception of a song's adherence to a national tradition; its acoustic aura, and the associations this aura can potentially evoke in an audience, are further factors determining connection to a linguistic "fatherland." Moreover, in setting Russian-language poetry, Britten and Tavener not only "translate" Russian song for Western audiences but are themselves incorporated into contrasting iterations of Russian national identity. In the case of Britten, *The Poet's Echo* situates him within the context of Soviet musical and literary culture, whereas for Tavener, his conversion to Orthodoxy entailed a right to claim a version of Russian culture that was, for its adherents, more authentic than the one represented by its geographical homeland.

Envoi

Britten and Tavener both enjoyed the practical and financial backing of important actors in the cultural and political fields; as a result, their settings of Russian poetry, regardless of the fact that they are not works by native Russian speakers, enjoy a special status within the Russian song tradition. This is particularly the case with Britten, whose *Poet's Echo* derives its status not because of some irreducible aura of national identity but because of the advocacy of leading Soviet artists. By contrast, Lourié knew no such institutional security, and many of his most significant and heartfelt works went unpublished, unperformed, and unacknowledged. Yet a renaissance of interest in his music has partially restored him, along with many other émigrés, to the historical record. As early as 1979, the Centre Georges-Pompidou in Paris held a major exhibition of French and Russian art, *Paris-Moscou 1900–1930*. As part of this, IRCAM (L'Institut de Recherche et Coordination Acoustique/Musique) organized a series of concerts devoted to the forgotten Soviet musical avant-garde (Fingerhut 2011), including a number of vocal works by Lourié. The musical consultant for this event was Detlef Gojowy, whose advocacy—as well as that of the violinist Gidon Kremer—led to a spate of concerts in the early 1990s, most notably in Cologne in June 1992, but also in Berlin, Milan, Boston, and even St. Petersburg. Performances and recordings of his works, including his songs, have been championed by the Swiss-based Arthur Lourié Gesellschaft in Basel, and a growing body of scholarship in the languages of the various "homelands" that Lourié inhabited—English, French, German, and Russian—has illuminated aspects of his biography.

So, let us return to Rubinstein's claim that "song is the only musical genre to have a fatherland." Superficially, this seems to gesture toward nationalist essentialism and a presumption that of all musical genres, song was uniquely tied to its origins. Yet as the preceding discussion has demonstrated, the notion of what constitutes song's putative "fatherland" is open to question. Song is a multimedia, collaborative genre that involves poetry, music, and performance, and this formal hybridity opens the way to an understanding of its national, geographical, and linguistic hybridity too. In the case of its poetic texts, these may be rooted in a given literary tradition, yet they can be communicated and represented abroad through acts of performance, translation, and criticism. Indeed, song may well represent one of the most important means by which nonnative audiences are able to encounter foreign poetry (Ronyak 2017). Setting aside the vexed question of whether music is indeed an international language, it is equally the case that Western art music circulates in a global context, and that the transnational careers of Russian singers, as well as those of foreign artists (Russophone or otherwise), provide a context in which song readily moves beyond the borders of its nominal nationality. The Russian song tradition, for all its intimate association with Russian-language poetry and the social contexts of Russian music-making, is one that is as susceptible to translation and mediation as any of the other Russian arts. Given the interpersonal character of the composition and performance of song, the boundaries of how it inscribes itself into cultural traditions can be drawn in vastly differing manners, depending on the institutional and political specificities of distinct eras and geographies.

Notes

1. The details of Lourié's output as a song composer are derived from various sources, including Gojowy 1993, Hulliger 2018, and collections of the composer's papers in the Paul Sacher Stiftung, Basel; the New York Public Library; and the Amherst College Center for Russian Studies. See also Aleksandr Timofeichev's online bibliography (www.proza.ru/2015/02/26/947), as well as the website of the Lourié Society (www.lourie.ch/).

2. A reference to Lourié's former lover, Olga Glebova-Sudeikina (who died in 1945). In an earlier version, the first song was dedicated to Nathalie Wilhouse (née Arsenieff).

3. Passages from Lourié's diaries in the Paul Sacher Stiftung, Basel, are my translations. For published extracts from these diaries, see Bobrik 2008, 2012. All translations are mine unless otherwise noted.

4. As a footnote to *The Poet's Echo*, it is interesting to note that Pears and Britten were briefly in a position to promote Lourié's vocal works, although not his settings of Russian verse. Lourié's diary records that Pears visited him in America in late 1948, when the tenor apparently suggested that he would premiere *Little Gidding* for tenor and small orchestra in London the following season, with Britten conducting. In the end, Pears seems not to have followed through with this plan, and the work was not heard until 1952, when it was given in Paris as part of the "Masterpieces of the XXth Century" festival organized by Nicolas Nabokov (Morrison 2014, 279–84).

Global Transnational Russian Culture

Non-Russians Writing Russian Literature

Miriam Finkelstein

> Today Soviet literature in Russian is being read not only by the Russian masses, but by the laborers of all the peoples of our Soviet Union. Millions of people from among the generation now maturing are being raised on it. *In this manner, Soviet-proletarian artistic literature in the Russian language ceases to be a literature exclusively for people who speak Russian and are of Russian origins, and is slowly acquiring an international character in its form.*
>
> **Maksim Gorky**, 1934

"Non-Russian" Russian Literature

More than seven decades after his speech opening the First All-Union Congress of Soviet Writers, Maksim Gorky's assertion that literature in the Russian language had become the literature of many who are not ethnic Russians still applies, albeit in ways Gorky could not have foreseen. It is affirmed, for instance, by the words of the Azerbaijani-Russian writer Chingiz Guseinov concerning contemporary Russian literature written by "non-Russian Russians": "Yet isn't there an extensive Russian literature being created by *non-Russian Russians*, raised in its traditions and carried in waves of emigration to all parts of the world, from the USA and Canada to Israel and Germany (examples: the 'old' Nabokov, the 'new' Brodsky)? . . . . And there are a huge number of Russian-speakers in the contemporary countries of the CIS, which moved Sergei Chuprinin to create an encyclopedia of 'Russian non-Russian' authors! *This literature does not cease being Russian just because it is created by ethnically non-Russian authors. It's simply that it must be made sense of differently*" (Guseinov 2014, emphasis added).[1]

Guseinov addresses Russian-speaking authors in the CIS as well as Russian-speaking émigrés in the West, regardless of ethnicity or even mother tongue. In this chapter I take Gorky's and Guseinov's conceptions several steps further. While Ilya Kukulin and Maria Rubins demonstrate in their chapters of this volume how Russian literature was and still is written outside the Soviet Union and post-Soviet Russia, my approach takes the "decentering" of Russian literature and culture even further. I argue that in the late twentieth and early twenty-first centuries, Russian literature is being produced and Russian culture is being performed around the globe by individuals who are neither Russians, nor Russian emigrants or their descendants, nor even speakers of the Russian language. My perhaps counterintuitive claim, in short, is that Russian culture may be understood as independent not only of Russian society but even of Russian individuals and communities, as they are commonly understood.

If not by ethnicity, nationality, or linguistic and social affiliation, how are we to define Russian culture? Let us begin by observing that, as the case studies offered in the present volume amply demonstrate, the limits and borders of cultural production that may be termed "Russian" are impossible to pin down: are Russian émigré authors who continued to write in their mother tongue (such as Brodsky) still Russian authors? If they have stopped writing in Russian and switched to a different language (as did Nabokov), can they still be considered Russian authors? Can immigrant authors born in the Soviet Union or in post-Soviet Russia be considered Russian writers if they write exclusively in other languages (English, German, etc.)? As Guseinov and Gorky attest, Russian was the lingua franca of the Russian Empire and the USSR; Russian literature, too, was imperial—written not only by ethnic Russians but also by representatives of other nationalities, by Azerbaijanis, Belarusians, Jews, and others. Yet let us boldly complicate things to the maximal degree: what are we to make of authors who have no biographical connection to Russia whatsoever but self-fashion themselves as Russians? Where, in short, does Russian culture end? In a poststructuralist key, we may ask whether the identity of the author, who was proclaimed dead by Roland Barthes in 1967, matters in the first place.

As I argue below, a theoretically coherent and maximally open conception of cultural belonging must conclude that Russian texts are produced and reproduced in multiple contemporary contexts beyond Russian territory, language, institutions, and communities. Plots, characters, poetic and narrative devices, and even texts as a whole that are marked in various ways as "Russian" are appropriated by non-Russian authors, incorporated into ostensibly non-Russian literatures, and disseminated on a global scale, becoming integral parts of American, French, and other literatures. These processes of hybridization, merging, and synthesis give rise to difficult taxonomical questions: to what literature do these hybrid texts belong?[2] Is language the only or the most important criterion upon which to base such judgments? (And what are we to do with the cases of multilingual texts?) We have three different options. In a first option we can decide to treat such texts as essentially American, French, or German (e.g., because they are written in English, French, or German) even though we recognize that particular plots, narrative forms, and so on are imported from the Russian literary tradition. Alternately, in a second option, we can call them "Russian" (although they are written in languages other than Russian) and treat them as a (distant) branch of Russian literature precisely because they display the above mentioned features. In a third option, perhaps one should call all such texts "hyphenated literature," as Yelena Furman suggests with regard to contemporary Russian-American literature (Furman 2011; Furman, this volume).

However, such questions of taxonomy inevitably lead to consideration of the more fundamental matter of categories of analysis. For our answers depend, among other things, on a definition of the very term "Russian." In what follows I propose a different way to think of what "Russian" (and therefore "Russian literature") means, globally, when we discuss cultural production and belonging. In my view, such terms are best seen as broadly circulating metaphors that attach constellations of significance to a particular culture in the shared imaginary geography of global literary culture. While the meaning of "Russianness" undoubtedly varies over time and across different audiences, in the current chapter I explore one conception of the core significance of Russian culture that is shared broadly in current global literary life and that conceives it as a particular mode of (ethical) behavior and writing. My argument focuses on specific constructions of what Russianness is or can be and, in a next step, on the active performances of these ideas in contemporary literature by French, German, Serbian, and Croatian poets and writers. Their appropriations of aspects of the Russian tradition go far beyond intertextual references and allusions, beyond imagination and representation of Russia and the Russians. These texts do something fundamentally different: they construct ideas of Russianness and deploy them as their own. In effect, non-Russians self-fashion themselves as Russian authors, writing literature in languages other than Russian yet conceiving of this literature as Russian. In order to delineate the specificity of these particular appropriations,

I propose that we locate them within and, at the same time, against a second, larger body of texts that also engage with Russia and Russian literature and culture but do so in a different fashion. This second body or group consists of texts that imagine and represent Russia and, at the same time, appropriate Russian literature. Unlike the first group, however, the authors of these texts never claim to actually write Russian literature and never self-fashion themselves as Russians. To make the differences between the two groups as clear as possible, I will first address the second group and will then proceed with a discussion of the first, with specificities of texts that are written in languages other than Russian yet conceived by their authors as Russian.

My readings are informed by recent approaches to the study of what has been termed "World Literature." In particular, I understand texts addressing Russian writers and Russian émigrés as part of a "transnational constellation" similar to those of transnational trauma literature and literature by migrant writers (Thomsen 2008, 3, 23, and chapters 3 and 4). As researchers of these and other world literature topics have found, certain methodological challenges present themselves to anyone undertaking an analysis of "transnational Russian literature." To read these texts requires us to cross the boundaries of nationally defined disciplines, such as the study of Russian or of French literature, and to push beyond the toolkit of any one scholar. For this reason, the following interpretations of texts outside my own regular competence take the form of observation by an outsider who in many cases lacks detailed knowledge about many social and cultural contexts—observation that focuses on a particular resonance or significance and leaves much else aside. Franco Moretti called such an approach "distant reading" (2000, 57). It must also be said that many texts relevant to my project are only available to me in translation. In spite of scholarly resistance regarding critical work with translations, my work proposes, with David Damrosch and particularly Lawrence Venuti, that translations are not (necessarily) inferior to originals and constitute a domain worthy of academic attention and a tool for scholarly comprehension of global literary life that itself persists through the institutions of translation and international book markets (Damrosch 2003, 288–300; Venuti 2011).[3]

Russia and Russian Émigrés in Contemporary World Literature

What, then, is the "meaning" of Russian literary culture across the globe today? Whereas Gorky believed that Soviet literature was in the process of internationalization, the same works and authors that Soviet authorities once denounced as "anti-Soviet" are the ones that attract the most global critical attention today.[4] Although interest in "classical" Russian writers such as Dostoevsky, Tolstoy, Chekhov, and Pushkin has never declined in global literary culture (consider, for example, J. M. Coetzee's 1996 novel *The Master of Petersburg*), in recent decades it has been supplemented by elevated attention to Silver Age poets, including Anna Akhmatova, Osip Mandelshtam, Boris Pasternak, and Marina Tsvetaeva. Of greatest importance in this regard is the experience of totalitarianism—the immeasurable suffering it caused these and many other authors in the Soviet Union. Writing about Anglophone poems on Russian poets (by Seamus Heaney, Amy Clampitt, Derek Walcott, and others), Stephanie Sandler remarks, "The morbid respect for Russian poets and the association of poetry's greatness with the suffering of its creators is still a powerful myth, West and East." Russian poets serve as role models for other authors who engage in "self-comparisons to the Russians, nearly always leaving them feeling the poorer" and, with central relevance for this discussion, seek to overcome the distance between themselves and the Russians: "Those whose poems are inspired by Russian poetry and theory may well notice their own 'desire to surpass the opposition between "me" and "you"'" (1999, 5, 7, quoting Lyn Hejinian). In the conclusion of this chapter I demonstrate how these boundaries are indeed overcome by some contemporary authors who effectively incorporate the Russian Other into the Self.

In the myth of the Russian writer, suffering is tied to expression. Resistance to injustice in the face of terror and oppression, often by means of preservation of memory and remembrance of victims, is a quality widely associated with some of Russia's most admired writers.[5] Many recent literary works from across the globe focus on the tragic events of Russian history of the twentieth and twenty-first centuries that led to the imprisonment, torture, and death of millions of Russians. The German author Hans-Joachim Schädlich writes in *Kokoschkin's Journey* (*Kokoschkins Reise*, 2010) about the effects of the Russian Revolution. In the United States, David Benioff's *City of Thieves* (2009), Elise Blackwell's *Hunger* (2008), and Debra Dean's *The Madonnas of Leningrad* (2007) reconstruct the horrific conditions under which ordinary people lived during the blockade of Leningrad. Bernardo Carvalho (Brazil) addresses the Chechen Wars and their disastrous effects in his novel *Mother's Son* (*O filho da mãe*, 2009).[6] As different as these texts are, their common denominator is the matter of memory. All recognize the necessity of public remembrance of victims—of the Stalinist terror, of World War II and Nazi atrocities, of the post-Stalinist Soviet regime, and, most recently, of the Chechen wars, and in short, of all who could not speak for themselves and whose suffering has received too little attention in official public discourse in both Russia and the West.

Anna Akhmatova, whose long poem *Requiem* (*Rekviem*, 1935–1940) is understood by many as paradigmatic—as the core of the Russian literary tradition of remembrance of victims—is evoked frequently. Some depict her life during the Stalinist terror (as in Robert Littell's novel *The Stalin Epigram*, 2009) and the years following Stalin's death (as in the 1994 play *Voile Noire Voile Blanche* by French feminist and literary critic Hélène Cixous).[7] Others emphasize that Akhmatova and her poem, far from being dusty exhibits in a museum of Russian literature, have urgent importance for today's memorial culture in Russia. In Carvalho's novel, which tells the story of two young men against the background of the Second Chechen War, one of the main characters, Yulia, is a cofounder of the Petersburg section of the Soldiers Mothers Committee (Komitet soldatskikh materei), whose mission is not only to offer assistance to soldiers and their families but also constantly to remind the Russian public of the tragic fate of many soldiers. At the beginning of the novel, Carvalho places this mission in the tradition of Akhmatova by establishing a biographical link between Yulia and the famous poet and her great work of remembrance. The former is identified as the granddaughter of the woman mentioned in the introduction to *Requiem*: "In the terrible years of the Yezhov terror I spent seventeen months in lines outside Leningrad's prisons. Once, I was somehow 'recognized.' A woman standing behind me in the line with blue lips, who had, of course, never heard my name, emerged from the stupor common to all of us and whispered a question in my ear (everyone spoke in whispers there), 'And can you describe this?' I answered, 'I can.' And then something like a smile flickered across what had once been her face" (Akhmatova 2011, 375). Yulia's work is motivated by both the poet and the poem; although not a poet herself, she is shown to be a direct inheritor of Akhmatova's mission. This tradition of victim remembrance by moral exemplars who tell the stories of those forced into silence is depicted here as both unique and quintessentially Russian.

While in Carvalho's novel this tradition is presented as confined to Russia, other texts depict its dissemination around the world, borne by the figure of the Russian émigré. The character of the Russian émigré, another common feature in multiple contemporary non-Russian texts, appears in a twofold hypostasis: either as a political émigré, preeminently of the 1920s, in flight from the Bolshevik state, or as a refugee from the desolation of late Soviet or early post-Soviet Russia. The latter group of refugees is depicted in national capitals or major urban centers such as Amsterdam, Berlin, London, New York, and Chicago—spaces they share not only with native inhabitants but also with migrants from other parts of the world.[8] In this multilingual, multicultural mélange, non-Russian authors commonly cast Russian émigrés and migrants as highly significant role models. The experience of life in (self-)exile of the earlier political émigrés—sundered from their country, culture, and language of origin and unwilling or unable to return—is presented as paradigmatic for the contemporary exilic condition.[9] As I will discuss at greater length below, political emigration is itself thus frequently understood as a specifically "Russian" experience. Further, post-Soviet émigrés are depicted as carriers of the Russian tradition of remembering history and its victims into new eras and territories.

This broadly disseminated notion of the recent Russian émigré as a role model is lucidly expressed, for instance, in *Constructions in the House, or Iwan Iwanytsch at the Window: Bagatelles and Novellas* (*Konstruktionen im Haus oder Iwan Iwanytsch am Fenster: Bagatellen und Novellen*, 2011), by the Polish-German poet and prose writer Iwona Mickiewicz. The short stories in this collection depict everyday life in a large apartment house in contemporary Berlin, a multicultural microcosm inhabited by individuals from all around the world and a metaphor for the city's tolerant, multicultural society.[10] At first glance, the prominence of Iwan Iwanytsch (the only Russian inhabitant), emphasized in the title, is puzzling. He only appears on the pages of a single story; otherwise, he is hardly ever seen by his neighbors and does not participate in the common life of the house. The story itself does not offer much biographical information about him: we only learn that he lived in Moscow in the 1980s and at some point chose to remain in Berlin (2011, 120–21). His exact status in Germany is left intentionally uncertain: Is he an emigrant? Is he in exile? As the narrator explains, "Iwan Iwanytsch at the window looks like sadness in a frame. Some call this picture: *emigration*. Some: *kitsch-picture* (not to be avoided). Some: *exile*. Some: *delegation abroad*. Or: *ambassador of fate*. Most of all, Iwan Iwanytsch is my neighbor, and he calls himself Iwan Iwanytsch at the window" (2011, 119). Thus Iwan Iwanytsch is depicted as a sad symbol, a personification of the experience of displacement in the most general sense.

In Mickiewicz's work, emigration or exile is not (only) the result of physical dislocation—back in the Soviet Union, Iwan Iwanytsch was already in exile. Exile as a human *conditio sine qua non* in that particular society is directly linked to its totalitarian past. It results from a politics that refused to acknowledge Stalinist crimes and prosecute those responsible: "In the nineteen eighties Iwan Iwanytsch had still seen two mass murderers in Moscow. They had a good pension, good support from the Party. They had signed death lists. Mainly lists for people to be shot. Back then, Iwan Iwanytsch already looked as if he were in exile" (2011, 120–21). In Berlin, in his position "at the window," which becomes an inseparable part of his name, he has multiple roles and functions. Outside of Russian territory and Soviet history, his experience has been rendered universal, both in spatial and temporal terms. A witness to the Soviet concealment of the

Stalinist past, in Germany he remains a guardian of the memory of Soviet victims and reminds his new environment about the globally significant crimes of the totalitarian regime. In other words, the memory of Russia's past must be upheld not only in Russia but elsewhere too, and not for a limited period but at all times. Iwan Iwanytsch's Soviet past renders him the bearer of moral truths with universal relevance. Significantly, it is not the role of the German neighbors or the narrator, with her experience of life in communist Poland, to caution against nationalism and racism in Germany. Instead, this duty falls to the Russian Iwan Iwanytsch, who becomes a voice for vigilance against trivializing the German past and forgetting Nazi crimes. He cautions against false glorification of the concept of "home country," whether uttered in Russian or German, as *rodina* or *Heimat* (2011, 119). The long-term safety and well-being of the house, which serves as a metaphor for human society, depend on people like him—those who remember the past and warn against its recurrence. At the end of the tale the window ceases to be a physical object and turns into a metaphor for Iwan Iwanytsch's moral gaze, which allows him, or forces him, to fulfill his world-saving function: "I do not tell Iwan Iwanytsch that I have seen two mass murderers in Moscow too. I fear that if I told him, he would disappear from our house together with his window" (2011, 122). Yet even if he left and took his individual "window" with him, the position "at the window" as such would remain and a replacement would have to be found immediately.

Russianness as Metaphor and Performance: A Theoretical Framework

The theoretical grounding that guides this analysis of Russianness as a metaphor is related to recent studies of contemporary literary constructions of Jewishness. Scholars including Aamir Mufti, Brian Cheyette, Anna Guttmann, and Isabelle Hesse have analyzed adaptations and constructions of Jewishness in postcolonial fiction, suggesting that Jewishness may be conceived as a broadly shared metaphor for minority identity, for diasporic experience, and for Otherness in a general sense. In his study on the postcolonial literatures of the Indian subcontinent, Aamir Mufti proposes that Jewish identity be understood as a historical model for modern ideas about minority identity in a global context: "In the question of the Jews' status in modern culture and society . . . what emerges is a set of paradigmatic narratives, conceptual frameworks, motifs, and formal relationships concerned with the very question of minority existence, which are then disseminated globally" (2007, 2). Similarly, Isabelle Hesse, who analyzes tropes of Jewishness in a range of contemporary literatures (including, among others, German-Jewish, Palestinian, and Hebrew letters), suggests that Jewishness should be conceived as a social construct, defined by particular contexts in which it is used. Such conceptions may, of course, attribute certain essential qualities to cultural identities, yet scholarly work such as Hesse's disavows the concept of an "eternal" Jewishness, fixed throughout history.[11] As she explains, the metaphor of Jewishness is widely used by subjugated groups in their own respective identity constructions: "The ideas of Jewishness are not only important for defining Jewish identity," but rather "ideas of Jewish minority and majority are used metaphorically to define and delineate contemporary identity more widely" (2016, 3). In this account, the significance of Jewishness derives from histories and cultural traditions of Jews and their reception. Yet in recognition that histories, identities and their receptions are themselves cultural constructs, the work of these scholars gains traction on the independent constellation of cultural identification that "lifts away" from essentially conceived identities in an age of global cultural circulation.

Contemporary constructions of Russianness may be conceived in a similar manner. For the authors of the works named above and their many and dispersed audiences, Russianness is a metaphor for the experience of political emigration or exile and for resistance to oppressive regimes and state-sanctioned violence by means of remembrance of victims. Furthermore, some authors step beyond devising and deploying metaphors of Russianness and proceed to actively perform, to act upon them. In what follows, I will discuss how different non-Russian authors who have personally experienced exile and political emigration and address this experience in their texts or those who dedicate their texts to the remembrance of the victims of state violence actually consider themselves to be Russians. If they self-fashion themselves as Russian writers it is precisely because (in their understanding) this is what Russian literature means, what it is really about—the state of exile and the memory of victims of oppressive, totalitarian regimes. Although Russian culture is, perhaps more than many others, often conceived as a unique and ineffable entity, in which the mysterious "Russian soul" finds expression, the texts in question demand an approach opposed to reductive essentialism. If culture is to be understood as a translocal, creative, and explorative phenomenon (Hörning and Reuter 2004, 12), its production must be conceived as a process unrestricted by national, ethnic, or linguistic limitations.

A maximal interpretation of such positions, one that flies in the face of certain principled positions within the contemporary contestation of identity and debates concerning cultural appropriation, might propose that individuals of whatever origin may actively participate in the production and dissemination of any culture of their choice.[12] Clearly, in concrete circumstances such adoptions of the culture of another may be inflected by power relations—rendering them either forms of cultural imperialism, when one community imposes cultural modes on another, or cultural appropriation, when a cultural formation or institution is taken up and redeployed in ways that may outrage or offend a subaltern group. Yet the current chapter is not a manifesto but rather a study of actual cultural processes per se—of the way Russian culture has been defined and performed by individuals beyond Russian geography and outside of conventional conceptions of collective identity based on nation, familial descent, place of birth, language, and so on. The Israeli historian Gadi Algazi has suggested that "culture is how to do what" (Algazi 2000, 13). He understands culture as a heterogeneous system of repertoires that contain options and models, "scripts" and "templates" for actions. However distinct one national culture is from others, we must recognize that anyone may and many do learn and adopt the scripts and templates of other cultures. For the purposes of the present study, this allows us to recognize that Russian culture is and has been "done" (i.e., performed) by many non-Russians.

Becoming Russian: Literary Performances of Russianness

In 1992 the Serbian poet and prose writer Bora Ćosić left his home country to protest Slobodan Milošević's policies and settled in Berlin. This city, as depicted in his collection of poems *Die Toten: Das Berlin meiner Gedichte* (*The Dead: Berlin of My Poems*, 2001), is occupied by the Russian migrants of today and by ghosts of past Russian émigré writers.[13] Many poems reflect on the condition of exile, since Ćosić considers himself a political emigrant. This experience is interpreted and given meaning by constant references to Russian literature. In the poem "Chekhov" ("Tschechow"), the lyric protagonist calls his exilic fate a (nearly) Russian one, and Berlin itself comes to resemble the Russian landscape of the steppe:

> And I read
> Gentlemen
> at my estate
> a lot of Chekhov
> in the two rooms
> of (the apartment in) Sybelstrasse in Charlottenburg
> [. . .] I am even somewhat melancholic
> because of a fate

that is nearly Russian
[. . .] I travel in Berlin
as in the Russian steppe
watch people
as though in a train to Tula [. . .].
(2001, 90)

According to Ćosić, the condition of exile has forced him to redefine his own position with regard to his own experience and to place himself within a particular, Russian tradition.

In this manner, the exile of Russian writers in Berlin becomes paradigmatic. In the poem "Russians in Berlin" ("Russen in Berlin"), the narrator sees himself in the company of Nabokov and Bely, imagined as his predecessors:

At the Wittenberg Square
at a late hour Nabokov
comes out of a house
from seventy years ago
deftly avoids the infrequent busses
and catches butterflies
in the pedestrian underpass
I meet Andrei Bely
with the silver walking stick
only later he won't admit to it [. . .].
(2001, 93)

At the end of the poem the previously clear distinction between the Russian predecessors and role models and the Serbian narrator is disrupted and the (Serbian) Self transforms into the (Russian) Other. Ćosić's self-inscription into the Russian tradition of exile culminates in the idea that in fact he himself is a Russian:

[. . .] the Russians in Berlin
believe they are
the only Russians in Berlin
which is wrong.
(2001, 93)

As these final lines suggest, those who call themselves Russians on the grounds of their national or ethnic origins, or simply because they speak Russian, do not have an exclusive claim to this denomination. The term "Russian(s)" refers here not to nationality, ethnicity, or language but rather to the condition of morally framed political exile. This is an epithet that can be extended to anyone living, as Ćosić does, in political exile in Berlin or elsewhere.

Neither in this poem nor in the other poems of this collection does Ćosić elaborate on the reasons why he positions himself within the Russian tradition and stages his poetic self as Russian. Given the formal and thematic structure of his works, it clearly was not Ćosić's intention to inscribe himself into and to perpetuate Russian *literary* traditions (i.e., to inherit the poetics, literary devices, forms, and strategies of the writers he references). Bely and Nabokov are projected as representatives of the best that Russian literature of their time had to offer and as artists who rescued, preserved, and continued the most distinguished literary, cultural, and spiritual traditions abroad. Ćosić relates to these figures in terms of their moral and ethical position. Of course, many writers returned to the Soviet Union from emigration (Viktor Shklovsky, Aleksei N. Tolstoy, Ilya Erenburg) as a result of difficult compromises with the state, yet Ćosić's concept of Russian authorship ignores these cases in favor of an image of moral role models, firm and incorruptible. These poems project Russian authors as entering self-imposed exile in defiance of a regime whose politics they could not accept, as was the case with Ćosić himself. The tradition imagined here is one of resistance—resistance to inhuman, oppressive, and totalitarian regimes.

In her biography of Marina Tsvetaeva, *Marina, or about Biography* (*Marina, ili o biografii*, 1986), Croatian writer Irena Vrkljan takes an even more radical approach. This work raises the tricky theoretical question of how far a biography can be separated from the biographer's own life (Hawkesworth 1991, 124). Vrkljan provides an explicit answer: distanced, "objective" biography is impossible, which is why, in effect, her book is a biography and an autobiography in one. For her, Tsvetaeva exemplifies an apotheosis within a (proto-feminist) tradition of resistance to restrictive and oppressive bourgeois society, which prevented women from pursuing creative professions. Fully aware of the differences between her own petit bourgeois family in prewar Belgrade and professor Tsvetaev's household in prerevolutionary Moscow, defined by intellectual and artistic interests, Vrkljan underlines parallels between her own and Tsvetaeva's mothers nonetheless (1986, 113–14). Both were unable to pursue intellectual/artistic careers because their respective societies deemed it incompatible with their prescribed roles as wives and mothers, and both had difficult relationships with their daughters. Searching for suitable female role models, the daughters were forced to turn to other women—Tsvetaeva to the painter Mariia Bashkirtseva and Vrkljan to Tsvetaeva herself. Also, Vrkljan's life abroad, which entailed the loss of friends and colleagues who stayed behind in Zagreb (many of whom were driven to insanity or suicide by the oppressive Socialist regime), echoes Tsvetaeva's own emigration experience.

The identification of Vrkljan with Tsvetaeva goes far beyond an intellectual kinship or observations about their parallel experiences. Like Ćosić's text, Vrkljan's crosses the line from imagination or representation of the role model to transformation of her own self into Tsvetaeva by way of physical incorporation. Gradually, in the course of the narration, the Russian poet is brought into the very body of the Croatian narrator. By the end, she becomes a physical part of Vrkljan, so much so that the two women become nearly indistinguishable. The differences between them begin to blur early on: "I now look at the photograph of Marina as a child as though it were my own" (1999, 25). Yet the biography of the Other, embedded in the narrator's body, is still understood as a foreign, painful matter: "The biographies of others. Splinters in our body. As I pull them out, I pull out my own pictures from the deep, dark funnel" (122). Eventually, Marina and her texts are seen as a vein (both in the sense of ore in a mine and of a blood vessel) and a trace running through Vrkljan's own body and life: "What I would like to discover is Marina's entry into my life. It is as though the text were being written along a blood vessel which gleams. But it is weak, that trace of a dead woman whom we did not know. I strengthen her outline with other times, I carry her about like a little rag animal, firmly pressed to my breast . . . But sometimes the tracks are very deep, brilliant" (160–61). Not only is Tsvetaeva's emigration reenacted by Vrkljan—Tsvetaeva's texts are contained in Vrkljan's texts, and her body is inscribed into that of her younger counterpart.

Writing Russian Literature: Modes of Global Appropriation

The deep identification of a non-Russian author with conceptions of Russian authorship described above is just one strategy of transnational Russian writing. Another that is widely attested is self-inscription into Russian literary traditions. Discussing Russian intertexts in Orhan Pamuk's novel *Snow*, Andrew Wachtel remarks that today national literary traditions are frequently decoupled from their language of origin and are available to all writers around the world (2012, 106). Today more than ever, as literature circulates globally among shared and interlinked markets and institutions, biographical circumstances such as place of birth and mother tongue no longer determine an author's position within a literary tradition. Fewer and fewer are writers confined to national traditions of their country of origin; increasingly, they gain a sense of liberty to inscribe themselves into a literary tradition of their choice. Thus, in *Snow*, a novel that is not about Russia and features no Russian characters, the Turkish writer Pamuk chooses to position himself in the literary tradition of Dostoevsky and Pasternak to a degree that makes Wachtel ask whether this novel is not in fact a Russian one, if not by language then by literary ancestry.[14]

Yet another strategy for the contemporary appropriation of Russian literature is that of rewriting. Unlike *Snow* and the other works mentioned above, rewritings emphasize their connection to (Russian) predecessors by borrowing titles (or parts of titles), plots that are relocated in new settings, or narrative or poetic forms and devices. Marjorie Perloff describes devices of "récriture" as central in global contemporary poetry: "In the climate of the new century, however, we seem to be witnessing a poetic turn . . . to dialogue—a dialogue with earlier texts or texts in other media, with 'writings through.' . . . Thus we are witnessing a new poetry . . . in which . . . the shift is . . . to the pragmatic discourse that appropriates and renews what is given in the discourse that constitutes a social and cultural world" (2009, 11–12). What Perloff describes for poetry is true for prose as well, and Russian prose is a prominent part of today's cultural world, frequently renewed in other linguistic and cultural contexts. Rewritings of Russian literature, predominantly of canonical authors such as Dostoevsky, Pushkin, Tolstoy, and Mandelshtam, have recently drawn much scholarly attention. Some of the most prominent authors revisiting the Russian canon have been the American L=A=N=G=U=A=G=E School poets Lyn Hejinian, Clark Coolidge, and Michael Palmer (Perloff 1993; Greber 2005; Edmond 2012, 72–94; Lutzkanova-Vassileva 2015) and the Russian-American writers Gary Shteyngart, Irina Reyn, Lara Vapnyar, and Anya Ulinich (Furman 2011, 2014, and this volume; Finkelstein 2016).

Returning to other non-Russian texts that construct Russianness as an ethical stance on the importance of bearing witness, we find several lesser-known appropriations of Akhmatova's *Requiem*. Cixous's play *Black Sail White Sail*, mentioned above, introduces Akhmatova, Nadezhda Mandelshtam, and Lydia Chukovskaya in the years between Stalin's death in 1953 and 1960, as they contemplate the possibility of publishing the previously banned poetry of Osip Mandelshtam and, most importantly, Akhmatova's *Requiem*. Cixous's text is not a direct rewriting of the poem; instead it uses Akhmatova's work for its underlying structure. Like *Requiem*, the play begins with Akhmatova waiting—this time not in a line but in the woods near Leningrad. Frequently referred to in the text, *Requiem* is not quoted directly, but many of its modified and paraphrased parts are distributed throughout the play, spoken by various characters (Rosslyn 2001, 80). Thus, as the Russian source text is merged with Cixous's new one, it becomes an integral part of the French text and, by extension, of contemporary French literature. The French writer's turn to Akhmatova is motivated by her conception of the Russian poet as a role model for describing and talking about other people's suffering. As Wendy Rosslyn puts it, "Cixous learns from Akhmatova that it is possible to write in the name of others" (2001, 83). Yet *Black Sail White Sail* is more than just a representation or imagining of Akhmatova. It is more than a rewriting of her text. The text itself is an act of remembrance, a performance of the principle of remembrance as formulated by Akhmatova. In writing this play, Cixous responds to Akhmatova's famous final stanza, in which she imagines how she will be remembered. Whereas the Russian poet was thinking about her posthumous fame in Russia, the French writer asserts that she is well remembered elsewhere too, and, with or through her text, all the others, both the famous and the nameless victims.

Another, more recent example of the appropriation of *Requiem* is the book *Weil es sagbar ist* (Because it can be told, 2013), by the German journalist and writer Carolin Emcke. In this collection of essays, written while she was serving as a correspondent in various war zones, Emcke tells stories of victims of the wars in Afghanistan, Iraq, Kosovo, and other places where refugees and prisoners of war have been subject to violence, torture, loss, and trauma. At the same time these are philosophical texts that discuss the nature of bearing witness. Emcke asks under what conditions it becomes possible for victims to speak, how we can listen, and what we need to do in order to understand victims' stories. For Emcke, witnessing is a decidedly ethical act and a moral imperative for both sides—for those who tell and, obviously, for those who listen (2013, 23–24). Although she also discusses well-known testimonials by Jewish Holocaust survivors (e.g., Primo Levi), her foundational model is Akhmatova. The book begins with a full quotation of Akhmatova's introduction to *Requiem*; here too, it serves as the introduction to the main text. Throughout the essays, Emcke returns time and again to Akhmatova's poem, which has been a source of inspiration for her journalistic and literary career since her university days and a companion for over twenty years (2013, 17–18). As is the case for Cixous, Akhmatova is the most central model for Emcke because, unlike Holocaust survivors, who mainly described their own fates, the Russian poet shows how one may speak for others.[15]

The entire first chapter of Emcke's work constitutes an analysis of Akhmatova's lines followed by the conclusion that it is both possible and legitimate to speak not only about but also for victims. The reason for the legitimacy of this kind of speech is twofold. First, in the case of both Akhmatova's text and Emcke's journalistic work, the original impulse for speaking for others comes from the victims themselves. Akhmatova's persona in her poem is explicitly asked by another woman in line to bear witness to the collective suffering in which they have both taken part; in her essays Emcke emphasizes that she, too, was frequently asked to tell the world about the suffering she saw. But second, and more importantly, this role is legitimate for Emcke because it has been affirmed by the authority of the famous Russian poet. In effect, Emcke's work is not simply an appropriation of Akhmatova's writings as a means of fashioning her journalistic mission after Akhmatova's poetic mission. Metaphorically speaking, we should instead recognize Emcke's book as an appropriation of a particularly Russian gesture. Like Cixous's play, Emcke's text is also a performance of a specifically Russian act of remembrance.[16]

Writing Russian Literature, Speaking for Others

As the cases examined here demonstrate, the crimes of the Soviet regime in general and the extermination of Russian-speaking poets, writers, and intellectuals in particular are thought to have not only local importance, limited to Russia itself. They gain a much wider, global significance, and so do the means of resistance to totalitarian violence—most importantly, the Russian culture of memory, which is rendered exemplary and international. Remembering the tragic fate of Russian poets and writers (and of millions of less prominent victims) thus becomes an ethical obligation for their non-Russian colleagues. In pre-perestroika times, when public remembrance of the victims of Stalinist terror was impossible in the Soviet Union, as well as in Russia today, when it becomes increasingly difficult yet again, these non-Russian acts of memory and solidarity were and are of special, urgent importance. This does not mean, however, that this obligation does not apply at other, more "fortunate" times: on the contrary, it applies always and everywhere. Furthermore, this Russian practice of remembrance and speaking for others is appropriated and exercised in other national contexts too. To speak of and to speak for victims of state-induced violence around the globe is an ethical obligation too. This act is fashioned after and legitimized by Russian literature—in particular by Anna Akhmatova. Ultimately, this gesture and the person, the author who performs it, are both conceived of as Russian. We must therefore question the assumed bonds that tie national literature and language not only to presumptive national territories but also to national or collective identities. Once we recognize that the literary is a site of self-creation rather than expression of one's "natural" or "essential" characteristics (or even, in a post-structuralist sense, a site where writing writes itself), we must confront the problem of the ontological principles that undergird not only where the national may be written but also by whom. There is perhaps no more "natural" context for such a discussion than in relation to Russia, which has historically been defined less by nation than by imperial, supernational, or transnational imperatives and identities. Without a doubt, there are many versions of Russianness in circulation in the contemporary world. Yet one broadly shared conception, perhaps the dominant conception, projects Russianness as a metaphor for the particular behavior, or set of literary actions and ethical gestures, just examined. If Russianness is here imagined as Otherness, it is not an exotic, barbarian, or frightening Other but a desirable one that is swiftly incorporated and turned the Self: the non-Russian Self imagines and creates itself as a Russian one. Being a "Russian" in this sense means resisting oppressive regimes and reminding the public of the victims of persecution, in any given national context, through the power of literature itself. To write "Russian" literature in this sense means to give a voice to the victims of violence and terror, to speak of and for those who would otherwise remain silent and forgotten.

Notes

1. For a different discussion of Gorky's and Guseinov's comments, see Frank 2016. All translations in this chapter are those of the author, unless otherwise noted.

2. On hybridity in contemporary Russian-American literature, see Furman 2011; Senderovich 2015a; and Furman, this volume.

3. These claims have been critiqued in Spivak 2000 and Apter 2006; see an overview of their arguments in D'haen 2012, 129–31.

4. See, for example, Jackson 2015 for a study of the reception of Dostoevsky, Chekhov, and other classical Russian writers in South African literature.

5. One of the earliest texts about a Russian poet of the second half of the twentieth century is Adrienne Rich's 1968 poem "For a Russian Poet," addressed to Natalya Gorbanevskaya, a fellow poet and prominent member of the Soviet dissident movement.

6. No English translation is available. A German translation, *Dreihundert Brücken*, was published in 2013. Other texts about the less dramatic but still chaotic and difficult postperestroika years include *The Offender* (*De overtreder*, 2007), by the Dutch Marente de Moor; *33 Moments of Happiness* (2000), by the German Ingo Schulze; and the novels *Encyclopedia of a Life in Russia* (2012), *Nocturnal Butterflies of the Russian Empire* (2000), and *Rex* (2007), by the Cuban José Manuel Prieto.

7. She first appears in Littell's novel as a friend of the still living Osip Mandelshtam, and later as a guardian of his memory and that of Gumilev and other dead poets and intellectuals of her generation. Cixous's novel appeared in English translation in 1994 as "Black Sail White Sail," in *New Literary History* 25, no. 2 (1994): 222–354.

8. Berlin is the setting of the novel *Nebe pod Berlínem* (*The Sky under Berlin*, 2002), by Czech writer Jaroslav Rudiš, and of the essay collection *Berlin* (2007), by the Slovene Aleš Šteger. *The Glassblower's Breath* (1993), by the British-Indian novelist Sunetra Gupta, is set in London. The American metropolises appear in Paul Greenberg's *Leaving Katya* (2002) and in Aleksandar Hemon's novels and short stories, which almost always feature Russian and post-Soviet migrants. See, most notably, his *Nowhere Man* (2002).

9. For instance, this is true of the Chinese-American writer Ha Jin, who in his book *The Writer as Migrant* (2008) establishes Alexander Solzhenitsyn as one of his most important role models.

10. The inhabitants include Germans, Turks, and Poles (e.g., the narrator, an alter ego of the author).

11. For similar discussions, see Cheyette 2013; Guttmann 2013.

12. These and other performative concepts of culture are discussed at length in Hausbacher 2009, 47–66.

13. The following are translations into English from the published German translations of these poems. The original texts remain unpublished.

14. Next to the more direct references to Turgenev and Gogol, Wachtel reconstructs a pervasive series of structural and thematic analogies to Dostoevsky's *Besy* (*The Devils*) and Pasternak's *Doktor Zhivago*. Something similar may be argued concerning the novel *Forgive* (*Odpusti*, 2014), by the Slovene writer Aleš Šteger, which combines the plots of Gogol's *Dead Souls* and Mikhail Bulgakov's *Master and Margarita*. Another example may be found in the Israeli writer Meir Shalev's *Russian Novel* (*Roman rusi*, 1988; English translation *The Blue Mountain*, 1991), which appropriates elements of the plot of Dostoevsky's *Crime and Punishment*.

15. This is not to say that Primo Levi and Ruth Klüger failed to speak about Nazi victims other than themselves; their narratives are, however, focused primarily on their own life stories and those of their immediate families.

16. In claiming legitimacy for speaking of the sufferings of those who cannot speak for themselves, Cixous and Emcke may be conceived as reacting to the postcolonial critique of speaking for others, expressed most famously by Gayatri Chakravorti Spivak in her influential 1988 essay "Can the Subaltern Speak?" As Cixous and Emcke show in their works, there are historical contexts and situations that make it imperative to speak on behalf of those who are silenced.

Works Cited

Abarinov, Vladimir, and Galina Sidorova. 2015. "'Russkii mir,' bessmyslennyi i besposhchadnyi." *Radio Svoboda*, February 18. www.svoboda.org/content/article/26855650.html.

Abashin, Sergey [Sergei]. 2016a. Review of *Making Uzbekistan: Nation, Empire, and Revolution in the Early USSR*, by Adeeb Khalid. *Ab Imperio* 4:256–67.

———. 2016b. "Sovetskoe = kolonial'noe? (Za i protiv)." In *Poniatiia o sovetskom v Tsentral'noi Azii*, edited by G. Mamedov and O. Shatalova, 28–48. Bishkek: Shtab-Press.

Abdullaev, Evgenii. 2009. "Russkii iazyk: zhizn' posle smerti. Iazyk, politika i obschestvo v sovremennom Uzbekistane." *Neprikosnovennyi zapas* 4. http://magazines.russ.ru/nz/2009/4/ab21-pr.html.

Abdullaev, Shamshad. 2003. *Nepodvizhnaia poverkhnost'*. Moscow: Novoe literaturnoe obozrenie.

Abramson, David M. 2000. "Socialism's Bastard Children." *PoLAR* 23 (1): 49–64.

Adamovich, G. B., and M. L. Kantor, eds. 2005. *Iakor': Antologiia russkoi zarubezhnoi poezii*. St. Petersburg: Alateia.

Adams, K. M. 2004. "The Genesis of Touristic Imagery: Politics and Poetics in the Creation of a Remote Indonesian Island Destination." *Tourist Studies* 4 (2): 115–35.

Agentstvo Respubliki Kazakhstan po statistike. 2011. *Itogi natsional'noi perepisi Respubliki Kazakhstan 2009 goda. Analiticheskii otchet.* Astana.

Aigi, Gennadii. 1982. *Otmechennaia zima: Sobranie stikhotvorenii v dvukh chastiakh.* Foreword by Pierre Emmanuel. Paris: Sintaxis.

Akhmatova, Anna. 2011. *Stikhotvoreniia.* Moscow: Eksmo.

Aktürk, Şener. 2012. *Regimes of Ethnicity and Nationhood in Germany, Russia, and Turkey*. New York: Cambridge University Press.

Alexander, Tamsin. 2012. "An 'Extraordinary Engagement': A Russian Opera Company in Britain, 1888." In *A People Passing Rude: British Responses to Russian Culture*, edited by Anthony Cross, 97–112. Cambridge: Open Book Publishers.

———. 2015a. "Decentralising via Russia: Glinka's A Life for the Tsar in Nice, 1890." *Cambridge Opera Journal* 27 (1): 35–62.

———. 2015b. "Tchaikovsky's *Yevgeny Onegin* in Britain, 1892–1906: Slipping between High and Low, Future and Past, East and West." *Musiktheorie* 3:223–34.

Algazi, Gadi. 2000. "Kulturkult und die Rekonstruktion von Handlungsrepertoires." *L'homme: Zeitschrift für feministische Geschichtswissenschaft* 11 (1): 105–19.

Altynbekova, Ol'ga. 2006. *Etnoyazykovye protsessy v Kazakhstane.* Almaty: Ekonomika.

Appadurai, Arjun. 1990. "Disjuncture and Difference in the Global Cultural Economy." *Theory, Culture & Society* 7: 295–310.

———. 1996. *Modernity at Large: Cultural Dimensions of Globalization*. Minneapolis: University of Minnesota Press.

Appiah, Kwame Anthony. 2006. *Cosmopolitanism: Ethics in a World of Strangers*. New York: W. W. Norton.

Apter, Emily. 2006. *The Translation Zone: A New Comparative Literature*. Princeton, NJ: Princeton University Press.

Armeyskov, Sergey. 2013. "Russian Stereotypes: Western Perception of Russia as Seen through Russian's Eyes. Part I." *Russian Universe*, November 14. https://russianuniverse.org/2013/10/14/russian-stereotypes/.

Arutiunian, Iurii. 1992. *Russkie: Etnosotsiologicheskie ocherki*. Moscow: Nauka.

Ashwin, Sarah. 2000. "Introduction: Gender, State and Society in Soviet and Post-Soviet Russia." In *Gender, State and Society in Soviet and Post-Soviet Russia*, edited by Sarah Ashwin, 1–29. London: Routledge.

Auden, W. H. 1949. "The Ironic Hero: Some Reflections on Don Quixote." *Horizon*, August, 86–94.

Aviv, Caryn, and David Shneer. 2005. *New Jews: The End of the Jewish Diaspora*. New York: New York University Press.

Axel, Brian Keith. 2002. "The Diasporic Imaginary." *Public Culture* 14 (2): 411–28.

Babitskaia, Varvara. 2009. "Mikhail Idov: Kofemolka. Retsenziia." *Open Space*, December 2. Accessed January 16, 2017. http://os.colta.ru/literature/events/details/14434/.

Bai, Eugene. 2015. "Sorry, but Soft Power Is Not a Part of the Russian Tradition." *Russia Direct*, April 7. http://www.russia-direct.org/opinion/sorry-soft-power-not-part-russian-tradition.

Baily, John, and Michael Collyer, eds. 2006. "Music and Migration." Special issue, *Journal of Ethnic and Migration Studies* 32 (2).

Bakhtin, Mikhail. 1984. *The Dialogic Imagination*. Translated by Caryl Emerson and Michael Holquist. Austin: University of Texas Press.

Baliakina, Elena. 2011. "'Miagkaia sila' narodnoi diplomatii." *Sovetskaia Belarus'*, January 13.

Barash, Aleksandr. 2002. *Sredizemnomorskaia nota: Stikhotvoreniia*. Jerusalem: Gesharim; Moscow: Mosty kul'tury. www.vavilon.ru/texts/prim/barash1.html.

———. 2009. "Byla ideia russkoi literatury Izrailia." *Lekhaim* 8 (208) (August). www.lechaim.ru/ARHIV/208/barash.htm.

Baraulina, Tatyana, and Andrei Khanzin. 1996. "Gender Differences in the Life Strategies of Russian Youth." In *Women's Voices in Russia Today*, edited by Anna Rotkirch and Elina Haavio-Mannila, 107–23. Aldershot, UK: Dartmouth.

Bar-Iosef, Khamutal, and Zoia Kopelman, eds. 1999. *Antologiia ivritskoi literatury: Evreiskaia literatura XIX–XX vekov v russkikh perevodakh*. Moscow: RGGU.

Bashkeev, Maksim. 2014. "Chto my znaem pro russkii mir?" *Tribuna*, December 4.

Bassin, Mark. 2006. "Geographies of Imperial Identity." In *The Cambridge History of Russia*, vol. 1, *Imperial Russia, 1689–1917*, edited by Dominic Lieven, 45–63. Cambridge: Cambridge University Press.

Bassin, Mark, Christopher Ely, and Melissa K. Stockdale, eds. 2010. *Space, Place, and Power in Modern Russia: Essays in the New Spatial History*. DeKalb: Northern Illinois University Press.

Bassin, Mark, Sergey Glebov, and Marlene Laruelle, eds. 2015. *Between Europe and Asia: The Origins, Theories, and Legacies of Russian Eurasianism.* Pittsburgh: University of Pittsburgh Press.

Bavil'skii, Dmitrii. 2009. "Mikhail Idov: 'Eto kak glaz na zatylke ili tret'ia ruka. . . .'" *Chastnyi korrespondent*, November 24. www.chaskor.ru/article/mihail_idov_eto_kak_glaz_na_zatylke_ili_tretya_ruka_12707.

Bearne, Suzanne. 2014. "Russian Tourism Spending in the UK Drops by 17% amid Ukraine Crisis." *Retail Week*, March 24.

Beissinger, Marc. 2002. *Nationalist Mobilization and the Collapse of the Soviet State.* Cambridge: Cambridge University Press.

Belinskii, V.G. (1841) 1954. "Stat'i o narodnoi poezii." In *Polnoe sobranie sochinenii v trinadtsati tomakh*, 5:289–450. Moscow: Izd-vo AN SSSR.

Bely [Belyi], Andrei. 1978. *Petersburg.* Translated by Robert A. Maguire and John Malmstad. Bloomington: Indiana University Press.

Benhabib, Seyla. 2004. *The Rights of Others: Aliens, Residents and Citizens.* Cambridge: Cambridge University Press.

Berdyaev, Nicholas. 1951. "From Posthumous Papers." *Third Hour* 5:2–7.

———. 1976. "World Discord and Christianity." In *Third Hour*, vol. 10, *In Memory of Helen Iswolsky*, edited by Thomas E. Bird, 78–84. New York: Third Hour Foundation.

Best, Stephen, and Sharon Marcus. 2009. "Surface Reading: An Introduction." *Representations* 108:1–21.

Bethea, David. 1983. *Khodasevich. His Life and Art.* Princeton, NJ: Princeton University Press.

Bezmozgis, David. 2004. *Natasha.* New York: Farrar, Straus and Giroux.

———. 2011a. *The Free World.* New York: Farrar, Straus and Giroux.

———. 2011b. "My Story: David Bezmozgis." HIAS, May 23. www.youtube.com/watch?v=8qU7fpKQ2_0.

———. 2012. "L'auteur David Bezmozgis et la question morale." Place des éditeurs, October 16. www.youtube.com/watch?v=8puI7aWHg1Y.

———. 2014a. *The Betrayers.* New York: Little, Brown.

———. 2014b. "The Novel in Real Time." *New Yorker*, March 13. www.newyorker.com/books/page-turner/the-novel-in-real-time.

———. n.d. "A Conversation with David Bezmozgis." Accessed May 31, 2018. https://www.hachettebookgroup.com/wp-content/uploads/2017/10/littlebrown-rgg-the-betrayers_bezmozgis_rgg_final.pdf.

Bhabha, Homi. 1994. *The Location of Culture.* London: Routledge.

Biddle, Ian, and Vanessa Knights, eds. 2007. *Music, National Identity and the Politics of Location: Between the Global and the Local.* Aldershot: Ashgate.

Bilaniuk, Laada. 2005. *Contested Tongues: Language Politics and Cultural Correction in Ukraine.* Ithaca, NY: Cornell University Press.

Bilenky, Serhiy. 2012. *Romantic Nationalism in Eastern Europe: Russian, Polish, and Ukrainian Political Imaginations.* Stanford: Stanford University Press.

Bissenova, Alima. 2017. "The Fortress and the Frontier: Mobility, Culture, and Class in Almaty and Astana." *Europe-Asia Studies* 69 (4): 642–67.

Bissenova, Alima, and Kulshat Medeuova. 2016. "Davlenie metropolii i tikhii natsionalizm akademicheskikh praktik."*Ab Imperio* 4:207–55.

Bitiutskii, Al'bert. 2014. "Pochemu Rada pobedivshego 'evromaidana' protiv russkogo iazyka?" *Russkaia narodnaia liniia*, February 26. http://ruskline.ru/special_opinion/pochemu_rada_pobedivshego_evromajdana_protiv_russkogo_yazyka/.

Blanton, Raymond, and Joshua P. Ewalt. 2014. "Rhetorical Maneuvers: Reflections on being Blue Collar in an Academic World." *Rhizomes* 27. http://rhizomes.net/issue27/blanton.html.

BMI. 2015. *United Kingdom Tourist Report Q3*. London: BMI.

Bobrik, Olesya. 2008. "Proshchanie s Peterburgom (iz vospominanii o Rossii Artura Lur'e)." In *Khudozhestvennaia kul'tura russkogo zarubezh'ia, 1917–1939: Sbornik statei*, edited by G. I. Vzdornov et al., 441–49. Moscow: Indri.

———. 2012. "Khronika pamiati: Iz amerikanskikh dnevnikov Artura Lur'e." *Iskusstvo muzyki: Teoriia i istoriia* 5:167–94.

———. 2014. "Arthur Lourié: A Biographical Sketch." In *Funeral Games in Honor of Arthur Vincent Lourié*, edited by Klára Móricz and Simon Morrison, 28–62. Oxford: Oxford University Press.

Bojanowska, Edyta. 2007. *Nikolai Gogol: Between Ukrainian and Russian Nationalism*. Cambridge, MA: Harvard University Press.

Bookriot. 2014. "Mikhail Idov 'Chës'" (January 21), bookriot.livejournal.com/32395.html (accessed January 16, 2017).

Borenstein, Eliot. 2016a. "What Isn't Russophobia?" *Plots against Russia*, July 26. http://plotsagainstrussia.org/eb7nyuedu/2016/7/26/what-isnt-russophobia.

2016b. "Russophobia and the Generic Villain." *Plots against Russia*, August 5. http://plotsagainstrussia.org/eb7nyuedu/2016/8/5/russophobia-as-generic-villain.

Bourdieu, Pierre. 1991. *Language as Symbolic Power*. Translated by G. Raymond and M. Adamson. Cambridge: Cambridge University Press.

Boym, Svetlana. 2001. *The Future of Nostalgia*. New York: Basic Books.

———. 2014. "A Soviet Drop-Out's Journey to Freedom: In Search of the Traces of My Refugee Transit Camp in Vienna, on My Way to America." *Tablet*, July 3. www.tabletmag.com/jewish-arts-and-culture/books/176945/camp-tale.

Brandenberger, David. 2002. *National Bolshevism: Stalinist Mass Culture and the Formation of Modern Russian National Identity, 1931–1956*. Cambridge, MA: Harvard University Press.

Brubaker, Rogers. 2000. "Accidental Diasporas and External 'Homelands' in Central and Eastern Europe: Past and Present." Institute for Advanced Studies, Vienna, Political Science Series, no. 71.

———. 2005. "The 'Diaspora' Diaspora." *Ethnic and Racial Studies* 28 (1): 1–19.

Brubaker, Rogers, and Frederick Cooper. 2000. "Beyond 'Identity.'" *Theory and Society* 29 (1): 1–47.

Buckley, Mary. 1989. *Women and Ideology in the Soviet Union*. Hertfordshire, UK: Harverster Wheatsheaf.

Bukovskii, Vladimir. 1987. *To Choose Freedom*. Stanford: Hoover Institution Press.

Bulkina, Inna. 2016. "'Stikhiia Maidana': Russkaia i ukrainskaia 'maidannaia poeziia.'" Gefter, April 1. http://gefter.ru/archive/18008.

Bullock, Philip Ross. 2006. "The Songs of Sergei Prokofiev: Texts and Contexts, Imitations and Interrogations." *Three Oranges* 11:17–22.

———. 2009. *Rosa Newmarch and Russian Music in Late Nineteenth and Early Twentieth-Century England*. Farnham: Ashgate.

———. 2016. "'An Era of Eros': Hellenic Lyricism in the Early Twentieth-Century Russian Art-Song." In *Musical Receptions of Greek Antiquity: From the Romantic Era to Modernism*, edited by Katerina Levidou, Katy Romanou, and George Vlastov, 260–95. Newcastle upon Tyne: Cambridge Scholars.

Butler, Judith. 1990. *Gender Trouble: Feminism and the Subversion of Identity*. New York: Routledge.

Cadiot, Juliette. 2007. *Le laboratoire impérial, Russie—URSS 1860–1940*. Paris: CNRS éditions.

Cadiot, Juliette, Larissa Zakharova, and Dominique Arel. 2010. *Cacophonie d'empire: Le gouvernement des langues dans l'empire russe et en URSS*. Paris: CNRS éditions.

Calhoun, Craig. 2002. "The Class Consciousness of Frequent Travelers: Toward a Critique of Actually Existing Cosmopolitanism." *South Atlantic Quarterly* 101 (4): 869–97.

Casanova, Pascale. 2004. *The World Republic of Letters*. Translated by M. B. DeBevoise Cambridge, MA: Harvard University Press.

Chandler, Andrea. 2013. *Democracy, Gender, and Social Policy in Russia: A Wayward Society*. Basingstoke, UK: Palgrave Macmillan.

Chapaer, Vasilii. 2010. "Kofemolka Mikhaila Idova." *APN*, December 27. www.apn.ru/opinions/article23504.htm.

Cheyette, Brian. 2013. *Diasporas of the Mind: Jewish and Postcolonial Writing and the Nightmare of History*. New Haven, CT: Yale University Press.

Ciolkowski, Laura. 2006. "A Compelling Coming-of-Age Story from Lara Vapnyar." *Chicago Tribune*, April 2. http://articles.chicagotribune.com/2006-04-02/entertainment/0604010034_1_muse-memoirs-short-fiction.

Cixous, Hélène. 1994. "Black Sail White Sail." *New Literary History* 25 (2): 222–354.

Clifford, James. 1994. "Diasporas." *Cultural Anthropology* 9 (3): 302–38.

Cohen, Richard. 1971. *Let My People Go*. New York: Popular Library Press.

Cohen, Robin. 1997. *Global Diasporas: An Introduction*. London: UCL Press.

Collin, Paul. 1894. *Trente poésies russes*. Paris: Alphonse Lemerre.

Commercio, Michele E. 2010. *Russian Minority Politics in Post-Soviet Latvia and Kyrgyzstan: The Transformative Power of Informal Networks*. Philadelphia: University of Pennsylvania Press.

Cosgrove, Simon. 2004. *Russian Nationalism and the Politics of Soviet Literature: The Case of* Nash sovremennik *1981–91*. New York: Palgrave Macmillan.

Ćosić, Bora. 2001. *Die Toten. Das Berlin meiner Gedichte*. Berlin: Aufbau-Taschenbuch.

Cowgill, Rachel, and Hilary Poriss, eds. 2012. *The Arts of the Prima Donna in the Long Nineteenth Century*. Oxford: Oxford University Press.

Cross, Jonathan. 2015. *Igor Stravinsky*. London: Reaktion.

———. 2013. "Stravinsky in Exile." In *Igor Stravinsky and His World*, edited by Tamara Levitz, 1–17. Princeton, NJ: Princeton University Press.

———. 2012. "Stravinsky's *Petrushka*: Modernising the Past, Russianising the Future; or, How Stravinsky Learned to Be an Exile." In *Twentieth-Century Music and Politics: Essays in Memory of Neil Edmunds*, edited by Pauline Fairclough, 23–35. Farnham: Ashgate.

Cunningham, Valentine. 1994. *In the Reading Gaol: Postmodernity, Texts and History*. Oxford: Blackwell.

Damrosch, David. 2003. *What Is World Literature?* Princeton, NJ: Princeton University Press.

Danuser, Hermann. 1999. "Composers in Exile: The Question of Musical Identity." In *Driven into Paradise: The Musical Migration from Nazi Germany to the United States*, edited by Reinhold Brinkmann and Christoph Wolff, 155–71. Berkeley: University of California Press.

Darczewska, Jolanta, and Piotr Żochowski. 2015. "Russophobia in the Kremlin's Strategy: A Weapon of Mass Destruction." Translated by Jim Todd. *OSW Point of View* 56 (October). Warsaw: Ośrodek Studiów Wschodnich im. Marka Karpia.

"Da ty rusofob." 2015. "Da ty rusofob." *Pora valit'*. http://pora-valit.com/да-ты-русофоб/.

Dave, Bhavna. 2007. *Kazakhstan: Ethnicity, Language and Power*. London: Routledge.

Davidson, Pamela. 1989. *The Poetic Imagination of Vyacheslav Ivanov: A Russian Symbolist's Perception of Dante*. Cambridge: Cambridge University Press.

Dayton, Eric. 1977. "Pragmatic Contradiction." *Ethics* 87 (3): 222–36.

Debrer, Sergei. 2008. "Byt' v Gamburge nemetsko-russkoi shkole?" *Russkaia Germaniia*, February 4.

———. 2010a. "Aleksandr Prokhanov: 'Nasha vlast' chem khorosha: Ona ne vmeshivaetsia v zhizn' naroda.'" *Russkaia Germaniia*, April 22.

———. 2010b. "Ot russkogo slova do russkogo delo—'distantsiia ogromnogo mera.'" *Russkaia Germaniia*, January 7.

Degai, Ekaterina. 2014. "Mikhail Idov, redaktor GQ: 'Eto sovershenno normal'no: Imet' druzheskie otnosheniia s Timati i pri etom byt' poklonnikom Alekseia Germana.'" Accessed January 16, 2017. *Malina*, February 21. malina.am/series/idov 994744.

Deleuze, Gilles. 1993. *The Fold: Leibniz and the Baroque*. Translated by Tom Conley. London: Athlone Press, 1993.

Deleuze, Gilles, and Félix Guattari. (1975) 1986. *Kafka: Toward a Minor Literature*. Translated by Dana Polan. Minneapolis: University of Minnesota Press.

de Vogüé, E. M. 1886. *Le Roman russe*. Paris: Plon, Nourrit et Cie.

———. 1887. *The Russian Novelists*. Translated by Jane Loring Edmand. Boston: D. Lothrop.

D'haen, Theo. 2012. *The Routledge Concise History of World Literature*. London: Routledge.

Dolbilov, Mikhail. 2010. *Russkii krai, chuzhaia vera: Etnokonfessional'naia politika imperii v Litve i Belorussii pri Aleksandre II*. Moscow: Novoe literaturnoe obozrenie.

Dolinskiy, Alexey. 2015. "Hard Thinking about Russian Soft Power: What to Do Next." *Russia Direct*, April 10. www.russia-direct.org/analysis/hard-thinking-about-russian-soft-power-what-do-next.

Dubinianskii, Mikhail. 2017. "Narody-nebrat'ia." *Ukraïns'ka Pravda*, December 25. www.pravda.com.ua/rus/articles/2017/12/25/7166659/.

Dufour, Valérie. 2006. *Stravinski et ses exégètes (1910–1940)*. Brussels: Université de Bruxelles.

du Quenoy, Paul. 2015. "In the 'Most Uncompromising Russian Style': The Russian Repertoire at the Metropolitan Opera, 1910–47." *Revolutionary Russia* 28 (1): 1–21.

Edmond, Jacob. 2012. *A Common Strangeness: Contemporary Poetry, Cross-Cultural Encounter, Comparative Literature*. New York: Fordham University Press.

Eksteins, Modris. 1990. *The Rites of Spring: The Great War and the Birth of the Modern Age.* New York: Anchor Books Doubleday.
Elias, Nelly. 2008. *Coming Home: Media and Returning Diaspora in Israel and Germany.* New York: State University of New York Press.
Eliav, Lova. 1965. *Between a Hammer and a Scythe: Personal Experience amongst Soviet Jews.* Tel Aviv: Am Over.
Ely, Christopher. 2003. "The Origins of Russian Scenery: Volga River Tourism and Russian Landscape." *Slavic Review* 62 (4): 666–82.
Emcke, Carolin. 2013. *Weil es sagbar ist: Über Zeugenschaft und Gerechtigkeit.* Frankfurt am Main: Fischer.
Emerson, Caryl. 2006. "Artur Vincent Lourié's 'Blackamoor of Peter the Great': Pushkin's Exotic Ancestor as Twentieth-Century Opera." In *Under the Sky of My Africa: Alexander Pushkin and Blackness,* edited by Catharine Theimer Nepomnyashchy, Nicole Svobodny, and Ludmilla A. Trigos, 332–67. Evanston, IL: Northwestern University Press.
———. 2014. "Jacques Maritain and the Catholic Muse in Lourié's Post-Petersburg Worlds." In *Funeral Games in Honor of Arthur Vincent Lourié,* edited by Klára Móricz and Simon Morrison, 196–268. Oxford: Oxford University Press.
Emerson, Caryl, and Klára Móricz. 2009–10. "Athur Vincent Lourié's Opera on Pushkin's Black Great Grandfather." *Pushkin Review* 12–13:71–96.
Engel, David. 2009. *Zionism.* London: Longman.
English, James. 2005. *The Economy of Prestige: Prizes, Awards, and the Circulation of Cultural Value.* Cambridge, MA: Harvard University Press.
Erenburg, Il'ia. 1962. "Trest D.E." In *Sobranie sochinenii v deviati tomakh,* 1:235–383. 9 vols. Moscow: Khudozhestvennaia literatura.
Erofeev, Venedikt. 2000. *Moskva-Petushki.* Moscow: Vagrius.
Etkind, Aleksandr, Dirk Uffel'mann [Uffelmann], and Il'ia Kukulin. 2012. "Vnutrenniaia kolonizatsiia Rossii: Mezhdu praktikoi i voobrazheniem." In *Tam, vnutri: Praktiki vnutrennei kolonizatsii v kul'turnoi istorii Rossii,* edited by Aleksandr Etkind, Dirk Uffel'mann [Uffelmann], and Il'ia Kukulin, 6–50. Moscow: Novoe literaturnoe obozrenie.
Etkind, Alexander. 2011. *Internal Colonization: Russia's Imperial Experience.* Malden, MA: Polity Press.
"Etnicheskii sostav Kyrgyzstana." 2016. KNEWS, March 9. http://knews.kg/2016/03/etnicheskij-sostav-kyrgyzstana-russkih-stanovitsya-menshe-uzbekov-bolshe-3.
Eurasian Development Bank. 2016. *EDB Integration Barometer–2016.* Report no. 40. St. Petersburg: EDB. https://eabr.org/en/analytics/integration-research/cii-reports/integratsionnyy-barometr-eabr-2016.
Ezrahi, Sidra DeKoven. 2000. *Booking Passage: Exile and Homecoming in the Modern Jewish Imagination.* Berkeley: University of California Press.
Fadeichev, Sergei. 2016. "Minkul'tury zakazalo issledovanie rossiefobii za 1,9 mln rublei." *TASS,* June 30. http://tass.ru/obschestvo/3420517.
Fairclough, Norman. 1992. *Language and Power.* London: Longman.
Fairclough, Pauline. 2007. "The 'Old Shostakovich': Reception in the British Press." *Music & Letters* 88 (2): 266–96.

Faranda, Regina, and David Nolle. 2003. "Ethnic Social Distance in Kyrgyzstan: Evidence from a Nationwide Opinion Survey." *Nationalities Papers* 32 (2): 177–201.

———. 2011. "Boundaries of Ethnic Identity in Central Asia: Titular and Russian Perceptions of Ethnic Commonalities in Kazakhstan and Kyrgyzstan." *Ethnic and Racial Studies* 34 (4): 620–42.

Father Superior (Igumen) Filipp. 2010. "Zamestitel' predsedatelia OVTsS: 'Russkii mir eto tsivilizatsionnaia obshchnost', obrazovannaia obshchimi tsennostiami i obshchim opytom obshchestvennogo stroitel'stva.'" *Patriarkhiia.ru*, June 17. http://mospat.ru/ru/2010/06/17/news20574/.

Federal'noe agentstvo po turizmu. n.d. Accessed August 19, 2015. www.russiatourism.ru/contents/statistika/statisticheskie-pokazateli-vzaimnykh-poezdok-grazhdan-rossiyskoy-federatsii-i-grazhdan-inostrannykh-gosudarstv/kolichestvo-grazhdan-rossiyskoy-federatsii-vyekhavshikh-za-rubezh/.

Fel'dman, Boris. 2014. "My—liudi russko-nemetskoi kul'tury, a ne rossiisko-germanskoi politiki." *Russkaia Germaniia*, March 11.

Felman, Shoshana. 2011. "Theaters of Justice: Arendt in Jerusalem, the Eichmann Trial, and the Redefinition of Legal Meaning in the Wake of the Holocaust." *Critical Inquiry* 27 (2): 201–38.

Fennell, John, ed. and trans. 1964. *Pushkin*. London: Penguin.

Fierman, William. 2012. "Russian in Post-Soviet Central Asia: A Comparison with the States of the Baltic and South Caucasus." *Europe-Asia Studies* 64 (6): 1077–100.

Fingerhut, Michael. 2011. "IRCAM-MOSCOW." *Fontes Artis Musicae* 58 (1): 55–71.

Finkelstein, Miriam. 2016. "Re-Writing Tolstoevskii: Postcolonial Narratives in Contemporary Russian-American Literature." In *Postcolonial Slavic Literatures after Communism*, edited by Klavdia Smola and Dirk Uffelmann, 453–77. Cologne: Peter Lang.

Flamm, Christoph, Christoph Keazor, and Roland Marti, eds. 2013. *Russian Émigré Culture: Conservatism or Evolution?* Newcastle upon Tyne: Cambridge Scholars.

Fleishman, L., R. Hughes, O. Raevskaya-Hughes. 1983. *Russkii Berlin 1921–1923*. Paris: YMCA-PRESS.

Florin, Moritz. 2011. "Elity, russkii iazyk i sovetskaia identichnost' v postsvetskoi Kirgizii." *Neprikosnovennyi zapas* 6:225–33.

Flynn, Moya, and Natalya Kosmarskaya. 2012. "Exploring 'North' and 'South' in Post-Soviet Bishkek: Discourses and Perceptions of Rural-Urban Migration." *Nationalities Papers* 40 (3): 453–71.

Flynn, Moya, Natalya Kosmarskaya, and Gusel Sabirova. 2014. "The Place of Memory in Understanding Urban Change in Central Asia: The Cities of Bishkek and Ferghana." *Europe-Asia Studies* 66 (9): 1501–24.

Fond Russkii Mir. 2011. *Otchet ob osnovnykh napravleniiakh deiatel'nosti 2010*. Moscow: Fond Russkii Mir. http://russkiymir.ru/export/sites/default/russkiymir/ru/fund/docs/Report_2010.pdf.

Forostyna, Oksana. 2015. "Poaching, Simmering, and Boiling: The Declining Relevance of Identity Discourse in Ukraine." In *What Does Ukraine Think?*, edited by Andrew Wilson, 25–33. Berlin: European Council on Foreign Relations.

Frank, Susanne. 2016. "'Multinational Soviet Literature': The Project and Its Post-Soviet Legacy in Iurii Rytkheu and Gennadii Aigi." In *Postcolonial Slavic Literatures after Communism*, edited by Dirk Uffelmann and Klavdia Smola, 191–219. Frankfurt am Main: Peter Lang.

Frick, David A. 1995. *Meletij Smotryc'kyj*. Cambridge, MA: Harvard University Press.

Furman, Yelena. 2009. "'We all love with the same part of the body, don't we?': Iuliia Voznesenskaia's *Zhenskii Dekameron*, New Women's Prose, and French Feminist Theory." *Intertexts* 13 (2): 95–114.

———. 2011. "Hybrid Selves, Hybrid Texts: Embracing the Hyphen in Russian-American Fiction." *Slavic and East European Journal* 55 (1): 19–37.

———. 2016. "Hybridizing the Canon: Russian-American Writers in Dialogue with Russian Literature." *Canadian Slavonic Papers* 58 (3): 205–28.

Furmanov, Kirill, Olga Balaeva, and Marina Predvoditeleva. 2012. "Tourism Flows from Russian Federation to the European Union." *Anatolia: An International Journal of Tourism and Hospitality Research* 23 (1): 17–31.

Galili, Lili, and Roman Bronfman. 2013. *The Million that Changed the Middle East: Russian Immigration to Israel*. Tel Aviv: Matar.

Galina, Maria. 2017. "Vernut'sia i peremenit': Al'ternativnaia istoriia Rossii kak otrazhenie travmaticheskikh tochek massovogo soznaniia postsovetskogo cheloveka." *Novoe literaturnoe obozrenie* 146 (4). http://magazines.russ.ru/nlo/2017/4/vernutsya-i-peremenit.html.

Galushko-Jäckel, Nina. 2015. *Russische Romanzen in der zweiten Hälfte des 19. Jahrhunderts: Studien zum Liedschaffen ausgewählter Komponisten*. Munich: Herbert Utz.

Gatagova, L. S., L. A. Rogovaia, L. P. Kosheleva, and Juliette Cadiot, eds. 2009. *TsK VKP(b) i natsional'nyi vopros*. Vol. 2, 1933–1945. Moscow: ROSSPEN.

Gates, Henry Louis, Jr. 1988. *The Signifying Monkey: A Theory of African-American Literary Criticism*. Oxford: Oxford University Press.

Gendelev, Mikhail. 1991. "Russkoiazychnaia literatura Izrailia (Konspektivnaia zapis' lektsii, prochitannoi 12 aprelia 1991 g. na zasedanii Ierusalimskogo literaturnogo kluba)." *Obitaemyi ostrov* 1 (April), 8–9. http://gendelev.org/proza/o-literature/370-literatura-doklad.html.

———. 2003. "Posleslovie avtora." In *Nepolnoe sobranie sochinenii*, 517–21. Moscow: Vremia.

———. 2017. *Gendelev: Stikhi, proza, poetika, tekstologiia*. Moscow: Novoe literaturnoe obozrenie.

Geraci, Robert. 2015. Review of *Internal Colonization: Russia's Imperial Experience*, by Alexander Etkind. *Nationalities Papers* 43 (2): 356–59.

Gerasimenko, Olesia. 2014. *Needinaia Rossiia*. Moscow: Common Place.

Gershenson, Olga. 2005. *Gesher: Russian Theatre in Israel—A Study of Cultural Colonization*. New York: Peter Lang.

———. 2009. "Accented Memory: Russian Immigrants Reimagine Israeli Past." *Journal of Israeli History* 28 (1): 21–36.

Gershenson, Olga, and Dale Hudson. 2008. "New Immigrant, Old Story: Framing Russians on the Israeli Screen." *Journal of Film and Video* 60 (3–4): 25–42.

Gershenson, Olga, and David Shneer. 2011. "Soviet Jewishness and Cultural Studies." *Journal of Jewish Identities* 4 (1): 129–47.

Giddens, Anthony. 1991. *Modernity and Self-Identity*. Cambridge: Polity.

Gilroy, Paul. 1993. *The Black Atlantic: Modernity and Double Consciousness*. London: Verso.
Girenko, Iurii. 2014. "Chto oznachaet prizyv Putina k vossoedineniiu 'Russkogo mira.'" *Vzgliad*, March 19. https://vz.ru/politics/2014/3/19/677961.html.
Giroud, Vincent. 2015. *Nicolas Nabokov: A Life in Freedom and Music*. Oxford: Oxford University Press, 2015.
Gitelman, Zvi. 1998. "The Decline of the Jewish Nation: Boundaries, Content, and Jewish Identity." *Jewish Social Studies* 4 (2): 112–32.
———. 2001. *A Century of Ambivalence: The Jews of Russia and the Soviet Union, 1881 to the Present*. 2nd exp. ed. Bloomington: Indiana University Press.
———, ed. 2016. *The New Jewish Diaspora: Russian-Speaking Immigrants in the United States, Israel, and Germany*. New Brunswick, NJ: Rutgers University Press.
Glad, John, ed. 1993. *Conversations in Exile: Russian Writers Abroad*. Durham, NC: Duke University Press.
———. 1999. *Russia Abroad: Writers, History, Politics*. Washington, DC, and Tenafly, NJ: Birchbark Press and Hermitage.
Glaser, Amelia. 2011. "Introduction: Russian-American Fiction." Special forum issue, "Russian-American Fiction." *Slavic and East European Journal* 55 (1): 15–18.
———, ed. 2015. *Stories of Khmelnytsky: Competing Literary Legacies of the 1648 Khmelnytsky Uprising*. Stanford: Stanford University Press.
Gleason, John H. 1950. *The Genesis of Russophobia in Great Britain: A Study of the Interaction of Policy and Opinion*. Cambridge, MA: Harvard University Press.
Goffman, Ervin. 1974. *Frame Analysis*. New York: Harper Colophon Books.
Gojowy, Detlef. 1993. *Arthur Lourié und der russische Futurismus*. Laaber: Laaber.
Gorham, Michael S. 2011. "Virtual Rusophonia: Language Policy as 'Soft Power' in the New Media Age." *Digital Icons: Studies in Russian, Eurasian and Central European New Media* 5:23–48. www.digitalicons.org/issue05/virtual-rusophonia-language-policy-as-soft-power-in-the-new-media-age.
———. 2014. *After Newspeak: Language Culture and Politics in Russia from Gorbachev to Putin*. Ithaca, NY: Cornell University Press.
———. 2016. "O 'padonkakh' i 'kiberdruzhinnikakh': Virtual'nye istochniki porchi iazyka." Translated by K. Gusarova. In *Nastroika iazyka: Upravlenie kommunikatsiiami na postsovetskom prostranstve*, edited by E. G. Lapina-Kratasyuk, O. V. Moroz, and E. G. Nim, 240–58. Moscow: Novoe literaturnoe obozrenie.
Gorshkov, M. K., et al. 2015. "Rossiiskoe obshchestvo v kontekste novykh realii (tezisy o glavnom). Institut sotsiologii Rossiiskoi akademii nauk. www.isras.ru/resume_rossiiskoe_obschestvo_v_kontekste_novykh_realy.
Gorsuch, Anne E. 2003. "'There's No Place like Home': Soviet Tourism in Late Stalinism." *Slavic Review* 62 (4): 760–85.
———. 2011. *All This Is Your World: Soviet Tourism at Home and Abroad after Stalin*. New York: Oxford University Press.
Gorsuch, Anne E., and Diane P. Koenker, eds. 2006. *Turizm: The Russian and East European Tourist under Capitalism and Socialism*. Ithaca, NY: Cornell University Press.
———, eds. 2013. *The Socialist Sixties: Crossing Borders in the Second World*. Bloomington: Indiana University Press.
Goscilo, Helena. 1996. *Dehexing Sex: Russian Womanhood during and after Glasnost*. Ann Arbor: University of Michigan Press.

———. 1993. "Speaking Bodies: Erotic Zones Rhetoricized." In *Fruits of Her Plume: Essays on Contemporary Russian Women's Culture*, edited by Helena Goscilo, 135–63. Armonk, NY: M. E. Sharpe.

Goscilo, Helena, and Andrea Lanoux. 2006. "Introduction: Lost in the Myths." In *Gender and National Identity in Twentieth-Century Russian Culture*, edited by Helena Goscilo and Andrea Lanoux, 3–29. DeKalb: Northern Illinois University Press.

Gourdine, Angeletta K. M. 2003. *The Difference Place Makes: Gender, Sexuality, and Diaspora Identity*. Columbus: Ohio State University Press.

Grabowicz, George. 1995. "Ukrainian Studies: Framing the Contexts." *Slavic Review* 54 (3): 674–90.

Grant, Bruce. 2009. *The Captive and the Gift: Cultural Histories of Sovereignty in Russia and the Caucasus*. Ithaca, NY: Cornell University Press.

Greber, Erika. 2005. "Das zweite Leben des Evgenij Onegin: Transpositionen der Oneginstrophe und Onegins Reinkarnation als Campus-Heldin." *Lebensstadien: Festschrift für Renate Döring-Smirnov. Wiener Slawistischer Almanach* 55:135–50.

Greenfeld, Liah. 1990. "The Formation of the Russian National Identity: The Role of Status Insecurity and Ressentiment." *Comparative Studies in Society and History* 32:549–91.

Grigas, Agnia. 2016. *Beyond Crimea: The New Russian Empire*. New Haven, CT: Yale University Press.

Guignery, Vanessa, Catherine Pesso-Miquel, and François Specq, eds. 2011. *Hybridity: Forms and Figures in Literature and the Visual Arts*. Newcastle upon Tyne: Cambridge Scholars.

Guseinov, Chingiz. 2014. "K voprosu o 'russkosti nerusskikh.'" *Druzhba narodov* 75 (4): 204–24.

Guseinov, Gasan. 2005. *Karta nashei Rodiny: Ideologema mezhdu slovom i telom*. Moscow: OGI.

Gutina, Nelly. 2011. *Israel Goes Russian*. Tel Aviv: Mercur.

Guttmann, Anna. 2013. *Writing Indians and Jews: Metaphorics of Jewishness in South Asian Literature*. New York: Palgrave Macmillan.

Hagglund, Roger. 1985. *A Vision of Unity: Adamovich in Exile*. Ann Arbor: Ardis.

Hale, Henry, and Robert Orttung, eds. 2016. *Beyond the Euromaidan: Comparative Perspectives on Advancing Reform in Ukraine*. Stanford: Stanford University Press.

Hardeman, Hilde. 1994. *Coming to Terms with the Soviet Regime: The "Changing Signposts" Movement among Russian Emigres in the Early 1920s*. DeKalb: Northern Illinois University Press.

Hast, Susanna. 2014. *Spheres of Influence in International Relations: History, Theory and Politics*. Farnham: Ashgate.

Hausbacher, Eva. 2009. *Poetik der Migration: Transnationale Schreibweisen in der zeitgenössischen russischen Literatur*. Tübingen: Stauffernberg.

Hawkesworth, Celia. 1991. "Feminist Writing in Eastern Europe: The Problem Solved?" In *Textual Liberation: European Feminist Writing in the Twentieth Century*, edited by Helena Forsås-Scott, 100–129. London: Routledge.

Haydon, Geoffrey. 1995. *John Tavener: Glimpses of Paradise*. London: Victor Gollancz.

Hayles, N. Katherine. 2010. "How We Read: Close, Hyper, Machine." *ADE Bulletin* 150:62–79.

Heller, Monica, Adam Jaworski, and Crispin Thurlow. 2014. "Introduction: Sociolinguistics and Tourism: Mobilities, Markets, Multilingualism." *Journal of Sociolinguistics* 18 (4): 425–58.

Herrero, Nieves, and Sharon Roseman, eds. 2015. *The Tourism Imaginary and Pilgrimages to the Edges of the World.* Bristol: Channel View.

Hesse, Isabelle. 2016. *The Politics of Jewishness in Contemporary World Literature: The Holocaust, Zionism, and Colonialism.* London: Bloomsbury.

Hirsch, Francine. 2003. "Getting to Know 'the People of the USSR': Ethnographic Exhibits as Soviet Virtual Tourism." *Slavic Review* 62 (4): 683–709.

———. 2005. *Empire of Nations: Ethnographic Knowledge and the Making of the Soviet Union.* Ithaca, NY: Cornell University Press.

Hollinshead, Keith. 1998. "Tourism, Hybridity, and Ambiguity: The Relevance of Bhabha's 'Third Space' Cultures." *Journal of Leisure Research* 30 (1): 121–56.

Hollinshead, Keith, Irena Atljevic, and Nazia Ali. 2009. "Worldmaking Agency—Worldmaking Authority: The Sovereign Constitutive Role of Tourism." *Tourism Geographies* 11 (4): 427–43.

Holt, Alix. 1985. "The First Soviet Feminists." In *Soviet Sisterhood*, edited by Barbara Holland, 237–65. Bloomington: Indiana University Press.

Hörning, Karl H., and Julia Reuter. 2004. *Doing Culture: Neue Positionen zum Verhältnis von Kultur und sozialer Praxis.* Bielefeld: Transcript.

Hosking, Jeoffrey. 2006. *Rulers and Victims: The Russians in the Soviet Union.* Cambridge, MA: Harvard University Press.

Hulliger, Stefan, ed. 2018. *Arthur Lourié: Catalogue of Complete Works.* Basel: Arthur Lourié Gesellschaft.

Hundorova, Tamara. 2013. *Tranzytna kul'tura: Symptomy postkolonial'noï travmy.* Kiev: Hrani-T.

Huntington, Samuel P. 1996. *The Clash of Civilizations and the Remaking of World Order.* New York: Simon and Schuster.

Iagun, Evgenii. 2015. "Rusofobiia i teoriia etnogeneza L. N. Gumileva." *Lib.ru: Zhurnal Samizdat*, October 5. http://samlib.ru/j/jagun_ewgenij/rusofobia.shtml.

Iakovenko, Natalia. 2002. *Paralel'nyi svit: Doslidzhennia z istoriï uiavlen' ta idei v Ukraïni XVI–XVII st.* Kiev: Krytyka.

———. 2008. *Ukraïns'ka shliakhta z kintsia XIV do seredyny XVII stolittia: Volyn' i Tsentral'na Ukraïna.* 2nd ed. Kiev: Krytyka.

Iakovlev, Fedor. 2011. "Rusofobiia na Ukraine granichit s paranoiei." *Regnum*, October 24. http://regnum.ru/news/polit/1459317.html.

Idov, Michael. 2005. "Bitter Brew. I opened a charming neighborhood coffee shop. Then it destroyed my life." *Slate*, December 29. www.slate.com/id/2132576/.

———. 2009a. *Ground Up: A Novel.* New York: Farrar, Straus and Giroux.

———. 2009b. *Kofemolka: Roman.* Translated by Mikhail Idov and Lilia Idova. Moscow: Corpus.

———. 2010a. "Klub Prokhorov: The Billionaire Nets Owner and the Creation (His Creation, Actually) of a New Kind of New York Russian." *New York*, May 30. http://nymag.com/news/features/66287/.

———, ed. 2010b. *Made in Russia: Unsung Icons of Soviet Design.* New York: Rizzoli.

———. 2011. "My Two Days as a Russian Tabloid Sensation." *The Awl*, May 4. www.theawl.com/2011/05/my-two-weeks-as-a-russian-tabloid-sensation.

———. 2013. *Chës: Povest' i rasskazy*. Moscow: Corpus.

———. 2015. "Kak snimalsia Londongrad: Uchebnik dlia stsenaristov." *Afisha Daily*, September 11. http://vozduh.afisha.ru/cinema/kak-snimalsya-londongrad-uchebnik-dlya-scenaristov/.

———. 2016. "Situation Comedy: My Strange, Phenomenally Successful Career as an American Screenwriter in Russia." *New York Times Magazine*, January 10, 30–35.

———. 2018. *Dressed Up for a Riot: Misadventures in Putin's Moscow*. New York: Farrar, Straus and Giroux.

Il'in, Ivan A. 1993. "Protiv Rossii." In *Sobranie sochinenii v desiati tomakh*, 2:1, 62–67. Moscow: Russkaia kniga.

Ingold, Tim. 2000. *The Perception of the Environment*. London: Routledge.

Inozemtsev, Vladislav. 2014. "Russkii mir I protiv Russkogo mira II." *Vedomosti*, July 29. www.vedomosti.ru/opinion/articles/2014/07/29/russkij-mir-protiv-russkogo-mira.

Interfax. 2016. "Rekordnaia dolia rossiian reshila nikuda ne ekhat' otdykhat' ėtim letom." Interfax, June 7. www.interfax.ru/russia/512255.

"Interv'iu Lukashenko negosudarstvennym SMI, v tom chisle Evroradio." 2015. Evroradio.fm, August 4. http://euroradio.fm/ru/intervyu-lukashenko-negosudarstvennym-smi-v-tom-chisle-evroradio-onlayn.

Iosseliani, Otar. 2002. "Vpechatleniya Nedeli." *Obschaya Gazeta*, March 14. www.pressarchive.ru/obschaya-gazeta/2002/03/14/262658.html.

Isakova, Anna. 2007. "A Russian Immigrant Looks at the Israeli (or Jewish?) Culture." In *Israel in the Middle East*, edited by Itamar Rabinovich and Jehuda Reinharz, 468–70. Waltham, MA: Brandeis University Press.

Ishchenko, Rostislav. 2014. "Russkii mir i natsional'nyi vopros." *Ekspert*, September 8. http://expert.ru/expert/2014/37/russkij-mir-i-natsionalnyij-vopros/.

"Israel Beiteinu" 1999. In *Lashon, Hevra, Ve-Tarbut*, edited by Malka Muchnik, 192–93. Ra'anana: Open University of Israel.

Iswolsky, Helen [Elena Izwolsky]. 1976a. "From Commitment to Oblation." In *The Third Hour*, vol. 10, *In Memory of Helen Iswolsky*, edited by Thomas E. Bird, 125–30. New York: Third Hour Foundation.

———. 1976b. "Soloviev and the Eirenic Movement." In *The Third Hour*, vol. 10, *In Memory of Helen Iswolsky*, edited by Thomas E. Bird, 73–77. New York: Third Hour Foundation.

Iurgens, Igor'. 2011. "Zhestkii vyzov 'miagkoi sily.'" *Rossiiskaia gazeta*, September 16.

Jack, Gavin, and Alison Phipps. 2005. *Tourism and Intercultural Exchange*. Clevedon: Channel View.

Jackson, Jeanne-Marie. 2015. *South African Literature's Russian Soul: Narrative Forms of Global Isolation*. London: Bloomsbury.

Jakobson, Roman. 1985. "Metalanguage as a Linguistic Problem." In *Selected Writings*, vol.7, *Contributions to Comparative Mythology: Studies in Linguistics and Philology, 1972–1982*, edited by Stephen Rudy, 113–21. Berlin: Mouton.

Jaworski, Adam, and Sarah Lawson. 2005. "Discourses of Polish Agritourism: Global, Local, Pragmatic." In *Discourse, Communication and Tourism*, edited by Adam Jaworski and Annette Pritchard, 123–49. Clevedon: Channel View.

Jaworski, Adam, and Annette Pritchard, eds. 2005. *Discourse, Communication and Tourism*, Clevedon: Channel View.

Kabanov, Aleksandr. 2010. *Betmen Sagaidachnyi*. Moscow: Art Haus Media.

———. 2017. *Na iazyke vraga: Stikhi o voine i mire*. Kharkiv: Folio.

Kabanov, Nikolai. 2014. "Latviiskoe issledovanie: 'U russkikh est' stremlenie dominirovat'.'" *Biznes i Baltiia*, September 25.

Kaganskii, Vladimir. 2001. *Kul'turnyi landshaft i sovetskoe obitaemoe prostranstvo*. Moscow: Novoe literaturnoe obozrenie.

———. 2005. "Rossiia-SSSR segodnia? Stat'ia tret'ia. Sravnitel'nyi portret prostranstv: Gosudarstvo RF i rossiiskoe prostranstvo." *Obshchestvennye nauki i sovremennost'* 4:100–112.

Kamatozov, Arsenii. 2014. "Sootechestvennik—eto zvuchit podozritel'no?" *Russkaia Germaniia*, December 16.

Kamel'nikov, I. 2009. "Ne Moskva li za nami." *Evropa-Ekspress*, December 14.

Kappeler, Andreas. 1997. *Rossiia—mnogonatsional'naia imperiia: Vozniknovenie. Istoriia. Raspad*. Moscow: Traditsiia-Progress.

Kara-Murza, Sergei. 2012. "Rusofobiia Zapada: Kratkaia istoriia." *Sdelano u nikh*, May 3. www.sdelanounih.ru/russophobe_1/.

Karlinsky, Simon, and Alfred Appel Jr., eds. 1973. *The Bitter Air of Exile: Russian Writers in the West, 1922–1982*. Berkeley: University of California Press.

Katsman, Roman. 2016. "Nekod Singer in Russian and Hebrew: Neoeclecticism and Beyond." *Symposium* 70 (2): 66–79.

Kazarin, Pavel. 2015. "Russkii mir protiv mira ukrainskogo." *Sovetskaia Belarus'*, April 9.

Kellman, Steven. 2000. *The Translingual Imagination*. Lincoln: University of Nebraska Press.

K'esa, Dzhul'etto [Giulietto K'esa]. 2016. *Rusofobiia 2.0: Bolezn' ili oruzhie Zapada*. Moscow: Eksmo.

Kharitonova, Natal'ia. 2008. "Vladimir Iakovlev: 'Snob'—eto ne shliagernaia zhurnalistka." *Open Space*, October 31. www.telekritika.ua/daidzhest/2008-10-31/41662.

Khazanov, Anatoly M. 2003. "A State without a Nation? Russia after Empire." In *The Nation-State in Question*, edited by Thazha V. Paul, G. John Ikenberry, and John A. Hall, 79–105. Princeton, NJ: Princeton University Press.

Khersonskii, Boris. 2014. *Missa in tempore belli / Messa vo vremena voiny*. St. Petersburg: Izdatel'stvo Ivana Limbakha.

———. 2015a. *Kosmonash: kniga stikhotvorenii*. Chernivtsi: Meridian Czernowitz.

———. 2015b. *Otkrytyi dnevnik*. Kiev: Dukh i litera.

———. 2016. "Soskochit' s iazyka: Mozhno li pisat' po-russki, ostavaias' pri etom ukraintsem." *Focus*, May 22. http://focus.ua/opinions/350822/.

Khersonskii, Boris, and Ekaterina Sergatskova. 2015. "Rossii nuzhno edinoe trevozhnoe prostranstvo na iuge Ukrainy." *Ukraïns'ka Pravda Zhittia*, February 10. life.pravda .com.ua/person/2015/02/10/189118.

Khersonskii, Boris, and Iurii Volodarskii. 2014. "'Nikakikh bratskikh narodov ne bylo': Odessit, russkii poet i ukrainskii grazhdanin—o iazykovoi probleme, rossiiskom messianstve i korennoi raznitse mezhdu Poroshenko i Ianukovichem." *Colta.ru*, September 25. www.colta.ru/articles/literature/4782.

Khersons'kyi, Borys [Boris Khersonskii]. 2016a. *Klaptykova kovdra*. Kiev: Dukh i litera.

———. 2016b. *Rodynnyi arkhiv ta inshi virshi*. L'viv: Vydavnytstvo Staroho Leva.

Kildea, Paul. 2002. *Selling Britten: Music and the Market Place*. Oxford: Oxford University Press.

———. 2013. *Benjamin Britten: A Life in the Twentieth Century*. London: Allen Lane.

Kirmse, Stefan B. 2011. "'Nested Globalization' in Osh, Kyrgyzstan: Urban Youth Culture in a 'Southern City'" In *Urban Spaces after Socialism: Ethnographies of Public Places in Eurasian Cities*, edited by Tsympyla Darieva, Wolfgang Kaschuba, and Melanie Krebs, 283–305. Frankfurt: Campus.

Kiselev, Dmitrii. 2008. "Rusofobiia: Istoriia i sovremennost'." *Vesti.Ru*, August 31. www.vesti.ru/doc.html?id=205437.

Kishinevsky, Vera. 2004. *Russian Immigrants in the United States: Adapting to American Culture*. New York: LFB Scholarly.

Kisliak, Ol'ga. 2011. "V sozvezdii Gagarina." *Sovetskaia Belarus'*, February 3.

Kiwan, Nadia, and Ulrike Hanna Meinhof, eds. 2011. "Music and Migration: A Transnational Approach." Special issue, *Music and Arts in Action* 3 (3).

Klots, Yasha. 2011. "The Ultimate City: New York in Russian Immigrant Narratives." *Slavic and East European Journal* 55 (1): 38–57.

Knox, Jennifer L. 2010. "David Bezmozgis." *New Yorker*, June 14 and 21. http://newyorker.com/magazine/2010/06/14/david-bezmozgis.

Kochanov, Evgenii. 2014. "Akela promakhnulas'." *Partner*, August 15.

Kochenov, Dimitry, and Aleksejs Dimitrovs. 2016. "EU Citizenship for Latvian 'Non-Citizens': A Concrete Proposal." *Houston Journal of International Law* 38 (1): 55–97.

Koenker, Diane. 2003. "Travel to Work, Travel to Play: On Russian Tourism, Travel and Leisure." *Slavic Review* 62 (4): 657–65.

———. 2013. *Club Red: Vacation Travel and the Soviet Dream*. Ithaca, NY: Cornell University Press.

Kohut, Zenon. 1981. "Problems in Studying the Post-Khmelnytsky Ukrainian Elite (1650s to 1830s)." In *Rethinking Ukrainian History*, edited by Ivan L. Rudnytsky with John-Paul Himka, 103–19. Edmonton: Canadian Institute of Ukrainian Studies, University of Alberta.

———. 1988. *Russian Centralism and Ukrainian Autonomy: Imperial Absorption of the Hetmanate, 1760s–1830s*. Cambridge, MA: Harvard University Press.

Korabelnikova, Ludmila. 2008. *Alexander Tcherepnin: The Saga of a Russian Emigré Composer*. Edited by Sue-Ellen Hershman-Tcherepnin. Translated by Anna Winestein. Bloomington: Indiana University Press.

Kosmarskaya, Natalya. 2006. *"Deti imperii" v postsovetskoi Tsentral'noi Azii: Adaptivnye praktiki i mental'nye sdvigi (russkie v Kirgizii, 1992–2002)*. Moscow: Natalis.

———. 2015. "The Russian Language in Kyrgyzstan: Changing Roles and Inspiring Prospects."*Russian Journal of Communication* 7 (2): 217–22.

Kosmarski, Artyom. 2011. "Grandeur and Decay of the 'Soviet Byzantium': Spaces, Peoples, and Memories of Tashkent, Uzbekistan." In *Urban Spaces after Socialism: Ethnographies of Public Places in Eurasian Cities*, edited by Tsympyla Darieva, Wolfgang Kaschuba, and Melanie Krebs, 33–56. Frankfurt am Main: Campus.

Kralin, Mikhail. 2000. *Artur i Anna: Roman bez geroia, no vse-taki o liubvi*. 2nd ed. Tomsk: Vodolei.

Krasikov, Sana. 2009. "There Will Be No Fourth Rome." In *One More Year*, 179–230. New York: Spiegel and Grau.

Krasovitskii, Aleksandr, ed. 2016. *Ukrainskaia proza i poeziia na russkom iazyke/Russkaia proza i poeziia sovremennoi Ukrainy*. Kharkiv: Folio.

Krasuska, Karolina. 2016. "Narratives of Generationality in 21st-century North American Jewish Literature: Krauss, Bezmozgis, Kalman." *East European Jewish Affairs* 46 (3): 285–310.

Kravchenko, Maria, and Sagi Tsirkin. 2015. "The Creators of *Beyond the Fear* Describe the Attempts to Silence Them." *Haaretz*, September 21. www.haaretz.co.il/gallery/cinema/.premium-1.2735606.

Krechetnikov, Artem. 2015. "Putin vidit v diaspore provodnika interesov Kremlia." *BBC: Russkaia sluzhba*, November 5. www.bbc.com/russian/russia/2015/11/151105_putin_russian_diaspora.

Kreid, Vadim, ed. 2003. *V Rossiiu vetrom strochki zaneset: Poety parizhskoi noty*. Moscow: Molodaia gvardiia.

"Kreml' reshil zaniat'sia russkimi v Latvii." 2008. *NovoNews*, September 10.

Kronenfeld, Daniel A. 2004. "Ethnogenesis without the Entrepreneurs: The Emergence of a Baltic Russian Identity in Latvia." In *Narva und die Ostseeregion*, edited by Karsten Brüggemann, 339–63. Narva: Narva College.

———. 2005. "The Effects of Interethnic Contact on Ethnic Identity: Evidence from Latvia." *Post-Soviet Affairs* 21 (3): 247–77.

Krüger, Simone, and Ruxandra Trandafoiu, eds. 2014. *The Globalization of Music in Translation: Music Migration and Tourism*. New York: Routledge.

"Kruglyi stol 'Russkii mir i protsessy globalizatsii.'" 2008. Fond Russkii Mir, November 3. http://russkiymir.ru/fund/assembly/the-second-assembly-of-the-russian-world/tables/155487/.

Kukulin, Il'ia. 2002. "Fotografiia vnutrennostei kofeinoi chashki." *Novoe literaturnoe obozrenie* 54:262–82.

———. 2004. "Gipsovye chasy." Review of *Maskavskaia Mekka*, by Andrei Volos. *Novoe literaturnoe obozrenie* 68 (4). http://magazines.russ.ru/nlo/2004/68/ku22.html.

———. 2012. "'Vnutrenniaia postkolonizatsiia': Formirovanie postkolonial'nogo soznaniia v russkoi literature 1970–2000-kh godov." In *Tam, vnutri: Praktiki vnutrennei kolonizatsii v kul'turnoi istorii Rossii*, edited by Aleksandr Etkind, Dirk Uffel'mann [Uffelmann], and Il'ia Kukulin, 846–909. Moscow: Novoe literaturnoe obozrenie.

———. 2016. "'The Long-Legged Time Is Fording the War': The Postcolonial Condition of the Russian-Language Poetry of Ukraine." In *Postcolonial Slavic Literatures after Communism*, edited by Klavdia Smola and Dirk Uffelmann, 161–87. Frankfurt: Lang.

Kulyk, Volodymyr. 2011. "Language Identity, Linguistic Diversity and Political Cleavages: Evidence from Ukraine." *Nations and Nationalism* 17 (3): 627–48.

———. 2014a. "Einheit und Identität: Sprachenpolitik nach dem Majdan." *Osteuropa* 64 (5–6): 227–37.

———. 2014b. "What Is Russian in Ukraine? Popular Beliefs Regarding the Social Roles of the Language." In *The Russian Language outside the Nation*, edited by Lara Ryazanova-Clarke, 117–40. Edinburgh: Edinburgh University Press.

———. 2015. "One Nation, Two Languages? National Identity and Language Policy in Post-Euromaidan Ukraine." *PONARS Eurasia Memo* 389. www.ponarseurasia.org/memo/one-nation-two-languages-national-identity-and-language-policy-post-euromaidan-ukraine.

———. 2016a. "Language and Identity in Ukraine after Euromaidan." *Thesis Eleven* 136 (1): 90–106.

———. 2016b. "National Identity in Ukraine: Impact of Euromaidan and the War." *Europe-Asia Studies* 68 (4): 588–608.

———. 2017. "Identity in Transformation: Russian-Speakers in Post-Soviet Ukraine." *Europe-Asia Studies*, December. https://doi.org/10.1080/09668136.2017.1379054.

Kuniaev, Stanislav. 2017. "Brat'ia solntsu i vetru." *Nash Sovremennik* 4:73–74.

Kurkov, Andrei. 2006. The 2006 J.B. Rudnyckyj Distinguished Lecture, University of Manitoba, February 23. http://proxycheck.lib.umanitoba.ca/libraries/units/archives/grants/rudnyckyj_lecture/lecture_13.html.

———. 2014. "Stan viiny bude permanentnym." *Deutsche Welle*, September 18. www.dw.com/p/1DEqV.

———. 2016. "Maiut' dominuvaty knyzhky pro liubov i zhyttia." *BBC*, September 23. www.bbc.com/ukrainian/society/2016/09/160920_kurkov_interview_book_she.

Kuznetsov, Sergei. 1999. "Kul'turnyi gid." *Russkii zhurnal*, July 30. http://old.russ.ru/culture/guide/19990730-pr.html.

Laitin, David. 1998. *Identity in Formation: The Russian-Speaking Populations in the Near Abroad.* Ithaca, NY: Cornell University Press.

Laruelle, Marlene. 2006. "'Russkaia diaspora' i 'rossiiskie sootechestvenniki'" / "'Russian diaspora' and 'Russian Compatriots.'" In *Demokratiia vertikali / Democracy of the Vertical*, edited by A. Verkhovskii, 185–212. Moscow: Sova.

———. 2015. "The 'Russian World': Russia's Soft Power and Geopolitical Imagination." *Center on Global Interests*, May 21. http://globalinterests.org/2015/05/26/the-russian-world-russias-soft-power-and-geopolitical-imagination/.

Laruelle, Marlene, and Sebastien Peyrouse. 2007. *Russkii vopros v nezavisimom Kazakhstane: Istoriia, pamiat', identichnost'.* Translated from French and with an introduction by Natalya Kosmarskaya. Moscow: Natalis.

Latour, Bruno. 2004. "Whose Cosmos, Which Cosmopolitics? Comments on the Peace Terms of Ulrich Beck." *Common Knowledge* 10 (3): 450–62.

"Latviiskie SMI o metodakh vliianiia Kremlia." 2009. *NovaNews*, December 10.

Lavrov, Sergei. 2009. "Sozidatel'nyi potentsial Russkogo mira." *Rossiiskaia gazeta*, November 30.

———. 2015. "Russkii mir na puti konsolidatsii." *Rossiiskaia gazeta*, November 1.

Layton, Susan. 1994. *Russian Literature and Empire: Conquest of the Caucasus from Pushkin to Tolstoy.* Cambridge: Cambridge University Press.

———. 2009. "The Divisive Modern Russian Tourist Abroad: Representations of Self and Other in the Early Reform Era." *Slavic Review* 68 (4): 848–71.

Lebedeva, Natal'ia. 2007. "Velikii, moguchii, populiarnyi–sobytie." *Rossiiskaia gazeta*, December 13.

Lederman, Marsha. 2010. "Canada Is Gary Shteyngart's Haven in Fiction and Real Life." *Globe and Mail*, November 19. https://www.theglobeandmail.com/arts/books-and-media/canada-is-gary-shteyngarts-haven-in-fiction-and-real-life/article1315734/.

Levantovskaya, Margarita. 2013. *Rootless Cosmopolitans: Literature of the Soviet-Jewish Diaspora.* PhD diss., University of California, San Diego.

———. 2016. "From Anxiety to Disidentification: Lara Vapnyar's *Memoirs of a Muse*, Irina Reyn's *What Happened to Anna K.*, and Anya Ulinich's *Lena Finkle's Magic Barrel.*" *East European Jewish Affairs* 46 (3): 311–30.

Levidou, Katerina. 2008. *Music in Interwar "Russian" Paris: The Encounter of Neoclassicism with Eurasianism*. PhD diss., University of Oxford.

Levinson, Aleksei. 2007. "1990-e i 1990-i: Sotsiologicheskie materialy." *Novoe literaturnoe obozrenie* 84:489–503.

Levintova, Hannah. 2014. "*Little Failure*: Gary Shteyngart on Immigrant Parents and 'Going Memoir.'" *Mother Jones*, January 3. www.motherjones.com/media/2014/01/interview-gary-shteyngart-memoir-little-failure.

Lewis, Clarence I. 1969. *Values and Imperatives: Studies in Ethics*. Stanford: Stanford University Press.

Lim, Shirley Geok-lin, John Blair Gamber, Stephen Hong Sohn, and Gina Valentino, eds. 2006. *Transnational Asian American Literature: Sites and Transits*. Philadelphia: Temple University Press.

Litman, Ellen. 2007. *The Last Chicken in America*. New York: W. W. Norton.

Lourié, Arthur. 1932. "The Russian School." *Musical Quarterly* 18 (4): 519–29.

Love, Heather. 2016. "Small Change: Realism, Immanence, and the Politics of the Micro." *Modern Language Quarterly* 77 (3): 419–45.

Luckyj, George. 1971. *Between Gogol' and Ševčenko: Polarity in the Literary Ukraine, 1798–1847*. Munich: W. Fink.

Lukash, Alexandra, and Moran Azulay. 2015. "Peres Calls on Jerusalem Festival Not to Screen Yigal Amir Documentary." *Ynet*, June 15. www.ynetnews.com/articles/0,7340,L-4668871,00.html.

Lunde, Ingunn. 2009. "Performative Metalanguage: Negotiating Norms through Verbal Action." In *From Poets to Padonki: Linguistic Authority and Norm Negotiation in Modern Russian Culture*, edited by Ingunn Lunde and Martin Paulsen, 110–28. Bergen: University of Bergen.

———. 2014. "Language on Display: On the Performative Character of Computer-Mediated Metalanguage." In *Digital Russia: The Language, Culture and Politics of New Media Communication*, edited by Michael S. Gorham, Ingunn Lunde, and Martin Paulsen, 141–55. London: Routledge.

———. 2017. *Language on Display: Writers, Fiction and Linguistic Culture in Post-Soviet Russia*. Edinburgh: Edinburgh University Press.

Lurkmore. n.d. "Rusofobiia." Lurkmore online encyclopedia. Accessed August 17, 2016. http://lurkmore.to/Русофобия.

Lutzkanova-Vassileva, Albena. 2015. *The Testimonies of Russian and American Postmodern Poetry. Reference, Trauma, and History*. New York: Bloomsbury.

L'vovskii, S. 2018. "Tret'ia psikhodelicheskaia Vladimira Sorokina, ili Telluriia: Piat'desiat glav o tom, chego ne mozhet byt'." In *"Eto prosto bukvy na bumage . . .": Vladimir Sorokin: posle literatury*, edited by E. Dobrenko, I. Kalinin, and M. Lipovetskii, 589–633. M. Novoe literaturnoe obozrenie.

Maertske, Vera. 2014. "'Nashli pishchu dlia uma, khotia dusha ostalas' v trevoge.'" *Russkaia Germaniia*, July 8.

Maiakovskii, Vladimir. 1973. "Nashemu iunoshestvu." *Sobranie sochinenii v shesti tomakh* 4:64–68. Moscow: Pravda.

Makashin, S. A., K. V. Pigarev, and T. G. Dinesman, eds. 1988. *F. I. Tiutchev. Literaturnoe nasledstvo*. Vol. 97, book 1. Moscow: Nauka.

Maksimova, Iuliia. 2013. "Pochemu russkikh turistov ne liubiat za granitsei." *Posol'skii Prikaz*, February 14. www.posprikaz.ru/2013/02/pochemu-russkix-turistov-ne-lyubyat-za-granicej.

"Malen'kaia pobedonosnaia voznia." 2014. *Vremia*, June 28. www.time.kz/articles/mir/2014/06/28/malenkaja-pobedonosnaja.

Malia, Martin. 1961. *Alexander Herzen and the Birth of Russian Socialism, 1812–1855*. Cambridge, MA: Harvard University Press.

Maltz, Judy. 2015. "One, Two, Three, Four—We Opened up the Iron Door." *Haaretz*, February 2. www.haaretz.com/st/c/prod/eng/25yrs_russ_img/.

Manaspaev, Marat. 2015. "Lukashenko iskliuchil vozmozhnost' voiny s Rossiei." *Kazakhstanskaia pravda*, August 4. www.kazpravda.kz/rubric/mir/lukashenko-iskluchil-vozmozhnost-voini-s-rossiei.

Marchenko, Alla, and Sergei Kurbatov. 2016. "Constructing the Enemy-Other in Social Media: Facebook as a Particular 'Battlefield' during the Ukrainian Crisis." In *Eurasia 2.0: Russian Geopolitics in the Age of New Media*, edited by Mikhail Suslov and Mark Bassin, 225–45. Lanham: Lexington Books.

Marom, Daniel, and Mickie Miller, eds. 2011. *Disput rasteriannykh*. Moscow: Tekst.

Marples, David, and Frederick Mills, eds. 2014. *Ukraine's Euromaidan: Analyses of a Civil Revolution*. Stuttgart: Ibidem Verlag.

Martin, Terry. 2001. *The Affirmative Action Empire: Nations and Nationalism in the Soviet Union, 1923–1939*. Ithaca, NY: Cornell University Press.

Martínez-San Miguel, Yolanda. 2014. *Coloniality of Diasporas: Rethinking Intra-Colonial Migrations in a Pan-Caribbean Context*. New York: Palgrave Macmillan.

Martynov, Aleksei. 2016. "Diskriminatsiia russkogo iazyka i russkogo naseleniia na byvshei Ukraine v kontekste sovremennoi voiny na Donbasse." *Russkii mir: Ukraina*, July 5. http://russmir.info/pol/7532-diskriminaciya-russkogo-yazyka-i-russkogo-naseleniya-na-byvshey-ukraine-v-kontekste-sovremennoy-voyny-v-donbasse.html.

Maslova, Lidia. 2001. "The Immigrant Is Singing about Jews." *Kommersant*, February 16. www.kommersant.ru/doc/168662.

Matich, Olga. 1984. "Is there a Russian Literature beyond Politics?" In *The Third Wave: Russian Literature in Emigration*, edited by Olga Matich with Michael Heim, 180–87. Ann Arbor: Ardis.

Mazepa, N. R., T. M. Riznychenko, I. D. Bazhynov, T. P. Zamorii, V. P. Turta, and Iu. I. Korzov. 1971. *Rosiis'ka literatura Ukraïny*. Kiev: Naukova dumka.

McGrane, Sally. 2015. "A Craftsman of Russian Verse Helps Ukraine Find Its New Voice." *New York Times*, April 10.

Meinecke, Friedrich. 1936. *Die Entstehung des Historismus*. Munich: R. Oldenbourg Verlag.

Mel'nikov, Rostislav [Rostyslav Mel'nykiv], and Iurii Tsaplin. 2007. "Severo-vostok iugo-zapada (o sovremennoi khar'kovskoi literature)." *Novoe literaturnoe obozrenie* 85:263–88.

Melvin, Neil J. 1998. "The Russians: Diaspora and the End of Empire." In *Nations Abroad: Diaspora Politics and International Relations in the Former Soviet Union*, edited by Charles King and Neil Melvin, 27–57. Boulder: Westview.

Mettan, Gi [Guy]. 2016. *Zapad-Rossiia: Tysiacheletniaia voina: Istoriia rusofobii ot Karla Velikogo do ukrainskogo krizisa*. Translated by Mariia Anninskaia and Svetlana Bulgakova. Moscow: Paulsen.

Mettan, Guy. 2017. *Creating Russophobia: From the Great Religious Schism to Anti-Putin Hysteria*. Atlanta, GA: Clarity.

Mickiewicz, Iwona. 2011. *Konstruktionen im Haus oder Iwan Iwanytsch am Fenster: Bagatellen und Novellen*. Berlin: Hanani.

Mitchell, Rebecca. 2016. *Nietzsche's Orphans: Music, Metaphysics, and the Twilight of the Russian Empire*. New Haven, CT: Yale University Press.

Mitrokhin, Nikolai. 2003. *Russkaia partiia: Dvizhenie russkikh natsionalistov v SSSR, 1953–1985 gody*. Moscow: Novoe literaturnoe obozrenie.

Moretti, Franco. 2000. "Conjectures on World Literature." *New Left Review* 1:54–68.

———. 2013. *Distant Reading*. London: Verso.

Morev, Gleb. 2015. "'Ot Sorokina ozhidat' deiatel'nosti po perechisleniiu deneg v fond nel'zia!': Konstantin Bogomolov i Dmitrii Kuz'min ob"iasnili Glebu Morevu, kak i pochemu oni golosovali na premii 'Nos.'" *Colta.ru*, February 6. www.colta.ru/articles/literature/6240.

Móricz, Klára. 2008a. "Decadent Truncation: Liberated Eros in Arthur Vincent Lourié's 'The Blackamoor of Peter the Great.'" *Cambridge Opera Journal* 20 (2): 181–213.

———. 2008b. "Shadows of the Past: Akhmatova's *Poem without a Hero* and Lourié's *Incantations*." *Twentieth-Century Music* 5 (1): 79–108.

———. 2014. "Introduction: Endgames and Funeral Games." In *Funeral Games in Honor of Arthur Vincent Lourié*, edited by Klára Móricz and Simon Morrison, 1–27. Oxford: Oxford University Press.

Morozova, Katia, and Nastia Iarova. 2013. "Al'ternativnaia karta Rossii i Evropy po Tellurii Sorokina." *Look At Me*, October 22. http://www.lookatme.ru/mag/how-to/books/197235-sorokin-map.

Morrison, Alexander. 2017. "Russian beyond Russia." Eurasianet, April 20. www.eurasianet.org/node/83296.

Morrison, Simon. 2009. *The People's Artist: Prokofiev's Soviet Years*. Oxford: Oxford University Press.

———. 2014. "Epilogue: The Silver Age and Tinseltown." In *Funeral Games in Honor of Arthur Vincent Lourié*, edited by Klára Móricz and Simon Morrison, 269–87. Oxford: Oxford University Press.

Muchnik, S. 2014. "Mezhdu Pol'shei i Rossiei: Chto vidiat tam nemtsy?" *Partner*, November 15.

Mufti, Aamir. 2007. *Enlightement in the Colony: The Jewish Question and the Crisis of Postcolonial Culture*. Princeton, NJ: Princeton University Press.

Muir, Stephen. 2013. "'About as Wild and Barbaric as Well Could Be Imagined . . .': Critical Reception of Rimsky-Korsakov in Nineteenth-Century England." *Music & Letters* 93 (4): 513–42.

Murugov, Viacheslav. 2015. "'My mozhem delat' proekty, sopostavimye s mezhdunarodnymi: Vopros—dlia kogo ikh snimat'": Viacheslav Murugov o 'Londongrade' i perspektivakh kompanii Art Pictures." *Cinemotion*, September 22. http://www.cinemotionlab.com/novosti/my_mozhem_delat_proekty_sopostavimye_s_mezhdunarodnymi_vopros__dlya_kogo_ih_snimat_vyacheslav_murugov_o_londongrade_i_perspektivah_kompanii_art_pictures/.

Muth, Sebastian, and Lara Ryazanova-Clarke, eds. 2017. "Commodification of Russian," Special issue, *International Journal of Bilingualism and Bilingual Education* 20 (4).

Mykhed, Oleksandr. 2016. *Bachyty, shchob buty pobachenym: Realiti-shou, reality-roman ta revoliutsiia onlain.* Kiev: ArtHuss.

Nabokov, Vladimir. 2002. *Stikhotvoreniia.* Edited by Maria Malikova. St. Petersburg: Gumanitarnoe agentstvo "Akademicheskii Proekt."

Nadkarni, Maya, and Olga Shevchenko. 2014. "The Politics of Nostalgia in the Aftermath of Socialism's Collapse: A Case for Comparative Analysis." In *Anthropology and Nostalgia*, edited by Olivia Angé and David Berliner, 61–96. New York: Berghahn Books.

Nakhimovsky, Alice Stone. 1992. *Russian-Jewish Literature and Identity.* Baltimore: Johns Hopkins University Press.

Nasritdinov, Emil. 2016. "Only by Learning How to Live Together Differently Can We Live Together at All: Readability and Legibility of Central Asian Migrants' Presence in Urban Russia." *Central Asian Affairs* 35 (2): 257–75.

Nathans, Benjamin. 2015. "Talking Fish: On Soviet Dissident Memoirs." *Journal of Modern History* 87 (3): 579–614.

National Statistical Committee of the Kyrgyz Republic. 2009. *Perepis' naseleniia i zhilishchnogo fonda Kyrgyzskoi respubliki.* Bishkek. www.stat.kg/en/statisticheskie-perepisi/.

Natsional'nyi statisticheskii komitet. 1992. *Svodny tom s nekotorymi itogami poslevoennykh perepisei naseleniia.* Bishkek.

Natsional'nyi statisticheskii komitet. 2000. *Naselenie Kyrgyzstana: Itogi pervoy natsional'noi perepisi naseleniia Kyrgyzskoi Respubliki 1999 goda v tablitsakh.* Bishkek.

Nedashkivska, Alla. 2010. "Language Situation of Cyber Ukraine." *Zeitschrift für Slavische Philologie* 67 (2): 407–40.

Nekrasov, N. A. 1949. *Sobranie stikhotvorenii.* Biblioteka poeta, Bol'shaia seriia. 2 vols. Leningrad: Sovetskii pisatel'.

Nekrasov, Viktor. 2014. *Prazdnik, kotoryi vsegda i so mnoi.* St. Petersburg: Lenizdat.

Nemenskii, Oleg B. 2013. "Rusofobiia kak ideologiia." *Voprosy natsionalizma* 13:26–65.

Nepogodin, Vsevolod. 2014. "Odessa—russkii gorod." *Literaturnaia gazeta*, April 9. www.lgz.ru/article/-14-6457-9-04-2014/odessa-russkiy-gorod/.

Neumann, Iver. 1996. *Russia and the Idea of Europe.* London: Routledge.

Newmarch, Rosa. 1900. *The Art Songs of Russia: A Lecture.* London: Steinway Hall.

———. 1902. "The Art Songs of Russia." *Sammelbände der Internationalen Musikgesellschaft* 3 (2): 377–87.

———. 1907. *Poetry and Progress in Russia.* London: John Lane.

Ngai, Sianne. 2013. "On Cruel Optimism." *Social Text: Periscope*, January 15. http://socialtextjournal.org/periscope_article/on-cruel-optimism.

Nikitin, Andrei. 2015. "Po moim prikliucheniiam snimaetsia serial: Oxxxymiron i Mikhail Idov o 'Londongrade.'" *Flow*, August 25. http://the-flow.ru/features/oxxxy-idov-londongrad.

Nikitin, V. S. 2006. "Sozdadim Russkii Mir." *Kommunisticheskaia Partiia Rossiiskoi Federatsii*, February 7. www.cprf.info/news/articles/culture/39299.html.

———. 2014. "Russkii Mir—eto sotrudnichestvo, a ne voina tsivilizatsii." Kommunisticheskaia partiia Rossiiskoi Federatsii, November 23. http://kprf.ru/party-live/opinion/136748.html.

"Novosti Russkogo mira." 2009. Post to no-reply@russkiymir.ru, November 3.
"Novosti Russkogo mira." 2015. Post to no-reply@russkiymir.ru, January 29.
"Nuzhny li segodnia sootechestvenniki Rossii?" 2012. *NovoNews*, December 3.
Nye, Joseph S., Jr. 2004. *Soft Power: The Means to Success in World Politics*. New York: Public Affairs.
———. 2006. 2011. *The Future of Power*. New York, NY: Public Affairs.
Obodovskaia, Elena. 2013. "Uspekhi nashikh detei." *Partner*, July 15.
"Obyvatel' voinstvuiushchii." 2015. *Vremia*, June 6. www.time.kz/articles/mir/2015/06/06/obivatel-voinstvujushij.
Offord, Derek. 2005. *Journeys to a Graveyard: Perceptions of Europe in Classical Russian Travel Writing*. Dordrecht: Springer.
"O konfederativnom soiuze Rossii, Belarussii i Ukrainy." 2012. *Sovetskaia Belarus'*, August 28.
Orusbaev, Abdykadyr, Arto Mustajoki, and Ekaterina Protassova. 2008. "Multilingualism, Russian Language and Education in Kyrgyzstan." *International Journal of Bilingual Education and Bilingualism* 11 (3–4): 476–500.
Ospovat, Kirill. 2007. "Lomonosov i 'Pis'mo o pol'ze stekla': Poeziia i nauka pri dvore Elizavety Petrovny." *Novoe literaturnoe obozrenie* 87:148–83.
Ostrovskii, Aleksei. 2008. "Most sodruzhestva." *Strategiia Rossii*, November 15.
Oushakine, Serguei Alex. 2007. "'We're Nostalgic but We're Not Crazy': Retrofitting the Past in Russia." *Russian Review* 66 (3): 451–82.
Patriarkh Kirill. 2009. "Vystuplenie Patriarkha Kirilla na torzhestvennom otkrytii III Assamblei Russkogo mira." *Russkaia Pravoslavnaia Tserkov'*, November 3. www.patriarchia.ru/db/text/928446.html.
"'Patrioty Rossii'—za natsional'noe vozrozhdenie!" 2011. *Rossiiskaia gazeta*, November 25.
Patterson, David. 1995. *Exile: The Sense of Alienation in Modern Russian Letters*. Lexington: University Press of Kentucky.
Pavlenko, Aneta. 2012. "Commodification of Russian in Post-1991 Europe." In *Globalisierung, Migration, Fremdsprachenunterricht*, Dokumentation zum 24. Kongress für Fremdsprachendidaktik der Deutschen Gesellschaft für Fremdsprachenforschung (DGFF), edited by M. Bär, A. Bonnet, H. Decke-Cornill, A. Grünewald, and A. Hu, 27–43. Baltmannsweiler: Schneider Hohengehren.
Pavlyshyn, Marko. 2016. "Literary History as Provocation of National Identity, National identity as Provocation of Literary History: The Case of Ukraine." *Thesis Eleven* 136 (1): 74–89.
Perloff, Marjorie. 1993. "Russian Postmodernism: An Oxymoron?" *Postmodern Culture* 3 (2). https://muse.jhu.edu/article/27392.
———. 2009. *Unoriginal Genius: Poetry by Other Means in the New Century*. Chicago: University of Chicago Press.
Peteri, György, ed. 2010. *Imagining the West in Eastern Europe and the Soviet Union*. Pittsburgh: University of Pittsburgh Press.
Petrovsky-Shtern, Yohanan. 2009. *The Anti-Imperial Choice: The Making of the Ukrainian Jew*. New Haven, CT: Yale University Press.
Philippov, Michael, and Anna Knafelman. 2011. "Old Values in the New Homeland: Political Attitudes of FSU Immigrants in Israel." In *Russian Israelis: Social Mobility, Politics and Culture*. London: Routledge.

Platt, Kevin M. F. 2008. "The Post-Soviet Is Over: On Reading the Ruins." *Republics of Letters: A Journal for the Study of Knowledge, Politics, and the Arts* 1 (1): 1–26. http://arcade.stanford.edu/rofl/post-soviet-over-reading-ruins.

———. 2013a. "Eccentric Orbit: Mapping Russian Culture in the Near Abroad." In *Empire De/Centered: New Spatial Histories of Russia*, edited by Sanna Turoma and Maxim Waldstein, 271–96. Aldershot: Ashgate.

———. 2013b. "Occupation vs. Colonization: Post-Soviet Latvia and the Provincialization of Europe." In *Memory and Theory in Eastern Europe*, edited by Uilleam Blacker, Alexander Etkind, and Julie Fedor, 125–46. New York: Palgrave Macmillan.

———. 2013c. "Russian Empire of Pop: Post-Socialist Nostalgia and Soviet Retro in Latvia." *Russian Review* 72:447–69.

———. 2014. "Gegemonia bez gospodstva / diaspora bez emigratsii: Russkaia kul'tura v Latvii." *Novaia literaturnaia obozrenie* 127:195–215.

———. 2015. "Lyric Cosmopolitanism in a Post-Socialist Borderland." *Common Knowledge* 21 (2): 305–26.

———. 2016. "Secret Speech: Wounding, Disavowal, and Social Belonging in the USSR." *Critical Inquiry* 42:647–76.

"Pliner o rossiiskom finansirovanii—vse eto kleveta i lozh'." 2012. *NovaNews*, March 22.

Plokhy, Serhii. 2006. *The Origins of Slavic Nations: Premodern Identities in Russia, Ukraine, and Belarus.* New York: Cambridge University Press.

———. 2008. *Ukraine and Russia: Representations of the Past.* Toronto: University of Toronto Press.

Podporenko, Iurii. 2001. "Bespraven, no vostrebovan: Russkii iazyk v Uzbekistane." *Druzhba narodov* 12.

Poe, Marshall T. 2001. *"A People Born to Slavery": Russia in Early Modern European Ethnography, 1476–1748.* Ithaca, NY: Cornell University Press.

Poliakov, Leonid. 2014. "Referendum, kotoryi vsegda s toboi." *Rossiiskaia gazeta*, March 19.

Poliakovskaia, Elena. 2010. "Mikhail Idov: 'Ia zasluzhil N'iu-Iork.'" *Booknik*, July 21. http://booknik.ru/context/all/mihail-idov-ya-zaslujil-nyu-yiorko/.

"Politika imitatsii deiatel'nosti." 2008. *Evropa-Ekspress*, September 8.

"Population Census 2011—Key Indicators." 2013. Central Statistical Bureau of Latvia, October 3, www.csb.gov.lv/en/statistikas-temas/population-census-2011-key-indicators-33613.html.

Porteous, Holly. 2013. "'There are no ugly women, only lazy ones'—The Duty of Beauty Labour in Contemporary Russian Women's Magazines." In *Körper—Geschlecht—Wahrnehmung: Sozial- und geisteswissenschaftliche Beiträge zur Genderforschung*, edited by Hella Ehlers, Gabriele Linke, Nadja Milewski, Beate Rudlof, and Heike Trappe, 133–56. Berlin: LIT Verlag.

Prigov, Dmitrii. 2005. "Pro nas i inozemnykh oslov." *Polit.ru*, March 26. http://polit.ru/article/2005/03/26/fobia.

Prilepin, Zakhar. 2017. *Vzvod. Ofitsery i opolchentsy russkoi literatury.* Moscow: Izdatel'stvo AST, Redaktsiia Eleny Shubinoi.

Prokhanov, Aleksandr. 2014. "Russkii mir." *Vzgliad*, August 28.

Pugh, Stefan M. 1996. *Testament to Ruthenian: A Linguistic Analysis of the Smotryc'kyj Variant.* Cambridge, MA: Harvard University Press.

Puleri, Marco. 2014. "Ukraïns'kyi, rossiis'komovnyi, rossiis'kyi: Self-Identification in Post-Soviet Ukrainian Literature in Russian." *Ab Imperio* 2:367–97.

———. 2016. *Narrazioni ibride post-sovietiche: Per una letteratura ucraina di lingua russa*. Florence: Firenze University Press.

Pumpiansky, Lev. (1939) 2000. "'Medni vsadnik' i poeticheskaia traditsiia XVIII veka." In *Klassicheskaia traditsiia: Sobranie trudov po istorii russkoi literatury*, edited by A. P. Chudakov and N. I. Nikolaev, 159–60, 671–78. Moscow: Iazyki russkoi kul'tury.

Pushkin, A. S. 1959–62. *Sobranie sochinenii v desiati tomakh*. 10 vols. Moscow: Khudozhestvennaia literatura.

Putin, Vladimir. 2001. "Vystuplenie Prezidenta Rossiiskoi Federatsii V. V. Putina na Kongresse sootechestvennikov, prozhivaiushchikh za rubezhom." Moscow, October 11. Reprint available at http://old.nasledie.ru/politvnt/19_44/article.php?art=24.

———. 2005. "Poslanie Federal'nomy sobraniiu." Moscow, April 25. www.kremlin.ru/events/president/transcripts/22931.

———. 2007. "Poslanie Federal'nomu sobraniiu Rossiiskoi Federatsii." Moscow, April 26. http://kremlin.ru/events/president/transcripts/24203.

———. 2012. "Poslanie Prezidenta Federal'nomu Sobraniiu." Moscow, December 12. http://kremlin.ru/news/17118.

———. 2014a. "Obrashchenie Prezidenta Rossiiskoi Federatsii." Moscow, March 18. http://kremlin.ru/events/president/news/20603.

———. 2014b. "Priamaia liniia." Moscow, April 17. http://kremlin.ru/events/president/news/20796.

——— 2014c. "Zaiavleniia dlia pressy i otvety na voprosy zhurnalistov po itogam rossiisko-avstriiskikh peregovorov." Vienna, June 24. http://kremlin.ru/events/president/transcripts/46060.

Pyke, Cameron. 2016. *Benjamin Britten and Russia*. Woodbridge: Boydell.

Raab, Josef, and Martin Butler, eds. 2008. *Hybrid Americas: Contacts, Contrasts, and Confluences in New World Literatures and Cultures*. Tempe, AZ: Bilingual Press/Editorial Bilingüe; Berlin: LIT Verlag.

Raeff, Marc. 1990. *Russia Abroad: A Cultural History of the Russian Emigration, 1919–1939*.

Rafeenko, Vladimir. 2017. *Dolgota dnei*. Kharkiv: Fabula.

Ram, Harsha. 2003. *The Imperial Sublime: A Russian Poetics of Empire*. Madison: University of Wisconsin Press.

Reed, Philip, ed. 1995. *The Travel Diaries of Peter Pears*. Woodbridge: Boydell.

Remennick, Larissa. 2002. "Transnational Community in the Making: Russian-Jewish Immigrants of the 1990s in Israel." *Journal of Ethnic and Migration Studies* 28 (3): 515–30.

———. 2007. *Russian Jews on Three Continents: Identity, Integration, and Conflict*. New Brunswick, NJ: Transaction.

———. 2011. "The Russian-Jewish Transnational Social Space: An Overview." *Journal of Jewish Identities* 4 (1): 1–11.

———. 2013. "Transnational Lifestyle among Russian Israelis: A Follow-Up Study." *Global Networks* 13 (4): 478–97.

Reyn, Irina. 2008. *What Happened to Anna K.* New York: Touchstone.

Riabchuk, Mykola. 2000. *Vid Malorosiï do Ukraïny: Paradoksy zapizniloho natsiietvorennia*. Kiev: Krytyka.

Ricoeur, Paul. 1994. "Imagination in Discourse and in Action." In *Rethinking Imagination: Culture and Creativity*, edited by G. Robinson and J. F. Rundell, 87–117. London: Routledge.

———. 2004. *Memory, History, Forgetting.* Translated by Kathleen Blamey and David Pellauer. Chicago: University of Chicago Press.

Robbins, Bruce. 2010. *Upward Mobility and the Common Good.* Princeton, NJ: Princeton University Press.

Roberman, Sveta. 2005. *Memory in Migration: WWII Red Army Soldiers in Israel.* Jerusalem: Magnes.

Rodeval'd [Rohdewald], Stefan. 2012. "'Vneshniaia kolonizatsiia vnutrennego' i 'vnutrenniaia kolonizatsiia vneshnego': Oppozitsionnye elity stolits vs. loial'nye elity Zapadnogo kraia, 1830–1910 gody. In *Tam, vnutri: Praktiki vnutrennei kolonizatsii v kul'turnoi istorii Rossii,* edited by Aleksandr Etkind, Dirk Uffel'mann [Uffelmann], and Il'ia Kukulin, 518–51. Moscow: Novoe literaturnoe obozrenie.

Rodoman, B. 2004. "Rossiia—administrativno-territorial'nyi monstr: Zapis' publichnoi lektsii, prochitannoi 28 oktiabria 2004 g. v moskovskom klube 'Bilingua.'" Polit.ru, November 4. http://polit.ru/article/2004/11/04/rodoman/.

Rogov, K. "Tri epokhi barroko." 2006. In *Tynianovskii sbornik. Vypusk 12: X-XI-XII Tynianovskie chteniia. Issledovaniia. Materialy,* 9–101. Moscow: Volodei.

Rokossovskaia, Arianda. 2011. "Iazyk pod stuk koles." *Rossiiskaia gazeta,* February 9.

Ronyak, Jennifer. 2017. "Meeting Barthes at Fischer-Dieskau's Mill: Co-Performance, Linguistic Identity, and a Lied." *Journal of Musicology* 34 (1): 32–70.

Rosslyn, Wendy. 2001. "Gender in Translation: Lowell and Cixous Rewriting Akhmatova." In *Gender and Sexuality in Russian Civilisation,* edited by Peter I. Barta, 71–86. London: Routledge.

Rovner, Adam. 2006. "So Easily Assimilated: The *New* Immigrant Chic." *AJS Review* 30 (2): 313–24.

Rozenfel'd, Boris. 2003. *Anna Akhmatova, Marina Tsvetaeva, Osip Mandel'shtam i Boris Pasternak v muzyke.* Stanford: Department of Slavic Languages and Literatures, Stanford University.

Rubins, Maria, ed. 2005. *Dictionary of Literary Biography.* Vol. 317, *Twentieth-Century Russian Émigré Writers.* Detroit: Thomson Gale.

———. 2015. *Russian Montparnasse: Transnational Writing in Interwar Paris.* Basingstoke: Palgrave Macmillan.

Rubinstein, Antoine. 1855. "Die Componisten Rußland's." *Blätter für Musik, Theater und Kunst,* May 11, 113; May 29, 129; June 8, 145–46.

Russian Federation. 1999. "O gosudarstvennoi politike Rossiiskoi Federatsii v otnoshenii sootechestvennikov za rubezhom." Konsul'tant Plius, May 24. Law last modified July 23, 2013. www.consultant.ru/online/base/?req=doc;base=LAW;n=102935.

"Russkie turisty razdrazhaiut ves' mir." 2009. *Newsland,* August 29. http://newsland.com/news/detail/id/404887/.

"'Russkii mir' i kak ego ponimat'?" 2014. *VTsIOM: Press-vypusk,* no. 2728 (December 3). https://wciom.ru/index.php?id=236&uid=657.

"'Russkii mir' kaput." 2015. *BelGazeta,* October 1.

Ruxpert. n.d. "Rusofobiia." *Russkii ekspert.* Accessed August 17, 2016. http://ruxpert.ru/Русофобия.

Ryan, Karen. 2011. "Failures of Domesticity in Contemporary Russian-American Literature: Vapnyar, Krasikov, Ulinich, and Reyn." *TranscUlturAl* 1 (4): 63–75. http://ejournals.library.ualberta.ca/index.php/TC/article/view/9701/7792.

———. 2013. "Forging a Transcultural Identity as a Russian-American Writer: Lara Vapnyar and Cultural Adaptation." In *Transcultural Identities in Contemporary Literature*, edited by Irene Gilsenan Nordin, Julie Hansen, and Carmen Zamorano Llena, 27–46. Amsterdam: Rodopi.

Ryazanova-Clarke, Lara. 2012. "The 'West' in the Linguistic Construction of Russianness in Contemporary Public Discourse." In *Understanding Russianness*, edited by R. Alapuro, A. Mustajoki, and P. Pessonen, 3–18. London: Routledge.

———. 2014a. "Introduction: The Russian Language, Challenged by Globalisation." In *The Russian Language outside the Nation*, edited by L. Ryazanova-Clarke, 1–32. Edinburgh: Edinburgh University Press.

———. 2014b. "Russian with an Accent: Globalisation and the Post-Soviet Imaginary." In *The Russian Language outside the Nation*, edited by Lara Ryazanova-Clarke, 249–82. Edinburgh: Edinburgh University Press.

Sabitova, Zinaida, and Akbota Alishariyeva. 2015. "The Russian Language in Kazakhstan: Status and Functions." *Russian Journal of Communication* 7 (2): 213–17.

Safran, William. 1991. "Diasporas in Modern Societies: Myths of Homeland and Return." *Diaspora* 1 (1): 83–99.

Said, Edward. 2000. *Reflections on Exile and Other Essays*. Cambridge, MA: Harvard University Press.

Salazar, Noel B. 2012. "Tourism Imaginaries: A Conceptual Approach." *Annals of Tourism Research* 39 (2): 863–82.

Salazar, Noel B., and Nelson H. H. Graburn. 2014. "Introduction: Toward an Anthropology of Tourism Imaginaries." In *Tourism Imaginaries: Anthropological Approaches*, edited by N. B. Salazar and N. H. H. Graburn, 1–28. New York: Berghahn Books.

Samoilov, David. 2010. "Kogda nibud'." *Chto Est' Istina?* 22 (9). http://istina.russian-albion.com/ru/chto-est-istina--022-sentyabr-2010-g/d-samoylov.

Sandler, Stephanie. 1999. "Introduction: Myths and Paradoxes of the Russian Poet." In *Rereading Russian Poetry*, edited by Stephanie Sandler, 1–27. New Haven, CT: Yale University Press.

Sandomirskaia, Irina. 2001. *Kniga o Rodine: Opyt analiza diskursivykh praktik*. Wiener Slawistischer Almanach. Sonderband 50. Vienna: Wiener Slawistischer Almanach.

Sarnov, Benedikt. (1988) 1989. "Da zdravstvuet samovyrazhenie!" *Vzgliad: Kritika. Polemika. Publikatsii*, vol. 2, edited by L. Voronin, A. Turkov, and S. Chuprinin, 234–60. Moscow: Sovetskii pisatel'.

Sassen, Saskia. 1996. *Losing Control: Sovereignty in an Age of Globalization*. New York: Columbia University Press.

Saunders, Robert A. 2006. "Denationalized Digerati in the Virtual Near Abroad: The Paradoxical Impact of the Internet on National Identity among Minority Russians." *Global Media and Communication* 2 (1): 43–69.

Schlögel, Karl, ed. 1994a. *Der Große Exodus: Die russische Emigration und ihre Zentren 1917—1941*. Munich: Beck.

———, ed. 1994b. *Russische Emigration in Deutschland 1918 bis 1941: Leben im europäischen Bürgerkrieg*. Berlin: Oldenbourg Akademieverlag.

Schlyter, Birgit. 2011. "Language Policy and Language Development in Multilingual Uzbekistan." *Language Policy and Language Conflict in Afghanistan and Its Neighbors: The Changing Politics of Language Choice*, edited by Harold. F. Schiffman, 176–207. Leiden: Brill.

Schmelz, Peter J. 2009. *Such Freedom, if Only Musical: Unofficial Soviet Music during the Thaw.* Oxford: Oxford University Press.

Schroeder, Philipp. 2010. "Urbanizing Bishkek: Interrelations of Boundaries, Migration, Group Size and Opportunity Structure." *Central Asian Survey* 29 (4): 453–67.

Semenchuk, Hryhorii, Iurii Izdryk, and Vitaly Chernetsky, eds. 2016. *Letters from Ukraine / Lysty z Ukraïny*. Ternopil': Krok.

Senderovich, Sasha. 2011. "Dissonance." *Tablet*, January 28. www.tabletmag.com/jewish-news-and-politics/56608/dissonance.

———. 2014. "Russian Jewish American Lit Goes Boom!" *Tablet Magazine*, June 17. www.tabletmag.com/jewish-arts-and-culture/books/175906/russian-jewish-am-lit.

———. 2015a. "Scenes of Encounter: The 'Soviet Jew' in Fiction by Russian Jewish Writers in America." *Prooftexts* 35 (1): 98–132.

———. 2015b. "Soviet Jews, Re-Imagined: Anglophone Émigré Jewish Writers from the USSR." In *The Edinburgh Companion to Modern Jewish Fiction*, edited by D. Brauner and A. Stähler, 90–104. Edinburgh: Edinburgh University Press.

Serov, Boris 2014. "Russkii mir ot Kryma do Donbassa." *Russkiy Mir*, June 8. www.russkiymir.ru/publications/141934.

Sewell, William H., Jr. 1999. "The Concept(s) of Culture." In *Beyond the Cultural Turn: New Directions in the Study of Society and Culture*, edited by Victoria E. Bonnell and Lynn Hunt, 35–61. Berkeley: University of California Press.

Shafarevich, Igor'. 2005. *Russkii vopros*. Moskva: Algoritm.

Shapira, Anita. 2012. *Israel: A History*. Waltham, MA: Brandeis University Press.

Shchedrovitskii, Petr. 2000. "Gosudarstvo v epokhu gumanitarnykh tekhnologii." *Russkii zhurnal*, July 21. http://old.russ.ru/politics/meta/20000721_sch.html.

Shchedrovitskii, Petr, Sergei Gradirovskii, and Boris Mezhuev. 2001. "Russkii mir: Vosstanovlenie konteksta." *Russkii Arkhipelag*, September. www.archipelag.ru/ru_mir/history/history01/shedrovitsky-russmir.

Shevchenko, Viktoriia. 2009. "V kontekste Gogolia." *Kazakhstanskaia pravda*, February 6. www.kazpravda.kz/archives/view/45913/.

Shih, Shu-mei. 2011. "The Concept of the Sinophone." *PMLA* 126 (3): 709–18.

Shklovskaia, Margarita, ed. 2001. *Orientatsiia na mestnosti: Russko-izrail'skaia literatura 90-kh godov*. Jerusalem: Biblioteka-aliia.

Shlapentokh, Dmitry. 2007. *Russia between East and West: Scholarly Debates on Eurasianism.* Leiden: Brill.

Shteyngart, Gary. 2002. *The Russian Debutante's Handbook*. New York: Riverhead Books.

———. 2004. "The New Two-Way Street." In *Reinventing the Melting Pot: The New Immigrants and What It Means to Be American*, edited by Tamar Jacoby, 285–92. New York: Basic Books.

———. 2006. *Absurdistan*. New York: Random House.

———. 2010a. "Only Disconnect." *New York Times: Sunday Book Review*, July 16, B27.

———. 2010b. *Super Sad True Love Story*. New York: Random House.

———. 2014. *Little Failure*. New York: Random House.

Shvab, Leonid. 2005. *Poverit' v botaniku*. Moscow: Novoe literaturnoe obozrenie.

Sidibe, Pierre. 2007. "'Politika russkogo mira." *Rossiiskaia gazeta*, June 26.

Silberstein, Laurence. 1999. *The Postzionism Debates: Knowledge and Power in Israeli Culture.* New York: Routledge.

Simanovskaia, Elena. 2009. "Eto bylo glavneishim delom russkoi emigratsii." *Partner*, July 15.

Simonov, Konstantin. 1990. *Stikhotvoreniia i poemy*. Biblioteka poeta, malaia seriia. Leningrad: Sovetskii pisatel'.

Singh, Amritjit, and Peter Schmidt, eds. 2000. *Postcolonial Theory and the United States: Race, Ethnicity, and Literature.* Jackson: University Press of Mississippi.

Siniavskii. (1957) 1989. "Chto takoe sotsialisticheskii realism." In *Tsena metafory: Prestuplenie i nakazanie Siniavskogo i Danielia*, edited by E. M. Velikanova, 425–59. Moscow: Kniga.

Sitkovskii, Gleb. 2015. "Shal'nye den'gi." *Novoe vremia*, August 15. http://newtimes.ru/articles/detail/101322/#hcq=GM5cxxp.

Slezkine, Yuri. 1994. "The USSR as a Communal Apartment, or How a Socialist State Promoted Ethnic Particularism." *Slavic Review* 53 (2): 414–52.

———. 2004. *The Jewish Century*. Princeton, NJ: Princeton University Press.

Sliusareva, Elena. 2016. "Chego khochet Putin? Venediktov rasskazal ob etom v Rige." *VES(tochka)LV*, May 25. www.ves.lv/kak-pereubedit-putina-venediktov-rasskazal-ob-etom-v-rige/.

Slobin, Greta. 2013. *Russians Abroad: Literary and Cultural Politics of Diaspora (1919–1939)*. Boston: Academic Studies.

Smirnova, Tat'iana. 2008. "V tsentre—iazyk." *Izvestiia Kazakhstana*, July 8.

Smola, Klavdia. 2011. "Israel and the Concept of Homeland in Russian Jewish Literature after 1970." *Journal of Jewish Identities* 4 (1): 171–90.

———. 2015. "The Reinvention of the Promised Land: Utopian Space and Time in Soviet Jewish Exodus Literature." *East European Jewish Affairs* 45 (1): 79–108.

Smooha, Sammy. 2008. "The Mass Immigrations to Israel: A Comparison of the Failure of the Mizrahi Immigrants of the 1950s with the Success of the Russian Immigrants of the 1990s." *Journal of Israeli History* 27 (1): 1–27.

Snow, K. 2012. "Russia as the 'Western Other' in Southeast Asia: Encounters of Russian Travelers in the Second Half of the Nineteenth Century." *Russian Review* 71 (2): 246–66.

Snyder, Timothy. 2003. *The Reconstruction of Nations: Poland, Ukraine, Lithuania, Belarus, 1569–1999*. New Haven, CT: Yale University Press.

Sokolova, Ekaterina. 2017. *Volchatnik*. Moscow: Novoe literaturnoe obozrenie.

Solzhenitsyn, A. I. 1995–97. "Kak nam obustroit' Rossiiu." In *Publitsistika v trekh tomakh*, 1:538–98. 3 vols. Leningrad: Sovetskii pisatel'.

Sorokin, Vladimir. 2013. *Telluriia*. Moscow: Corpus.

Sotnik, Sasha. 2015. "V DNR ne poedu, k solov'evu ne poidu." Interview with Timur Shaov, May 23. www.youtube.com/watch?v=-sU8uqM3r2Y.

Sperling, Valerie. 2015. *Sex, Politics, and Putin: Political Legitimacy in Russia*. New York: Oxford University Press.

Spivak, Gayatri. 2000. "The Politics of Translation." In *The Translation Studies Reader*, edited by Lawrence Venuti, 397–416. London: Routledge.

Stahl, Henrieke. 2015. "Poesie als politische Partizipation: Der virale poetopolitische Diskurs um Anastasija Dmitruks Videogedicht 'Nikogda my ne budem brat'jami' auf *Youtube*." *Zeitschrift für Slavische Philologie* 71 (2): 441–77.

Steinberg, Jessica. 2016. "Miri Regev's Cultural War Heats Up." *Times of Israel*, January 29. www.timesofisrael.com/miri-regevs-cultural-war-heats-up/.

Stepanenko, Viktor, and Yaroslav Pylynskyi, eds. 2015. *Ukraine after the Euromaidan: Challenges and Hopes*. New York: Peter Lang.

Stratunovskii, S. 1999. "Noch' nad Insar-rekoi." Introduction to poems by Sergei Zav'ialov. Arion 3. http://magazines.russ.ru/arion/1999/3/zavyal.html.

Strauss, Claudia. 2006. "The Imaginary." *Anthropological Theory* 6 (3): 322–44.

Stroi, Anna. 1997a. "Otkryvaia rubriku." *Diena*, July 30, 6.

———. 1997b. "Rossiia priznala pasport negrazhdanina Latvii v kachestve proezdnogo dokumenta." *Diena*, July 7, 2.

Struve, Gleb. 1959. *Writers in Exile: Problems of an Émigré Literature*. Berkeley: University of California Press.

Struve, Nikita. 1996. *Soixante-dix ans d'émigration russe*. Paris: Fayard.

Sudebnyi otchet po delu antisovetskogo "pravo-trotskistskogo bloka" 2–13 marta 1938 g. 1938. Moscow: Iuridicheskoe izdatelstvo NKIu SSSR.

Šulmane, Ilze. 2006. "The Russian Language Media in Latvia." In *Latvian-Russian Relations: Domestic and International Dimensions*, edited by Nils Muižnieks, 64–73. Riga: LU Akadēmiskais apgāds.

Summ, Liubov'. 2015. "Neobkhodimost' poniat' (K prezentatsii 'Otkrytogo dnevnika' Borisa Khersonskogo)." *Dukh i litera*. http://ru.duh-i-litera.com/neobhodimost-ponyat-k-prezentatsii-otkryitogo-dnevnika-borisa-hersonskogo/.

Suny, Ronald. 1993. *The Revenge of the Past: Nationalism, Revolution, and the Collapse of the Soviet Union*. Stanford: Stanford University Press.

Suslova, Apollinaria. 1982. *Dnevnik: Gody blizosti s Dostoevskim*. New York: Silver Age.

"Sviateishii Patriarkh Kirill: Russkii mir—eto osobaia tsivilizatsiia, kotoruiu neobkhodimo sberech'." 2014. *Russkaia Pravoslavnaia Tserkov'*, September 6. www.patriarchia.ru/db/text/3730705.html.

Sylvester, Richard D. 2014. *Rachmaninoff's Complete Songs: A Companion with Texts and Translations*. Bloomington: Indiana University Press.

Sysyn, Frank. 1981. "The Problem of Nobilities in the Ukrainian Past: The Polish Period, 1569–1648." In *Rethinking Ukrainian History*, edited by Ivan L. Rudnytsky with John-Paul Himka, 29–102. Edmonton: Canadian Institute of Ukrainian Studies, University of Alberta.

———. 1985. *Between Poland and the Ukraine: The Dilemma of Adam Kysil, 1600–1653*. Cambridge, MA: Harvard University Press.

Tallès, Olivier. 2015. "Boris Khersonsky, le psychiatre au chevet de l'Ukraine." *La Croix*, August 21. www.la-croix.com/Actualite/Monde/Boris-Khersonsky-le-psychiatre-au-chevet-de-l-Ukraine-2015-08-21-1346625.

Tannen, Elizabeth. 2011. "A Conversation with Gary Shteyngart." *Blue Mesa Review* 24:170.

Taruskin, Richard. 1987. "Stravinsky's 'Rejoicing Discovery': In Defense of His Notorious Text-Setting." In *Stravinsky Retrospectives*, edited by Ethan Haimo and Paul Johnson, 162–99. Lincoln: University of Nebraska Press.

———. 1996. *Stravinsky and the Russian Traditions: A Biography of the Works through "Mavra."* 2 vols. Oxford: Oxford University Press.

———. 2014. "Turania Revisited, with Lourié My Guide." In *Funeral Games in Honor of Arthur Vincent Lourié*, edited by Klára Móricz and Simon Morrison, 63–120. Oxford: Oxford University Press.

Tavener, John. 1999. *The Music of Silence: A Composer's Testament.* Edited by Brian Keeble. London: Faber and Faber.

Taylor, Philip S. 2007. *Anton Rubinstein: A Life in Music.* Bloomington: Indiana University Press.

Teren, Tetiana, ed. 2014. *Litopys samovydtsiv: Dev'iat' misiatsiv ukraïns'koho sprotyvu.* Kiev: KOMORA.

Terwilliger, Cam. 2014. "The Rumpus Interview with David Bezmozgis." *The Rumpus,* September 29. http://therumpus.net/2014/09/the-rumpus-interview-with-david-bezmozgis.

Thomas, Gareth James. 2005. "The Impact of Russian Music in England, 1893–1929." PhD diss., University of Birmingham.

Thomsen, Mads Rosenthal. 2008. *Mapping World Literature: International Canonization and Transnational Literatures.* London: Continuum.

Thorsen, Elise. 2016. "Territory and Empire in Early Soviet Poetry." PhD diss., University of Pittsburgh.

Thurlow, Crispin, and Adam Jaworski. 2003. "Communicating a Global Reach: Inflight Magazines as a Globalizing Genre in Tourism." *Journal of Sociolinguistics* 7 (4): 579–606.

———. 2010. *Tourism Discourse: Language and Global Mobility.* Basingstoke: Palgrave Macmillan.

———. 2011. "Banal Globalization? Embodied Practices and Mediated Actions in Tourists Online Photo-Sharing." In *Digital Discourse: Language in the New Media,* edited by Crispin Thurlow and Kristine Mroczek, 220–50. New York: Oxford University Press.

Timofeev, Sergei [Sergej Timofejev]. 2011. *Sinie malen'kie gonochnye mashiny.* Moscow: Novoe literaturnoe obozrenie.

Timofejev, Sergej, Artur Punte, Semyon Khanin, and Vladimir Svetlov. 2015. *Hit Parade: The Orbita Group.* Edited by Kevin M. F. Platt. New York: Ugly Duckling Presse.

Tiurina, Irina. 2012. "Vyezd rossiiskikh turistov za rubezh v 2011 godu." *RATA News,* March 6. www.ratanews.ru/news/news_6032012_2.stm.

———. 2015. "Vyezdnoi turpotok iz Rossii pokazal samoe bol'shoe snizhenie za poslednie 20 let." *RATA News,* April 9. www.ratanews.ru/news/news_4092015_2.stm.

Tokhtakhodzhaeva, Marfua. 2008. *XX vek v vospominaniiakh, ustnykh istoriiakh, pis'makh i dnevnikakh zhenshchin Uzbekistana.* Moscow: Natalis.

Tölölyan, Khachig. 2007. "The Contemporary Discourse of Diaspora Studies." *Comparative Studies of South Asia, Africa and the Middle East* 27 (3): 647–55.

Tolts, Mark. 2011. "Demography of the Contemporary Russian-Speaking Jewish Diaspora." Paper presented at the conference on the Contemporary Russian-Speaking Jewish Diaspora, Harvard University, November 13–15. http:// http://archive.jpr.org.uk/download?id=2962.

Tolz, Vera. 2001. *Russia.* London: Arnold.

"To Our Readers." 1951. *Third Hour* 5:1.

Toynbee, Jason, and Byron Dueck, eds. 2011. *Migrating Music.* London: Routledge.

Traditsiia "Rusofobiia." 2016. "Rusofobiia." *Traditsiia.* Accessed August 17, 2016. http://traditio.wiki/Русофобия.

Tsipris, Anna. 2012. "Immigratsiia i dvuiazychie." *Evropa-Ekspress*, September 3.

Tsirkin-Sadan, Rafi. 2014. "Between Marginal and Transnational: Post-Soviet Immigration in Hebrew Literature." *East European Jewish Affairs* 44 (2–3): 253–68.

Tsvetkov, Aleksei. 2016. "Iazyk pod sudom." *InLiberty*, June 16. www.inliberty.ru/blog/2329-Yazyk-pod-sudom.

Tsygankov, Andrei P. 2009. *Russophobia: Anti-Russian Lobby and American Foreign Policy*. New York: Palgrave Macmillan.

Tumanov, Alexander. 2000. *The Life and Artistry of Maria Olenina-d'Alheim*. Translated by Christopher Barnes. Edmonton: University of Alberta Press.

Tunbridge, Laura. 2013. "Singing Translations: The Politics of Listening between the Wars." *Representations* 123 (1): 53–86.

Tunley, David. 2002. *Salons, Singers and Songs: A Background to Romantic French Song*. Aldershot: Ashgate.

Uffelmann, Dirk. 2011a. "Post-Russian Eurasia and the Proto-Eurasian Usage of the Runet in Kazakhstan: A Plea for a Cyberlinguistic Turn in Area Studies." *Journal of Eurasian Studies* 2 (2): 172–83.

———. 2011b. "'Self-Orientalisation' in Narratives by Polish Migrants to Germany (by contrast to Ireland and the UK)." In *Contemporary Polish Migrant Culture and Literature in Germany, Ireland, and the UK*, edited by Joanna Rostek and Dirk Uffelmann, 103–32. Frankfurt: Lang.

———. 2014. "Is There a Russian Cyber Empire?" In *Digital Russia: The Language, Culture and Politics of New Media Communication*, edited by Michael S. Gorham, Ingunn Lunde, and Martin Paulsen, 266–84. London: Routledge.

———. 2016. "The Imagined Geolinguistics of Ukraine." In *Eurasia 2.0: Post-Soviet Geopolitics in the Age of New Media*, edited by Mikhail Suslov and Mark Bassin, 249–73. Lanham: Lexington Books.

———. Forthcoming. "iRhetoric—Metonymie als generative Trope von Selbstperformanz im Social Web: Mit Boris Chersonskijs Facebook als Testfall." In *Ich-Splitter in Bild, Schrift und Klang: (Cross-)Mediale Selbstentwürfe in den slawischen Kulturen*, Wiener Slawistischer Almanach Sonderband, edited by Gernot Howanitz and Ingeborg Jandl.

Ulinich, Anya. 2007. *Petropolis*. New York: Viking.

———. 2014. *Lena Finkle's Magic Barrel*. New York: Penguin.

Umetbaeva, Damira. 2015. "Paradoxes of Hegemonic Discourse in Post-Soviet Kyrgyzstan: History Textbooks' and History Teachers' Attitudes towards the Soviet Past." *Central Asian Affairs* 2 (3): 287–306.

Umland, Andreas. 2012. "Russia's New 'Special Path' after the Orange Revolution." *Russian Politics and Law* 50 (6): 19–40.

———. 2016a. "The Putinverstehers' Misconceived Charge of Russophobia: How Western Apology for the Kremlin's Current Behavior Contradicts Russian National Interests." Translated by Andrew Kinder. *Harvard International Review*, January 21. http://hir.harvard.edu/the-putinverstehers-misconceived-charge-of-russophobia/.

———. 2016b. "Russlands abenteuerliche Aussenpolitik: Die 'Putin-Versteher' und ihre Irrtümer." *Neue Zürcher Zeitung*, January 11. www.nzz.ch/meinung/kommentare/die-putin-versteher-und-ihre-irrtuemer-1.18675062.

Urry, John. 2002. *The Tourist Gaze*. 2nd ed. London: Sage.

———. 2005. "The Consuming of Place." In *Discourse, Communication and Tourism*, edited by Adam Jaworksi and Annette Pritchard, 19–27. Clevedon: Channel View.

Urry, John, and Jonas Larsen. 2011. *The Tourist Gaze 3.0*. London: Sage.

Uvarov, Sergei. 1848. "Doklad ministra narodnogo prosveshcheniia S. S. Uvarova imperatoru Nikolaiu I." *Biblioteka Iakova Krotova*. www.krotov.info/acts/19/1830/1833119.html.

Vaiskopf, Mikhail. 2001. "'My byli kak vo sne': tema iskhoda v literature russkogo Izrailia." *Novoe literaturnoe obozrenie* 47:241–52.

Valiaev, Evgenii, and Aleksei Zhivov. 2015. "Mezhdunarodnaia konferentsiia 'Rusofobiia i informatsionnaia voina protiv Rossii': Kak eto bylo." *Narodnaia diplomatiia*, October 4. www.publicdiplomacy.su/2015/10/04/rusofobiya-i-informatsionnaya-voyna-protiv-rossii/.

van Dijk, Teun. 1998. *Ideology: A Multidisciplinary Approach*. London: Sage.

———. 2003. "The Discourse-Knowledge Interface." In *Critical Discourse Analysis: Theory and Interdisciplinarity*, edited by G. Weiss and R. Wodak, 85–109. Basingstoke: Palgrave Macmillan.

———. 2008. *Discourse and Power: Contributions to Critical Discourse Studies*. Houndmills: Palgrave.

———. 2010. "Discourse, Knowledge, Power and Politics: Towards Critical Epistemic Discourse Analysis." In *Critical Discourse Studies in Context and Cognition*, edited by Christopher J. Hart, 27–64. Amsterdam: John Benjamins.

Van Leeuwen, Theo. 1996. "The Representation of Social Actors." In *Texts and Practices: Readings in Critical Discourse Analysis*, 32–70. Routledge: 1996.

———. 2008. *Discourse and Practice: New Tools for Discourse Analysis*. Oxford: Oxford University Press.

Vapnyar, Lara. 2003. *There Are Jews in My House*. New York: Pantheon Books.

———. 2005. "On Becoming Russian Jewish American." In *Who We Are: On Being (and Not Being) a Jewish American Writer*, edited by Derek Rubin, 293–99. New York: Schocken Books.

———. 2006. *Memoirs of a Muse*. New York: Pantheon Books.

———. 2008a. *Broccoli and Other Tales of Food and Love*. New York: Pantheon Books.

———. 2008b. "Hillary's Underpants: The Sad Tale of 'Clintonsha,' or She-Clinton." In *Thirty Ways of Looking at Hillary: Reflections by Women Writers*, edited by Susan Morrison, 190–96. New York: HarperCollins.

———. 2014. *The Scent of Pine*. New York: Simon and Schuster.

———. 2016. *Still Here*. New York: Hogarth.

Venuti, Lawrence. 2011. "World Literature and Translation Studies." In *The Routledge Companion to World Literature*, edited by Theo D'haen, David Damrosch, and Djelal Kadir, 180–93. London: Routledge.

Verdery, Katherine. 1994. "From Parent-State to Family Patriarchs: Gender and Nation in Contemporary Eastern Europe." *East European Politics and Societies* 8 (2): 225–55.

Verkholantsev, Julia. 2008. *Ruthenica Bohemica: Ruthenian Translations from Czech in the Grand Duchy of Lithuania and Poland*. Slavische Sprachgeschichte 3. Berlin: LIT Verlag.

Verscheuren, Jef. 2004. "Notes on the Role of Metapragmatic Awareness in Language Use." In *Metalanguage: Social and Ideological Perspectives*, edited by Adam Jaworski, Nikolas Coupland, and Dariusz Galasiński, 53–73. Berlin: Mouton de Gruyter.

"Vesna massovogo porozheniia." 2014. *Belorusskaia gazeta*, May 14.

"V Ialte otkrylsia i Livadiiskii forum 'Russkii mir: Problemy i Perspektivy.'" 2015. *Krym Inform*, June 6. www.c-inform.info/news/id/24186.

Vinokur, Semion. 2003. *Kalik be-shahor lavan ve-tseva*. Israel Film Service. Documentary film.

Vishnevetskii, Igor'. 2005. *"Evraziiskoe uklonenie" v muzyke 1920–1930-x godov*. Moscow: Novoe literaturnoe obozrenie.

Vishnevskaia, Galina. 1985. *Galina: Istoriia zhizni*. Paris: La Presse Libre.

Vishnevskii, Anatolii. 1998. *Serp i rubl': Konservativnaia modernizatsiia v SSSR*. Moscow: OGI.

VisitBritain. 2014. "Market and Trade Profile: Russia." http://visitbritain.org/research. Accessed December 26, 2015.

Visnushenko, Lina. 2014. "Tol'ko nachalo diskussii." *Aktual'nye kommentarii*, August 20. http://actualcomment.ru/tolko_nachalo_diskussii.html.

Vogler, Candace. 2002. "Social Imaginary, Ethics, and Methodological Individualism." *Public Culture* 14 (3): 625–27.

Volkmann, Hans-Erich. 1966. *Die russische Emigration in Deutschland 1919–1929*. Würzburg: Holzner-Verlag.

Volodin, A.I. 1985. "Herzen i Zapad: Ideinoe tvorchestvo russkogo myslitelia i social'no-politicheskii opyt Zapadnoi Evropy." In *Herzen i Zapad*, Literaturnoe Nasledstvo 96, edited by S. A. Makashin and L .R. Lanskii, 9–44. Moscow: Nauka.

Vozhdaeva, Anna. 2008. "Russkie v Uzbekistane." Informatsionno-analiticheskii tsentr Laboratorii obshchestvenno-politicheskogo razvitiia stran blizhnego zarubezh'ia, May 21. Accessed April 21, 2017. https://ia-centr.ru/experts/1179/.

Vrkljan, Irena. 1986. *Marina, ili o biografiji*. Zagreb: Grafički Zavod Hrvatske.

———. 1999. *The Silk, the Shears and Marina, or, About Biography*. Evanston, IL: Northwestern University Press.

Vrubel'-Golubkina, Irina. 2003. *Simvol "My": Evreiskaia khrestomatiia novoi russkoi literatury*. Moscow: Novoe literaturnoe obozrenie.

Vujačić, Veljko. 2015. *Nationalism, Myth, and the State in Russia and Serbia: Antecedents of the Dissolution of the Soviet Union and Yugoslavia*. Cambridge: Cambridge University Press.

"Vsesoiuznyi perepis' naseleniia 1989 goda: Natsional'nyi sostav naseleniia po respublikam SSSR." 2016. *Demoskop Weekly*, no. 703–4 (October 13–November 13. http://demoscope.ru/weekly/ssp/sng_nac_89.php?reg=0.

"Vykhodu—net!" 2014. *Vremia*, September 3. www.time.kz/articles/mir/2014/09/03/vihodu-net.

Wachtel, Andrew. 2012. "Orhan Pamuk's *Snow* as a Russian Novel." *Slavic and East European Journal* 56 (1): 91–108.

Walsh, Stephen. 2006. *Stravinsky: The Second Exile: France and America, 1934–1971*. London: Jonathan Cape.

Wang, L. Ling-Chi. 1995. "The Structure of Dual Domination: Toward a Paradigm for the Study of the Chinese Diaspora in the United States." *Amerasia* 21 (1–2): 149–69.

Wanner, Adrian. 2011. *Out of Russia: Fictions of a New Translingual Diaspora*. Evanston, IL: Northwestern University Press.

———. 2012. "Russian Jews as American Writers: A New Paradigm for Jewish Multiculturalism?" *MELUS* 37 (2): 157–76.

———. 2013. "*Lolita* and *Kofemolka*: Vladimir Nabokov's and Michael Idov's Self-Translations from English into Russian." *Slavic and East European Journal* 57 (3): 450–64.

———. 2014. "Moving beyond the Russian-American Ghetto: The Fiction of Keith Gessen and Michael Idov." *Russian Review* 73 (2): 281–96.

———. 2018. "The Poetics of Displacement: Self-Translation among Contemporary Russian-American Poets." *Translation Studies* 11 (2): 122–38.

Weaver, Anne Marie. 2015. "Art Song in Nineteenth-Century Russia: An International Exploration." PhD diss., University of Rochester.

Westphal, Bertrand. 2007. *La Géocritique, Réel, Fiction, Espace*. Paris: Éditions de Minuit.

Wikipedia "Anti-Russian Sentiment." *Wikipedia*. Accessed August 7, 2016. http://en.wikipedia.org/wiki/Anti-Russian_sentiment.

Wikipedia "Putin." 2015. "Putin khuilo!" *Wikipedia*. Accessed August 7, 2016. http://en.wikipedia.org/wiki/Putin_khuilo!

Wikipedia "Rusofobiia." 2016. "Rusofobiia." *Wikipedia*. Accessed August 7, 2016. http://ru.wikipedia.org/wiki/Русофобия.

Williams, Martin. 2014. "From Russia with Cash, the Tourist Economy Is Booming." *The Herald*, August 21.

Williams, Robert C. 1972. *Culture in Exile: Russian Emigrés in Germany, 1881–1941*. Ithaca, NY: Cornell University Press.

Wilson, Andrew. 2000. *The Ukrainians: Unexpected Nation*. New Haven, CT: Yale University Press.

———. 2005. *Ukraine's Orange Revolution*. New Haven, CT: Yale University Press.

———, ed. 2015. *What Does Ukraine Think?* Berlin: European Council on Foreign Relations. www.ecfr.eu/publications/summary/what_does_ukraine_think3026.

Wodak, Ruth, and Paul Chilton, eds. 2006. *A New Agenda in (Critical) Discourse Analysis: Theory, Methodology and Interdisciplinarity*. Amsterdam: John Benjamins.

Wodak, Ruth, Rudolf de Cillia, Martin Reisigl, and Karin Leibhart. 2009. *The Discursive Construction of National Identity*. Edinburgh: Edinburgh University Press.

Woll, Josephine. 1984. "Guests from the Future." *Russian Review* 43:377–391.

Wortman, Richard. 1995–2000. *Scenarios of Power: Myth and Ceremony in Russian Monarchy*. 2 vols. Princeton, NJ: Princeton University Press.

Yanovsky, V. S. 1976. "The Time of Nikolai Fedorov." In *The Third Hour*, vol. 10, *In Memory of Helen Iswolsky*, edited by Thomas E. Bird, 85. New York: Third Hour Foundation.

Yekelchyk, Serhy. 2007. *Ukraine: Birth of a Modern Nation*. New York: Oxford University Press.

———. 2015. *The Conflict in Ukraine: What Everyone Needs to Know*. New York: Oxford University Press.

Yonah, Yossi. 2007. "Reclaiming Diaspora: The Israeli State, Migration, and Ethnonationalism in the Global Era." *Diaspora: A Journal of Transnational Studies* 16 (1–2): 190–228.

Yurchak, Alexei. 2006. *Everything Was Forever Until It Was No More*. Princeton, NJ: Princeton University Press.

Zaharchenko, Tanya. 2016. *Where Currents Meet: Frontiers in Post-Soviet Fiction of Kharkiv, Ukraine*. Budapest: Central European University Press.

Zamiatin, Dmitrii. 2006. *Kul'tura i prostranstvo: Modelirovanie geograficheskikh obrazov*. Moscow: Znak.

———. 2011. *V serdtse vozdukha: K poiskam sokrovennykh prostranstv*. St. Petersburg: Izdatel'stvo Ivana Limbakha.

Zamiatin, D. N., N. Iu Zamiatina, and I. I. Mitin. 2008. *Modelirovanie obrazov istoriko-kul'turnoi territorii: Metodologicheskie i teoreticheskie podkhody*, edited by D. N. Zamiatin. Moscow: Institut Naslediia.

"Zapad, zapad, zapadnia." 2014. *Belorusskaia gazeta*, May 7.

"Zasedanie mezhdunarodnogo diskussionnogo kluba 'Valdai.'" 2013. *Kremlin.ru*, September 19. http://kremlin.ru/news/19243.

Zav'ialov, Sergei. 1998. *Melika. Vtoraia kniga stikhotvorenii*. Moscow: ARGO-Risk.

———. 2007. "Skvoz' mokh bezzvuchiia: Poeziia vostochnofinskogo etnofuturizma." *Novoe literaturnoe obozrenie* 85:339–53.

Zevelev [Zeveliov], Igor'. 2014. "Granitsy russkogo mira: Transformatsiia natsional'noi identichnosti i novaia vneshnepoliticheskaia doktrina Rossii." *Rossiia v global'noi politike* 12 (2): 34–45.

Zhadan, Serhii. 2016. "In the Fight Against the Enemy, We Forget about Finding Potential Allies." Translated by Natalia Ivanova. *Korydor*, June 14. www.korydor.in.ua/en/opinions/serhij-zhadan-vorohy-sojuznyky.html.

Zhadan, Serhii, Iurii Vynnychuk, Irena Karpa, Fozzi, Andrii Kokotiukha, Vladimir Rafeenko, and Maks Kidruk. 2016. *DNK*. Kharkiv: KSD.

Zhirinovskii, Vladimir. (1993) 2008. *Poslednii brosok na iug*. Moscow: Izdatel'stvo Liberal'no-Demokraticheskoi Partii.

Zhivov, Viktor. 2008. "Chuvstvitel'nyi natsionalizm: Karamzin, Rostopchin, natsional'nyi suverenitet i poiski natsional'noi identichnosti." *Novoe literaturnoe obozrenie* 91:114–40.

———. 2009. "The Myth of the State in the Age of Enlightenment and Its Destruction in Late Eighteenth-Century Russia." Translated by Liv Bliss. *Russian Studies in History* 48 (3): 10–29.

Žižek, Slavoj. 1997. "Multiculturalism, Or, the Cultural Logic of Multinational Capitalism." *New Left Review* 1 (225): 28–51.

Zorin, Andrei. 2001. *Kormia dvuglavogo orla . . . Literatura i gosudarstvennaia ideologiia v Rossii v poslednei treti XVIII–pervoi treti XIX veka*. Moscow: Novoe literaturnoe obozrenie.

Contributors

Philip Ross Bullock is Professor of Russian Literature and Music at the University of Oxford, and Fellow and Tutor in Russian at Wadham College. His publications include *The Feminine in the Prose of Andrei Platonov* (2005), *Rosa Newmarch and Russian Music in Late Nineteenth and Early Twentieth-Century England* (2009), *The Correspondence of Jean Sibelius and Rosa Newmarch, 1906–1939* (2011), and *Pyotr Tchaikovsky* (2016), as well as *Russia in Britain, 1880–1940* (2013), coedited with Rebecca Beasley.

Vitaly Chernetsky is an associate professor of Slavic languages and literatures and the director of the Center for Russian, East European and Eurasian Studies at the University of Kansas. He is the author of *Mapping Postcommunist Cultures: Russia and Ukraine in the Context of Globalization* (2007) and of articles on modern and contemporary Russian and Ukrainian literature and film, in which he seeks to highlight cross-regional and cross-disciplinary contexts. His translations into English include two novels by one of Ukraine's leading contemporary writers, Yuri Andrukhovych, *The Moscoviad* (2008) and *Twelve Circles* (2015).

Miriam Finkelstein is an assistant professor in the Department of Slavonic Studies at the University of Innsbruck, Austria. Her main research areas are contemporary Russian poetry, Russian-Jewish literature, exile, and migration. She is the author of *Im Namen der Schwester: Studien zur Rezeption der Regentin Sof'ja Alekseevna bei Katharina der Großen, Evdokija Rostopčina und Marina Cvetaeva* (2011) and coeditor, with Diana Hitzke, of *Slavische Literaturen als Weltliteratur: Hybride Konstellationen* (2018). Currently she is writing her second book about translingual Russian-American and Russian-German literature.

Yelena Furman is a lecturer in the Department of Slavic, East European, and Eurasian Languages and Cultures at the University of California, Los Angeles. Her areas of interest include contemporary Russian and Russian-American literature and feminist theory. She has published on Russian-American fiction, Russian women's fiction and film, and Virginia Woolf's translation of Dostoevsky.

Michael Gorham is a professor of Russian studies at the University of Florida and an associate editor of the *Russian Review*. He is the author of *After Newspeak: Language Culture and Politics in Russia from Gorbachev to Putin* (2014) and *Speaking in Soviet Tongues: Language Culture and the Politics of Voice in Revolutionary Russia* (2003). He recently coedited (with Ingunn Lunde and Martin Paulsen) *Digital Russia: The Language, Culture, and Politics of New*

Media Communication (2014), and was coeditor (with Daniel Weiss) of a special issue of *Zeitschrift für Slavische Philologie* (2017, nos. 72:2–73:1) dedicated to "The Culture and Politics of Verbal Prohibition in Putin's Russia."

Natalya Kosmarskaya is a senior researcher at the Centre for Central Eurasian Studies, Institute of Oriental Studies, Russian Academy of Sciences (Moscow, Russia). Her areas of research are ethnic and diaspora studies, migration studies, urban sociology, and Central Asian studies. Her books include *"Children of the Empire" in Post-Soviet Central Asia: Mental Shifts and Practices of Adaptation (Russians in Kyrgyzstan, 1992–2002)* (2006) and *Post-Soviet Diasporas: History, Politics, Identity*, to appear in 2018 (both in Russian).

Artyom Kosmarski is a researcher at the Center for the Study of General Problems of Modern East, Institute of Oriental Studies, Russian Academy of Sciences (Moscow, Russia). He received his master's degree in social anthropology from the Central European University (Budapest) in 2007. He writes on Central Asian studies, colonial history, and urban anthropology, focusing mainly on Uzbekistan and Kyrgyzstan.

Ilya Kukulin is an assistant professor in the School of Cultural Studies of the National Research University–Higher School of Economics in Moscow and a senior researcher at its International Center for the History and Sociology of World War II and Its Consequences. He is the author of *Machines of a Noisy Time: How Soviet Montage Became the Aesthetic Method of Unofficial Culture* (in Russian, 2015) and has coedited six volumes, focused on various topics, from the history of schooling in twentieth-century Eastern Europe to the cultural practices of internal colonization in Russia. He is also the author of many articles on Russian literature, especially poetry, Russian twentieth-century unofficial social life, and the political discourses of Russian social media.

Alex Moshkin is an SSHRC postdoctoral fellow at the Centre for Comparative Literature at the University of Toronto. He received his PhD from the University of Pennsylvania in 2018. His dissertation, "Forty Years in the Wilderness: Russian-Israeli Literature, Film, and Painting, 1977–2017," examines Russian-Israeli institutions and works of literature, film, and visual arts that emerged in Israel in the last forty years in both Russian and Hebrew languages.

Kevin M. F. Platt is the Edmund J. and Louise W. Kahn Term Professor in the Humanities at the University of Pennsylvania. He writes on representations of Russian history, Russian history and memory, contemporary Russian poetry, and global Russian cultures. His most recent monograph is *Terror and Greatness: Ivan and Peter as Russian Myths* (2011). He also recently served as editor and chief translator for the poetry anthology *Hit Parade: The Orbita Group* (2015). He is currently completing the monograph *Near Abroad: Russian Culture in Latvia.*

Maria Rubins is Professor of Russian and Comparative Literature at the School of Slavonic and East European Studies of University College London. She works on Russian literature and culture of the nineteenth through twenty-first centuries from a comparative and interdisciplinary perspective. Her research interests include modernism, exile and diaspora, bilingual writing, canon, Russian-French cultural relations, and Russian-language literature in Israel. She is the author of several books, including *Crossroad of Arts, Crossroad of Cultures: Ecphrasis in Russian and French Poetry* (2000) and *Russian Montparnasse: Transnational Writing in Interwar Paris* (2015), and over one hundred articles and book chapters. She is a translator of fiction from English and French into Russian, including books by Elizabeth Gaksell, Judith Gautier, and Irène Némirovsky. Rubins is the editor of several book series, including Studies in Slavic Literature and Poetics at Brill, the Fringe series at UCL Press, and the newly created Anthem Press series Modern Israel: Cultures, Languages, Identities.

Lara Ryazanova-Clarke is Professor of Russian and Sociolinguistics at the University of Edinburgh. Her book publications include *The Russian Language Today* (with T. Wade) (2011), *The Russian Language outside the Nation* (2014), *The Vernaculars of Communism: Language, Ideology and Power in the Soviet Union and Eastern Europe* (with P. Petrov) (2015), and the two-volume *French and Russian in Imperial Russian* (with D. Offord, V. Rjéoutski, and G. Argent) (2015). She is a series editor of the Russian Language and Society book series at Edinburgh University Press.

Dirk Uffelmann is a professor of Slavic literatures and cultures at the University of Passau. His research interests include Russian, Polish, Czech, and Ukrainian literatures, migration, masculinity, and internet studies. He has authored two monographs and coedited fourteen volumes, including *Contemporary Polish Migrant Culture and Literature in Germany, Ireland, and the UK* (2011), *Tam, vnutri: Praktiki vnutrennei kolonizatsii v kul'turnoi istorii Rossii* (2012), *Vladimir Sorokin's Languages* (2013), and *Postcolonial Slavic Literatures after Communism* (2016).

Lisa Ryoko Wakamiya is Associate Professor of Slavic and Courtesy Associate Professor of English at Florida State University. She writes on transnational literary migration, post-Soviet literature and film, and the intersections between narrative and material culture. She is the author of *Locating Exiled Writers in Contemporary Russian Literature: Exiles at Home* (2009) and the coeditor (with Mark Lipovetsky) of *Late and Post-Soviet Russian Literature: A Reader* (2015).

Adrian Wanner is the Liberal Arts Professor of Russian and Comparative Literature at Pennsylvania State University. He specializes in diaspora studies and the theory and practice of translation. His latest books are *Out of Russia: Fictions of a New Translingual Diaspora* (2011), a German verse translation of the poetry of Vladislav Khodasevich (2013), and a study of self-translation among Russian poets (2018).

Index